the definitive guide to project management

the fast track to getting the job done on time and on budget

Second Edition

SEBASTIAN NOKES AND SEAN KELLY

FT Prentice Hall
FINANCIAL TIMES

An imprint of Pearson Education

Harlow, England • London • New York • Boston • San Francisco • Toronto • Sydney • Singapore • Hong Kong
Tokyo • Seoul • Taipei • New Delhi • Cape Town • Madrid • Mexico City • Amsterdam • Munich • Paris • Milan

PEARSON EDUCATION LIMITED

Edinburgh Gate
Harlow CM20 2JE
United Kingdom
Tel: +44(0)1279 623623
Fax: +44(0)1279 431059

Website: www.pearsoned.co.uk

First published 2003
Second edition published in Great Britain 2007

© Aldersgate Partners LLP 2003
© Casnus Limited 2007

ISBN 978 0 273 71097 4

British Library Cataloguing-in-Publication Data
A catalogue record for this book is available from the British Library

Library of Congress Cataloging-in-Publication Data
Nokes, Sebastian.
  The definitive guide to project management : the fast track to getting the job done on
  time and on budget / Sebastian Nokes and Sean Kelly. -- 2nd ed.
    p. cm.
  Includes bibliographical references and index.
  ISBN 978-0-273-71097-4
  1. Project management--Handbooks, manuals, etc. I. Kelly, Sean, 1960-II. Title.

  HD69.P75N65 2007
  658.4'04--dc22
                                                          2006053299

10 9 8 7 6 5 4 3 2 1
11 10 09 08 07

Typeset by 30
Printed and bound in Great Britain by Ashford Colour Press, Hampshire

The Publishers' policy is to use paper manufactured from sustainable forests.

The authors may be contacted at Sebastian@Nokes.net

the definitive
guide to
project management

Ashley,

With compliments,

Sachin Noh

8/9/07

FT Prentice Hall
FINANCIAL TIMES

In an increasingly competitive world, we believe it's quality of thinking that gives you the edge – an idea that opens new doors, a technique that solves a problem, or an insight that simply makes sense of it all. The more you know, the smarter and faster you can go.

That's why we work with the best minds in business and finance to bring cutting-edge thinking and best learning practice to a global market.

Under a range of leading imprints, including *Financial Times Prentice Hall*, we create world-class print publications and electronic products bringing our readers knowledge, skills and understanding, which can be applied whether studying or at work.

To find out more about Pearson Education publications, or tell us about the books you'd like to find, you can visit us at **www.pearsoned.co.uk**

PEARSON
Education

about the authors

Sebastian Nokes and Sean Kelly have worked together on a number of strategic projects and programmes.

SEBASTIAN NOKES

Sebastian Nokes is a practicing project and programme manager who also advises corporations, government bodies and professional service firms on project and programme management, decision making and information management. He has led major projects in the investment banking, nuclear and high technology sectors. He is currently a partner at Aldersgate Partners LLP, a management consulting firm, and previously worked for IBM and Credit Suisse First Boston. He was educated at Eton College and London University (Birkbeck, SOAS, Imperial and LBS) and has served as an officer in the 2nd Goorkha Rifles and the Royal Air Force. Sebastian has written or edited a number of books and articles on project management and other business topics. He lives in London and works in the UK, Europe and Asia/Pacific.

His current interests include how to change the mindset and culture of management teams to enhance project performance, and how to structure major strategic projects in large organizations. His current research work focuses on valuing projects and securitization.

SEAN KELLY

Sean Kelly is a serving British Army officer with wide experience in both the public and private sectors. He was educated in the UK and Australia and his past employers include Deutsch Bank, OCL and Hoechst. His current areas of interest are the practical implications of implementing a complex information strategy and risk transfer in public–private partnerships. He has worked as a Project Manager in the US, Europe, Africa and the Far East. His qualifications include MA, MBA and PMP.

As the first officer sent to the UK Ministry of Agriculture, Food and Fisheries during the Foot and Mouth crisis of 2001, he was responsible for project managing how and where the military could assist. This led to the deployment of thousands of servicemen. He was awarded the MBE in 2002 for his role in the worldwide operations that followed 9/11. He is currently commanding a British Army Regiment and working with a number of leading training providers across Great Britain.

acknowledgements

The authors gratefully acknowledge all those whose advice, examples or other assistance have contributed to this book. We most especially thank the clients of Aldersgate Partners LLP and we recognize the trust that they place in us, and we also thank all of those who have attended our training courses, either public or in-house corporate courses.

While cautioning that all faults and other deficiencies in the book are solely the responsibility of the authors – and one hardly appreciates how important that statement is until one has tried to write a book – we would like to thank also our colleagues at Aldersgate, all of whom have contributed, in various ways, to the book, and to our friends at Pearson Education in the UK, USA and elsewhere, Digby Law in Sydney and TypingNZ in New Zealand. Thanks to: Professor Chris Higson, Peter Robin, Guy Treweek, Dr. Diana Burton, Dr. Stephen Coulson, Andrew Howard, Steve Bullen, David Tulloch, and Debra Palmer; Richard Stagg, Steve Temblett, Laura Blake, Liz Gooster and Lesley Pummell; and Stephen Digby in Australia and Kim Megson in New Zealand.

We thank and acknowledge the assistance given by the Project Management Institute, both to us in preparing this book and more widely, and we thank Douglas Murray, Leslie Higham, Diana Humphrey and the team at the PMI.

Our particular thanks go to Tony Gamby, JP Rangaswami, Cedric Burton, Mike Stone, Jeremy Havard, the Revd. Gordon Taylor, Aziz Muzakhanov, Louis Plowden-Wardlaw, Julian Fidler, Peter Burditt, Paul Najsarek, Mark Kerr, Paul Leighton, David Maitland, Dillon Dhanecha, Mike Baker, Kennedy Frazer, Tegwen Wallace, Graham Mackintosh, Nick McLeod-Clark, Dave Hastings, Dave Best, Steve Holland, Mark Dutton, Nicola Smith, Mike Molinaro, Emma Ross, Jonathan Webb, Gareth Moss, Adrian Cory, Frances Kinsella and Andrew Ward.

We also thank Andrew Munro, Patrick Smith, Alan Greenwood, Dominic Allen, Jennifer Johnson, Mark Goodman, Graeme Graas, Aaron Dover, Ian Major, David Kriel and Philip Stromeyer, Jesus Rodriguez, and Heidi Peel.

A number of individual and organizations have helped in various ways with the production of the book. Humphrey and Bella Nokes provided extensive use of their houses in Switzerland, Andrew and Vicky de Pree of theirs in New Zealand, Dave and Vee Burton of their houses also in New Zealand, and Chris Booton and Gina of theirs in Melbourne – all of which were delightful and productive places in which to get thinking and writing done in a way that is simply not possible in the office in London. Vaughan Smith and the Frontline Club in London, the Cornell Club and its staff in New York, the Wellington Club and its staff in Wellington have all helped in bringing this book into being. Tina Arthur is invaluable in logistic support and much wise advice has come from Rachel Sheard.

contents

preface to the Second Edition

In a competitive market, all new growth comes from projects. The world economy has become much more competitive in the last ten years, because of three factors, namely the lowering of trade barriers, the rise of China and other low cost jurisdictions, and Internet and other technology developments. The level of competition facing businesses is as great as it was in Victorian times, if not greater. In Victorian times great new business and social organizations were built quickly from scratch, and many long-established institutions failed or sank into terminal decline, forever eclipsed by more vigorous upstarts who understood the new rules of the game better. So while those who say that organizations today face unprecedented rates of change and innovation have scant understanding of history, it is certainly true that we are in one of history's periods of great change, uncertainty and competition. By definition, projects are about the new, and by extension all new growth in a competitive market comes from projects. And this, fundamentally, is why project management has gone from being an esoteric and specialized backwater ten years ago to one of the foremost concerns of top management. By 2007 in the industrialized economies, everything that could be outsourced, downsized, reengineered or web-enabled has been or is in the process of being outsourced, downsized, reengineered or web-enabled. The only remaining way to create new value and new growth is to get better at doing new things better – which is project management.

And it is not just commercial businesses which are increasing their project and programme management capability. Governments across the world are re-embracing project management and investing heavily in it. Governments are increasingly recognizing that they must enhance their project management capability, which somewhere between the 1970s and 1990s seemed to become neglected. Project management, even in the days of the building the pyramids of Egypt, has been a discipline developed equally by government and private enterprise. In more recent times the armed forces and the financial services industries have been especially prominent in advancing project management, both in its application and in the theoretical body of knowledge. Project management is a unique conduit for swords into ploughshares, as techniques funded by the armed forces and especially the nuclear weapons industry are applied by local government and the caring professions to help build a fairer, more just and freer society.

This second edition is an almost complete re-write of the highly successful first edition. The main change is that the second edition is consistent with the PMBOK® Guide, which is a standard administered by the Project Management Institute (PMI). The Institute is the world's largest and fastest-growing professional body for project management with a strong presence in all geographical regions and industries. The book is written above all for practicing project and programme managers, and as practitioners are increasingly wanting to take the professional exams offered by the PMI, we have tried to ensure that the way the book is written supports those readers who intend to sit the exams, both PMP® and CAPM® of the PMI. The second edition retains the focus on the human aspects of project management that featured in the first edition. Whatever methodology or standard is used in project management, it is first of all people who matter, because it is people who get projects done or who block them. Project management is first of all about people.

list of figures

List of figures

an introductory case study

This partly imaginary case study shows what this book is about.

San joined the Navy from school. His parents could never have afforded a university course but he was a clever young man and was selected for officer training. Two years later he joined his first ship as a junior officer. He was an assistant communications officer. The first project the Captain gave him was rewriting the phone directory for the Model 600 telephone network aboard. He worked hard on this and using all his limited experience he produced an impressive booklet. It was an alphabetical list of crew members and each entry was cross-referenced with office or work space. He reported to the Captain ahead of schedule and presented his masterpiece. The Captain took one look at his offering, threw it overboard and sent him away.

Crestfallen San returned to the communications team. Here a wise old Petty Officer who had been with the Captain for years took him to one side. This is a warship, he explained. In combat, people die and things get blown up. The phone directory has to allow for this. San realized the error of his ways and returned to his work. Twenty-four hours later he returned to the Captain with his revised directory. This time it was organized by role, cross-referenced first by location and then by the names of those filling that role. If individuals were killed or injured and others took on their role, the book would still work. The Captain smiled. San had learned a good lesson as a Naval Officer and the ship had a new phone directory.

San served in the Navy for a further six years, both at sea and ashore in the main headquarters. He learned a great deal about people, particularly in the close confines of the ship, and when in the headquarters he learned the importance of understanding the politics surrounding issues. He left the Navy as it downsized and moved into project management. He worked on a variety of projects, from introducing traffic speeding cameras to building a new school. He became a Certified Associate in Project Management (CAPM) as soon as he could and built his qualifications in PRINCE2. After a few years he took the Project Management Professional (PMP) exam, passed and became a keen member of his country's chapter of the Project Management Institute (PMI). This personal development path not only built his qualifications but did so in line with his experience. It also afforded him a considerable support network of like-minded professionals. His experience continued to grow and, having completed a major project for an international communications company, he became an independent consultant. After some years he came back to the Defence Department as a contracted project manager on a major networking project for the Navy. His specific responsibility was the e-mail system.

He brought all his experience to this task. He made a point of getting to know all his team. He arranged social events and occasionally got them to bring their partners along. Long ago he'd learned the importance of a good memory and made a point of knowing something about all of them. He'd made it a personal rule to get round his team's office space each day and talk to as many as he could. He also arranged meetings with all the stakeholders he had identified and personally met with them all. Whilst he couldn't say he liked them all, he had at least created a relationship with them.

The project was a political minefield. There was much internal politics within the Defence Department and much interference from politicians. This was not surprising, since the project accounted for a large part of the defence budget. Moreover, the senior officers had had to be convinced that the system was worth it: couldn't the money be better spent just buying more weapons? Would the e-mail system really provide a better picture of what was going on in battle than the alternative, a networked system? Many senior officers were sceptical.

San was fortunate. He arrived at the project with a background in project management and an understanding of how the Navy worked at both the front line and in headquarters. He took several weeks before the project started to meet with a number of his old comrades to update himself on how things really were. He enjoyed being back in his old environment and this made him all the more determined to do a good job.

Once the project started he got into the detail of the specifications for the system he was to produce. As far as he could see, it was good. It had been developed using front-line users who would actually have to make it work at sea rather than in a test building. Remembering back to his first days at sea, he was pleased to note that it was role-based. The Captain's e-mail address would be '[Ship Name]–Captain' rather than the name of the individual holding the post.

The software development for the whole project was run by a major international IT company. At the outset San was concerned. As normal, the IT company was trying hard to get the Navy to change its working practices to fit the software product, in order to minimize the number of modifications required. Often this causes no significant problems to the customer and helps by keeping costs down and resilience up, but San could see problems in this case because the proposed changes in working practices were not practicable in the environment of sea warfare.

As was his custom, San developed his reporting mechanisms with everyone in mind. He had learned over the years the advantages and disadvantages of various methods of communication, even learning sign language for one contract with a charity for children with impaired hearing. He did not waste time. His project support office worked extremely hard in the early days developing systems that would produce all the likely reports at the touch of a button, in a format appropriate to the recipient. He insisted that the database for his project was as open as possible to speed up reports. He prided himself on being able to produce reports rapidly on anything to do with the project. He regularly tested his staff with regular quizzes, on both project and general knowledge. His team began to enjoy his quizzes and became very competent with the reporting software as a result. These abilities proved their value when one day the head of the overall project, a difficult character and in a bad mood on that day, stormed into their office while San was away, demanding the most obscure of reports. The fact that the report was produced faster than he could drink a cup of coffee took him back a little and, despite his best efforts not to, he smiled.

All of these skills were of course why San had got the contract and he rapidly became well known in the Department as an individual who was at the top of his game and a good guy to work for.

Soon San realized that the scale and complexity of the project had been underestimated. The hardware element of the project was not going well. The network was to spread from the headquarters' offices to ships at sea. The hardware providers had assumed that running network cables through a warship was the same as doing so in an office block. The ramifications for the system of damage control procedures and airtight compartments for chemical environments had been missed. Most surprisingly, the IT supplier had forgotten that warships move around, sometimes violently, and when the ship moves so does the computer system. Hardware must be secured to the ship and not left on a desktop, and the system must cope with computers changing physical location as the ships move.

Such complexity was not the only problem. The software developers were having difficulty making the real-time data network operate at sea as it had in the lab. Every time they tried to add more than three ships the system crashed. This was a major problem, since the Navy's standard warfighting tactics required at least four vessels to be working together, which is what real-life experience and also computer modelling showed is the minimum effective force. Somewhat surprisingly, the chief programmer actually asked a senior Admiral if the Navy couldn't just make do with three ship formations. The Admiral's reply is unprintable.

Despite the problems on the horizon, San's project had been progressing well. He could do little about the infrastructure issues, but he was confident he would have the e-mail system ready on time. Then it all started to go wrong. He had taken his senior team members out for a coffee. Over coffee they told him that they thought the software provider was intending to use a name-based directory for the e-mail system, like the one that San had produced on his first ship and his Captain had thrown overboard. They knew this was a problem since at one of their first team meals San had told them the story of his first project. This problem had not been known until now because they were still using test addresses. San was worried. On his return to the office he contacted the relevant stakeholder and in conversation they confirmed his fears. It was the IT supplier's standard way of doing things and would therefore be much easier and cheaper to implement – for them. 'Besides', he said, 'whoever wrote that element of the specification clearly didn't understand modern e-mail systems and was just copying the phone book. What difference could it make?' He added that the Defence Department had agreed to the specification.

San called a meeting with the software provider at which he explained in the greatest detail why role-based software was critical. This fell on deaf ears. The overall project already had enough problems and this wasn't going to be another. San pushed and pushed this issue for several weeks. At one point a Vice President of the software provider tried to hire him for another project at a much higher salary just to remove him as an obstacle to their plan. San turned this down but it did confirm that the issue was serious. San discovered that the individual who had agreed this in the Department was someone who had never served on a warship and knew little about the Navy. San returned to his office to think through how he would resolve this issue. He couldn't report a variation since the specification change had been agreed even though no one had informed him of the project support office. He decided to speak to the section head concerned. This got him no further since the section head took the view that San was creating yet another problem where one didn't exist. He couldn't even understand San's motivation, since sticking with a name-based system would enable the e-mail element to be completed even faster, earning them both a bonus.

San took the weekend to think this through. It was true he could be confident of a large bonus if he followed the name-based plan, but it troubled him deeply. Finally his wife asked him if he could live with either decision and he told her he could not. 'Decision made then', she said, 'go and see your old Captain and get some advice, this is all his fault anyway.'

The retired Admiral, as the Captain had become, was surprised to see San but pleased that the lesson taught years ago had not been forgotten. 'Leave it with me', he said, 'I might be retired but I think I can still pull a few strings.' True to his word, that's exactly what he did, so fast that even San was surprised. A directive came down from the head of the Navy three days later, stating that all communication systems were to be role-based. Unfortunately for San it was not too difficult for those involved to work out who had outmanoeuvred them. As a consequence his project came under close scrutiny. However, his team was a solid one as a result of all the activities they had done together and stuck by him when things became difficult.

San's battle was not a secret and he developed a reputation with the user community who reinforced his position at every possible occasion. After much argument at the highest levels, the IT company finally conceded and a role-based solution was accepted. San's team worked every hour available to implement it on schedule and they made it. Their rollout would be subject to the infrastructure delays but these had mostly been overcome. The great delay in the overall project was the data network. This team were still struggling with the complexity of what they were trying to create. The higher management of the Department were keen to demonstrate some progress, so San's system was rolled out as soon as the infrastructure was at an acceptable level. It was a great success and the lack of a data network to improve overall situational awareness was overcome aboard by using picture attachments on the e-mail system. It wasn't real time but it was a great step forward. And everyone was happy.

San was especially happy. He had the respect of those who mattered, even if he was not quite as rich as they and even if the software provider was never going to offer him employment. Then the situation in the country changed radically.

There had always been a separatist movement in the west of the country. The movement changed policy from demonstrations to armed insurrection. A civil war started. The west enlisted the help of a neighbouring country and its armed forces. San's country suffered many casualties. The conflict ended in victory for the government's forces, but in the aftermath it became all too clear that without the up-to-date picture of the battle that the improvised e-mail attachments provided, the government might well have lost the war. The IT company immediately laid claim to their brilliance in all the trade publications. However, a little-known retired Admiral wrote in the national press that had their original name-based solution been adopted, messages and orders would never have got through to the individuals who took over the roles of those lost in battle. The IT company lost credibility, and had anyway been involved in a number of major public procurement disasters. In his letter the Admiral accepted that theoretically high-tech forwarding and administrator actions could have solved the problem in an office of e-mail being addressed to a wounded or missing or dead officer, but he pointed out that in a fast-moving battle, people tend to die without forwarding their mail and administrative support can be far away.

San was vindicated. He is now working overseas on a desert pipeline project, and over a glass of lemonade in the evening wonders how he would have felt if he hadn't stood his ground all those years ago. He had learned a great deal over his career and it had all come together at the right time. Yes, he knew all the techniques of project management and kept up with developments, but it was his experience, ethics and desire to do more than just meet the specification that made him into the fine project manager that he is today.

introduction

1

2

3

4

5

6

7

8

9

10

11

12

13

▶ Aims of this chapter

This introductory chapter can be skipped by those who want to get straight into how to do project management. However, as an introductory chapter, the aims are to:

◆ explain the current major trends and forces in project management, so as to situate the role of the project manager in that context, and especially to show how globalization and increased competition are causing increased demand for project management;
◆ give the perspective of the organization on project management, as well as the project manager's perspective;
◆ explain what project management is and how it relates to general management, contrast it to business processes, and summarize what makes it a distinct skill set with a distinct body of knowledge;
◆ introduce the Project Management Institute's PMBOK approach to project management, as the largest and fastest growing of the three main global standards.

For those who want to skip this chapter, try the following test. Try it anyway, whether or not you like reading introductory chapters.

---

1. Is the need for your project understood and agreed by everyone who will have to contribute resources to it?   Yes/No

2. Do you understand the project authorization and monitoring procedures in your organization?   Yes/No

3. If you take on the management of the project, will you be given the authority to make decisions about the project direction? (What does the history of your organization tell you on this point?)   Yes/No

4. If this is your first project, will you get support and guidance from more experienced project managers?   Yes/No

5. Do you know why you have been chosen to manage this project? (What does this tell you about the motivations of the other people involved?)   Yes/No

6. Can you commit the time needed to manage this project? Do you know from experience how much time you will need?   Yes/No

7. Will you be responsible for the initial definition of scope, timing and cost? If these have already been set, can you review and renegotiate them if required?   Yes/No

8. Has the person who had the idea for the project described the concept to you directly in their own words?   Yes/No

9. Do you know enough about your organization's track record with projects? (Which succeeded, which did not, and why?) Have you got the maximum learning from others' experience?   Yes/No

10. Have you had formal training (or if highly experienced but not training, some sort of peer assessment) in project management?   Yes/No

---

If you score eight or more, well done – you seem to be a highly experienced project manager and you have a safe project in hand. If you scored less, welcome to project management as it is in the real world; you are by no means alone. In either case, we hope you will get much out of this book.

▶ What's new about the new edition?

This is the second edition of *The Definitive Guide to Project Management*. This edition has been updated to incorporate the latest thinking on project management and current best practice. Project management is nothing if not a practical discipline, and it is also a new discipline. As such, how to do project management is evolving. The fundamental principles are now fairly stable, but the knowledge of how to apply them continues to evolve.

In the last few years corporations have taken a much more strategic interest in project management, and, for different reasons, the same is true of government departments. Faced with great pressures to reduce costs because of globalization and the resultant increased competition, corporations have downsized, outsourced, restructured and cut every possible cost. The only remaining area where significant cost reductions and, more interestingly, gains from innovation and creative thinking can help to rescue competitive advantage, is project management, and its cousin programme management. Government too has been forced to radically rethink its approach to project management. Around the world, government is expected to deliver more, under greater scrutiny, and in many democratic countries there are signs that the electorate is close to refusing to pay any higher taxes. The result of these pressures in both the corporate and the government world is a severe need for better project management. The only way to get new things done, to innovate and reap the benefits of innovation, is through project management.

Projects are essentially defined as getting new things done, and as such they are risky. But is there really any similarity between getting new things done in, say, critical illness surgery and, say, building oil rigs? That is, is project management a general discipline, with general principles which apply to a wide variety of different kinds of industry? Yes, is the short answer. Of course, one would be insane to try to innovate in one kind of business without using available expertise, in other words, there are many things in projects that will vary from industry to industry, but there are also general principles. This is not so odd, as we can see by making comparisons with accounting and general management. Irrespective of the particular business, there are general accounting principles which apply when doing accounting, and general management principles which apply when managing, irrespective of industry. There are also accounting techniques used in some industries and not others[1], and management techniques[2] used in some types of organization only.

A result of the recent increase in interest in project management, and its universal applicability across all kinds of organization, is a rapid development of methodologies for doing project management, and a consolidation of them.

▶ What do project managers really want?

In a two-day informal survey of project managers at one of the world's biggest trade shows for industry, commerce and major projects[3], one of the authors asked experienced project managers what problems they faced in carrying out their project management responsibilities. The top five problems were as follows.

◆ The people side of project management: understanding people, getting others in the project to understand people, getting people to rub along with each other, and adapting one's approach to project management to allow for every person being slightly different.

◆ Lack of a common approach across their organization, causing inefficiency and risk, as the same fundamental administrative problems are solved anew in each project.

◆ Having to deal with unexpected crises that could reasonably have been foreseen and, if not avoided, seen longer in advance, so giving the project manager more time to deal with them.

◆ Getting highly skilled technical people and other highly intelligent employees to think outside their disciplines when necessary for the project – especially (but not only) on the people side, as listed above.

◆ Selling the benefits of project management to customers, so that they are prepared to pay for project management, either in terms of up-front cost, which saves money in the long term, or in terms of front-loading[4] design and planning of projects, which also saves customers time, money and risk in the longer term.

There was also a strong interest in providing training for project managers and others involved in projects, both the less experienced and the more experienced.

Emerging standards for project management

The current trend in project management is a rapid consolidation on a few global standards, and a major growth in professionalization of project management. As part of this trend, one of the main emerging world standards is the Project Management Institute's approach, known as the Project Management Body of Knowledge or *PMBOK Guide*®. The *PMBOK Guide* is also the US national standard (ANSI) for project management. This edition of the book is aligned to the *PMBOK Guide*. We will also refer to three other standards, which although not nearly as widespread as PMBOK, have some interesting features. These are PRINCE2, the ISO standard for project management, and the APM approach. PRINCE2 has evolved to meet the specific needs of UK government projects, and is especially useful for generating the bureaucracy that is often a requirement of the public sector's duty of accountability. The APM is rooted in the European tradition of industrial management, and offers some useful contrasts to the PMBOK, which is more rooted in the efficient world of US global corporations and investment banks. A recent innovation in project management is the critical chain method[5]. Appendix A describes that approach to project management and its rationale. It is not fundamentally different from the current mainstream methodologies, but it has some radical innovations in how risk and contingency are managed and is worth knowing about once you have mastered the basics of project management.

Project management is founded on common sense

When cooking a meal of roast lamb, peas and beans, the lamb goes in the oven first, the beans go into boiling water or the steamer some time later, and the peas last of all. (For 'lamb' please may we beg forgiveness of vegetarian readers and ask them to read instead 'nut cutlet', which we are informed has the necessary cooking properties to make this example work.) That way all the food is ready at once, and the meal works. Start cooking the lamb, the beans and peas at the same time, and they will all be ready at different times. That is the heart of project management: doing different things at the right times so that the end result is what is wanted. This means knowing what is wanted, what inputs we need to get there, what processes must be performed, and in what order. Some risk management is also a good idea: what if the lamb cooks faster, or slower, than expected? We check the lamb from time to time to see whether it is progressing as expected, and bring forward or delay the start of cooking the beans and peas. It is exactly the same in project management: we determine what is likely to vary from our plan, we monitor progress to check for variance, and we take steps and change things to ensure that despite variances we end up with what we wanted.

There is a view often heard among older employees who have had the job title of 'project manager' for a number of years that they have little to learn in project management. This may well be true: if someone has been a dependable and capable project manager for many years, then clearly they do know what they are doing. However, their employer may see things differently, because at the organizational level, there is a huge benefit to having everyone involved in project management doing things the same way. To take an analogy, two drivers may be very competent in driving cars, but if one drives on the left side of the road and the other drives on the right, then there is a huge benefit to having them both drive on the same side of the road, whichever side that is – not a benefit to the driver who changes, nor much benefit to the other driver, but a benefit to everyone else, especially pedestrians and ambulance crews. It's the same for driving projects in organizations. Say an organization has 100 projects and 100 project managers, one running each project. Suppose further that each project manager is very competent and professional but has their own unique way of doing project management. In a rival organization there are also 100 projects, but in that organization there is a standard basic project management methodology. This second organization will have many cost and risk advantages over the first that together add up to a significant advantage in terms of higher customer service and lower overall cost and risk. Some of the specific advantages are as follows:

◆ Project managers can work together more easily and with less risk and inefficiency, because they use a common approach, which means that large projects and programmes are easier to plan, manage and execute, and that there is greater flexibility in how staff are deployed.
◆ Training new project managers can be standardized, and new project managers will be able to work with experienced managers from an earlier stage.
◆ The costs of training new project managers can be reduced through standardization.

◆ Sponsors and customers and others who interact with the project interact more efficiently and effectively, both from their own point of view and from the project manager's, because of the commonality between projects.

▶ How readers can use this book

This book is for both the beginning project manager and the experienced project manager. Project sponsors, senior managers, project engineers, project support staff and programme offices, financial controllers and project accountants, programme managers, marketing and salespeople, and others who are involved in projects but may not be project managers will also find it useful. This book provides a single reference source for project managers and others who need to know about project management. It provides guidance in all key aspects of project management.

There are two important limitations to be aware of when using this book:

◆ The contents of this book explain best practice in the discipline, but much of what matters most in project management simply has to be learnt through experience. People who are new to project management should also make full use of the support available from their organizations, and especially from more experienced project managers. If in doubt, ask someone who has done it before!

◆ Almost by definition, projects involve tackling new problems. This means that sometimes a project will encounter a problem which does not fit easily into the framework used in this book. It is essential to remember that books are not a substitute for common sense: if there are sound reasons for doing things differently from the way presented here, then do things differently. The framework presented has great value, but common sense is more valuable still, and use your common sense when applying the techniques set out in this book. Project management is not about being right in theory, it is about delivering a result that people want.

▶ What kinds of project is this book aimed at?

Most projects are small projects with few project staff, perhaps a part-time project manager and no other dedicated staff. At the other end of the scale are very large projects, such as building the Three Gorges Dam in China, or preparing London for the Olympic Games, or merging two large corporations. The framework presented in this book is based on fundamental principles that apply to all projects in all industries. (In the same way, the principle in cooking is that one starts cooking different parts of the meal at different times so that the meal comes together at the same time, whether one is cooking for oneself only, or cooking a feast for five thousand.) However we have tended to give examples of small to medium-sized projects, because experience shows that this is where most readers work.

Project management's nine knowledge areas

There are a number of different ways to look at project management, a number of different perspectives on it. It is useful to have several different perspectives on project management. One of them is the different kinds of knowledge that together make up project management, which we will introduce presently. Another perspective is the project management lifecycle, that is the sequence in which the different project management tasks happen. It is probably easier to understand project management on first encountering the subject from the perspective of the sequence of project management activities, and in Chapter 2 we do just that, describing the project lifecycle from start to finish. However, for the most part this book explains project management from the perspective of the nine knowledge areas. We owe those readers who are coming to project management for the first time an explanation of why we have decided to do this, and we also suggest that they might like to go straight to Chapter 3 and skim it – don't yet read in detail – to acquire a sequential perspective on project management, before returning and continuing either here or in Chapter 2.

There are reasons for structuring this book predominantly by the knowledge areas of project management rather than by the project lifecycle. It is rather like learning to drive: although the way we drive from A to B is to start the car, drive, and then stop, and at a high level all driving lessons begin with us starting the car, then have us driving, and end with us stopping the car, in learning to drive we need to practise different parts of driving technique together. So one lesson will focus on hill starts, another on emergency stops, another on parking, and so on. So it is in project management. Although all projects are planned to have a beginning, middle and end, the reality of project management and business generally is that in some projects you will need to use more of one tool than another, and some projects will need replanning and yet more replanning, rather than planning being restricted to the start of the project. In short, you will end up as a more effective project manager by learning the subject in terms of knowledge areas; and if you are an experienced project manager, you will find that there are some knowledge areas that you need to improve more than others. The project lifecycle is also important, and we give you that perspective in Chapter 2.

The nine knowledge areas of project management (as per the PMI's *PMBOK Guide*) are:

- Project Integration Management.
- Project Scope Management.
- Project Time Management.
- Project Cost Management.
- Project Quality Management.
- Project Human Resource Management.
- Project Communication Management.
- Project Risk Management.
- Project Procurement Management.

1 **Project Integration Management**. This knowledge area is the heart of project management. You must understand what it is and why it is important. It contains

the skills, tools and techniques required to integrate all the components of the project so as to be able to deliver the end product. Integration means getting everything done at the right time in the right sequence, connected in the right way.

2 **Project Scope Management**. Scope management is the process by which the project manager defines the boundaries to the project work and ensures that any changes to the original scope are carefully managed. Scope means what is included in the project and what is excluded from it.

3 **Project Time Management**. This knowledge area is about making sure that things happen on time, with keeping the project on schedule. It includes techniques to estimate how long things will take, to plan accordingly, and then to keep things on track.

4 **Project Cost Management**. This knowledge area is about keeping the project on budget, and includes techniques for estimating costs, planning and budgeting, and monitoring and controlling costs. (Costs always matter – even in government, eventually.)

5 **Project Quality Management**. Quality in project management is about the project's deliverables being fit for purpose. A project that delivers something that cannot be used has failed, no matter how well the project management methodology was followed and no matter how quickly and cheaply it was completed.

6 **Project Human Resource Management**. Project Human Resource Management is about how to find, lead and manage the people involved in the project. It also deals with their professional development.

7 **Project Communication Management**. Failure to pay attention to this knowledge area is often how a perfectly good project is turned into a failure. Communication Management is about identifying who needs what information, how it is to be communicated to them and when they need to have it – and ensuring that the right people get the right information at the right time.

8 **Project Risk Management**. Projects are risky. Project risk management is about identifying and evaluating risks, planning responses where necessary, and ensuring that the plans translate into action if the risks crystallize.

9 **Project Procurement Management**. This knowledge area deals with the procurement of resources for the project.

▶ Projects as a distinct class of activity

▶ Projects and processes

Everything that people do in an organization can be categorized as either a project or a process. A process is an activity which happens continually or a set of activities which happen continually, that is, they are always happening or being made to happen. For example, payroll activities are a process because they happen every month, or week or fortnight. Merging a business with another is not normally a process, because the activities involved are not always happening in the organization – it is a one-off activity, and so by definition is a project[6].

So that we are quite clear on the difference between a project and a process, consider an oil refinery or a telephone exchange. Running an oil refining plant is a process. Upgrading it or repairing it is a project. Running a telephone exchange is also a process. What about upgrading the telephone exchange to handle broadband? Upgrading the first exchange is a project, but if the telephone company owns a few hundred identical exchanges, and the same team is upgrading them, then after the first few times, upgrading them becomes a process. Telephone exchanges are more numerous and more standardized than oil refineries.

The examples of upgrading oil refineries and telephone exchanges show that the distinction between project and process is not fixed and absolute. There can be activities which have elements of both project and process. The distinction between project and process is useful, however, because it helps us to manage well. Project management is used where there is a high degree of novelty, uncertainty and therefore risk. Process management helps us reduce costs and risks and increase quality where there is a history of having done more or less exactly the same thing before, and where the same thing will be repeated in future. Upgrading Cyclops Oil's one and only refinery is predominantly a project for Cyclops Oil, but it might be predominantly a process for the Millennium Oil Refinery Upgrading Specialists Corporation, which does one a week.

Cyclops Oil and the telephone exchange upgrade also illustrate another strategic importance of projects. Projects are the primary means by which organizations grow and create value, in fact, projects are the only way in which organizations survive. As the world changes, organizations, like individuals, must adapt or die. Companies must create new products and new markets to replace old ones that wither and eventually vanish. (Government sector bodies too must innovate and change or, like Tsarist Russia or the Soviet Union after it, revolution will replace them, ultimately.) Figure 1.1 shows how projects continually provide replacement for the value lost in an organization as its environment and customers change.

Why does the difference between processes and projects matter to you? Why does this distinction between project and process matter? Is it not just theory, irrelevant to getting on with the job? It matters to senior managers and it matters to project managers and others involved in projects for slightly different reasons. For senior managers in an organization, an understanding of the difference between a project and a process will enable them to deploy the best management techniques to each thing that the organization does, and to have a more realistic mental picture of what is likely to happen in each of those things and how they should be guided and directed. For project managers and all those involved in doing project work, understanding this distinction is like knowing where you are on a map: you will have more confidence in when to apply project management techniques and a greater understanding of how what you are doing relates to all the other activities of your organization.

The dividing line between projects and processes (Table 1.1) depends on whether the organization repeats an activity often enough for it to become routine. For example, a large construction company might build a new housing development consisting of hundreds of near-identical houses. Their process of building a house is very well defined, but there may be different drainage or access requirements at different ends of the site so that the construction methods may be slightly

Fig. 1.1 Growth, or new value creation, in the organization comes only from projects

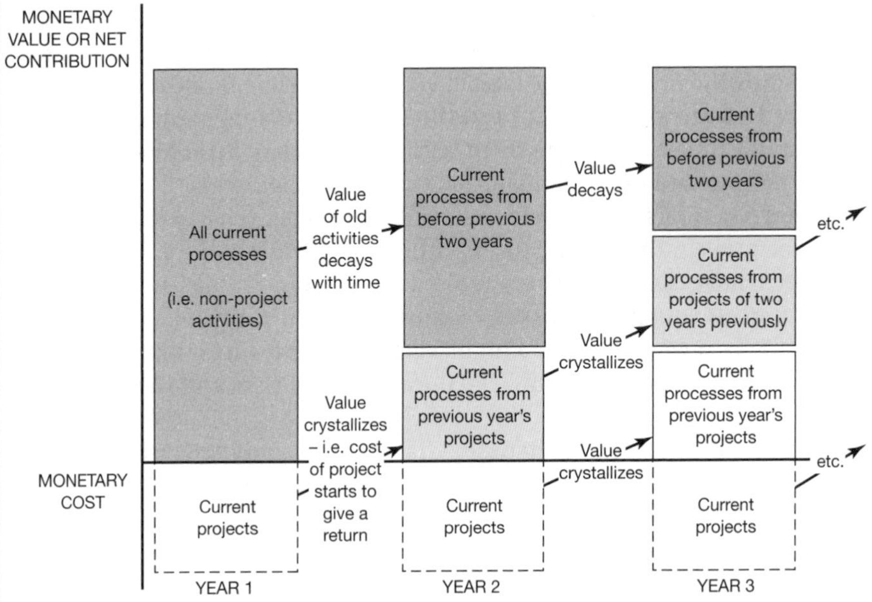

This diagram shows the role of projects in creating value in the future to replace value that will be lost as the organization s environment changes, through technological advances, changing customer preferences and in the case of the private sector, competition, and in the case of the government sector, changing stakeholder and societal needs. The area above the horizontal axis shows value, that is revenue (or societal value) minus costs, created by doing the things that the organization has done before, plus, in the case of Year 2 and Year 3, new value created by projects. New value can be either reduced costs, or increased revenues (or equivalent for the government sector), because value is revenue minus cost. Projects incur cost now to create value in the future. All value originated, at some point in the past, in a project; projects change or create business-as-usual processes.

Table 1.1 Features of projects and processes

Project	Process
◆ Novel: has not been done before, not in exactly the same way.	◆ Repeated continually: has been done before, will be done again.
◆ May be managed across divisions or directorates.	◆ Managed by a single division or department.
◆ Some key risks involved are not well understood.	◆ Most risks involved are well understood.
◆ Value to the organization is by delivering the project on time and on budget.	◆ Value to the organization is created by continuous improvement of the process.

different as a result. For this company, house-building is a process that can be repeated with a little adaptation. But if you were to build your own house, then it would almost certainly be a project. You are very unlikely to be as practised at building houses as the company that builds the housing development.

One way to interpret Table 1.1 is that we may distinguish between a project and a process according to the degree of execution risk involved. Procedures that get repeated frequently are usually refined through experience to the point where they are unlikely to fail catastrophically. Thousands of cans of beer pass along a canning line every minute and the likelihood that any particular can will be found to be outside its specified limits is very small. Continuous improvement initiatives such as Six Sigma use the continual repetition in processes to create value by making incremental changes to the process to reduce risk, increase quality (fitness for purpose) and reduce costs. But as the novelty of a process increases, so does the risk of not producing the expected result, and with entirely new ventures there are no pre-existing processes that can be refined.

Projects, in their purest form, create entirely new processes. Creating a new process necessarily involves doing new things. Discovering the right way to do them necessarily involves making some mistakes. New combinations of technologies or new markets usually mean that the people who have to do the project have not worked together before and there is no pre-existing organizational framework or protocol to guide their interactions. So before ground-breaking projects can begin to achieve their business objectives they must first create a new organization and this is itself fraught with risks. These activities involve such high risk that trying to manage them within the framework of the firm's usual activities is very likely to lead to disaster. A different management approach is needed for these high-risk activities, and this is why project management is different from day-to-day management. Having defined projects in absolute contrast to processes, we can see that in real life there is a continuum between pure processes and pure projects. Some projects have fewer pre-existing processes in them. Figure 1.2 illustrates the differences between projects and processes and recognizes this continuum. The Cisco example is one of many that illustrates how activities which are part of a project the first time around can become more process-like as they are repeated.

Fig. 1.2 Projects and processes

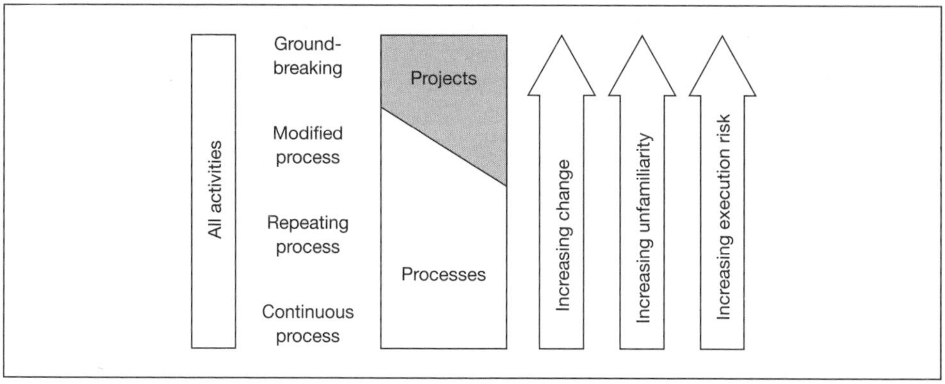

Case study

Acquisition projects at Cisco

The acquisition of another company is a rare event in the life of most organizations. Acquisition clearly changes the organization and requires careful planning and execution. It would be a major project in almost any firm.

Cisco, the Internet equipment supplier, grew from $28 million in revenues to $8.5 billion in only nine years, having deliberately adopted a strategy of growth by acquisition. At one time Cisco was acquiring another firm on average every 16 days! Acquisitions are notoriously difficult to get right, particularly when the most valuable part of the acquired firm is the people. But Cisco's growth plan required lots of acquisitions, and so one of the four main parts of the plan was to 'systematize the acquisition process'. Rather than reinvent the wheel with every acquisition, Cisco had strict procedures that included things such as:

◆ Standard pre-acquisition criteria and due diligence processes.

◆ A strict timetable for getting acquired companies' supply chains integrated into the Cisco system so that cost savings were immediately realized and the greater reach of the Cisco sales network could increase sales of the acquired company's products.

◆ A formal system of 'buddying' new employees with Cisco employees who had similar experience. The Cisco buddy had specific responsibility for making sure that new joiners knew the Cisco procedures.

◆ Structuring the deal to ensure employee retention and to align motivations of new employees with Cisco.

◆ Appointing a respected senior manager from the acquired company to lead the integration process.

These measures had been proven to address many of the common reasons for failure of company mergers. Cisco repeated the acquisition project so many times that it was able to formalize procedures in a way that greatly improved the speed of company integrations and the chances of success. Cisco had taken what would normally be a rare and risky project and turned it into a routine process.

▶ Definitions of project

It is sometimes helpful to have a definition of a key term so that we understand it better. Many organizations have their own definitions of what is a project for their purposes. If you do not already know, you should check whether your organization does. One of the main reasons why projects fail is that they were not identified as being projects and so were not managed as projects. Understanding what projects are and knowing their features and how they differ from processes can help to reduce the amount of waste and risk in your organization. It does not matter whether the word 'project' is used within your organization to describe an activity – the argument about whether to call something a project or not is not worth having – but what does matter is that project management techniques are applied to projects, whether or not they are called projects.

- 'A temporary endeavour undertaken to create a unique product, service or result' – Project Management Institute.
- 'A set of coordinated activities, with a specific start and finish, pursuing a specific goal with constraints on time, cost and resources' – International Standards Organization (ISO 8402). This definition extends the set of identifiable characteristics of a project to include constraints on time, cost and resources. (Were we to have unlimited time, cost and resources then there would be little need for proper management.)
- 'A management environment that is created for the purpose of delivering one or more business products according to a specified business case' – PRINCE2.
- 'A unique process, consisting of a set of coordinated and controlled activities with start and finish dates, undertaken to achieve an objective conforming to specific requirements, including constraints of time, cost and resources' – BSI[7].
- 'An endeavour in which human, material and financial resources are organized in a novel way to deliver a unique scope of work of given specification, often within constraints of cost and time, and to achieve beneficial change defined by quantitative and qualitative objectives' – alternative definition, Association of Project Managers[8]. (The primary APM definition follows the BSI definition.)

▶ Programmes and projects

A programme is a set of related projects, sometimes called a portfolio of projects. The term programme is sometimes used, confusingly, as a synonym for project. Although these two terms are related, they do not mean the same thing. Programme management is different from project management. The project manager is focused on making their project succeed; delivering the project is all, and if the project does not deliver the project then they have failed. A programme manager has more complex and subtle success criteria. Take the hypothetical example of a government programme to manage the consequences of harsh weather, floods, drought, snowstorms and climate change. Within this programme there might be a project to manage flooding and another to manage droughts. Now by logic alone we know that there will not be both floods and drought at the same time. For the programme to succeed it is not necessary that all of its projects succeed, or even happen. Or, to take a commercial example, commercial organizations often have some projects designed to manage a downturn in the economy, and others aimed at exploiting boom periods. These two kinds of projects are not both going to run at the same time, nor are they designed to, but they may be part of the same programme.

So programmes comprise a number of projects. Similarly, projects may comprise a number of sub-projects. What then is the difference between on the one hand programmes and projects, and on the other, projects and sub-projects? To some extent this is a matter of taste and organizational preference. Indeed, there is one investment bank that defines terms such that what it calls a programme is what the rest of the world calls a project, and vice-versa. Generally speaking, sub-projects are categorized as such because they are tightly or closely related to the project, and the success of each and every sub-project is necessary to the success of the project. In the case of programmes and the projects of which the programme is comprised, the programme can succeed without every single project happening or succeeding. In this sense, in contrast to projects and sub-projects, projects are loosely related to the programme. As we have said before, one should not be excessively concerned about how these terms are used and whether your particular organization uses them in a pure way; what matters is that you understand the principles, and you understand how to relate the terms as we will use them in this book to what happens in your organization, so that you can be a better project manager, and your organization can get projects done as well as possible, meaning at the lowest cost and risk, delivering the greatest business benefits.

▶ Identifying projects

There are advantages to identifying projects, whether or not they are so called, in order that they can be properly managed. Projects do not always have a label attached with the words 'This is a project'. That is, the customer service improvement project is not always called 'The customer service improvement project'. It may also be called an initiative, plan, scheme, strategy, measure, proposal, step, action or approach. As we have already seen, there is a continuum between processes and projects. The new 'Zap initiative', which is, let us suppose, the corporate name for the customer service improvement initiative, may include some process elements and some elements of a project. It is your job as the senior manager responsible for this, that is, the sponsor, or as the project manager or a member of the Zap team, to understand what within it is project management, so that you can do the best possible job in making the Zap initiative succeed. The point is that the ability to identify projects as such is a valuable one. And it is not difficult.

So how do you recognize a project when it is not called a project, or how do you check that something called a project is in fact a project? Projects have some or all of the following characteristics:

◆ Projects are the means to bring about change faster than it would happen otherwise; projects accelerate change to beyond the rate at which the organization naturally evolves and changes.
◆ Projects have a definite start and end point. (This contrasts with processes, which continue in a cycle.) Once a project reaches its objective, it finishes.
◆ Projects have high risk. This is a corollary of accelerated change.
◆ Projects are about doing something new. Consequently, projects have to develop new approaches and means of doing things.

Projects come in all sizes and every variety of difficulty. Some can be planned, managed and executed all by the same person working part time. Others require tens of thousands of people working on many sites doing many different things. All of them share some common features and will benefit from some parts of the body of knowledge that has built up around project management in general, but which parts of the body of knowledge should be applied will vary according to the specifics of the project. One of the skills that both organizations and individuals should try to acquire in project management is a sense of judgement of what tools to apply to different kinds of project. Figure 1.3 illustrates some dimensions in which projects can differ, and shows the different risks of failure associated with each.

Fig. 1.3 Project difficulty

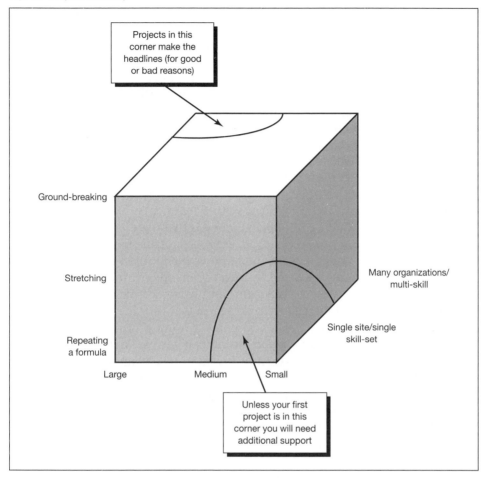

Projects in this corner make the headlines (for good or bad reasons)

Ground-breaking

Stretching

Many organizations/ multi-skill

Single site/single skill-set

Repeating a formula

Large   Medium   Small

Unless your first project is in this corner you will need additional support

Managing projects

Project management takes time. It cannot be treated as something that requires no time to be allocated to it, or that can be done by squeezing it around other activities without freeing up the necessary time; if such an approach is taken then your projects are much more likely to fail. This is a point to be understood not only by project managers but also by sponsors and others in senior management. The point is that project management, like any management activity, requires time. This is not to say that one can never manage a project at the same time as other activities; it simply means that if your diary is already full, you need to make some space in it before you take on something else. The trick is to strike a balance so that enough time is allowed to the project manager but not so much as to risk work expanding to fill excess time allotted to it. Different kinds of project need different amounts of time, and how much time is required is a matter of judgement. Small projects similar to projects that you have managed previously will take less time than large, unfamiliar projects.

Project management is a distinct management discipline. Even managers who are experienced but not in project management will have to learn new skills, that is project management skills, to be successful when running any but the smallest and simplest projects. Other general management skills are relevant to project management but are not sufficient to make success reasonably likely. Many of the skills of general management are also to be found in project management; these include leadership, teamwork, motivation, time management, HR, planning, budgeting and costing, risk management, change management and conflict resolution.

So what is distinctive about project management? In a word, risk. The nature of risk in projects is such that a distinct approach to those general management techniques that are found within project management is required. But let us expand for a few lines on this short answer, the single word 'risk', for there is a debate about whether project management is a subject at all and an argument that it is not distinct from general management. We believe that argument is mistaken for two reasons. First, empirical evidence from practitioners is that there are increasingly large numbers of people who have to manage or be accountable for projects as part of their work and who want to acquire and improve their project management skills as a distinct skill set. Those managers by their actions are saying that there is something distinct about project management, and what is driving them to acquire increased skills in project management is the risk that they have found previously in projects. Secondly, from a theoretical point of view, projects are about doing things that have not been done before, using new teams, under tight time constraints, and often working across existing organizational boundaries. This is likely to mean that while general management skills are applicable, they need to be applied in special ways. This is not so odd: the laws of physics apply equally on land and at sea, but the skills we use for piloting a car are similar to but in practice significantly different from those we use for piloting a boat. Both embody the same principles, but each is adapted to a different environment.

This book is a practical guide to project management, so we will not spend more time on this question, but it is useful for project managers and others responsible for projects to know that it is a distinct management competence, and that competence in other management skills does not automatically translate into competence in project management.

The project management lifecycle

All projects follow the same basic sequence of steps:

◆ decide what needs to be done;
◆ decide how to do it (that is, design the approach);
◆ do it.

Between each of these three basic steps there is a management decision to continue with the project. This basic model can be expanded to make it more detailed and useful to practitioners. For example, the 'do it' step involves monitoring and controlling. Like so much in project management, this is no more than applied common sense, in this case management by exception. We monitor the execution of something, in our case the project, and then we focus most of the controlling effort on the exceptions or deviance from the plan.

In this book we will assume that your organization has a generic model of a project which we will call the project lifecycle. This should be more detailed than the three-step model given opposite, but it need not be, and this model will serve if your organization does not yet have its own model. It merely represents a generic way in which projects are structured. The project lifecycle may break the work down into phases that correspond to the progress of a general project. Many organizations also have their own project management terminology, and increasingly they are standardizing on either the PMI or the PRINCE2 one. If your organization uses its own project vocabulary, it should not be too hard to map across the PMBOK's. Related to, but different from, the project lifecycle are the project management process groups:

◆ Initiating
◆ Planning
◆ Executing
◆ Controlling
◆ Closing.

These fit together as shown in Figure 1.4.

Fig. 1.4 The five project process groups

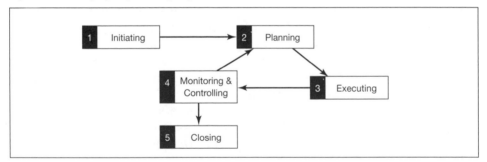

Summary

This chapter has introduced project management. Projects are distinguished from routine activities, which may be called processes, because they run continually, and cycle around, whereas projects have a definite start and finish, and aim to accelerate the normal rate of change. Projects are thus trying to do something new. This makes them risky. Projects are the main source of new competitive advantage, of tomorrow's profits or of tomorrow's new government and voluntary sector services. Projects are increasingly important in organizations.

◆ This book follows the approach and method of the Project Management Body of Knowledge (PMBOK), which is the distilled best practice from the Project

Management Institute, the largest professional body in the world for project management.

◆ It also draws on other smaller but established bodies of knowledge, including PRINCE2.

◆ As well as the project manager's perspective, the project manager (or sponsor) must consider the wider perspective of the organization in which the project sits (the performing organization).

◆ Project management is a rapidly evolving discipline at present.

◆ Understanding and managing scope is critical to the success of projects.

▶ Notes

1 By way of examples, the Black–Scholes method (or developments of it) is used to value options in the capital markets and commodities industries, but is not useful to value options on sequels in the film industry. (This is not to say that no-one is arguing otherwise. Why they would be fundamentally mistaken is outside the scope of this book.)

2 One does not manage a gang of unskilled labourers in quite the same way that one manages a troupe of prima ballerinas, or highly paid solicitors. (This, again, is not to say that no-one is arguing to the contrary, and, again, why they would be misguided to do so is beyond the scope of this book, but will be obvious to anyone who has left the confines of a Marxist university department and tried to make a living as a manager in an organization responsible to its customers.)

3 Farnborough International Air Show, Farnborough, UK, 20–21 July 2006.

4 'Front-loading' means doing an activity earlier than absolutely necessary, usually in order to gain benefits of risk or cost reduction in the longer term. The price paid is increasing early-stage costs, which is why selling the benefit is important.

5 Critical Chain was developed by Eliyahu Goldratt. See, for example, *The Goal: A Process of Ongoing Improvement* by Eliyahu M. Goldratt, North River Press Publishing, second edition, 1992, or *The Haystack Syndrome* by Eliyahu M. Goldratt, North River Press Publishing, 1990.

6 For simplicity here we ignore the corporate finance business, whose function includes to merge businesses. But even then, it is not the corporate finance firm itself that merges on a regular basis.

7 *BS 6079-2:2000. Part 2 – Vocabulary*. British Standards Institute, 15 March 2000. The BSI text includes within brackets numbers referring to other definitions; these brackets and numbers are omitted from our quotation of the BSI definition.

8 APM website, glossary section, http://www.apm.org.uk/PtoQ.asp (July 2006).

project organization, people and management

1

2

3

4

5

6

7

8

9

10

11

12

13

▶ Aims of this chapter

By the end of this chapter, the reader should:

◆ understand that people are paramount in project management;
◆ understand that the soft factors of organizational culture and personal character and style are more important to success in project management than the hard factors such as analysis and planning techniques;
◆ categorize their own organization into the spectrum of generic organizational structures, and state the main consequences for project management;
◆ be able to draw a diagram of the typical organizational structure of a project and describe the project management roles of the principal people in it;
◆ describe the type of personality types most commonly successful in project managers;
◆ define the term project stakeholder and explain why stakeholders are important to projects in both positive and negative terms;
◆ describe in detail the role of the sponsor and project manager, and also the relationship between them in project management;
◆ describe some key principles in managing the people and organizations in a project;
◆ state the words that make up the acronym SMART;
◆ describe a project lifecycle and state whether it is the same as the project management process groups;
◆ state five differences from the point of view of where the project manager and sponsor ought to focus their efforts between the beginning and middle of the project lifecycle;
◆ give examples of how project lifecycle and organizational structure affect each other.

▶ Structure of this chapter

This chapter begins by considering the organizational structure of projects, and the performing organization (the term used to mean the organization in which the project sits, the organization that owns the project). We then proceed to look at the people in the project and some of the softer factors in project management, which are the most critical for project success. This leads naturally to some guidelines for managing people in projects. The chapter ends with project lifecycles and phasing, which is naturally related to organizational structure and also to people and their styles.

▶ First thoughts

People do projects, and only people. Tools, techniques, software, old tried and tested management theories, new and sexy management fashions do not get projects done. People may use those things, well or badly, but fundamentally it is people who get projects done. 'How do we organize for success?' is one of the oldest questions in business, and to this day is one of the absolutely most important[1].

Managing projects means managing people. A project manager needs to realize that this means that all those soft 'people issues' that in some organizations are rarely discussed are going to affect your ability to do your job. So let us start by looking at how projects are organized and the role and characteristics of people in projects.

▶ Organizational structure and project structure

One would expect a colony of elderly Italian artists to settle naturally on quite a different way of organizing themselves if they were to have to cook communal meals than one would expect a class of five-year-old British schoolchildren to need to be organized for feeding purposes. The purpose of this imaginary example is simply, by means of an extreme pair of cases, to remind ourselves that the kind of people we are dealing with will affect what type of organizational structure is the most effective for a given purpose. Different times and places have different cultures and norms. The right way to organize teams of people in the 1950s stopped working in most Western countries in the 1960s, as people rebelled against authority that could not justify itself. These examples may sound distant from the everyday problems of project management, but in fact cultural matters, and the organizational factors that stem from them, are often very much behind the everyday performance issues in project management. As a project manager or sponsor, you need to understand people, you need to understand organizational culture, and you need to know what implications these have for your project. There are many reasons for this, only two of which we will set out right now. One is that culture and organizational design affect the efficiency and effectiveness of individuals and projects; that this is a factor in general management and not just project management should not for a moment allow us to ignore its central importance to project management. Another reason is that you need to be able to judge when something that worked very well in another project either will be unlikely to work in your next project, or will need modification, because the structure or the culture of the organization is different.

Let us define some terms. By organizational design or organizational structure we mean how an organization is structured into sub-units, such as divisions and departments, or, to say the same thing in a different way, how the functions within the organization report to each other up the hierarchy. Also included in what we mean by organizational structure is where ownership of various resources, especially people and capital, sits within the organization. By the character of an individual we mean their personality traits, their behavioural style, their habits of mind and dispositions to act in certain ways, especially with regard to other people. By organizational culture, we mean a similar thing to the character of an individual, but as it applies to a whole organization or a part of an organization, not to the individual – 'how we do things around here'. Figure 2.1 depicts how the individual's character is affected by the character of other individuals and of the organization's style and structure, and vice versa, and how all these are also affected by society at large. You need to understand this because projects typically cut across different divisions of an organization, and different divisions will have their own styles. In investment banks, the best way to communicate with corporate finance professionals is not the same as the best way to communicate with foreign exchange spot traders; in IT the salespeople have a different culture from programmers; and in healthcare, surgeons will respond best to a different way of presenting the benefits of a project from the way that is best for nurses. What works in IBM is not necessarily what will work in Microsoft's culture, and Microsoft's view of the world can be expected to be different from Skype's or Google's. In short, understand the people you are dealing with, and their organization.

Fig. 2.1 Structure and style

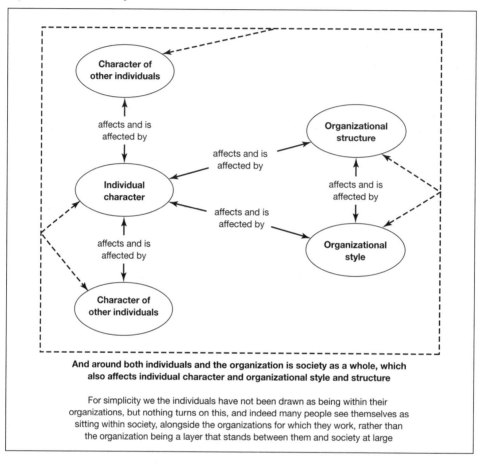

And around both individuals and the organization is society as a whole, which also affects individual character and organizational style and structure

For simplicity we the individuals have not been drawn as being within their organizations, but nothing turns on this, and indeed many people see themselves as sitting within society, alongside the organizations for which they work, rather than the organization being a layer that stands between them and society at large

Main kinds of organization and consequences for project management

There is an infinite variety of types of organization, because every organization, like every person, is in some sense unique. However, it is useful to consider several different kinds of organization and their consequences for project management. To set the scene for doing that, let us first remind ourselves of the difference between a project and a process. A process is a continuing activity, in which key operations are repeated periodically. The process will continue indefinitely. Paradigm examples of processes are payroll, sales and marketing, and financial control and direction. Projects, in contrast, have definite start and end points, and are set up to achieve a specific purpose, after the attainment of which (or after the failure to attain which) they are shut down. The first and foremost distinction between kinds of organizations from the point of view of project management is between organizations that are in a sense nothing but a collection of projects, and organizations that exist to manage one or more processes[2]. We call these the projectized and the process-focused. (The PMBOK calls the latter non-projectized.) This is summarized in Figure 2.2, while Table 2.1 gives some examples of each kind to illustrate this difference.

Note that some businesses are naturally projectized ones. Law firms and management consulting firms, for example, will often be in effect a portfolio of projects, legal cases in the case of law firms and consulting engagements in the case of management consultancies. Accounting firms, by contrast, will be of the other kind if they specialize in audit, as audit happens every year, follows the same pattern, and necessarily dovetails exactly into the previous iteration of the process. Note that there are many fields in which it will make sense to have a single company (one of many kinds of organization) straddling the two different kinds of activity. Take oil and gas, for example. Distributing gas and petrol to customers is definitely a non-projectized business, predominantly, whereas exploration is predominantly a projectized business. We qualify this with the word 'predominantly' in both cases

Fig. 2.2 A taxonomy of organizations with respect to their implications for project management

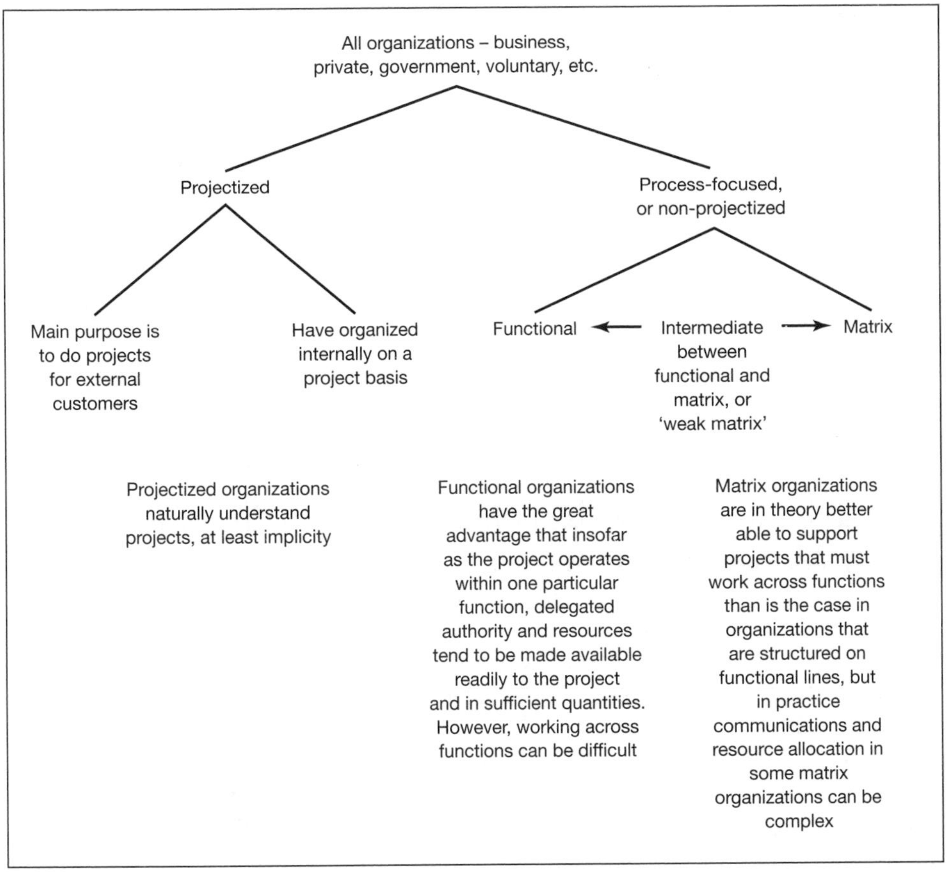

Table 2.1 Some typical examples of kinds of organizations that are projectized and of kinds that are process-focused, with respect to project management

Projectized	Process-focused (non-projectized)
◆ Oil and gas exploration.	◆ Oil and gas refining.
◆ Corporate finance.	◆ Capital markets trading.
◆ Starting a new business.	◆ Fund management.
◆ New product development.	◆ Retailing and wholesaling.
◆ Transport – charter services.	◆ Transport – scheduled services.
◆ Legal representation – bar.	◆ Administration of justice.
◆ Intelligence responses to major events, foreign intelligence.	◆ Domestic intelligence and counter-intelligence.
◆ PhD programmes.	◆ Education – primary to tertiary.
◆ Research and development, e.g. into drugs and medical treatments, or software and services development.	◆ Hospital and GP surgery management.
	◆ Pharmaceutical sales.
◆ Expeditionary warfare, including mercenary and private military company assistance.	◆ Software sales, software maintenance.
	◆ Pensions administration.
◆ Outsourcing of local government services.	◆ Maintaining armed forces in peacetime.
◆ Property development.	◆ Local government services.
◆ Film production and entertainment product creation.	◆ Farming.
	◆ Distribution.
	◆ Entertainment promotion.

---

because there are some projects in the business of oil and gas distribution, such as building a new refinery or running a sales campaign to attract new customers. And in exploring for new oil and gas fields, while each new exploration is a project, all oil and gas exploration projects have certain common features, such as the need for derricks, pipes, environmental PR, and careful control of naked lights at the well head. But the distinction holds: some kinds of business are naturally organized as projects, others are naturally organized as processes.

So what? From a project management point of view, trying to run a project in an organization that naturally understands projects is going to be easier than trying to run one in an organization that has no experience of projects. You need to know what experience of projects exists in your organization and especially in all the parts of it that your project will depend on. This should not be too difficult if you have been there some time, although the question is a useful lens through which to think about how things can be improved, but if you are setting up a project in a new organization, or a new part of your organization, it is a vital question.

Organizations that lack experience of project management are likely also to lack some of the basic processes and organizational assets that make projects easier to run. This will mean that compared to running the same project in an organization that does have such experience and assets, your project either will need extra budget to compensate, or will need to accept greater risk. For example, if you have run a highly successful project in a projectized business at a total cost of £x, you will find that doing the same project on the same scale in a non-projectized business will cost more. One example of the kinds of things lacking might be systems or processes for project accounting, which will mean either hiring a project accountant into the team, training someone from the financial controller's function to do the job, or running the project without proper project accounting. A project accounting system is one of the elements included in a project management system.

Figure 2.3 sets out some types of functional organizational structure with their implications for project management.

Fig. 2.3 Types of organizational structure and their implications for project management

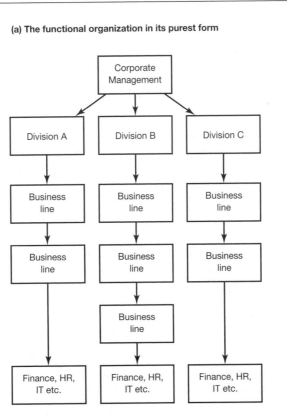

(a) The functional organization in its purest form

The functional organization in its purest form is a multidivisional business in which each division is completely independent of the others. Corporate management sets strategic direction for each division and allocates capital to each division on behalf of the owners, and holds each division to account. Divisions operate entirely independently from each other

Implications for project management
- Working within your own division is easy
- Working outside your own division is hard
- If your division does not understand projects, it will be difficult to get them to understand
- Getting input and buy-in to your project from other divisions means communicating up and then down the organizational hierarchy

Fig. 2.3 Continued

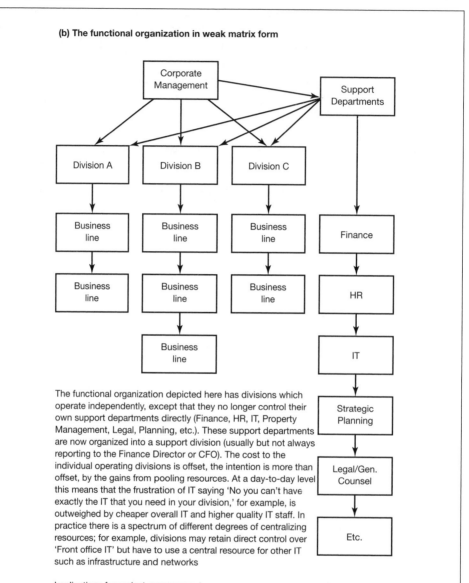

(b) The functional organization in weak matrix form

The functional organization depicted here has divisions which operate independently, except that they no longer control their own support departments directly (Finance, HR, IT, Property Management, Legal, Planning, etc.). These support departments are now organized into a support division (usually but not always reporting to the Finance Director or CFO). The cost to the individual operating divisions is offset, the intention is more than offset, by the gains from pooling resources. At a day-to-day level this means that the frustration of IT saying 'No you can't have exactly the IT that you need in your division,' for example, is outweighed by cheaper overall IT and higher quality IT staff. In practice there is a spectrum of different degrees of centralizing resources; for example, divisions may retain direct control over 'Front office IT' but have to use a central resource for other IT such as infrastructure and networks

Implications for project management
• Similar to the functional organization, except
• People understand cross-divisional working better, although cross-divisional politics can be a major frustration
• Divisions contend for the same support resources, so your project may have to wait or make a strong case
• The centralization or grouping together of support functions can reduce the length of the communication lines for getting input to your project, so making it easier

Fig. 2.3 Continued

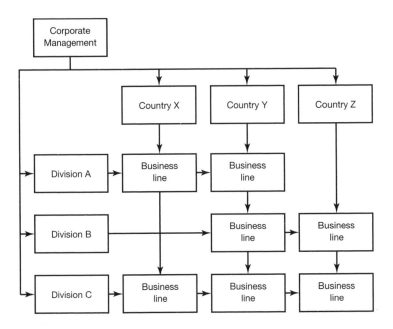

(c) One possible example of the pure form of the matrix organization

The distinguishing feature of the matrix organization, in its pure form, is that the business lines have two bosses (or more) each. This may seem like a crazy idea, but it evolved as a response to critical problems in the complexity of modern business organizations and severe coordination and resource allocation constraints. In practice, one of the bosses on the organization chart tended by force of personality or power over more resources than the other to dominate the business line, and since its heyday in the 1960s, the pure form of matrix is tending to be abandoned and regarded as an impracticable idea. However, it is alive and well in many government sector organizations, and perhaps less unsuitable in that sector than in commercial organizations. Conceptually it is a useful model for the project manager to have in mind as an aid to understanding how new organizations might be structured even if they are not pure-form matrix ones

Implications for project management
• In theory your project will have good connectivity to many parts of the organization. In practice these connections may be weak or overloaded
• In theory your project can get the authority it needs to work across the right parts of the organization, in practice you may end up competing for time, attention and other resources with many other projects who have the same authority

▶ Project management system

A system is vital to managing anything effectively and efficiently. Projects are no exception. There needs to be a system in your project, and at the very least both the sponsor and the project manager need to understand the system and agree on it. The following case study shows why the sponsor and project manager must agree on the basics of the system to be used for project management in their project.

Case study

Why project management systems matter: a case study from the UK public sector

This case study may sound incredible but is sadly a true real-life example. Sad because it wasted a million pounds of taxpayers' money. There was a £1 million budget project in a UK government body where the government organization used the term 'sponsor' to mean, in effect, low-level administrator with no power. This organization did have people called 'responsible directors' who fulfilled a role that most other organizations call 'sponsor'. The organization also had adopted no fewer than four different standard methodologies for project management, including PMBOK, PRINCE2, APM and the British Standard. It hired an outside project manager to run the project, the responsible director washed their hands of the project, the 'sponsor' mandated one project management methodology one week and another the next, and because of great confusion about which project management system was to be used, and also for other reasons, another million pounds of public money was wasted. It only became clear some months after the project that a major cause of project failure had been confusion about the project management system – had it been clear at the start, the project manager could perhaps have avoided many of the problems but at least would have halted the project. The project manager was blamed for everything that went wrong. A new project manager was hired, who confirmed that the first project manager was indeed useless and incompetent, and then proceeded himself to fail even more spectacularly to deliver the project, for roughly the same reasons. The government organization shrugged off this double failure as just the way that projects are. It did not document any of the lessons learnt in its lessons learnt database. Such is the way that public money is sometimes spent.

A project management system need not be large and complicated, and certainly should not be bureaucratic. The most important thing is that the sponsor and project manager agree on what the system is, or they can even start by agreeing that there is no system and that they will develop one as they go along. It is also perfectly good to say 'We will use the Company's standard project management system' or 'We will use the Company's standard project management system but adapt it as necessary for the needs of this particular project'. Whether you document adaptations or not is of course up to you, but again the project manager and sponsor should agree, in order to avoid wastage by, for example, the project manager documenting where the project will differ in its system from the company's standard when the sponsor sees no need. The kind of thing that needs to be surfaced and discussed, to continue with that example, is if the project intends to take many other people into the project team from the same organization at a later stage, then having documentation of how the project management system differs from the company standard will save much time and risk in inducting those people into the project.

One of the standard methodologies for project management, such as the PMBOK one which is followed in this book, can save much time and effort by providing much, but not all, of a project management system. However, the golden rule in project management is to focus on being effective: pick something that works and be prepared to bend, break and chop up existing standards and approaches to get it right for your project (within the constraints of your organization's policy, of course). One very successful project manager eschewed all specialist project management methodology and based his system on the 1980s edition of the British Army's *Platoon Commander's Aide Memoire*. It worked for him. By all accounts he was a pain to work for, and the women who worked for him complained that they felt they were actually in the army in his platoon, but the fact is that his projects ran well and even the women who worked for him respected him. Conversely, there are people who score top marks in all the project management training and tests of methodologies yet who could not run a successful project if their lives depended on it. Find a system that works and stick to it, and develop it as you go.

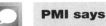

PMI says

Project management system

'Project Management System (Tool). The aggregation of the processes, tools, techniques, methodologies, resources, and procedures to manage a project. The system is documented in the project management plan and its context will vary depending upon the application area, organizational influence, complexity of the project, and the availability of existing systems. A project management system, which can be formal or informal, aids a project manager in effectively guiding a project to completion. A project management system is a set of processes and the related monitoring and control functions that are consolidated and combined into a functioning, unified whole.' *PMBOK Guide* (p.369)

▶ Project organization and project roles

Figure 2.4 sets out a typical organizational structure of a project. The details of the project structure will vary according to specific roles that people play in a particular project. We look at both in this section. Different organizations will label the same roles with different names. Irrespective of what actual names are used, the underlying responsibilities of the roles described here are found in most projects. Here we use the names and roles given in the *PMBOK Guide* for convenience, together with a few others, such as the project steering committee to reflect the reality of real-life project management. You need to understand the rationale for each of the roles in a project, and what their responsibilities are. You also need to know what these roles are actually called in your organization, as it is unlikely that your organization will follow the *PMBOK Guide* nomenclature for every project role. The most important roles in a project are the Sponsor and the Project Manager. It is vital to understand what these roles do and don't do in project management.

Fig. 2.4 A representative organizational structure of a project

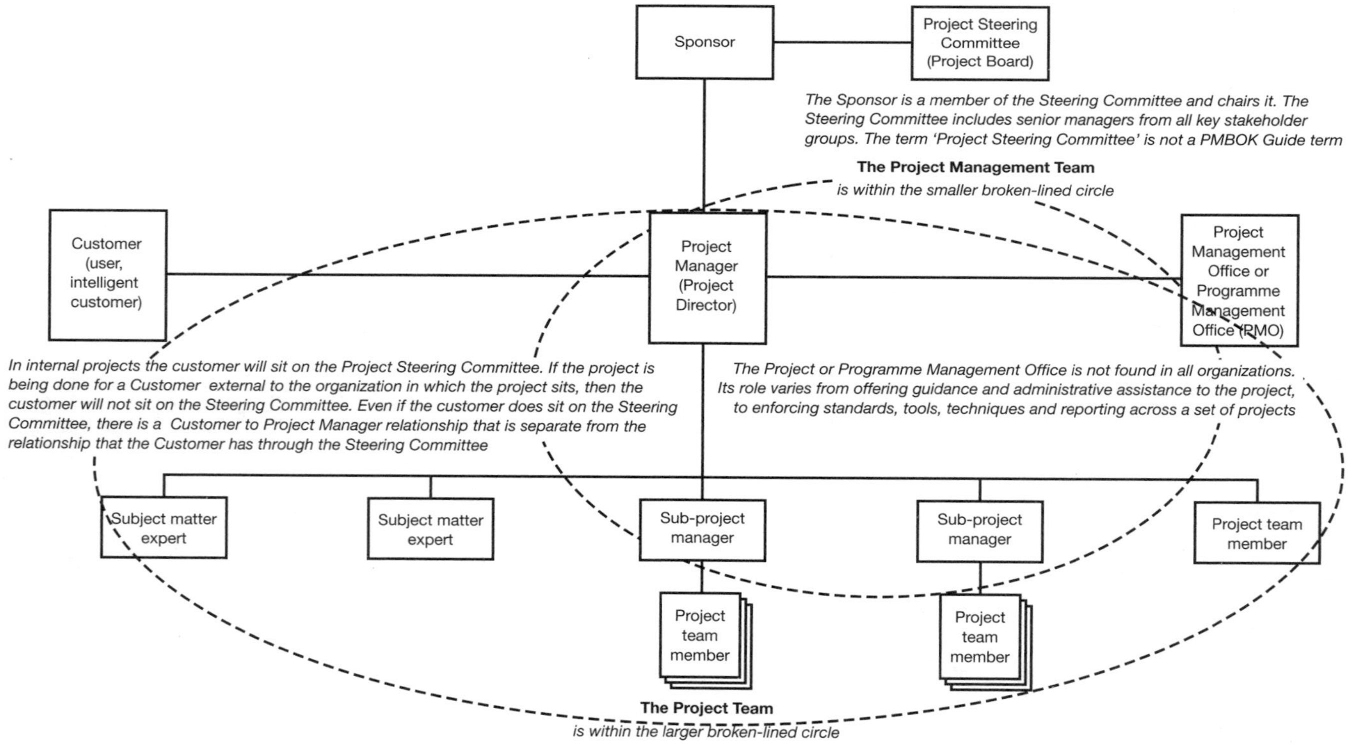

Project Steering Committee (Project Board)

Sponsor

Customer (user, intelligent customer)

Project Manager (Project Director)

Project Management Office or Programme Management Office (PMO)

Subject matter expert

Subject matter expert

Sub-project manager

Sub-project manager

Project team member

Project team member

Project team member

The Project Management Team is within the smaller broken-lined circle

The Project Team is within the larger broken-lined circle

The Sponsor is a member of the Steering Committee and chairs it. The Steering Committee includes senior managers from all key stakeholder groups. The term 'Project Steering Committee' is not a PMBOK Guide term

The Project or Programme Management Office is not found in all organizations. Its role varies from offering guidance and administrative assistance to the project, to enforcing standards, tools, techniques and reporting across a set of projects

In internal projects the customer will sit on the Project Steering Committee. If the project is being done for a Customer external to the organization in which the project sits, then the customer will not sit on the Steering Committee. Even if the customer does sit on the Steering Committee, there is a Customer to Project Manager relationship that is separate from the relationship that the Customer has through the Steering Committee

There are many different names for the titles or roles of those in the project who come under the Project Manager. The three main types are shown here. Sub-project managers have management responsibility for a part of the project. Subject matter experts may or may not perform project work, but their primary contribution to the projects is their specialized expertise – remember that the Project Manager is not expected to know about all areas of the project, their role is to do project management, so subject matter experts provide the expertise necessary to design and plan the project and to make sound and informed decisions on their subject matter. Project team member is the term for anyone else on the project. It is useful to have a term for the group who collectively do project management in the project, and this is the project management team. The project team means everyone involved in doing project work, although normally the Customer, Sponsor and Steering Committee are excluded from both these groups as they are not involved in doing day-to-day project work. Where there is a Project or Programme Management Office, it may or may not be involved in project management or project execution, which is why in this diagram the PMO box is partly included in the broken-lined circles. On large projects or where the individual has negotiated a title increase, the Project Manager may be called Project Director.

▶ Sponsor

The sponsor is responsible to the organization that owns the project for the resources committed to the project and, ultimately, for the project delivering results and for the performance of the project. Often the sponsor is a senior manager who wants the project done, usually because it will benefit them in some way. In some cases the sponsor may see the need for the project themselves, but in other cases the suggestion may come from elsewhere in the organization and the sponsor then adopts or is asked to adopt the idea. If there are several senior managers who will all benefit from the project, then it is important that this group agrees to nominate a single sponsor to avoid inefficiency in the project. Although the rule is 'one and only one sponsor in a project', there are many organizations where two or more sponsors are appointed because of the power structure in the organization and how the project relates to it. If your organization decides to appoint two sponsors, it is usually best to live with it rather than to argue the theoretical case for getting rid of one of them. It can be that the Project or Programme Management Office (PMO) is the sponsor – see below.

A good sponsor is one who understands how the performing organization works and can get things done. The sponsor clears the way for the project and establishes links from the project to key areas within the performing organization. This requires pragmatism, political sensitivity and good management skills.

The sponsor's role is necessary because it is impractical for the whole management of the organization to be involved in every decision about directing the project. The organization therefore charges the individual who hopes to get the benefits of a successful project with the responsibility and authority for project supervision. This is not the same as project management – it is rather someone who acts as the buyer of the project on behalf of the organization. Conceptually, the sponsor has a business need for the project, the firm grants the sponsor the money and resources for the project, and the sponsor then contracts with the project team to execute the project. Hence in project organization terms the project manager works for the sponsor, who works for the business.

The sponsor's focus is on the business objectives, and it is common for there to be little contact with the sponsor other than at major project events, unless the project is drifting off track and it looks like the business objectives will not be met. Sponsors tend to be busy people. Nonetheless, it is vital for there to be good communication between the sponsor and the project manager, and the sponsor should ensure that if the project manager needs to talk to them then the sponsor is available. It is the sponsor who has the final responsibility to protect the business by intervening if required to get the project back on track or, if necessary, to cancel the project before extra money is wasted.

PMI says

Sponsor

'Sponsor. The person or group that provides the financial resources, in cash or in kind, for the project.' *PMBOK Guide* (p.376)

The BSI definition of a sponsor is an 'individual or body for whom the project is undertaken and who is the primary risk taker'[3]. This definition is useful because it highlights that the sponsor has the most to lose, the most at stake in the project.

A common problem for sponsors right now is that they are appointed as project sponsors but feel that they themselves lack experience and training in project management. The difficulty felt by many sponsors who are in such a position is that they cannot afford to reveal their lack of experience either to the project team or to their peers. If you are a sponsor who feels this, fear not. Project management is applied common sense, and the essential features of sponsorship are entirely within the skills and experience that you will already have acquired in your career. Your main job as sponsor is to do three things: listen to the project manager and intervene if they are out of their depth or heading in the wrong direction; keep the stakeholders on side with the project and smooth communication between them and the project team, especially the project manager; and keep your eye on the purpose of the project and see that it keeps heading in the right direction. Like all senior management jobs, much of project sponsorship is a matter of understanding the power and politics in your organization. Finally, if you feel that some training in project management would be useful, there are a number of specialist courses for project sponsorship; half a day is probably more than sufficient.

▶ Project manager

The project manager in effect contracts with the sponsor to manage the project that is defined in the project charter or project plan. The limits of the project manager's authority and responsibility must be understood by both the project manager and the sponsor. In most organizations, the project manager has authority to use money and resources up to the limits set out in the plan or charter but no more. If the project manager learns that the project will take more than has been authorized, then it is vital to seek reapproval on the new basis, otherwise the project manager will have no authority to proceed. The project manager plans, organizes, controls and reports project activities, working closely with the sponsor as appropriate. In practice this usually means that the two work more closely at the start of a project, to define scope and plan the project, and to work out what the project is and how it will fit into the organization. Once these things have been worked out and the project moves into the execution phase then contact tends to reduce, unless major problems or changes arise. The size of the project determines what the project manager does. On smaller projects, the project manager may undertake activities such as drafting the scope statement and planning on their own, but on large or complex projects a team of specialists may be required.

Finally, we should be quite clear about what the project manager's role is and is not in project management. It is about managing the project, not doing the work. Often in very small projects the person who is managing the project is also doing some of the work. There is nothing wrong with that, but only the work of managing the project can be called project management. For example, if a project manager is appointed to supervise the move of a thousand staff from one office building to another, the project management role is to plan the move and manage the people who are to physically carry the furniture from one location to another, and deal with all the communication needs and unexpected issues as they arise. The project manager is not, as project manager, doing the lifting of furniture. Management is a real activity that takes much time and effort, and has its own distinct discipline and body of professional knowledge. Nor is it the project manager's job to know everything about the subject matter in their project, but it is their job to ensure that the project has or has access to people with the right expertise. A project manager must be a subject matter expert in project management, and should ideally also have experience of the industry in which the project is working: it is project management expertise that is the primary consideration, because that is the prime need for the project management role.

PMI says

Project manager
'Project Manager. The person assigned by the performing organization to achieve the project objectives.' *PMBOK Guide* (p.369)

Who makes a good project manager? This varies according to the industry and the nature of the project, but in general good project managers are:

◆ task focused,
◆ able to manage to deadlines,
◆ politically aware,
◆ able to compromise pragmatically,
◆ good communicators, and
◆ able to inspire and motivate others.

Good project managers will normally have been trained in some recognized project management methodology. The main methodologies current at the time of writing are the following:

◆ PMI's *PMBOK Guide* (also the US National Standard ANSI/PMI 99-001-2004)
◆ Critical Chain
◆ PRINCE2
◆ British Standard BS6079
◆ Various national methodologies under the IIPM umbrella, such as APM in the UK.

Previous standards for project management include:

◆ IBM's MITP (amalgamated with PRINCE to become PRINCE2)
◆ IBM's WISSDM
◆ PRINCE®.

What matters much more than which methodology or whether project managers have been trained is their ability to manage projects, which should be evidenced in their career history. Project managers' careers typically start in a project role other than project management, perhaps as the administrative assistant to a project manager, which is an ideal way to learn because one gets to see all of project management but without being exposed to the risk of responsibility. They then progress to managing a small project, perhaps an internal one, and from there get larger or more important projects according to their abilities.

▶ Project team member

Team members carry out tasks or groups of tasks specified by the project manager, with agreed deliverables and to agreed timescales. Team members are expected to take responsibility for their own tasks, to keep the project manager informed about progress and to exercise initiative if they become aware of other factors outside their specific task that might also affect the project.

PMI says

Project team members

'Project Team Members. The persons who report either directly or indirectly to the project manager, and who are responsible for performing project work as a regular part of their assigned duties.' *PMBOK Guide* (p.371)

The team is vital to the project. People who want to be on the project will be much more valuable to it than people who don't want to be on the project. This means that the sponsor and project manager have a selling job from the moment the project is first conceived.

▶ Programme board

In organizations where several projects together form a programme, also known as a portfolio of projects, there will be a committee to oversee the programme. The programme board reviews, approves and prioritizes project proposals as well as authorizing resource allocation. It monitors project exceptions and instigates corrective action. It aligns the projects within the programme and may mandate standard methodologies, tools, techniques, reporting and training for each programme. ('Programme board' is not a *PMBOK Guide* term.)

▶ Programme or project management office

Where an organization runs many projects, there are economies of scale to be gained from standardization across them. There may also be a need to coordinate projects as a portfolio, or programme, and to apportion scarce resources between them on a systematic basis – such is the case for having a programme or project management office (PMO). The PMO is becoming an increasingly common structure in organizations, as more and more organizations see benefits from it.

The role of the PMO ranges from at one extreme nothing more than assistance and support at the whim of the project manager, to at the other extreme a management and controlling function that allocates resources to projects, directs how they should be done and how and when they should report, and enforces training and standards on project teams. A PMO that is mandated to operate more towards the controlling end of this spectrum is by no means necessarily a bad thing from the point of view of the project manager and the project, as it frees up much time for the project manager to concentrate on the tasks most essential to the project, and it also provides a large measure of insurance against failure. As ever, the personal relationships and communications established by the project manager are vital. If you are a project manager and are expected to work under a PMO, find out what it can do for you and your project, build excellent personal relationships with the key people in it, and use it. The PMO may take on some of the responsibilities of the project sponsor, or may even fill the role of the sponsor. The role of a PMO may include such things as:

◆ Administering centralized project reporting logging.
◆ Providing project people and resources.
◆ Coordinating project resource usage across the organization – possibly by maintaining the resource databases linked to the organization's project planning software.
◆ Disseminating best practice in project management across the firm, for example by arranging training or by ensuring that all project managers use the company projects handbook if there is one.
◆ Being a source of advice and a knowledge repository for project teams and individuals.
◆ Selecting and supporting project planning software.
◆ Representing the project's function in discussions within the firm on infrastructure, quality procedures, and so on.
◆ Creating and maintaining standard forms for project charters, plans, checklists, risk and issue logs, reports and commonly used project procedures.
◆ Checking and enforcing minimum standards in the documentation submitted.

Although there is a clear theoretical difference between a programme and a project, and a useful one, in practice it is unlikely that a single organization would run two separate bodies for programme and project management office, so we treat them both in one section here.

PMI says

Programme and Project Management Office
'Programme Management Office (PMO). The centralized management of a particular program or programs such that corporate benefit is realized by sharing the resources, methodologies, tools and techniques, and related high-level project management focus.' *PMBOK Guide* (p.368)

'Project Management Office (PMO). An organizational body or entity assigned various responsibilities related to the centralized and coordinated management of those projects under its domain. The responsibilities of a PMO can range from providing project management support functions to actually being responsible for the direct management of a project. ...' *PMBOK Guide* (p.369)

The term 'project office' is slightly different from 'project management office'. In project management, the project office is a role, not a room or a place. The role is to provide administrative support for the project. It has some relationship to a project management office in that a PMO can perform some or all of the functions of a project office. The project office is a good role in which to place graduate trainees and others at the start of their careers to give them safe exposure to project management, but it is also a career path in its own right. On a project of any size the project office or administrative function is substantial, and it is valuable to free the project manager from having to do project office tasks.

▶ Performing organization

By this term we mean the organization, company, firm, business, government department or charity that owns the project, that organization within which the project is performed.

PMI says

Performing organization
'Performing Organization. The enterprise whose personnel are most directly involved in doing the work of the project.' *PMBOK Guide* (p.366)

▶ Stakeholders

Stakeholders are all those who have an interest in the project, that is, who stand to gain or lose from the project. Stakeholders may be individuals or groups; some will be inside and some may be outside the performing organization. Examples of stakeholders include:

- ◆ The project's customer or other direct users of its deliverables.
- ◆ The steering committee and the project team.
- ◆ Others within the performing organization whose work will be affected by the project.
- ◆ People or organizations outside the performing organization who will be affected (this may include protest groups – you don't have to invite them to your project management meetings, but if they can derail your project or embarrass you, you may want to include them as a factor in your plans).
- ◆ Managers and team members of other projects who have an interest in this project (for example, if they depend on it to provide outputs or to release resources by a certain date).
- ◆ Previous buyers of goods or services who may react positively or negatively to news of the project.
- ◆ Suppliers and distributors (they may be fearful of the changes implied by the project, especially if they think it will mean a loss of business).

The role of stakeholders in a project must be dealt with on a case-by-case basis. Projects can have far-reaching effects and one of the potential pitfalls of project management is to believe that the only people who matter are those on the project team and the project's customers. Stakeholders is a loose category but the unifying idea is that their opinion matters in some way, and they often choose themselves rather than being appointed by the project manager. Their impact can be very great on some projects, and in some sectors companies have developed standard contingency plans that are applied on all projects. On the positive side, a network of enthusiastic supporters of the project is one of the hallmarks of a truly successful project and can itself contribute to that success.

Stakeholder management has elements of public relations, but project managers do not need to become public relations specialists. On small projects it is usually enough to remember that there are interested parties outside the formal project boundary, and to make an effort to communicate with them at appropriate times.

PMI says

Stakeholder

'Stakeholder. Person or organization (e.g. customer, sponsor, performing organization, or the public) that is actively involved in the project, or whose interests may be positively or negatively affected by the execution of the project. A stakeholder may also exert influence over the project and its deliverables.' *PMBOK Guide* (p.376)

▶ Influencers

If the notion of stakeholders as described above is too broad, for example the idea of including a protest group as a stakeholder gets in the way of thinking clearly about the project, then the term 'influencer' may be useful as a kind of weak stakeholder, or a class of stakeholder who we would rather did not exist.

▶ Subject matter expert

The project manager is required to be an expert in project management first and foremost, not in the subject matter of the project, although experience in it helps. The project will need expert input that the project manager and sponsor do not possess. This comes from people called subject matter experts. They may or may not do more than provide information and guidance to the project. Expert advisors can often add value quickly if they are used appropriately to address a specific problem within their area of expertise. Such inputs from internal or external experts may not require full-time membership of the project team, though if subject matter experts are used on a part-time basis then it may be necessary to set aside time to ensure they are up to speed with the latest developments in the project, and they should at least be given regular briefings. ('Subject matter expert' is not a PMBOK term.)

▶ Seller (also Supplier)

'Seller' is the PMBOK standard term for a supplier to the project of products or services, although in this book we use the terms 'seller' and 'supplier' interchangeably, to accord with common usage. It is common for projects to rely on external suppliers for some of their critical outputs. The supplier might take on a sub-project but you, the project manager, are still responsible for overall delivery and should manage the supplier with no less care and attention than internal resources. Suppliers should be set SMART objectives and be required to give timely and accurate progress reports like other members of the team.

PMI says

Seller

'Seller. A provider or supplier of products, services or results to an organization.' *PMBOK Guide* (p.375)

▶ Users and customers (and 'intelligent customers')

The project's customer is the person or group for whom it is being done. They are the intended ultimate and main beneficiaries of the project. They benefit from the project's results. This makes them a critically important group. Their most formal relationship with the project is usually in specifying the user needs at the beginning of the project, and in accepting the project outputs at the end. During the project the role of the customer will vary but they will usually be called upon to provide continuing guidance throughout the life of the project in order to ensure that the results of the project stay on track and, just as importantly, that the expectations of the customer and of the project team remain aligned. Customers need to be managed by the project; this is a key task for the project manager and sponsor, and it usually requires that the customer be openly and honestly engaged in the project.

Where the customer is a large organization or a large group of people, then in order to keep communications working effectively it is normal for the customer to appoint a single point of contact to handle the interface with the project. In some cases this representative may need to have the authority to make binding decisions on behalf of the user group, including the decision to accept or reject changes in the project objectives. In some cases too an 'intelligent customer' may be designated. This term is not used to imply that all the other customers are not intelligent, but means that the designated intelligent customer has a detailed understanding of the results required of the project. Test pilots could be examples of intelligent customers for aircraft, for example. ('Intelligent customer' is not a *PMBOK Guide* term.)

PMI says

User and Customer

'User. The person or organization that will use the project's product or service. ...' *PMBOK Guide* (p.378)

'Customer. The person or organization that will use the project's product or service or result. ...' *PMBOK Guide* (p.358)

'Result. An output from performing project management processes and activities. Results include outcomes ... and documents .... Contrast with product and service. See also deliverable.' *PMBOK Guide* (p.372)

The *PMBOK Guide* definitions for the terms 'user' and 'customer' given here imply a useful difference. Both the project's customers and users use products and services delivered by the project, but only the customer uses results of the project. One difference between results on the one hand and products and services on the other is that only results include outcomes.

To illustrate this difference and why it is useful, consider the example of a project to reduce credit card fraud. The customer of the project is the bank that issues the credit card, because the bank and not the customer benefits most of all, and directly, from the project's outcome, which is reduced fraud. (Generally speaking, the bank's customers do not pay directly if they are the victims of credit card fraud; it is the bank that bears the loss. For clarity in this example, ignore the minor costs of inconvenience, etc.) However, the project may produce certain services, such as a verification code, as part of achieving the desired end state, and the credit card holders may have to use the verification code. Hence both the credit card holders and the issuing bank are users but only the bank is the customer, in project terms. Why does this matter? In short, because in such a project all users need to be satisfied with the service they get from the project: for example, if the verification code service is such that credit card owners refuse to use it, the project will fail. So all users need to be engaged appropriately in the project, but in different ways. What sets apart the customer from other users in this example is that it is only the customer who has a direct interest in the outcome of the project, which is to reduce credit card fraud. If the reduction is not great enough from the customer's point of view – the customer being the bank – then the project will be a failure, no matter what the other users feel about the verification process. So, in your project, understand who the customers and users are.

Managing the project team

In this section we cover some tools and techniques for managing the project team.

Team selection

The team is the people who will make the project happen. It is therefore essential that between them they have the right skills and experience for the needs of the project. A team skills matrix is a useful tool to check that the team's skills and experience are right. The sponsor and project manager should look at the skills matrix for their project and ensure that any gaps are filled. Table 2.2 is an example of a skills matrix and the text at the bottom of the table gives further details.

Human dynamics and soft skills are vital in project management. Every project manager wants the best experts on the team, but what if the best aren't available? And what if the best technical expert is available but only because nobody else will work with them? This is not some fuzzy side-issue that you can ignore. Your team have got to be able to work together, and it is part of your job as a project manager to think about this. If your project team has not worked together before, or if they show signs of not working together well, then you should include team-building in your project plan. The best team-building activities may not be labelled as such.

Table 2.2 An example skills matrix

Skills and experience required	Project team members									
	Abel	Beth	Cain	Don	Ellie	Fay	Gill	Harry	Indira	Jude
Technical knowledge of the Furtwangler Mk. IX jet engine	x		x			xx	x	xx	xxx	xxx
Technical knowledge of Boltzmann machines and simulated annealing	xxx	xxx	xxx	x	xxx			xx	x	xxx
CAD-CAM operator	xx	xx	xx	x	xxx			xx		
Knowledge of the customer – organization, processes and culture										
Finance and accounting skills						xxx	xxx			
Project planning skills				x				xxx	x	
Knowledge of how to get things done in our organization		xxx						xxx		xxx
Presentation skills				x	xxx			xxx		xxx
Ability to put people at ease in interviews				x	x			xxx		

This example of a skills matrix lists the skills and experience that the project needs down the left-hand side, and lists the members of the project team across the top. Where a team member has a skill or some experience, a single x ' is entered to show a small degree of skill or experience, and 'xxx' to show a high degree. This matrix shows that this team is strong in technical skills, i.e. the first three rows. The matrix also lists softer skills that will be important to this project, such as being able to put people at ease in data gathering interviews, and it seems that the team is short of these skills. If having only one person, Harry, who is strong in this skill is likely to be insufficient (and look at all the other areas where Harry is the only person with substantial skill), then the project can decide whether to remedy this by training team members listed here or by adding a new team member. There is one area, knowledge of the customer organization, where no-one on the team has any experience – this is an area that needs to be fixed.

Is there such a thing as a perfect team member? We might imagine a genius who knows every corner of their technical field, never gets sick, and always files their documents properly. What would you feel like having to work next to this person? Your answer probably reveals much about the sorts of people you like to work with, and so the real answer to the question about the perfect team member is that it depends on who else is in the team. Every project team is different and what is perfect in one will not work in another. So it is neither possible nor desirable to provide precise rules for team selection other than to say that fit with individuals in the team should be a factor.

Some factors to consider with regard to human dynamics and people in projects are as follows.

- People like to work with friends, or at least people with whom they have worked in the past. Getting to know new people takes time and intellectual and emotional energy, and most people will save themselves the effort if possible.
- An entirely new team in which nobody has worked together before will not work at full capacity until some time after the start.
- An established team or group of people may not assist in recognizing skills gaps that require new members to join their team. Use the skills matrix to make sure that you as project manager or sponsor can see skills gaps in the team, and then work out how to sell the idea to the team. You must be prepared to tell the team as a last resort if selling does not work.
- The project manager needs to spend time getting to know their team, and the sponsor and project manager need to spend time getting to know each other. Use this time to establish who is who and how people like to work together.
- If your project team is widely dispersed then they will probably never really understand how each other works unless you make a special effort to bring them together to work as a group at the start of the project. Bringing together does not have to be physical; it can be by video conferencing or telephone conferencing.
- If a team is made up mostly of people who have worked together before, with one or two new faces, then take care to ensure that the new joiners fit. Groups develop their own sub-culture and a new joiner can sometimes break the rules without noticing; this can sometimes lead to rejection of the new joiner unless someone realizes what is going on and intervenes. Rejection can be a matter of subtle group dynamics and it may not be obvious that it has happened. A new joiner may feel isolated and demotivated when it becomes obvious that everyone on the team is friendly with everyone else except them.
- A special case of the problem is where you, the project manager, are the new person on an existing team. This is examined in more depth below (see 'Gaining and maintaining authority').
- Teams under pressure tend to reach for and adapt the first likely looking solution. If a team has worked together on a similar problem before, they are very likely to revert to their previous solution if they need to save time. Sometimes this is definitely what the project needs, but if not, then altering the composition of the team may be necessary to stimulate new thinking.
- Not every project team that has worked together before wants to work together again. If the earlier project has strained relationships then you may be better off not burdening your project with this emotional legacy. Don't assume that all previous experience is positive.

▶ Gaining and maintaining authority

One of the stressful aspects of becoming a project manager is often the idea that you will somehow have to establish authority over people who have hitherto been your peers. 'Won't it be obvious that I know less than everyone else about most of the aspects of the work? Won't they see through me?' Many successful project managers admit that they started with just the same fears. It did not stop them doing a good job.

The good news is that most people will be on your side. Your team want you to succeed because that means project success, which is good for them as well. Most people do not expect you to be an expert in their domain as well as yours – after all, they would probably not have been brought into the team unless they had some specialist skills. Furthermore, the performing organization also wants you to succeed and will give support and guidance if you ask for it. Your position as a manager gives you a natural source of authority. The simple fact that you are the manager predisposes people to fulfil your requests – you have the weight of convention and organizational protocol behind you. Even friends can usually respond appropriately and professionally when you move into the project manager role as long as you do not give out mixed signals when in the professional setting.

As project manager you have five sources of power:

◆ Legitimate power: this is what the authority that comes from your position as project manager is called. It is your primary source of power in the project.
◆ Reward power: the capacity to grant a reward that someone wants.
◆ Expert power: specialist knowledge that means your opinion carries weight. The importance of expert power varies. In technical and professional domains some degree of demonstrable technical knowledge is essential, and in extreme cases some professions are known for reluctance to be managed by non-members.
◆ Referent power: the power of your personal network. If you are the daughter of the chief executive you will have considerable power in the organization even though you may hold a junior post. By all means use your network to help your project, but beware of using this power in ways that harm others or allow you to short-cut the normal channels. You do not want to acquire a reputation for excessive use of referent power.
◆ Coercive power: in some ways the reverse of reward power – it is the capacity to inflict some unwanted outcome on someone who does not do as you wish. Any use of coercive power is likely to destroy whatever enthusiasm an individual may have had, even if it produces the desired action in the short term.

You can either build on your initial advantages, or destroy them (Table 2.3). Common sense usually makes the difference between these two outcomes.

Maintaining your authority as a project manager is essentially the same as in any management function. What is different in project management is that you might have to become very skilled at the basics because new projects, with new teams, will come along far more frequently than they would if you were in a line management position, which means that you may need to keep redefining your authority. Another reason is that project team members may feel that their real manager is their line manager and not you, the project manager. A further way in which project management differs from process or line management is that project management involves more uncertainty about what to do and how to do it.

Projects, by their nature, involve doing things in new ways and some part of the work is likely to go beyond established procedure. The team looks to the project manager to give guidance and set direction under these circumstances, and if they get the impression that you are vague and confused, you will begin to lose credibility. But be wary of being decisive merely for appearance's sake, since this can be equally damaging to your credibility. Your best defence against this is the project

Table 2.3 Maintaining authority – do's and don'ts

Do	Don't
◆ Treat everyone as adults. Tell them what needs to be done and why, and let them get on with it.	◆ Take credit for anyone else's work.
◆ Ask for people's opinions about their area and listen to the answer.	◆ Give the impression that you don't trust people by not accepting the professional opinion of people who know more about the area than you.
◆ Praise good work publicly.	◆ Attack or insult anyone on the team, even if you feel angry about something.
◆ Share information about things within and beyond the project.	
◆ Remember that making people ask for your signature or give you an account of how they spent their time can be a way to subtly remind them who is boss.	◆ Attempt to win favour with the team by breaking confidences with others in the firm. (Can the team then trust you?)
◆ Ask people to do things in just the same way you would normally – politely and professionally.	◆ Bark orders like a drill sergeant (or a chef de corps de ballet). If you let your fear drive you to this, people might even not take you seriously.
◆ Refer to and be seen with the senior people with whom you have to deal.	◆ Refuse to get involved with group social activities – you will be seen as aloof.
◆ Respond to bad news by looking for a solution, not a culprit.	◆ Shoot the messenger.
	◆ Use coercive power (not even if they deserve it).

plan. If you have thought through all the issues, considered all the possible approaches and planned the project in a way that gives the best balance of risks and progress, then you will already know most of the answers. Refer back to the plan, remind yourself why it was set up this way, and give a clear answer. Project managers who try to work without making or referring to a plan lose credibility with their teams not because the teams pay direct attention to the plan itself, but because the manager appears indecisive and keeps contradicting earlier decisions.

▶ Maintaining authority when you make a mistake

Everybody makes mistakes, even experienced and highly qualified project managers. Sometimes you can recover the situation before anyone notices, but sometimes somebody will realize that they are having to work harder because of a mistake you made. Some people never ever admit that something was their fault, even if it is obvious, and some go so far as to intimidate anyone who dares to point it out or to suggest another way that is clearly better. If you behave this way you will bring about two things: you will eventually erode the morale of your team, starting with the most intelligent, and you will ensure that no ideas other than your own get implemented. Since nobody can challenge these ideas of yours, the bad ones will not be filtered out, and your project will suffer.

If you suspect that this description might apply to you – or, more importantly, that your team believes that it applies to you – then change your behaviour. The change is easy: all you have to do is to admit that you were wrong once in a while.

Try it. You will find that instead of losing respect you gain it, by showing that you are mature enough to take responsibility for your own actions. This does not mean you have to fawn constantly, just that you should not hide behind your manager- ial power. If you have made a mistake, you might even find it easier to get people to help you out by apologizing and asking for their support than by announcing the extra workload and leaving them to deduce the reasons themselves.

▶ Personal work styles

Your personal style of working will affect the project, as will those of every team member. We all have slightly different styles, which can be modified rather than changed outright. Even without modifying them, being aware of one's own style, and that of others, and knowing how to use them and when to delegate to some- one with a better style, is important in project management and management gen- erally. One's personal style is separate from one's skills and knowledge, although it is affected by them and by experience. A style that is amusing and tolerable in a keen 20-year-old can look ridiculous in a 70-year-old, and vice versa.

As an example of how style matters, consider someone who never actually seems to do any work and yet is incredibly productive. Ask yourself whether they have ever produced answers to questions faster than you could have done, just by know- ing who to ask instead of trying to generate the answer themselves. This is part of style. If, instead, you are yourself one of the people who always finds the answer through your network, maybe you secretly admire or despise those people who try to work everything out for themselves instead of making use of perfectly good pre- existing information. The point of all this is that different people have different operating styles. They both get results. You are much more likely to have to deal with different styles in cross-functional project management than if you stay within your own domain, as different domains attract different sorts of people.

There are many theories about personalities and people's preferred team roles, but it is sufficient here to point out that these differences are real and can bring down the unwary project manager. Do not assume that everyone works in the same way that you do, and manage the working styles in your team actively. That means choosing the right mix of people and adapting your own style to suit circumstances. One technique that many project managers use is to run a Belbin or Myers–Briggs or other personality type assessment exercise at the start of their project. This can serve a dual purpose as a team-building exercise as well as revealing supposed per- sonality types. Many people dislike the idea of these kinds of exercises because they seem manipulative, but if run in the right way they can be very enjoyable. The HR department of the owning organization will often run such exercises if requested.

One way to think of the working style problem is that there are two ways people can spend work time together: either they can be business-like, with a focus on get- ting the job done ('task oriented'), or they can focus on the person in front of them and deal with the human issues ('maintenance oriented'). Figure 2.5 illustrates the spectrum of these characteristics. In the course of a normal day, or even a single conversation, most people spend part of their time in task and part in maintenance. Maintenance time is the glue that holds groups of people together as a coherent group. By investing time and energy in authentic conversations that touch areas of

Fig. 2.5 Personal working styles: task focus, maintenance focus

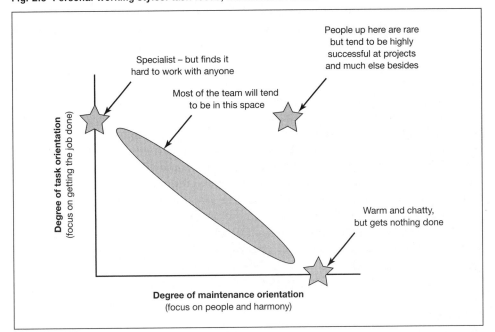

life outside the immediate task, the bonds that tie the group together are maintained. So as a project manager with a newly formed group, you should expect to have to invest time and energy (maybe even deliberately chosen time outside work hours, as a signal of your commitment to the human side) to get the team together. Once people feel good spending time together it becomes easier for them to talk about task problems and interact effectively without worrying too much about what other people think. Suggestions for improvements are easier to make to friends than to strangers. Some maintenance time after a gruelling period in the run-up to a project deadline is well spent, and will keep the team working for the rest of the project.

Some industries seem naturally to attract task-focused individuals, such as securities trading, fighter pilots, high-value sales, pianists, project management, and engineering. Other kinds of work seem to attract both task-focused and maintenance-oriented people: local and central government, law, the stage, and marketing. Just to be clear, it is not a bad thing that government has more maintenance-focused people in it than, say, securities trading. A government in which everyone is task focused to the complete exclusion of being maintenance oriented is called a dictatorship. Projects, and the world at large, need both. (And by the way, in case it is not obvious, projects are best not run as dictatorships either, even in the securities industry.)

Everyone has a natural predisposition towards either task or maintenance activities. As project manager, you need to ensure a balance in your team between task and maintenance orientation. This depends not just on the people, but on the nature of the project. You will also need to adapt your style to match circumstances. When the deadline is looming you and the whole project must be more task focused, so you must have built up enough of a reserve of goodwill through your previous behaviour that you can behave in a directive manner, giving orders with little explanation if necessary. Judge when it is safe to have some fun together and when the team has really got to get down to some hard work, then set an appropriate example.

▶ Socializing

This can be a way to get to know people's personal styles ... and to let them get to know yours, which is just as important. It is good for team spirit to spend time together socializing. Knowing this, the obvious thing to do is to go out for a drink together after work, or, depending on the country and culture you are in, a communal hookah. This is just what friends do together, and everyone will work better together as a result. But don't expect it to be good for everyone. Some people just don't like it: maybe they have family commitments, or they just don't enjoy going to the sorts of places that you enjoy. Sometimes pressing everyone to come along may be counter-productive: nobody can be ordered to have fun. If there are people who are clearly uncomfortable with the suggested outing, it is pointless to insist. Next time, choose a different time or event, and if you must, just make sure that these people get included in group events during work hours.

▶ Morale

Morale is vital to any human endeavour, and the maintenance of morale is one of your main responsibilities as project manager. With good morale in the project team, all kinds of problems and setbacks amount to less than water off a fat goose's back. With poor morale, even the most trivial problem can derail things. People do good work because they want to. It might give them a sense of achievement directly or they might feel good about doing their bit for the team. Poor morale will soon sap your own motivation. Experience shows that the things that build morale are different from the things that can destroy it (Table 2.4).

Morale in a project should be managed by using the same basic personal communication tools you use for everything else – and especially:

◆ Treat people fairly and use their skills.
◆ Listen to people.
◆ Build your relationship with the person as well as the job function.
◆ Use common sense when deciding the necessary level of project documentation, and make sure that everyone understands why this is necessary and they feel comfortable with it.
◆ Let people know that you notice good work and extra effort.
◆ Make sure that people understand why their task is important.
◆ Show that you trust and rely on the person.
◆ Protect team members from demoralizing uncertainty over the project direction or justification.
◆ Avoid romantic or sexual relations with project team members.

Should you conceal your own morale problems? Both enthusiasm and despair are infectious. A radiantly enthusiastic project manager can energize the team, making

---

Table 2.4 Factors that do and don't build morale

Factors that build morale	Factors that do not
◆ A sense of achievement.	◆ Excessively close supervision that implies a lack of trust.
◆ Shared adversity and struggle.	
◆ Recognition.	◆ Irrational policies.
◆ Performing work that is in itself satisfying and worthwhile.	◆ Frequent change in plans.
	◆ Time-wasting administrative procedures.
◆ A sense of responsibility.	◆ Seeing other team members humiliated, or being humiliated oneself.
◆ The prospect of advancement.	
◆ Learning something worthwhile.	◆ Work that is too easy.
◆ A sense of personal growth.	◆ A sense of being taken for granted.
◆ Working for and with people one respects professionally.	◆ Feeling that there is no merit in how different team members are rewarded.
◆ Being entrusted with important information or tasks.	◆ Romantic or sexual affairs between leaders and team members.

---

everybody's tasks seem easier and more enjoyable. But if you are despairing, be aware that the team will be guided by your attitude. This does not mean that you should ever conceal what is happening: it is essential that everyone on the team understands the facts of the situation so that their own project decisions reflect reality. But it does mean that despondency on your part will be amplified through the team, and will make problems worse.

▶ Supervision, or monitoring and control

The project manager's responsibility to maintain the balance of the time/cost/ performance trade-off means that project activities must be supervised. This is also known as monitoring and control, which is a knowledge area within project management that is covered in Chapter 3. Here we introduce certain aspects of monitoring and control that are especially relevant to the personal style and management skills of the project manager.

As project manager, you need to know whether the project is on track with its deliverables, and you will need to intervene if you believe that there is a problem. This amounts to little more than a restatement of the project manager's job title, so why spend time on it here? As is often the case, the principle is easy, but the practical implementation needs care.

Most project managers develop a personal system for supervising activities. Even more, they develop a sixth sense to warn them of when things are about to go off track. Some project managers take a formal approach with a lot of scheduled reporting. Others practise 'management by walking around' – that is, just making a tour of the desks of the project team, chatting about whatever they are doing, and following their instinct about who to talk to next. Either approach is potentially viable, but each can be dangerous if they are applied without being adapted to suit individual team members. Some people need more supervision than others, and applying the same process to everyone risks annoying the senior people while leaving the junior people feeling adrift and unsure that their work is useful.

Sometimes, you may have to deal with someone who thinks that they know everything, but whose attitude in fact reveals that they do not even know how much else there is to learn. In these circumstances careful supervision is required to cover the technical gaps, but this individual probably believes that supervision is not needed. Some lateral thinking can help: use the project plan to insert some extra formal quality assurance checks in a way that is less personally threatening than constantly checking up on progress. At the same time, try to pair the individual with a more senior team member so that they can share tasks. This way, day-to-day supervision is delegated.

It is a basic instinct to want to check up on everything as a deadline approaches, just to make sure that it is all going to be alright. This is an excellent habit for a project manager to get into. But don't take it too far. There comes a point when everyone knows what has got to be done, all the inputs are available, and all that remains is to do the work; going round and checking again actually slows things down. The best thing you can do at this stage is simply to clear all the minor obstacles out of the way of the people who will do the work, and let them get on with it. If the person responsible for the last-but-one critical chain activity has to leave the office to get their car serviced, then your best action is not to check their work again, but to offer to take care of the car while they stay and get on with work!

▶ The boundaries of responsibility

You can and should relax sometimes! One of the reasons why project management can be stressful is the uncomfortable feeling that you will be held responsible for other people's mistakes. You are the manager and you are responsible for delivering the project, and the buck stops with you. If someone on your team lets you down then it is still your problem, even when you did everything possible to help that person succeed. A project manager who publicly blames a team member for the delay in delivery looks foolish, so you may end up taking the blame yourself.

To some extent, this tension is a fact of life for any manager and you will have to live with it. But do not ruin your life by letting yourself feel responsible for every mistake that happens. If you have in fact delegated responsibility and authority together, then the person to whom the task was delegated must accept responsibility for the task outcome. If you suspect that an individual has not fully understood that their actions have a direct impact on the customer, then maybe let the person talk to the customer directly or at least take them to a meeting with the customer, so that they can experience the reaction at first hand. In the same way that a good project manager should never take the credit for somebody else's good work, you should find a way to allow team members to feel the negative consequences of their actions as well.

▶ Project lifecycle

▶ Introduction

Before we look at what a project lifecycle is, let us be clear on what the term means generally, in ordinary language. A lifecycle means a series of types of event that follow each other in the same order; this series can be expected to repeat, perhaps with some variation, for other things of the same kind. So the human lifecycle begins with birth, proceeds through childhood, adolescence, adulthood (which begins often with naive enthusiasm and concludes with tempered resignation), into senility and then ends with death. Shakespeare describes the human lifecycle more poetically in the seven ages of man. Different individual people may have different lives – some mature early, others exhibit teenage tendencies in their mid-twenties, some become senile at 60, others are as sharp as a pin into their late 90s or beyond. Death can end the cycle early, but the point is that there is a pattern, and it is so useful to know where an individual is in their lifecycle when dealing with them that we do this unconsciously: we don't treat the two-year-old who rushes into our bedroom in the middle of the night in the same way that we treat the adult who does the same thing.

So it is with projects. Projects, whatever their differences, all share roughly a common lifecycle by virtue of being projects, and as a project manager or sponsor you need to know what the general project lifecycle is and how the focus of your job in the project changes at different stages in the lifecycle.

The simplest lifecycle is:

beginning → middle → end

Note that already this simplest of project lifecycle models identifies one of the distinguishing features of projects. Remember that everything in an organization is either a process or a project. Projects differ because they have definite start and end points, whereas processes run continuously. Has the project started yet? Has it finished yet? These turn out to be key questions in many project governance situations. Large business corporations and government organizations often have a large number of projects that are like Frankenstein, neither truly alive nor dead. This is perfectly reasonable if the projects have deliberately been put into a state of suspended animation, that is put on hold, while waiting for some other factor to be resolved. What happens too often, however, is that the projects should have been killed off and the resources reallocated to more promising projects, but poor project governance, or poor management, allows a number of essentially pointless activities to continue under the guise of projects.

Table 2.5 lists some examples of where project management should focus at different stages of the project lifecycle. Note that where a project is broken down into several different stages, each stage can follow this phasing. So, taking one of the points illustrated in Table 2.5, if we are in the middle of stage 1 of the project, we certainly should already have had a plan for stage 1 worked out, but we should not be at all concerned if we have no plan yet for stage 5. This point introduces the relationship between project structure and project lifecycle, both of which are also related to how to manage the project team and to organizational structure. The experienced sponsor and project manager will be aware of these relationships and their practical implications for the project that they are managing at the time.

Table 2.5 Examples of key differences in focus for project management at different phases of the project, on the simplest of all lifecycle models

Beginning	Middle	End
◆ Acceptable right at the start not to know exactly what the aims, rationale and approach of the project are, though these should be worked out early on.	◆ Must be clear on what the aims, rationale and approach of the project are.	◆ The only thing that matters is: did the project achieve the aim?
◆ The right time to work out what the plan is.	◆ Should be following the plan and doing the work.	◆ The plan is irrelevant. Lessons learned should be captured and applied to future projects.
◆ Acceptable not to know who will be doing the work and how they will be organized, but should be worked out early on.	◆ The project team should have bonded and formed as a team, with its own distinct style. Some changes to team members are normal.	◆ The project team breaks up and individuals return to their line roles or move on to other projects.

PMI says

Project lifecycle and project phase

'Project Lifecycle. A collection of generally sequential project phases whose names and number are determined by the control needs of the organization or organizations involved in the project. A lifecycle can be documented with a methodology.' *PMBOK Guide* (p.368)

'Project Phase. A collection of logically related project activities, usually culminating in the completion of a major deliverable. Project phases ... are mainly completed sequentially, but can overlap in some project situations. Phases can be subdivided into subphases and then components; this hierarchy, if the project or portions of the project are divided into phases, is contained in the work breakdown structure. A project phase is not a project process management group.' *PMBOK Guide* (p.369)

▶ Project phasing and the project lifecycle

The project's lifecycle is made of phases. This is a straightforward idea, but it is valuable to understand it clearly, as by doing so many problems in project management can be spotted earlier and managed better. A key implication that follows from the idea of the lifecycle is that there is a sequence in which to do phases in a project. It may be that there are two or more equally good sequences, but what matters for project management is that the sponsor and the project manager pick a sequence and either stick with it or agree to change to a different sequence.

What should that sequence be? There is no standard model that applies across all projects. The choice of phases and how to sequence them varies according to the industry in which the project is, and also according to the way in which a particular performing organization works. Some things in project management are completely general and apply across all projects, for example the kinds of questions that should be answered in a project charter (or project initiation document), but phasing is not like that.

The question of how to divide up the project into phases and what sequence they should be in will fall into one of two circumstances:

◆ Either your project will be of a kind for which there is an established model, perhaps one created by your organization for its own particular needs, or created by a professional body, or there may be a model available informally which can be understood by talking to someone who has done similar projects before.
◆ Or the project will be of a 'blue sky' nature, that is, something that has not been tried before, in which case how to phase it and what the lifecycle options are will be one of the earliest tasks and can be a major undertaking or sub-project in its own right.

If there is an established model lifecycle for your project, then obtain it (or them) and review it to ensure that you understand how it applies to or differs from your project's needs. It may be useful to adapt such models to some extent to your needs, but most often it is a case of adaptation rather than starting from scratch. In any large organization that runs projects, there will usually be several such models, each with their own group of supporters. How easy it is to find such models depends on the intellectual capital management system or knowledge management system in your organization. If you meet the supporters of a particular model or template for a lifecycle, they will usually be enthusiastic about their particular lifecycle model, but you should try to understand the implicit assumptions underlying their support for their particular model, especially what kind of project it is designed for and what kind of problem it was designed to solve. Selecting a lifecycle model is like selecting any tool. The tool can be excellent without being an appropriate tool for your particular job. And there is also the danger of making the best the enemy of the good, by wasting time on trying to select the perfect tool, wasting time on minor differences between very similar lifecycle models, when any good enough tool would do and the time saved should be spent on some other project activity. Also consider the needs of your organization rather than just your project – the organization stands to gain from standardizations of tools, including lifecycle models, and you must be prepared to use a lifecycle that is slightly less than perfect for your particular project because of the broader strategic gains to the organization from using a standard set of lifecycle models. The boxed text describes some standard lifecycle models and Figure 2.6 sets out some examples.

Fig. 2.6 Some examples of various project lifecycles

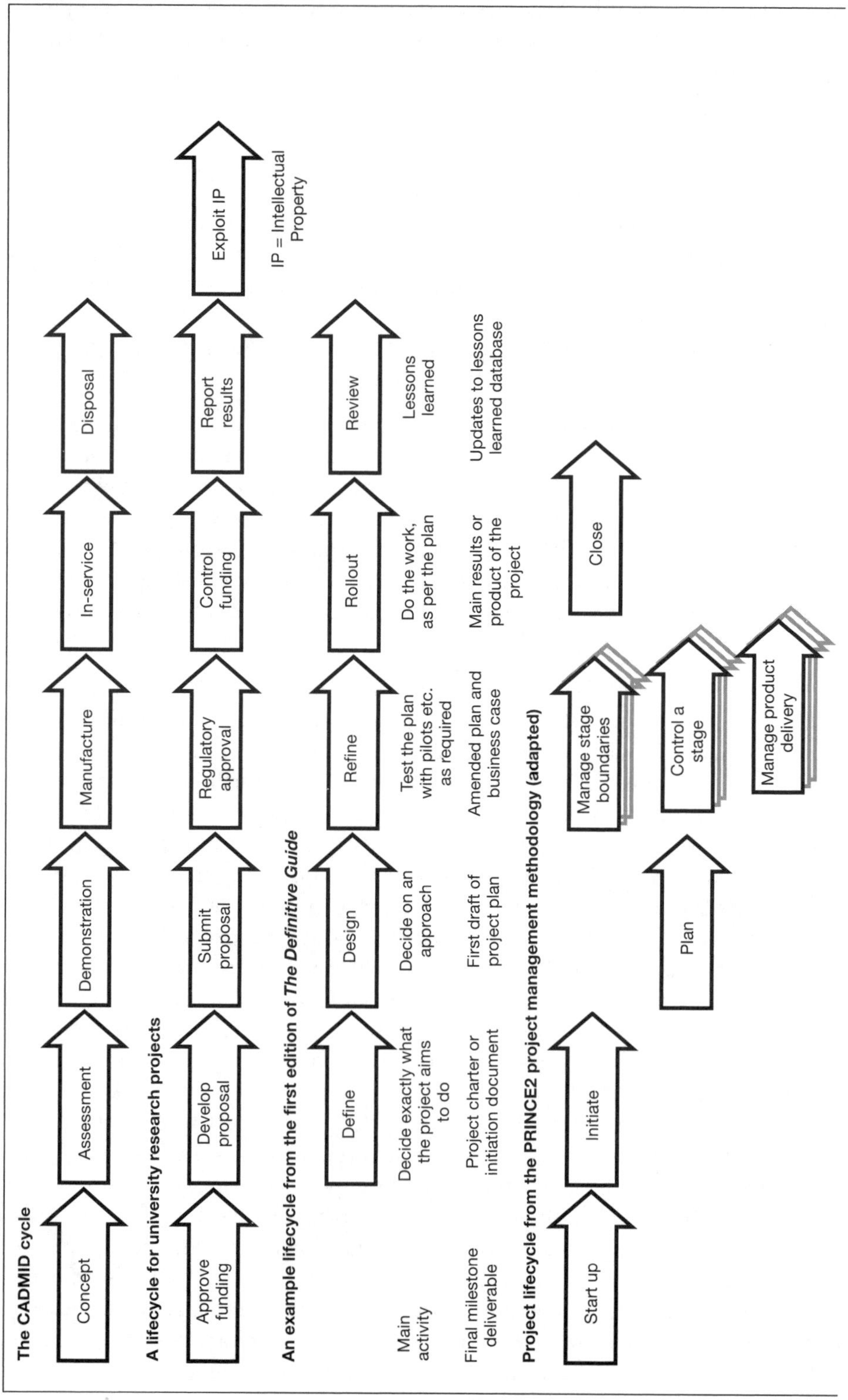

The CADMID cycle

Concept → Assessment → Demonstration → Manufacture → In-service → Disposal

A lifecycle for university research projects

Approve funding → Develop proposal → Submit proposal → Regulatory approval → Control funding → Report results → Exploit IP

IP = Intellectual Property

An example lifecycle from the first edition of *The Definitive Guide*

Define → Design → Refine → Rollout → Review

| Main activity | Decide exactly what the project aims to do | Decide on an approach | Test the plan with pilots etc. as required | Do the work, as per the plan | Lessons learned |
| Final milestone deliverable | Project charter or initiation document | First draft of project plan | Amended plan and business case | Main results or product of the project | Updates to lessons learned database |

Project lifecycle from the PRINCE2 project management methodology (adapted)

Start up → Initiate → Plan

Manage stage boundaries → Close

Control a stage

Manage product delivery

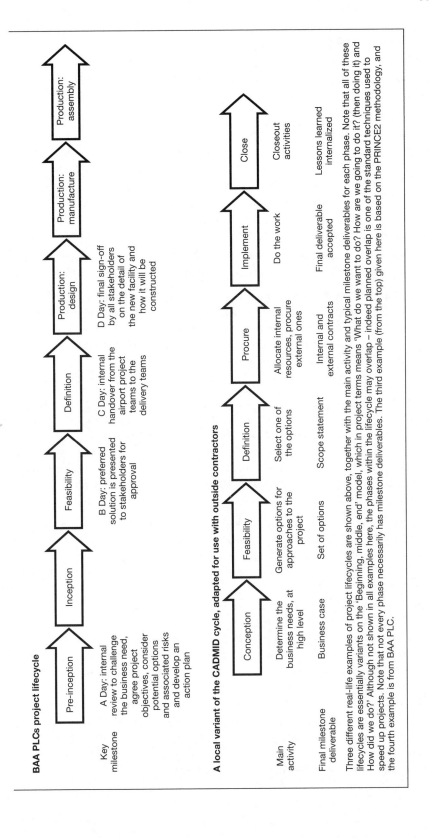

BAA PLCs project lifecycle

	Pre-inception	Inception	Feasibility	Definition	Production: design	Production: manufacture	Production: assembly

Key milestone

A Day: internal review to challenge the business need, agree project objectives, consider potential options and associated risks and develop an action plan

B Day: preferred solution is presented to stakeholders for approval

C Day: internal handover from the airport project teams to the delivery teams

D Day: final sign-off by all stakeholders on the detail of the new facility and how it will be constructed

A local variant of the CADMID cycle, adapted for use with outside contractors

	Conception	Feasibility	Definition	Procure	Implement	Close
Main activity	Determine the business needs, at high level	Generate options for approaches to the project	Select one of the options	Allocate internal resources, procure external ones	Do the work	Closeout activities
Final milestone deliverable	Business case	Set of options	Scope statement	Internal and external contracts	Final deliverable accepted	Lessons learned internalized

Three different real-life examples of project lifecycles are shown above, together with the main activity and typical milestone deliverables for each phase. Note that all of these lifecycles are essentially variants on the 'Beginning, middle, end' model, which in project terms means 'What do we want to do? How are we going to do it? (then doing it) and How did we do?' Although not shown in all examples here, the phases within the lifecycle may overlap – indeed planned overlap is one of the standard techniques used to speed up projects. Note that not every phase necessarily has milestone deliverables. The third example (from the top) given here is based on the PRINCE2 methodology, and the fourth example is from BAA PLC.

Some lifecycle models

Spiral development

Spiral development is one of many responses to the problem of costs and time overruns in project management in defence and other industries. It aims to overcome three problems:

◆ Cycle time/obsolescence – rapid advances in technology mean that as the project progresses, new working methods and new solutions become available that could not have been foreseen at the start, creating a risk of building something obsolete. The business need is to speed up the cycle time.

◆ Interfacing – the problem of how different organizations with different approaches to project management, including different lifecycle models, can work together on joint projects efficiently.

◆ Waste – the particular risk of waste that arises when a project progresses too far without checking that what it is doing is actually what is wanted and is valuable.

Spiral development is a new name for an old idea, which can be summed up as 'build a little, test a little'[4]. The US Department of Defense has indicated a definite preference for spiral development in certain areas[5] and its websites contain further information. An alternative starting point for further information is the Software Engineering Institute of Carnegie Mellon University (CMU)[6].

CADMID

The CADMID cycle used in UK defence procurement is aimed at achieving the same things. Although the CADMID cycle is most popular in defence procurement and contracting, it embodies practical principles which can reduce risk and cost in a wide variety of industries such as capital markets, pharmaceuticals, government, software and financial services. Three notable features of the CADMID cycle, which may be worth considering as potentially significant factors in designing the phasing of your project, are as follows.

◆ Work out the concept first. Written down in CADMID form, this looks obvious, but unless the separation between working out the concept of a new product or service on the one hand and creating and delivering it on the other is made explicit, then there is a greater risk of problems in cost, work control and stakeholder miscommunication.

◆ Demonstrate before full-scale production. Having a demonstration or trial phase specifically to learn about the project's product reduces risk and cost later on. This can be unpopular with senior stakeholders who are under pressure to deliver results soon, but experience shows that often in projects that intend to deliver new technology or new services, more haste results in more cost and less speed, and a thorough demonstration phase, separate in scope and prior to main production, is almost invariably a sound idea.

◆ Plan for retiring the product. If the project produces something that will be integral to the organization's business processes, then when the time comes to retire the product, another project will be necessary. Retirement need not be part of the project that creates the product, but it will be valuable in the long term when creating the new product or service to capture and store information likely to be critical when retiring the product or service. The biggest example in recent times of not doing this was in the software industry where many pieces of software had to be retired in preparation for the year 2000 but to do so incurred great cost because much of the knowledge necessary for safe, controlled retirement of that software from the mission-critical processes had been lost. This is an example of the importance of knowledge and information management in project and programme management, but that is a subject beyond the scope of this book.

Business process reengineering

A number of methodologies have been developed for doing business process reengineering, most of which are based in some way on the work of Michael Hammer[7]. Most of the major management consulting firms, such as IBM Consulting, have their own flavours of business process reengineering, and many large commercial and government organizations are following this trend.

If the project is more of a blue-sky nature, or if you are dealing with the first kind and wish to make a thorough review of a pre-existing lifecycle model, the following is a checklist of questions to help you develop an appropriate phasing for your project:

- How will you know when you have finished the project? What are the success criteria? What will success look like? What will it have delivered or how will the world be different?
- What are the 'exam questions' that your project has to answer? Or that you have to answer before the project can proceed?
- What is the logical structure of your project, in terms of sequence of work?
- Who are the key stakeholders, and what do they expect the product to produce from their point of view?
- What are the implications for phasing of cashflow or budget factors? And of your financial year cycle?
- What are the key deliverables? What implications could they have for phasing?
- If you will bring into the project sub-contractors or different teams of people, will their arrival and departure be potential phase boundaries?
- What regulatory or legal compliance tests have to be met? Should these define phase boundaries?
- What degree of front-end loading (FEL) should your project have? (FEL is explained on page 57.)

▶ Milestones, phases and stage gates

We have used the term 'milestone' above without defining it. A milestone is a special kind of deliverable or event that is an obvious marker that some piece of work, such as a phase of a project, has been completed – the more obvious the better. An end of course exam is a paradigm case of a milestone: there is no doubt whether or not the exam has happened, it is a quite definite fact, and it is an event, rather than a drawn-out activity (if that seems untrue, then take the end of the examination as being the milestone).

PMI says

Milestone
'Milestone. A significant point or event in the project. ...' *PMBOK Guide* (p.364)

Senior management often like to have project progress reports in terms of milestones. This has the advantage that if the milestones are well chosen, the reporting is simple and short but gives a good idea of progress. Milestones should be binary yes/no events. 'Have we delivered the prototype to the customer?', 'Does the database work?', 'Is the contract with suppliers signed yet?' and 'Have we been paid in full yet?' are all examples of milestone questions.

Milestones thus make natural boundaries to phases. This introduces the idea of scope, which we have seen is critical in project management. The scope of the project is simply a special term for the boundary of the project, so the boundary or scope of the overall project should align with the outer boundaries of the phases. This point sounds obvious, but may need to be remembered in large complex projects, or in smaller ones where what might look like a convenient milestone, because it is simple, has the unintended consequence of increasing the scope of the project. The difference between a final milestone of 'Deliver database' and one of 'Get paid' is an example of where this might matter.

▶ Phasing in cost and risk control

Phasing can be used as a means to manage risk of wasted effort, poor coordination and unnecessary rework. These can arise in three ways:

◆ people who want to do work at the wrong time (too early or too late to be of maximum value);
◆ the natural tendency of cost of changes to increase and probability of completion to increase with project progress; and
◆ not understanding early enough in the project key details.

Note that the design and use in a project of phasing and the type of lifecycle selected play a key role in managing each of these risks.

▶ Phases to control when people start work

If you allow a child to choose which parts of cooking in the kitchen to attend to, you may find that the resulting meal is all chocolate cake and no vegetables or starter. In a more grown-up version, the same risks exist to your project, not only with individual people but also with suppliers and sub-contractors, who may feel strong incentives to start their work before your project is ready for it.

Suppose that a project has two phases apart from the 'beginning' and 'end' phases; let us call them M1 and M2. Suppose that M1 is tedious and dull, but that phase M2, which is very interesting and also fun to do, cannot be planned properly until phase M1 is finished. Both M1 and M2 are being staffed by project team members who are volunteering to do overtime. There is a risk that some of the team members, if left uncontrolled, will try to start work on M2 before M1 is finished, maybe even before M1 is started. A vital way to use the concept of the lifecycle in project management is to know when you have to say 'No – this won't start until that has finished'.

You should understand what the logical sequence of work is and where there is a piece of work that should not start until some event has occurred. The Work Breakdown Structure focuses on this, and phasing can be used to enforce project discipline around critical no-start-before points. Make sure you understand the incentives which may exist in your project for people to start too early.

▶ Front-end loading (FEL)

Front-end loading is the common sense idea of investing more in planning at the start of a project to avoid risk and cost later. This idea makes special sense in projects because changes are cheaper at the start of a project than at the end. Figure 2.7(a) and (b) illustrates this point. When building a house, if we are going to change the shape of the foundations of the house, the time to do it is before the foundations are built, not after the roof is finished, because a change then means

Fig. 2.7 Cost and probability of completion

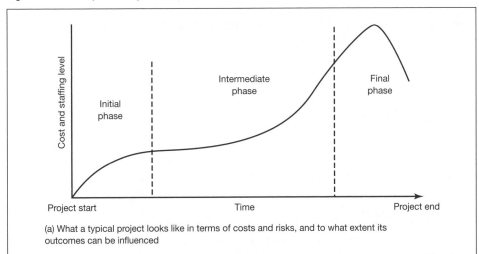

(a) What a typical project looks like in terms of costs and risks, and to what extent its outcomes can be influenced

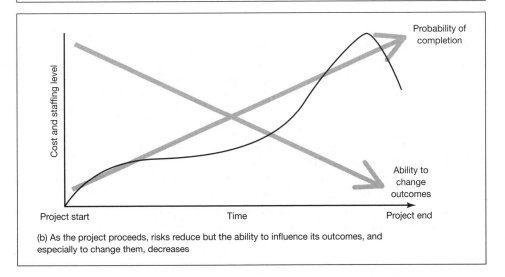

(b) As the project proceeds, risks reduce but the ability to influence its outcomes, and especially to change them, decreases

knocking the house down and starting again. So front-end loading is the formal name for a lifecycle approach that deliberately applies more planning, testing and development effort to the early stages of a project with the intention of reducing cost or risk later. It is often used in conjunction with stage gates.

The main implication of FEL for phasing your project is that if your project uses FEL you may need to increase the number of early phases, or make the early phases longer, and in either case probably increase their budget. You should also include in the business case the case for using FEL and a justification for the extra costs to be incurred, that is, what specific benefits later on should be expected from the extra up-front costs. One implementation of FEL with stage gates is:

1 Concept approved.
2 Feasibility proved.
3 Definition finalized.
4 Pre-operational installation and commissioning.
5 Operational commissioning.

▶ A key distinction: lifecycle versus project process groups

The next chapter describes project process groups. These are:

1 Initiating.
2 Planning.
3 Execution.
4 Monitoring and control.
5 Closing.

This list looks like a project lifecycle model, and while the words initiating, planning, etc. could be used as names for phases in a project lifecycle, this is not what the project management process groups are. It is vital to be clear on this distinction, and many people who pass the PMI's professional exams are confused on this point, even sometimes those who pass with high marks.

The lifecycle of a project is the way that it is broken up into different phases, and a project should have whatever phases are decided. It is definitely not the case that all projects should be forced into a lifecycle of 'initiate, plan, execute, monitor and control, close'. The project management process groups are doing something quite different from the phasing. The process groups describe what processes are more likely to be useful for initiating project management work, for planning it, and so on. When a project has a lifecycle of several phases, it is likely that many of the five process groups will be needed in each phase. The planning phase, if there is one, is likely to need rather more of the planning process group, of course, but even the manufacture phase (assuming there is one) may need some of the planning process group, especially if teething lessons in manufacture of the project's product necessitate revisions to the project plan.

In a project with a single phase, that is a project not broken down into phases, you are likely to want to use all the process groups in the project, which means using all five in one phase – this example may help to make clear the difference between phases and process groups.

Phasing must vary according to the project type, and many industries and organizations have their own models for phasing. The project management process groups are collections of processes that are naturally likely to be used together, and potentially all five might be used in any one phase of the project. Whether any process group is actually used in a particular phase of a project will vary according to the specifics of the project. Why does this distinction matter? There are five reasons. Confusing the two:

◆ limits your ability to exploit for your project the value built into a lifecycle model if one exists, or to design an optimal lifecycle model;
◆ limits your ability to get maximum benefit from project management tools and techniques, such as the PMBOK;
◆ may weaken your credibility as a project manager with key stakeholders;
◆ creates extra and unnecessary work and risk in reconciling the two in areas where no reconciliation is necessary; and
◆ increases risk by reducing the range of tools and techniques you may consider applying in any phase of the project.

If after reading the above you still feel confused, don't worry. Things should become clearer after reading the next chapter. If you are not intending to read the next chapter right away, all that it is essential to remember is that a project phase is absolutely not the same thing as a project management process group.

▶ Project lifecycles and product lifecycles

Sometimes members of the project team may get confused between a product lifecycle and a project lifecycle. Note that these are two clearly and distinctly different things, although in the case where a project is creating or modifying a product, they are related to that extent. Suppose that Project Icarus is a project to design and build the Fantastic Large Aircraft (FLA). The contract for the project states that Icarus, the project, ends when the first FLA completes its airworthiness testing and gains a civil transport licence. The design and manufacture of the product, the FLA, and all maintenance of FLA, will be done thereafter not by project Icarus, but as a business line (that is, a process) within FLAC, the FLA Company. The FLA is expected to have a 50-year life, whereas the Icarus project is expected to last 10 years. The lifecycle of the FLA is longer than the Icarus project lifecycle, and the FLA starts life well after the Icarus project begins. This distinction is a very simple one, but it is worth watching out for confusion in your project team between the two, and being clear in communication with stakeholders when discussing either lifecycle about which one it is.

Note that the project lifecycle and the product lifecycle interact. As sponsor or project manager, you need to understand how they interact, not in a complex theoretical way but in a practical way. There will be processes related to the product that either will be part of your project or will interact with it. These are usually defined in the project lifecycle model. For example, in defence procurement in the UK, many processes related to creating products such as submarines and aircraft are defined in terms of the CADMID lifecycle. Managing the production of these products is a project (or programme) and uses project management.

▶ Summary

People get projects done, so project management is first and foremost about managing people, which requires understanding them. How to organize is a central question of business management generally, as well as project management. Projects are owned by organizations, and the organizational structure and the cultural style of the performing organization is one of the major factors in determining the optimal structure for a project. Organizations range from those that are in effect a set of projects, to the functional organization, with the matrix organization as an adaptation of the functional – each of these types has advantages and disadvantages for the project and for project management.

The two key roles in the project are the sponsor, who is accountable to the performing organization for the costs and results of the project, and the project manager. These two need to work together, especially at the start of a project or when it hits problems. The project manager as such is there to manage the project, not to perform the project work, which falls to the project team. Within the project team there may be sub-project managers and subject matter experts as well as ordinary team members. The project manager is not, as project manager, expected to be an expert on all subjects critical to the project, but is expected to use the subject matter experts to ensure that the project has all the knowledge and expertise that it needs. The project manager must keep the sponsor informed of all major decisions, issues and risks in the project. The sponsor's most important task once the project is underway is to clear the way in terms of organizational politics and interests for the project to succeed.

▶ Further reading

Berne, E., 1964. *Games People Play*. London: Penguin. This is a classic study of the psychology of human relationships, with much of practical use for the project manager.

Gallwey, W.T., 2000. *The Inner Game of Work*. New York: Texere. Chapters 1, 8, 9 and 10 are particularly relevant to topics covered here.

Greene, R. and Elffers, J., 2000. *The 48 Laws of Power*. London: Profile Books. An excellent and highly readable manual of how to acquire and use power in organizations.

Harris, T.A., 1995. *I'm OK, You're OK*. London: Arrow. This book is much better than the title might suggest. It discusses how people are triggered to adopt different attitudes, labelled 'parent', 'child' or 'adult'. The 'child' behaves as if everything in the world can be fixed or changed by a 'parent'. 'Adults' realize that this is not always possible, no matter how desirable.

Maslow, A.H., 1998. *Maslow on Management*. New York: Wiley.

The following websites are useful introductions and contain some tools for personality type assessments:

- http://skepdic.com/myersb.html
- www.capt.org/The_MBTI_Instrument/Isabel%20Myers.cfm
- www.belbin.com

▶ Notes

1. Professor Jay W. Lorsch, Harvard Business School, personal correspondence, June 2004.
2. This distinction is nothing to do with process industries, such as oil and gas. An oil exploration company, although categorized as being in a process industry, can be a projectized company nonetheless. To see why, read on.
3. BSI (March 2000), *British Standard BS 6079-2:2000. Project Management – Part 2: Vocabulary*. Third Edition. London: BSI.
4. See, for example, Jackson, Joab. 'Pentagon backs spiral development', *Washington Technology*, Issue 06/09/03, Vol. 18, No. 5.
5. 'The publication of Department of Defense (DoD) Directive 5000.1 and DoD 5000.2 established a preference for the use of evolutionary acquisition strategies relying on a spiral development process', *Cross Talk – The Journal of Defense Software Engineering*, August 2002.
6. www.sei.cmu.edu/cbs/spiral2000/february2000/finalreport.html.
7. Hammer, Michael. 'Re-engineering work: don't automate, obliterate'. *Harvard Business Review*, July–August 1990. Since this initial milestone article, many feel that Hammer has softened his stance on the 'obliterate' injunction in the title.

project management processes

1

2

3

4

5

6

7

8

9

10

11

12

13

▶ Aims of this chapter

This chapter introduces the concept of process groups for project management and then describes each one in detail. The previous chapter described project lifecycles, and it is vital to understand the difference between process groups and the phases in a lifecycle. By the end of this chapter, the reader should be able to:

◆ list the five project management processes in sequence;
◆ state the principal outputs of each process group;
◆ describe the purpose of each of the process groups;
◆ use some of the key tools in each process group.

PMI says

Project process groups
'Project Process Groups. The five process groups required for any project that have clear dependencies and that are required to be performed in the same sequence for each project, independent of the application area or the specifics of the applied project life cycle. The process groups are (1) initiating, (2) planning, (3) executing, (4) monitoring and controlling, and (5) closing.' *PMBOK Guide* (p.370) [numbering of groups added]

▶ Process groups – rationale and general principles

The five project management process groups (Figure 3.1) are:

1 Initiating.
2 Planning.
3 Executing.
4 Monitoring and controlling.
5 Closing.

The general principle behind the process groups is nothing more than the common sense idea of plan, then act. This is a simple but critically important principle – so important in project management that it is worth spelling out the obvious: if you start doing things without planning them, chaos followed by failure is the likely result. The complication in project management is that there is in practice a tension between doing more planning and getting on with the doing part. The risk if you get the balance wrong one way is paralysis by analysis, the risk the other way is headless chicken syndrome, that is, much activity to little intended effect. The project management process groups of the PMBOK, and their equivalents in other approaches to project management, have evolved as best practice implementations and development of this simple principle in project management.

There are a number of specialized enhancements on the basic plan-then-do concept, several of them highly valuable. Many organizations have their own preference for one of these, and many teach their preferred model as part of their

Fig. 3.1(a) The five project process groups and their deliverables

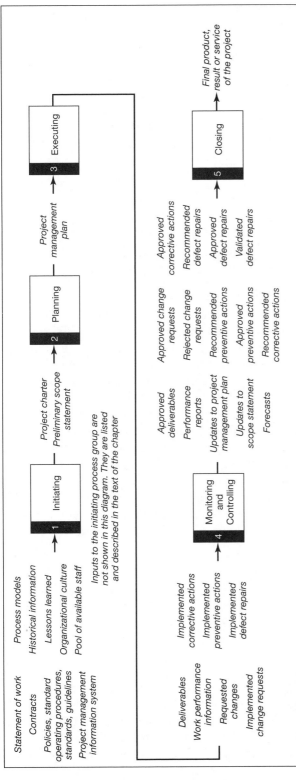

(a) Basic outline

Project management process groups are shown in numbered boxes, one to five. The deliverables from each process group are shown after each box, and these are also inputs to the next process group. Note that this is a simplified or idealized representation of the processes and their interaction, but this idealized representation is the best way to learn about the project management processes as they apply in real life, because if this simplified view is understood, then it is easy to understand the complexities and variances that apply in real-life project management processes. Most of the complexities arise in how process groups interact, for example a requested change (output from the Executing process group) is addressed in the next process group (Monitoring and Controlling) but may trigger updating the project management plan, that is, replanning, which involves processes from a previous process group (Planning). This is no more than common sense requires. So why have process groups in sequence if they interact and sometimes work in parallel, or parts of them work in parallel? The answer is that, first, it is logical and efficient to group the main different kinds of processes together, for example so that all planning processes are together, because at whatever stage in the project we do it, planning is planning, and we don't do a fundamentally different kind of planning at different times in the project. Secondly, it helps us to remember why we are doing some particular activity, to determine whether it is essential in our project or essential right now, and to ensure that where there are different ways of using the same piece of information we use it in all ways necessary for our project – in short, it is a good way to organize the complexities of project management.

▶

Fig. 3.1(b)   Some of the major interconnections between process groups and other assets

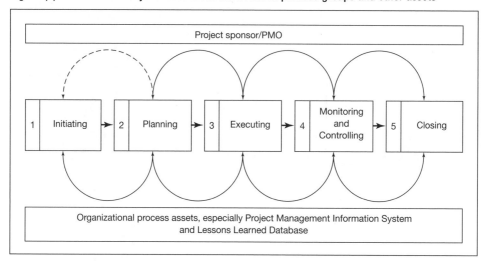

management development training. If you already have your own variant of the basic plan-then-do model, it is worth understanding that the fundamental principles are exactly the same as those of the project management process groups. This will save you much effort in trying to remember something completely different (it isn't) and also save you the effort of trying to resolve differences in approach (there are no major ones, none that are not fairly easily reconciled); and perhaps most of all if you are new to an organization, it will save you from wasting effort in arguing that the project management process groups should replace whatever is already in place, or, much harder, trying to replace in the PMBOK or some other methodology the process groups with your own organization's version of plan-then-do. You can of course do any of these things, but our advice is to understand the principles and not worry about differences in particular versions, although each version in widespread use is very valuable for the purposes for which it was designed.

We will look briefly at two different versions of the basic plan-then-do principle, both of which are in widespread use in large organizations. They are the OODA loop and the Plan–Do–Check–Act cycle.

▶ The OODA loop

The OODA loop was developed by John Boyd[1], and is a cycle of four stages:

◆ Observe.
◆ Orient.
◆ Decide.
◆ Act.

The loop and how it works are described in Figure 3.2. A notable feature of the OODA loop is that it splits the Plan half of the simple two-step plan-then-do model into three parts. Planning itself is the Decide part of the OODA cycle. This is preceded by Observe and Orient. The point of this division is to defer planning until

Fig. 3.2 The OODA loop

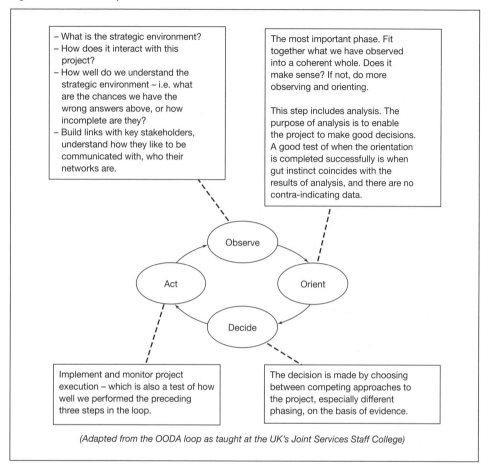

– What is the strategic environment?
– How does it interact with this project?
– How well do we understand the strategic environment – i.e. what are the chances we have the wrong answers above, or how incomplete are they?
– Build links with key stakeholders, understand how they like to be communicated with, who their networks are.

The most important phase. Fit together what we have observed into a coherent whole. Does it make sense? If not, do more observing and orienting.

This step includes analysis. The purpose of analysis is to enable the project to make good decisions. A good test of when the orientation is completed successfully is when gut instinct coincides with the results of analysis, and there are no contra-indicating data.

Observe

Act

Orient

Decide

Implement and monitor project execution – which is also a test of how well we performed the preceding three steps in the loop.

The decision is made by choosing between competing approaches to the project, especially different phasing, on the basis of evidence.

(Adapted from the OODA loop as taught at the UK's Joint Services Staff College)

one understands enough about the context of the plan. This is, in a way, treating the Plan step as the then-do half of the simple plan-then-do, in other words it is introducing, in a sense, the idea of having a plan for a plan. It is, however, more than this, and shows a more practical grasp of how real life works. It does take time in a new environment or circumstance to soak in the environment and to adjust one's mind to it.

In the case of setting up a substantial new project, the distinction between Observe and Orient is a useful and highly practical one, even if one runs both in parallel to an extent. Observing is about understanding the environment and the wider context in which the project is to sit. The Orient step is about thinking through how the project fits in that context. The difference is that Observe does not involve any consideration of the specifics of the project, whereas Orient does.

These distinctions in the early stages of the OODA loop are most useful when you are setting up a new kind of project in a large and complex organization. They are least useful if your project follows a well-established lifecycle model and is of a kind that you, the project team and the organization have done frequently before (unless there have been problems of customer satisfaction or quality, in which case a close examination perhaps using the OODA tool may be useful this time round). For example, a project to reengineer processes in an organization that has not done reengineering before, or in a division which has not changed its working methods for many years, will benefit more from an OODA-type approach than a project to implement a standard piece of technology with a project team that has done the same thing many times before, working to a project lifecycle that is very much tried and tested.

So if you are in a situation where the OODA loop might be useful, how do you use it in project management? It is simply a case of bearing the principles of OODA in mind as you move through the project management process groups. For example, in the initiating process group, remind yourself that there is a strong Observe and Orient requirement. This could mean using a draft or strawman version of the project charter and the draft scope specification as communication tools to help you Observe and Orient – that is, circulating them more widely and engaging potential stakeholders in discussions about them more than would be the case on a project where you did not need the benefits of the OODA loop.

The final observation to make on the OODA loop is that it is a loop or cycle: it continues around.

▶ The Plan–Do–Check–Act cycle

The Plan–Do–Check–Act (PDCA) cycle (Figure 3.3) was popularized by Deming[2], and comprises the following steps:

- **Plan** to change something.
- **Do**. Test the planned change empirically.
- **Check**. Assess the results of the test, to decide whether to implement change, or make further studies.
- **Act** on the basis of the test and assessment. If this does not produce the desired results, repeat the cycle, with a different plan.

Note that the Do step is not simply going out and doing it, but rather together with the Check stage is a test of the plan. Like the OODA loop described above, the PDCA cycle emphasizes planning and preparation, although with the emphasis placed slightly differently.

▶ How to use the process groups

The wrong way to use the process groups in real-life project management is to try to apply them all. Even worrying about remembering them all and how they fit together is inadvisable, we feel. With experience, you will gradually develop a memory for them in real-life project management, to the extent that you need them in your particular work. The right way to use them is to skim through them, and pick out elements of them that look useful to you. Most projects process quite well without the preliminary scope statement, for example, so don't start using it and its associated processes if you don't need it. However, if you can feel in your waters, to coin a phrase, that there is scope trouble ahead right from the start of the project, then consider using it and regard the associated processes as ideas for you to develop. (Of course, if

Fig. 3.3 The Plan–Do–Check–Act loop

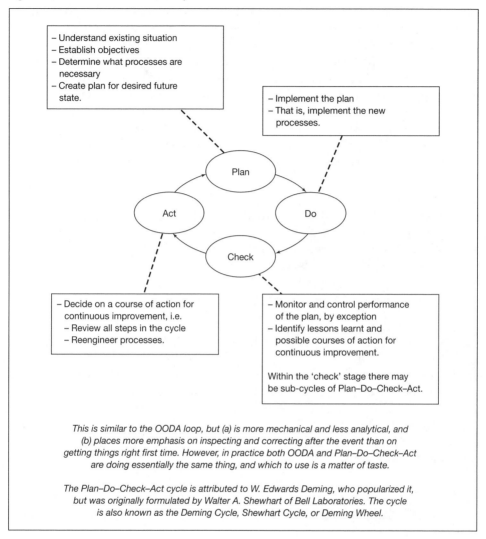

– Understand existing situation
– Establish objectives
– Determine what processes are
  necessary
– Create plan for desired future
  state.

– Implement the plan
– That is, implement the new
  processes.

Plan

Act

Do

Check

– Decide on a course of action for
  continuous improvement, i.e.
  – Review all steps in the cycle
  – Reengineer processes.

– Monitor and control performance
  of the plan, by exception
– Identify lessons learnt and
  possible courses of action for
  continuous improvement.

Within the 'check' stage there may
be sub-cycles of Plan–Do–Check–Act.

*This is similar to the OODA loop, but (a) is more mechanical and less analytical, and
(b) places more emphasis on inspecting and correcting after the event than on
getting things right first time. However, in practice both OODA and Plan–Do–Check–Act
are doing essentially the same thing, and which to use is a matter of taste.*

*The Plan–Do–Check–Act cycle is attributed to W. Edwards Deming, who popularized it,
but was originally formulated by Walter A. Shewhart of Bell Laboratories. The cycle
is also known as the Deming Cycle, Shewhart Cycle, or Deming Wheel.*

you are taking the PMI exams, you will need to learn the process groups in detail, and
if you are new to project management that will be useful.) In a nutshell, if you already
have some experience of doing project management, then:

◆ Don't try to use all parts of the process groups.
◆ Don't worry about whether you understand the detail of the process groups and
  how they fit together – you already know most of what you need to know and
  there are easier ways to cope with any gaps.
◆ Do use the high-level idea of the process groups as a mental checklist to ensure
  that you are doing the right thing at the right time.
◆ Do use the detail process groups as a guide, to refresh your thinking, or when you
  hit particular problems.

Those four rules are sufficient advice on how to treat the process groups, but we can say more by way of explanation. The great risk in setting out the process groups as they are set out is the risk of overcomplicating a simple idea. Why then do we set them out like this? There is a general problem with trying to write a guide to project management or to document it, which is that the nature of the subject inherently has this risk. In practice the choice is merely one of which form of potential overcomplication one picks. We have picked the PMBOK as being one of the least risky formalizations, and, being the most commonly used one in the world, we hope that there will be a larger community to ensure that the representation of the process groups is not allowed to harm projects in practice.

The risk is summarized by Max Wideman:

> ... a well-run project is simply not run like that [i.e. as per the PMBOK model of process groups]. If a project life span is properly configured for ... management control, and the proper levels of conceptualization, definition and planning are done ... then the process group interactions as presented are an unnecessary complication. All that is necessary is to exercise the standard management cycle of plan, organize, execute, monitor and control ...
>
> From www.maxwideman.com/musings/process1.htm

Just to be clear, for practical purposes we recommend reading the process groups in this chapter and understanding the broad principles in them, but not trying to learn all the detail by heart. Pick and choose what you think will be useful, based on your experience of project management in your industry, and refer back to this chapter for further information if you need it. On the other hand, if you are preparing for the PMI exams, you will need to learn some of this by heart. In either case, if you get confused, remember that all the process groups are doing is expanding the basic common sense idea of plan and then act to projects.

▶ The initiating process group

▶ What is the initiating process group?

The initiating process group is all about getting the project started. 'Initiation' means getting the project started. It is about being able to give a firm, definite and completely unambiguous 'Yes!' answer to the question 'Has this project started?' – and, just as importantly, to the two questions 'And do we know roughly what this project is aiming to achieve, and why?'. Just as the person who knows *how* will always work for the person who knows *why*, so a project which starts without a clear idea of why it exists will be at the mercy of many other projects and vested interest groups in the organization, and is likely to fail. It is no more than common sense to ensure that right at the start of a project, the project – that is the sponsor and the project manager – are clear about what the project is doing and why. The initiating process group is nothing more than applied common sense to enable you to answer these questions effectively and efficiently.

Table 3.1 shows three key differences to you as sponsor or project manager that result from doing initiation effectively.

Table 3.1 What initiation is, in terms of before and after project initiation

Before initiation	After initiation
◆ You may not be certain at a high level of what the project is and why it is being done.	◆ You will have maybe not complete certainty but a clear idea for starters, so to speak, and if you are not certain, you will know what kinds of things you need to find out next to increase your certainty.
◆ The project manager and the sponsor may have quite different ideas about the project from each other.	◆ Either both will have roughly the same idea, or at least they will understand clearly where their ideas differ, and that the sponsor's idea is the more important of the two.
◆ There is no written recognized picture '3 of what the project is about that can be used as a general basis for communicating to others, especially selling the project and getting constructive feedback on its merits and possible approaches.	◆ There is a 'recognized picture' of what the project is or might be, and how it will fit into the organization and create benefit, to serve as a basis for discussion across the organization.

PMi says

Initiating processes

'Initiating Processes (Process Groups). Those processes performed to authorize and define the scope of a new phase or project or that can result in the continuation of halted project work. A large number of initiating processes are typically done outside the project's scope of control by the organization, program or portfolio processes and these processes provide input to the project's initiating processes group.' *PMBOK Guide* (p.362)

▶ What is the output of initiation?

The most important output is the Project Charter. This is also known as a Project Initiation Document (in PRINCE2) and the Project Brief (BS 6079). The other output is the Preliminary Scope Statement. The kind of information contained in the project charter is as follows, but given that initiation happens right at the start of a project (or phase) all this information is understood to be provisional, and subject to testing in the planning process group:

◆ What exactly is this project going to do?
◆ Why? What is the business case? (in outline.)
◆ Who is going to do it? (This section of the charter should at least say who the sponsor is, and if possible the project manager. If these two appointments are not

to be filled during project initiation, then the charter should say when they will be filled, and give in outline the type of skills and experience and seniority required of them.)

◆ When?

A single page is often all that is needed for a project charter for small to medium-sized projects. The outputs therefore should be regarded as in 'strawman' form; that is, they should be understood, if not deliberately designed, to be in provisional form, and all who read them should understand that they are intended to change very much.

One of the uses for a project charter is as a basis on which management decides whether or not to proceed with a project. Acceptance by the performing organization of the project charter may also be the trigger to release money and resources at least for the first phase of the project.

▶ Why is initiation important in project management?

Initiation is the most important process group, so we spend extra effort explaining it here. Initiate well and you can cope with much that is not quite right later on. Initiate badly and your project may never recover even if you excel at all the subsequent process groups. A project or phase that does not initiate effectively will carry for the rest of its duration a high risk of, at best, extra cost, and at worst, complete failure. This is simply logical common sense: if the project does not start with a clear idea of what it is doing and why, then it will either have to work out these things as it goes, that is to say, it will have to make up its reason for existence as it goes along, which is expensive and likely to damage the credibility of those involved, or it will never get adequate traction and resources in the organization to deliver anything.

How does initiation work? What are the inputs, tools and techniques? There are two processes within the initiating process group:

◆ Develop project charter.
◆ Develop preliminary project scope statement.

Producing a project charter or project initiation document is often no more than filling in a template, in terms of getting words onto paper. The charter is essentially no more than the What? Why? How? When? Who? of the project – the 5 Ws[4]. However, the intellectual and conceptual tasks of answering these questions about the project can be as difficult and complicated as the questions themselves are simple. What exactly is it that the project is to do? And why – what is the business case? Even though these questions need not be answered in detail in the initiation phase, be clear that the task of answering them can be a substantial one. While initiation for some projects is completely routine, and answering the questions will be simple and straightforward, in other projects it may be a major task.

Figure 3.4 gives a list of inputs to the two processes of the initiating group. The most important thing is to get a project charter, which is sometimes known as a project initiation document (PID). If you focus on one thing in initiation, focus on getting the charter. Focusing on that will help you also to work out what inputs you

Fig. 3.4 The initiating process group

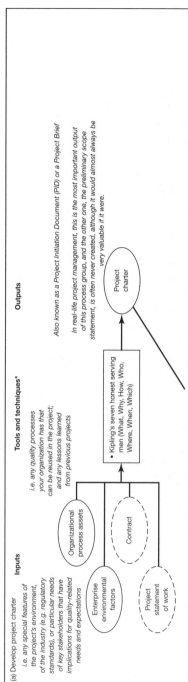
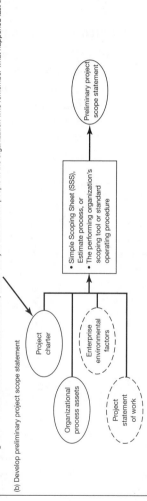

(a) Develop project charter

Inputs

i.e. any special features of the project's environment, of the industry (e.g. regulatory standards), or particular needs of key stakeholders that have implications for quality-related needs and expectations

- Enterprise environmental factors
- Organizational process assets
- Contract
- Project statement of work

i.e. any quality processes your organization has that can be reused in the project; and any lessons learned from previous projects

Tools and techniques*

- Kipling's seven honest serving men (What, Why, How, Who, Where, When, Which)

Outputs

- Project charter

Also known as a Project Initiation Document (PID) or a Project Brief

In real-life project management, this is the most important output of this process group, and the other one, the preliminary scope statement, is often never created, although it would almost always be very valuable if it were.

(b) Develop preliminary project scope statement

- Project charter
- Organizational process assets
- Enterprise environmental factors
- Project statement of work

- Simple Scoping Sheet (SSS), Estimate process, or
- The performing organization's scoping tool or standard operating procedure

- Preliminary project scope statement

The most important and most commonly used inputs are in solid ovals, others are in broken-line ovals. If your project is being done on the basis of a contract, then it certainly should be one of the inputs used in creating the project charter, but we use a broken line for it in this diagram because in real life, many projects initiate without a formal contract; the same applies to the statement of work. In contrast, there is always a set of 'Enterprise environmental factors', comprising at the least the culture and the 'way we do things round here' in your organization – ignore these at your peril. Find out what they are, and, as they say in California, go with the flow. Chief among the organization process assets to look for as inputs are: (1) your organization's model for a project charter (also called a Project Initiation Document (PID)); (2) your organization's process lifecycle for this type of project and any relevant industry standard or trade association or professional bodies' models; (3) lessons learned from previous projects of a similar kind, and as well as looking at formal lessons learned databases or similar, ensure that you talk to a few people in the organization who remember what happened last time.

Work can start on the scope statement before the charter is complete, and for small or simple projects, the scope statement can be simply a paragraph or set of bullet points in the charter. However, scope is so critical in project management that even if the preliminary scope statement is to be combined within the charter, it should be a separate conceptual exercise.

* For those doing the PMI's exams, note that the PMBOK methodology lists the inputs and outputs given in the diagrams above, but does not list the tools and techniques that we show here. Also, the PMBOK does not distinguish as we do here by means of broken-line ovals between the most important inputs and outputs

need and what tools and techniques to use to write the charter. The tools and techniques in this process group boil down to common sense and whatever management tools your organization uses for defining problems and producing papers.

If feasible to do so, a key activity in initiation is to create a well-documented description of end-user requirements and derive a full project plan including timing, resources and costs. It is only once this information is available that a proper decision about whether to proceed with the project can be made.

For project managers, in the early stages of the project it will be useful to get into the habit of carrying the current version of the project charter wherever you go. Print it out and stick it to the inside cover of your daybook, so that you can refer to it if required during any conversation next to the coffee machine, or while you are walking around the team members' work areas. (Later in the project you can replace the charter with a Gantt chart or some other summary of the project plan.)

▶ Who should be involved in initiation?

The sponsor and the project manager should definitely be involved in the initiation process group, although at times and in certain organizations one or both of these may not be appointed until after initiation. Sometimes a project or programme management office will handle initiation.

Once a broad need for a project has been identified, the project must be set up or initiated. Much of the setup work is done in some organizations by a project management office or some management structure other than the project itself, but at some point the project will need to start as a project in its own right. Initiation is about doing this, and how initiation works in your organization will define who in addition to the sponsor and project manager should be involved. Initiating a project does not mean starting work on creating the desired products of the project immediately; there is usually much to be done both in administrative tasks and in clarifying the project's objectives and what will be involved in achieving them. The initiating process group is about getting this administration and clarification started and to a useful point. Note that such work may also extend to the planning process group, but usually in a project there is a minimum amount of initiation that needs to be done before things can go further, before the real work can start – this is initiation.

▶ The planning process group

▶ What is the planning process group?

'To fail to plan is to plan to fail.' We take it that the idea of planning needs no explanation. The planning process group is the set of processes used in project management to create a plan by which to manage the project. A vital element of the plan is the scope, and it is so critical in project management that it merits being listed as a separate output of the planning process to the overall plan (see the PMBOK definition), although it is a section of the plan. There are risks both of doing too much planning, and of doing too little. There are a number of complications in all but the smallest and simplest projects and one of the main aims of the planning process group is to deal with these complications.

PMI says

Planning processes
'Planning Processes (Process Groups). Those processes performed to define and mature the project scope, develop the project management plan, and identify and schedule the project activities that occur within a project.' *PMBOK Guide* (p.367)

The particular complications facing a project or a phase of a project in planning will depend on the particular project and especially on the particular team and organization involved. Note too that planning, unlike the previous process, initiating, is one that continues throughout the project. Whereas initiation should in a well-run project have a definite end point, in a well-run project of any size planning is something that continues almost to the very end, as new factors arise and existing factors change or their ramifications to the project become better understood: there is a constant need for replanning. The complications in planning include:

- How often to replan?
- How to manage information needed as inputs to planning when some of the information is constantly being updated?
- How to manage a variety of levels of quality and reliability of inputs to planning?
- How to determine the level of granularity and accuracy at which to plan? And how far ahead?
- How to control changes to the plan?
- How to control the impact on execution of the plan of intended but not yet approved changes to the plan?
- How to manage and communicate planning options so that they can be discussed effectively without the communication process sending the wrong signals?
- How to minimize the bureaucracy of planning?
- How and when to involve stakeholders in planning?

As a rule, if your project faces any of these questions, it is more important to decide on an answer to the question and stick to it until you make a definite decision to change it than to worry about getting the perfect answer – 'you' here meaning the sponsor and the project manager jointly. Try to be pragmatic, make a decision, see if it works, and if not change it. For example, take the first question, how often to replan? Suppose that you don't really know, which is quite likely. Gut feel may suggest to replan every two months, with a major replan every six months. Unless anyone can say definitely why that is a bad idea, give an alternative replanning schedule and convince the project manager and sponsor that it really is better, stick with it, and don't spend too much time in discussion. Then, if it becomes clear that more frequent replanning is necessary, change. Equally, if the replanning burden at two-monthly intervals is outweighing the benefits, then change and reduce to replanning every three or four or maybe even six months.

Table 3.2 summarizes the results of the planning process.

Table 3.2 What planning is, in terms of before and after planning

Before planning	After planning
◆ No plan exists in sufficient detail to use to manage and control execution.	◆ A plan exists that is usable for executing the project.
◆ The scope is defined loosely and incompletely, in the Preliminary Scope Statement.	◆ The scope of the project is well understood together with the ramifications for the project and the performing organization and key stakeholders, and all these are documented in the scope statement (included as a section within the project plan).
◆ The project manager does not have an intuitive feel for proceeding confidently in the next (say) 3 months.	◆ The project manager feels confident intuitively that they know what should be happening in the next 3 months.
◆ The stakeholders are not confident in the plan.	◆ All stakeholders have been engaged, understand the plan as it affects them or may (through project risks) affect them, and have their own copy of the plan or part of it.

▶ What is the output of planning?

The main output of the planning process group is of course the project plan, and, important not to forget, updates to the plan. One of the main reasons that projects go wrong is that actual activity diverges from the plan because the plan is not updated to reflect necessary or desired changes. This would not matter if the plan had no value – in other words, if there is any point in having a plan, which there is, then the whole point is to have a plan that guides execution, and if you allow the execution of project work to proceed unplanned then you might as well not bother with a plan. A complication here is the risk that the project may come to feel as if it is about producing the plan instead of producing the final product of the project. This risk needs to be managed, by having a plan that is the right size, neither too small nor too big, and the right structure for the project, the organization and the project team. Throwing away the plan is not managing this risk, it is increasing it; and failing to update the plan to the point where the plan is not showing what is actually happening and what is intended to happen in the project is in effect the same as throwing away the plan. The planning processes, if you select just the ones relevant to your needs, will help you to manage this risk efficiently.

The *PMBOK Guide* gives a full list of inputs and outputs for the planning processes, and it should be studied carefully by anyone doing the PMI's exams, and is likely to be valuable to any practising project manager.

▶ Who should be involved in planning?

Who should be involved depends entirely on the kind of project. Very small projects can be planned fully in one's head, written on a postcard, and executed from memory. Large projects, to build a large tunnel or to launch a new bank or to create a major new retail service, may need teams of people on individual elements of the plan.

▶ The executing process group

▶ What is the executing process group?

The executing process group turns a theoretical plan into something tangible. The entire reason for a project is that it should produce some deliverables, either physical products or something that is recognizable, such as a change in working practices.

The executing process group contains more than the production of the project deliverables; however hard or simple a task that might be to complete, it is also concerned with the realization of the project plan and how it evolves to meet the realities of the project tasks and operating environment. As such the execution process group should not be considered in isolation, but as a process that is intimately entwined with the monitoring and controlling process group. Between them these two process groups work the project plan, changing and documenting those changes as the project plan evolves.

The processes within the execution process group produce the project deliverables and perform quality assurance to ensure that the deliverables achieve the required standard. The execution process identifies change requests, often as a result of experience gained from executing part of the project plan, and then implements these changes. Changes to the plan that arise in this fashion are called corrective actions. Change requests occur to prevent a risk developing into an issue: shutting the stable door prior to the horse bolting are preventive actions.

An important part of the execution process group is the selection and development of the project team to complete the project work packages. In most cases, the risks associated when working with an experienced and motivated project team are much lower than those when attempting to execute the same work with an inexperienced project team.

Table 3.3 summarizes the results of the executing process.

PMI says

Executing processes
'Executing Processes (Process Groups). Those processes performed to complete the work defined in the project management plan to accomplish the project's objectives defined in the project scope statement.' *PMBOK Guide* (p.360)

Table 3.3 What execution is, in terms of before and after execution

Before execution	After execution
◆ Work packages and project deliverables are incomplete.	◆ Work packages and deliverables are completed.
◆ The level of risk associated with a work package is high.	◆ The level of risk associated with a work package is reduced.
◆ The project team is undeveloped and inexperienced.	◆ The project team have worked together and, as a minimum, started to develop some of the skills required to complete the project deliverables.
◆ The project communications are largely theoretical and evolving from the planning phase.	◆ Communications have been tested and can be amended as a result of the experience gained.

▶ What is the output of executing?

The main output of the executing process group is of course the project deliverables: this is the output of the entire project! As well as the deliverables the other main output of the execution process is change requests and the implementation of change requests. Along with the monitoring and controlling process group, execution is an iterative process; a successful project manager continuously checks that deliverables are of the appropriate quality and manages the associated risks.

▶ Why is executing important in project management?

As well as the importance of a project actually executing the production of a product or implementing a change, the execution process group is important as it is this process that makes the project management plan work. Earlier earned value management protocols for project managers implicitly used the execution process as a test of the rigour of the project management plan and, ergo, a test of the competence of the project manager. This is unhelpful as it ignores the reality that changes to projects mostly occur owing to events beyond the project manager's control, such as stakeholder decisions or changes in the wider business, social or physical environment.

General Eisenhower famously stated that 'no plan ever survives contact with the enemy, but you still have got to have one'. A conjugate to that quote was made by a much earlier military commentator who said 'in strategy there are no victors'. Taking these two mantras together, it can be said that the best project management plan is worthless, unless it can be adapted to the realities of the project environment. It is the execution process that implements the changes to a project plan and identifies many of the change requests, as risks to the project become better defined.

▶ Who should be involved in executing?

As with the planning process group, who should be involved depends entirely on the kind of project. As a minimum, this will usually be the project manager and the project team. Larger projects may require interactions with members of the organization outside the project team who are members of the organization or sub-contracting parts of the project to external sellers.

It is the interactions between the project team and members of the same interaction that are often the most complicated. Most organizations have rigorous procedures in place for procurement or contracting services; it is their processes for obtaining goods or services internally that tend not to be well planned. From the point of view of the project manager, any deliverables or work packages that are executed internally to the organization, but outside the project team that they control, should be planned and managed with the same care as those contracted in from outside the organization. The risk associated with work executed externally to the project team is typically higher than for similar work carried out internally. The main reasons for this increased risk are the extra communications required between the project manager and those external to the project and the lack of control the project manager has over them to deliver work packages within the project timescales. Sellers and contractors external to the project organization are normally controlled and legally bound by contract to complete work to the required standard and on time; while those internal to the organization but outside the project manager's control often lack suitable incentives.

The monitoring and controlling process group

What is the monitoring and controlling process group?

The monitoring and controlling process group is the feedback mechanism that compares the performance of the project during the execution process to the project plan. Changes will always occur during project execution, as the risks that are identified during the planning process become better understood as a result of project execution. It is often stated that project risks decrease as the project proceeds, but this is often not the case, as in projects with poorly defined or changing baselines the risk can increase unless the project is properly controlled.

As its name implies, monitoring and controlling involves two actions: the project must be observed and its progress recorded; and the changes must be actively managed by the project manager. It is not enough for a project manager to notice changes within a project passively; their variation from the baseline plan needs to be appreciated and appropriate actions taken to correct drift away from the plan. All changes to the project plan should be taken through the integrated change control process, to ensure that the project deliverables conform to the project scope statement.

Table 3.4 summarizes the results of the monitoring and controlling processes.

PMI says

Monitoring and controlling processes

'Monitoring and Controlling Processes (Process Groups). Those processes performed to measure and monitor project execution so that corrective action can be taken when necessary to control the execution of the phase or project.' *PMBOK Guide* (p.364)

Table 3.4 What monitoring and controlling is, in terms of before and after monitoring and controlling

Before monitoring and controlling	After monitoring and controlling
◆ Risks are either unknown or of uncertain probability.	◆ Risks can be determined to a point where they can be adequately managed.
◆ Changes to the project plan occur due to external influences and to overcome risks identified during execution.	◆ Change control is integrated into a single, well-defined process that is understood by the project team.
◆ The performance of the project is uncertain.	◆ Project performance is measured in relation to the baseline project plan and the future of the project can be forecasted.

▶ What is the output of monitoring and controlling?

The main output of the monitoring and controlling process group comprises the actions necessary to correct issues or defects identified during the execution process. The monitoring and controlling process determines the difference between the state of the project and the project plan. It is the feedback that allows all parts of the execution phase (quality, costs, schedule and risks) to be measured against the project plan. In the words of Lord Kelvin, 'only once you can measure and quantify a thing can you understand it'. By comparing the progress of a project to the project plan, it is possible to forecast the future of the project.

Besides the variation between the project deliverables and the plan, the monitoring and controlling processes have a number of other outputs, which are listed in full in the *PMBOK Guide* together with their associated inputs. We have already suggested, above, how to use the project management processes, but let us emphasize here that, unless you are taking the PMI's exams, the way to use this section of project management methodology is sparingly.

▶ Why is monitoring and controlling important in project management?

Moving from the theoretical world of project planning to the real project environment will often change the project stakeholders' understanding of what the project is about. At this point it is important for the project manager to be able to document and factor any changes to the plan that this shift in understanding may bring.

Just as medieval doctors examined the four humours to determine the fate of their patients, the 12 monitoring and controlling processes allow a project manager to know the state and progress of their project, so that they can make meaningful forecasts on its performance. The level of detail required for recording and monitoring progress is often determined by the detail and accuracy needed for forecasting.

▶ Who should be involved in monitoring and controlling?

The short answer is the project manager, since monitoring and controlling processes include some of the most fundamental project manager responsibilities. Overseeing and controlling the project work and managing the project risks are key tasks that can make the difference between a project succeeding or failing. Large or highly technical projects may have specialists to monitor risks and schedule control, while budget control often comes from the finance function of many organizations. Command and understanding of the monitoring and controlling process group are fundamental to the decision making of project managers.

▶ The closing process group

▶ What is the closing process group?

The closing process group consists of two main activities: project closure and administrative closure. Project closure is the formal completion of the project deliverables and their transfer to others, such as the client, customer or other recipient of the project products or services, the termination of the activities of the project team and the completion of lessons learned or experience gained on the project. Administrative closure completes all project documentation and formally signs off any contracts external to the project organization. The archiving of project documents and lessons learned on a project are valuable intellectual property for an organization. The project documents can often prove invaluable in providing an aid to planning and identifying risks for future, similar projects. Experience has shown that without proper documentation, corporate memories are exceptionally short; even with the best will in the world, individuals' memories are highly selective and often focus on the highs or lows associated with projects, without remembering the underlying reasons for events. The experiences of an engineering firm involved with technical research and development have shown that even if the individuals on a particular project are retained by the organization, the working knowledge to complete similar projects is lost after a period of around two years.

Table 3.5 summarizes the results of the closing process.

PMI says

Closing processes
'Closing Processes (Process Groups). Those processes performed to terminate formally all activities of a project or project phase, and the transfer of the completed product to others or close a cancelled project.' *PMBOK Guide* (p.354)

> Table 3.5 What closing is, in terms of before and after closing

Before closing	After closing
◆ Project deliverables have not been formally transferred to others.	◆ Project deliverables are formally transferred to others or a cancelled project is closed.
◆ Lessons learned or experiences gained on the project are not formally documented.	◆ All lessons learned from the project and relevant project documents are archived by the organization.
◆ Contracts placed by the project to contractors external to the organization are still active.	◆ All contracts established by the project are formally closed.

▶ What is the output of closing?

The main output of the closing process group is the formal transfer of the project deliverables to others, either internal or external to the project organization. At this point the execution and monitoring and controlling processes should have converged and the completed deliverables correspond to the revised baseline plan. A useful exercise for the project manager at this point is to examine the revisions to the baseline plan and compare these to the initial assumptions made in the planning process. The difference between the assumptions and those risks and external changes that resulted in change requests are often useful for future projects, since in many cases they will have resulted from the organizational structure or environment the project was conducted in.

Table 3.6 describes the two processes associated with the closing process group and their inputs and outputs.

> Table 3.6 The various processes of the closing process group, showing for each one its inputs and outputs

Inputs	Outputs
Close project	
◆ Project management plan	◆ Administrative closure procedures
◆ Contract documentation	◆ Contract closure procedures
◆ Enterprise environmental factors	◆ Final product, service or result
◆ Organizational process assets	◆ Organizational process assets (updates)
◆ Work performance information	
◆ Deliverables	
Contract closure	
◆ Procurement management plan	◆ Closed contracts
◆ Contract management plan	◆ Organizational process assets (updates)
◆ Contract documentation	
◆ Contract closure procedures	

▶ Why is closing important in project management?

The end stages of a project are often the most difficult for a project manager. At this point interest in the project may be waning or the feeling that the job is complete may lower the effort of the project team. The role of the project manager is to ensure that all of the project deliverables have been met and that the project scope statement has been satisfied. Some projects have suffered from unexpected requests or aspirations expressed by stakeholders at the closure stage. To avoid this it is essential to ensure that stakeholder management and project communications are maintained until the formal close of the project.

▶ Who should be involved in closing?

Closure is essentially an action for the project manager and the project team. During the later stages of a project, the commitment of project team members may decrease rapidly as they concentrate on reassignment to new projects or different roles within the organization. It is important for the project manager to motivate the project team members and keep them directed to completing project work until formal closure.

▶ Summary

The five project management process groups are:

- ◆ Initiation.
- ◆ Planning.
- ◆ Execution.
- ◆ Monitoring and controlling.
- ◆ Closure.

The general principle behind the project management process groups is simply plan, then act: the OODA loop and the Plan–Do–Check–Act cycle are two methodologies that can help achieve the balance between planning and acting.

The individual processes that make up the process groups are described in terms of their inputs and outputs. If you are preparing for the PMI exams, you will need to learn some of this by heart. For real-life project management, we recommend reading the process groups in this chapter and understanding the broad principles in them, but not trying to learn all the detail. Pick and choose what you think will be useful, based on your experience of project management in your industry, and refer back to this chapter for further information if you need it. The process groups allow a project manager to gain a sense of proportionality: to determine the balance between thinking and doing.

▶ Notes

1 Colonel John (Richard) Boyd (1927–1997), United States Air Force fighter pilot.

2 Dr W. Edwards Deming (1900–1993), a pioneer of modern quality management (whose work in that field is discussed in Chapter 8). Deming acknowledged Walter A. Shewhart (1891–1967) and his Shewhart Cycle as the origin of the PDCA cycle, although its origins can be traced further back.

3 This term derives from the term 'recognized air picture' used in NATO air warfare, and which plays a key role in RAF and USAF doctrine. Without a recognized air picture much time is wasted and risk created by uncertainty over who thinks what is where in the air. Even if the recognized air picture is wrong, it soon gets corrected as everyone is alert for errors in it, everyone is updating it through a standardized common process, and everyone gets the updated picture at the same time. There is much to be gained in all parts of project management from adopting the concept of the 'recognized picture'.

4 Or five of Kipling's six honest serving men – Rudyard Kipling, *The Elephant's Child*.

project integration management

1

2

3

4

5

6

7

8

9

10

11

12

13

▶ Aims of this chapter

Project integration management is the heart of project management. When you have completed this chapter you should:

◆ know what project integration management is, how it relates to project management as a whole, and why it is important;
◆ be able to categorize project activities according to whether or not they fall within project integration management;
◆ know what factors cause integration management to become more important the larger the project;
◆ be able to apply the principles of project integration management in practice in your projects, in such a way as to increase the efficiency, increase effectiveness, and reduce risks, of the way you do project management;
◆ be able to explain to other project managers and project sponsors the business case for treating project integration management as a distinct task within project management;
◆ use integration management sparingly, as and where necessary, to run your project, and not use your project to run the bureaucracy of integration management.

▶ What is project integration management?

Project integration management means coordinating all the other processes and activities of project management, so as to ensure that the aim of the project is achieved as efficiently as is practicably possible. In terms of the project management process groups and knowledge areas, then, integration is the means by which the project manager uses the right parts of the process groups and knowledge areas, at the right time, in the right way, to achieve the aim. The PMI's PMBOK says that integration 'includes ... unification, consolidation, articulation, and integrative actions that are crucial to meeting customer and stakeholder requirements and managing expectations'[1]. What does this mean in practical terms? Read on!

Key Idea

Project integration management
Above all, project integration management is about deciding where to focus project management effort, and deciding in a systematic way that draws on experience and best practice.

Integration, as the term is used in project management, is also about:

◆ making and managing changes in the project,
◆ making decisions,
◆ knowing where to focus resources and effort,

- identifying risks and issues, and
- reducing or eliminating the impact of risks, issues and changes.

All of this work must be controlled, managed and integrated (Table 4.1) in order to prove beneficial to the overall project.

PMI says

Project integration management

'Project Integration Management includes the processes and activities needed to identify, define, combine, unify and coordinate the various processes and project management activities within the Project Management Process Groups. In the project management context, integration includes characteristics of unification, consolidation, articulation and integrative actions that are crucial to project completion, successfully meeting customer and stakeholder requirements and managing expectations.' *PMBOK Guide* (p.337)

Table 4.1 Seven project integration management processes

		Process Group		
Initiating	*Planning*	*Executing*	*Monitoring and controlling*	*Closing*
1 Develop project charter	3 Develop project management plan	4 Direct and manage project execution	5 Monitor and control project work	7 Close project
2 Develop preliminary scope statement			6 Integrated change control	

The role of integration in project management

Integration is about doing the right thing at the right time to make the project happen.

As we have seen in Chapter 3, there are five process groups that may be used in a project or a phase of a project, and the skills required across the five together fall into nine knowledge areas. This sounds complicated, and the five process groups and nine knowledge areas are the way that the PMI divides up the expertise that you, the project manager, needs into manageably sized chunks. In return for the complexity of two dimensions, knowledge areas and process groups, we get a manageable way of looking at all the project management tools and techniques, and how they fit together. Don't worry about the complexity: if you are a practitioner, get a rough feel for things and pick out the bits that seem useful to your project. If you are learning for the PMI exams, do enough rote learning to pass the PMI exams. In practice the project manager's task requires managing the interactions that extend beyond the boundaries of the process groups and the knowledge areas, and this is how project integration management is useful in real life.

Project integration management is about linking and coordinating project and product processes and knowledge areas to ensure the best possible planning and execution of the project. This can be a difficult task. It requires a trade-off between competing requirements and objectives. On the one hand, it incurs the cost of complexity and bureaucracy by having the two dimensions of knowledge areas and process groups instead of the single dimension of a simple 'prepare, plan, do, review' for the project manager to think about. So on the other hand the benefits from having our project management tools and techniques organized into knowledge areas and processes must exceed those costs, by enabling us to do things much more efficiently or on a much bigger scale, and at much lower cost and risk than a simple linear approach could possibly achieve. Do we in fact get this net benefit? Only if we know how to select the right tool at the right stage in project management. This is also what integration is about.

In real life, being able to do integration requires a certain level of knowledge and experience on the part of the project manager. Integration management is an exception to the general rule in project management that most of project management is applied common sense, that is, it can be worked out just by thinking about the task. While it is common sense that in a large or complex project, there is a discrete task that is integration, even if it is called by some other term, the processes involved in such integration are not so easily deduced from first principles in the way that much of planning and HR management, for example, can be. The integration knowledge area derives from careful analysis of how projects have succeeded and failed over many years.

There are many different project management methodologies, but the key to all of them is integration. Integration is important because in order to satisfy the sponsor and stakeholder requirements, a project manager needs to manage the interactions across all organizational and process boundaries. This requires making trade-offs. As the performance trade-offs will be different for each project, experience and history are only partial guides. The larger and more complex the project, the more iterations will be necessary to ensure stakeholder requirements are met, as well as getting agreement on the process outcomes.

The project manager's main responsibility is to make sure the objectives and agreed deliverables are met, on time and within budget. This is what integration is about.

The most important tools for project integration management are planning, communication and leadership. Other skills are influencing, negotiating and problem solving.

▶ A first look at project integration management

This section covers the following aspects:

◆ Understanding how the project will interact with the organization.
◆ Integrating external inputs to the project.
◆ Influencing and coordinating resources outside the project's command.
◆ Selecting the right project management tools given the project's complexity.

▶ Understanding how the project will interact with the organization

The first step in project integration management is to understand how the project's deliverables will interact with the current or future operations of the organization. If your project is, to take an imaginary and extreme example, to replace bus drivers with robots, this would mean understanding the existing workforce, their trade unions, how the robots would interact with the passengers, and with the police and insurers in the event of accidents. If the structure of the organization will alter during the life of the project, the interactions initially established between the project and stakeholders will need to change and adapt according to the reorganization, and there needs to be a plan, and before that a vision in the mind of the project manager, for realizing and managing that change. So, as a project manager, consider all likely organizational changes, so that their impact is reflected in your project management work, especially in planning.

One of the greatest impacts on projects from organizational changes is changes in stakeholders. New organizational structures mean new stakeholders. New stakeholders should be involved in project planning activity as soon as they are identified, in order to minimize the risk that they might refuse to accept the project's deliverables.

▶ Integrating external inputs to the project

We have seen that integration means pulling together and prioritizing and coordinating all project management activities. The project manager, helped where necessary by the project sponsor, will have authority over resources allocated to the project and over processes that fall within the jurisdiction of the project. However, such is the nature of project management that many of the resources and processes critical to the success of the project are not under the command of the project manager or even of the sponsor. At best, the sponsor and project manager have some degree of influence over many of the critical resources and processes. Therefore a key factor during the initiation and planning processes of the project is to integrate resources and processes that are necessary for the project from those beyond the ones controlled by the project. In plain English, you will have to plan to beg, borrow or steal. Figure 4.1 illustrates the point that the project needs resources beyond what it actually controls. This is the hard part of integration, and one of the hardest parts of project management altogether.

▶ Influencing and coordinating resources outside the project's command

Influencing resources outside the project's control is related to the previous subsection, on integrating external inputs to the project. The problem of influencing and coordinating resources over which the project team have no direct authority needs to be managed at all stages of the project.

Projects never have enough resources or access to processes. This is natural given the nature of projects as temporary endeavours concerned with innovation or change. Projects have direct control of only a fraction of what they need in order to succeed. Figure 4.1(a) depicts this problem. Figure 4.1(b) shows the solution, which is to develop a zone of influence and beyond that a zone of interest. The zone of influence encompasses assets and processes necessary to the project but which are

Fig. 4.1 Projects must obtain the use of assets and processes beyond their control

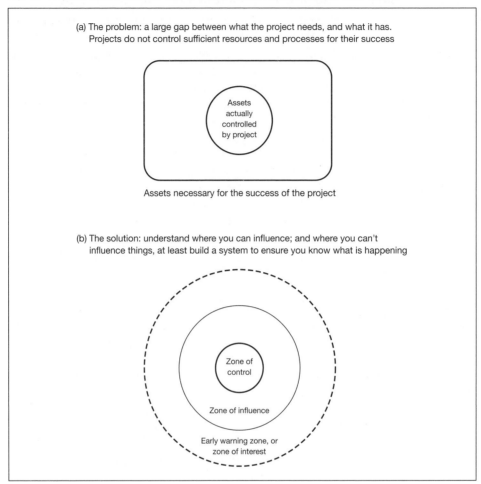

not controlled by the project, those that you will have to 'beg, borrow or steal'. The interpersonal skills of the sponsor and project manager, and the project team, and the power and influence of the project sponsor are critical to ensuring that the zone of influence is sufficiently large for the project. There will still remain risk areas, assets and processes which are not within the zone of influence right now, but which need to be brought within it in due course, or even controlled, for the project to be a success. The project must develop an intelligence or information gathering system so that it knows what is happening to these assets and to give the project the best chance of bringing them within the zone of influence or control at a later date.

▶ Selecting the right project management tools given the project's complexity

A problem in project management is that project management methodology can become the focus of effort instead of the focus being on delivering the project. Put another way, what ultimately matters is results, not whether project management methodology was or was not used. Project management methodology must be a means to an end, but a big risk is that it becomes an end in itself. Big, complex projects need more project management tools and techniques than small, simple projects. A key skill for project managers is to know which tools to use when, and how to use them.

We have seen that the size and complexity of a project should determine how much project management process should be used. There is always a temptation for the inexperienced project manager or the project manager in a failing project to apply more and more effort to the bureaucracy of project management, for example to producing project documentation, holding project workshops and writing project reports. Project integration management is an antidote to this often lethal bureaucracy, but for it to work the person using the tools and techniques of project integration management has to be aware of the risk of applying project management tools and techniques inappropriately and to have some experience of real-life project management. Project integration management will help you to determine what tools to use and when. 'Yes, we need to appoint some project staff, but first let's decide what exactly it is that we are doing in this project' – project integration management helps you to make this kind of argument.

Project integration management ensures all the right areas of the project and of project management methodology are covered, or have been considered and deferred or rejected, as part of the project management process. The importance of integration can be shown by the initial project management plan produced during the planning process of the project. Once the project has moved in to the execution process, a certain aspect may have changed or altered which was not part of the original plan. The project team would evaluate the impact; this in turn could generate an adjustment to the initial project management plan. The whole process is an iterative approach that requires the need for integration and implementation by the project manager.

An aim of project integration management is to use the smallest number of project management tools and techniques that is needed to deliver the project's objectives.

▶ Processes and process groups of integration management

This section describes the key processes that fall within project integration management. The aim is to describe each process and enable you to understand its role in integration, so that you can do it. The context of this is project integration management. The individual processes (and in brackets the process groups to which they belong) within project integration management are:

- ◆ Develop project charter (Initiating)
- ◆ Develop preliminary project scope statement (Initiating)
- ◆ Develop project management plan (Planning)
- ◆ Direct and manage project execution (Executing)
- ◆ Monitor and control project work (Monitoring and Controlling)
- ◆ Integrated change control (Monitoring and Controlling)
- ◆ Close project (Closing).

Note that this list can also be read as a sequence of things to do to run a project. The charter is a 'plan for a plan' or a high-level, first-cut plan for the project. Often it need be no more than a one-page 'What? Why? Who? How? Where? When?' outline of the project as it is first conceived, but for larger projects it may be a longer document. The purpose of the scope statement is to say what does and does not fall within the project, and, following from that, what the key interfaces of the project are. The key elements of the charter and the scope statement are also key ingredients of the project plan. Why are they separated out in project management methodology as separate activities before the main planning[2]? For all but the smallest, simplest projects, planning is a complex activity and it can be hard to know how to begin planning the work. If you are having difficulty in deciding or even thinking about how to start planning your project, don't worry – that is entirely normal, even for very highly qualified and experienced executives.

If you are finding it hard to start planning, here are two ideas that may help. First, start by writing just a one-page plan, with a few lines under the headings 'What are we trying to do in this project: Why? How? When?'. And secondly, develop in your mind, and later on paper, a high-level, very rough view of the aim and rationale for the project, which is provided by the charter, and an initial or 'strawman' view of the rough scope of the project and the key interfaces. In both of these, use the strawman approach (see key idea box). Things can always be revised as more is learnt.

Key Idea

The strawman

A dictionary definition of 'strawman' is an argument set up to be defeated[3]. In project management, we use the term to mean something, typically a plan or report, that is set up to be modified or changed completely. The key idea is that it is a starting point only, and criticism, comment and total change not only do not matter, they are positively welcomed. We use a strawman to get the ball rolling, that is to get things started. People who receive strawman ideas should understand that they ought not to get angry with the strawman idea or use it to attack the project, but instead if they think it is misguided, they should come up themselves with a better idea and feed it back to the project. Getting traditional cultures to use the strawman can require a little cultural change.

▶ The sequence of integration processes

Project management starts with project initiation. In project initiation the various project stakeholders are brought together to develop the project charter and the preliminary scope statement. Once those things are done the project then moves into the planning phase. Planning uses the outputs from initiation to start integrating all the detail needed to prepare, develop and coordinate the subsidiary plans produced in the project management plan.

The next stage of integration management is to direct and manage the execution process group by completing the work specified in the project management plan, together with the implementation of the approved changes. During execution a major output presented to the project manager is information about work performance. This information is assessed and reviewed to determine whether the project is running as planned or whether it is running at variance to the performance baselines. This information gathering and assessment is what is called monitoring and controlling.

PMI says

Control

'Control (Technique). Comparing actual performance with planned performance. Analyzing variances. Assessing trends to effect process improvements. Evaluating possible alternatives, and recommending appropriate corrective actions as needed.' *PMBOK Guide* (p.355)

Control will generate a set of preventive actions. They require an approval process and change control process, or otherwise the project will change in an uncontrolled way, which increases cost and risk. Like so much in project management, this is no more than common sense, but experience shows that it is useful to make the point explicitly.

We will next look at some of the processes within project integration management in more detail.

▶ How do projects get started?

How do projects come to be? There are many root causes leading to business needs for projects, including the commercial needs of the organization ('market driven'), new legal or regulatory requirements, changing fashions, or responses characterized by varying degrees of gambling in the face of advances in technology or the opening of new markets. The vanity and ego of chief executives and elected and non-elected government officials has also been proposed by some, although it is beyond the scope of this book to opine on the likely validity of such claims. Once the business need has been established, the next stage is to decide how to respond to this need. A typical approach here is to generate a number of possible approaches and run a selection process to pick the one that will be used in the project. As an aside, it is common for such selection processes to be a source of concern and problems in large organizations, but that is also beyond the scope of this book.

The project manager should understand the constraints and assumptions included in the project charter. 'Should', because that is the ideal but may not be possible; for instance, if the project is large and complex, say to modernize working practices across a varied, multi-business organization, working out the constraints and assumptions is a mini-project in itself. In such cases the key thing is for the project manager and sponsor to be aware of their state of ignorance, and the size of the task necessary to work out the constraints and assumptions to a degree that allows proper planning. This lack of knowledge can be documented in the charter.

▶ Develop project charter

Key Idea

Project charter (or PID)

A project charter, or project initiation document (PID), states, at a high level, what the project is and the rationale for doing it. A project charter can also be used to give formal authorization to the project. It is a short document, and can be changed later as the tasks within the project become better understood.

A project charter:

- ◆ is a short document, in the style of an executive summary,
- ◆ summarizes what the project is,
- ◆ explains why the project is necessary or desirable,
- ◆ describes how the project will work,
- ◆ is the first deliverable in a project,
- ◆ is also known as a project initiation document or PID,
- ◆ is the 'plan for the plan',
- ◆ formally authorizes the project,
- ◆ can be a stage-gate,
- ◆ can be used to set the tone of the project with stakeholders,
- ◆ can set the context and approach to benefits realization.

PMI says

Project charter

'Project Charter (Output/Input). A document issued by the project initiator or sponsor that formally authorizes the existence of a project, and provides the project manager with the authority to apply organizational resources to project activities.' *PMBOK Guide* (p.368)

Here we give one possible layout and description of a project charter, and an example of a completed charter (Tadley). Many organizations have their own templates for project charters. Another widely used format for a charter is the PRINCE2 template for a project initiation document, which is the same thing as a charter.

Project charter template

Author, date and version

What?

Aim
◆ State the aim. The aim of this project is to – do what?

What is the project?
◆ Describe the project briefly. (Use the 'grandmother test'. Would your grandmother understand what you have written? If not, simplify and clarify until both your grandmother and the average 12-year-old can understand it.)
◆ What is the overall market size problem or the product–market space addressed by the project?
◆ What is the end point? How will we know when the project is finished?

What are the deliverables?
◆ Say whether any work needs to be done to define the deliverables.

Cost
◆ Rough order of magnitude (ROM) estimate of number of man-days effort and of costs.

Why?

Why we are doing it?
◆ Give the simplest, clearest possible reason. Most projects are done for one of five reasons: (1) legal or regulatory; (2) to 'keep the lights on' or stay in business; (3) to reduce risk; (4) to improve profit; or (5) to generate capability to serve new markets. State which of these applies.

What is the business need?
◆ If there is a business need, as opposed to regulatory/legal, explain it briefly.
◆ What business need does the project meet or what customer problem does it solve? What is the financial case?
◆ What is the risk reduction case?
◆ What is the case in terms of increasing capability?
◆ What is the regulatory case?
◆ What options will be created?

What is the burning issue?
◆ If there is a burning issue, state it in one sentence.

Estimated value of the project (and basis)
◆ Internal
◆ External

Who?
◆ Who is to be involved, in what roles, with what responsibilities?
◆ Who is critical in delivering this programme – the team, partners, suppliers?

◆ Who is the relevant regulator?
◆ Who are the business partners for this project? Are they involved yet? On what basis?
◆ Who are potential trial customers?
◆ Who is the competition?

Where?
◆ Where does this programme fit within our strategy?

How?

Overall approach
◆ What will be the overall approach for how the project will get done? List the:
  – methodologies,
  – previous similar work,
  – key milestones,
  – tools and techniques.
◆ How will the deliverables of the programme be implemented? (i.e. designed, delivered, sold or supported?)

Milestones
◆ What are the milestones in this project?
◆ Which are potential quick-wins?

How will we plan and assure quality?
◆ How will we know what the customer wants? How will we know all their requirements?
◆ How will we prevent errors?
◆ Do we already have the full set of capabilities to ensure a reasonably good probability of right-first-time, or are we likely to need to acquire new resources or capabilities to do this?
◆ What measurements should we make, especially for continuous improvement?

When?
◆ When will the project be completed? (Give a date)
◆ When will the first customer sign up or when will the first users go live?
◆ When will cash flow or cost reduction or efficiency gains or risk reductions crystallize? That is, when will our firm begin to realize the benefit of this project?

Project charter example: Tadley revenue project

Tadley Project Charter (Part 1)
11 October 2007, prepared by I. Kant, project sponsor, and R. Descartes, project manager, Tabula Rasa Technologies, Inc.

What is the project aiming to achieve?
◆ To define and document the Corporation's approach to creating a new product and service offerings for performance management in the public healthcare sector.
◆ To identify the work required to set up the collateral required to launch the offering, and to identify fully the costs and benefits of doing so.

Why is it important to achieve it?

◆ Healthcare clients, unlike our traditional financial services clients, do not understand what the corporation does, so this project will remedy this understanding gap for performance management deliverables.

◆ There is clear evidence from existing healthcare clients that a performance management offering is desirable and therefore that a wider market demand is likely.

◆ There is an opportunity to transfer knowledge into the Corporation to augment current offerings and to use that combined knowledge to further enter the public healthcare space.

Where will it be developed?

◆ This is a project to be developed by the Corporation staff working jointly with external analysts and consultants, ahead of any product offering to the market.

Who is going to be involved in managing the project and what are their responsibilities?

◆ Project Manager – R. Descartes

◆ Project Sponsor – I. Kant

◆ Project Office – Anna X. Zimander

How and when is it all going to happen?

◆ Project initiated Monday 1 October. All documentation to be produced by R. Descartes for interim and final review by the project steering group.

Final deliverables

1 Performance Management Product Offering overview.

2 Go to market plan including high-level costs and targets.

Timescale

◆ Project to produce draft final deliverables 25 October.

◆ Final sign-off to commence Part 2 by 6 November.

The charter defines what success will look like and may indicate how this will be measured by detailing with the higher-level requirements of the project. The charter thus sets the scene for benefits realization.

We have just explained why the format or template for a project charter and for other project documentation may need to be adapted to the particular type of project. A project management template designed for one kind of project may not be ideal for another. So if your organization's template for a project charter seems to be too complex or not aligned to the needs of your project, perhaps it has been designed for a different kind of project. For example, in POTCOM (not its real name), a large old-fashioned telecoms company in which most projects had been large engineering or national marketing projects, the project templates were written for big projects. One day POTCOM decided to stop being a traditional telecommunications company, and to do many exciting new small projects around web services. Management initially felt that POTCOM needed a new project management methodology, when in fact all it needed was to adjust the templates to reflect the change in size and complexity of the new kind of initiatives. This saved a great amount of money, risk and upheaval.

Another factor to consider in the design of project documentation, including the charter, is the kind of internal processes it is to be used for. Increasingly organizations are adopting a stage gate approach (see key ideas box) to control projects. A project charter can be used in the Initial Stage Gate or Gate 0 approval decision. If your charter is to be used this way, then make sure that it contains the information required by the process (as opposed to you as the project manager and sponsor being the arbiters of what should be included). Here we give an example of a charter (Whitby) for a different kind of project from the Tadley project earlier. The latter is a project to create a new product and service offering, that is, it is designed to generate new revenue, whereas the Whitby project whose charter is given here is a back-office or purely internal project. Different kinds of project and different circumstances require different kinds of charter. One of the biggest differences is between projects aiming at revenue generation, or other client-facing projects, on the one hand, and those aiming at back-office or administrative concerns on the other.

Key Ideas

Stage gate and stage gate review

A stage gate is a set of conditions that must be met before further work can be done. These conditions include completing certain work packages, and may include obtaining certain approvals or meeting certain quality standards. The stage gate is the project management equivalent of telling a small child 'you can't have any ice cream until you have eaten up all your vegetables'. Stage gates are a way to control cost and effort expended and to enforce good work and management discipline in projects. (Stage gates are not explicitly part of the PMI *PMBOK Guide*, but are often useful in large, complex projects. The concept is implicit in *PMBOK Guide*.)

A stage gate review will assess activities and deliverables to date and decide whether to approve the project proceeding to the next stage.

The UK's Ministry of Defence adopted the stage gate approach to projects in response to a series of high-profile cost overruns and performance problems in major projects. The results so far seem to show an improvement on the previous state of affairs.

Project charter example: Whitby internal project

Whitby Project Charter

15 September 2005, prepared by John McTaggart, Company Secretary, Time Research Ltd.

Project description

ISO 9000 is a quality certification that requires accredited companies to establish clear processes, follow them, and verify compliance through a formal audit process.

To extract the maximum benefit from undergoing ISO 9000 accreditation, the Company aims to use the audit to identify their business processes that have the greatest impact on the business and to prioritize them. Levantine Quality Assurance Register (LQAR) have been contracted to act as ISO 9000 assessors.

Project authority
◆ The Project Sponsor is John McTaggart.
◆ The Project Manager will be George Berkeley.

Objectives
◆ Project Whitby will prepare the Company for an ISO 9000 audit, maximizing the value obtained through the stages of process establishment, implementation and verification by audit.
◆ The project will be completed by the first quarter of 2006.

Business case
◆ Accurate knowledge of a firm's business processes is a vital input for assessing the current state of the company and planning its future direction. Effective application of the ISO 9000 audit will allow the Company to rank its processes in order of value and to establish those that have the greatest impact on the business. Conducting an internal audit will provide the Company with a 'live' project to practise and refine techniques for the survey and interpretation of business processes.
◆ Attaining the ISO 9000 qualification will provide existing and potential clients with assurance of the quality of the Company's business processes.

Product description and deliverables
As a minimum Whitby will achieve the ISO 9000 qualification for the Company. The success of the project will be judged on the increase of our understanding of our business processes. At the highest level, the project deliverables are as follows:

1 Complete the questionnaire – this should allow us to check that our processes cover all the ISO 9000 areas.
2 Decide on an assessment date and location. LQAR suggested that this was typically 6–10 weeks after completing the questionnaire. The Company should be able to achieve this within four weeks.
3 Return the questionnaire and supporting documents to LQAR.
4 Assessment meeting – explore with LQAR how to release value from our processes, rather than just going through a checklist assessment.
5 Arrange ongoing surveillance meetings, as necessary.

Effort/resources required
Two man-months spread across the Company in preparation for the assessment, two man-months for the assessment itself, and then a series of short review meetings to respond to any of their suggestions and to record progress.

▶ The project charter as a control and approval device

As we have seen, the charter is a key document in project management because it gives a high-level description of the project and is the 'plan for the plan'. The project charter can also perform a control function. In many organizations, the sponsor and members of the project steering committee sign off the charter to give formal authorization to the project or to its next stage, the establishment of the project. When used as an authorization mechanism, the signing of the project charter by the project steering committee releases resources to the project and authorizes a budget for the project.

▶ The project charter and interfacing

Interfacing means the connections between the project and the rest of the world, including:

◆ other parts of the organization to which the project belongs,
◆ any external customers for the project, and any regulatory bodies,
◆ any external suppliers,
◆ the means of communication with those other parties,
◆ how those communications will work,
◆ which specific individuals in the project will own each communication link, and who will be their counterpart,
◆ how the project's processes will interact with processes in the rest of the organization (e.g. financial control and budgeting processes).

A critical success factor of the project is how it interfaces with the rest of the organization. Get interfacing wrong and your project becomes like the albatross in *The Rime of the Ancient Mariner*[4] – everyone wants to avoid it because they think it will ruin their lives. Even if you do everything else perfectly in your project management, but get the interfacing wrong, the project will fail. Getting the right support and interaction, that is, interfacing, is above all about communication. The project charter is an excellent communication tool available right at the start of the project, so use it as such. Remember that you can use the charter in draft form even before the formal start of the project, on a strawman basis, to help you get early warning of likely interfacing problems.

The sponsor is responsible for issuing the project charter, but the work of writing and thinking through the details required to integrate the various aspects stated in the charter is the project manager's. The project manager drafts the charter and gets the information and questions that form its content, working closely with the sponsor. It is sent out to other stakeholders in the name of the sponsor and with their full authority. It is best to send the draft charter to a few close allies of the sponsor first and modify it if necessary in the light of their feedback before sending it out to the full set of stakeholders. When sending out the charter, it should be the sponsor's signature block and the sponsor's e-mail account and not the project manager's that are used.

▶ Statement of work

In some organizations, one of the main inputs produced prior to formal approval of the project charter is the statement of work (SOW). The statement of work, together with the organizational structure, policies and the company's processes and procedures, are used in creating the project charter – ideally. In other organizations the charter comes first, and then one of the next tasks is to produce the statement of work. The point is that the statement of work needs to be produced early on in the project, because it is the formal specification of work to be done. There may be more than one statement of work, especially in large projects.

Key Idea

Statement of work (SOW)

A statement of work (SOW) is a contractual (for external suppliers) or near-contractual (for suppliers within the same organization as the project) statement of what work is to be done. For external suppliers, the SOW can be the contract. For internal suppliers, the SOW is often the mechanism by which a cost code is set up and project accounting is done. Internal SOWs may have other names.

PMI says

Statement of work (SOW)

'Statement of Work (SOW). A narrative description of products, services, or results to be supplied.' *PMBOK Guide* (p.376)

Case study

Statement of work

The statement of work (SOW) is generated by the sponsor or customer and forms a key input into the project charter, prior to formal approval. The statement of work needs to be produced early, because it sets out the formal specification of work to be done. Following the Defence Strategic Review in 1997, the MOD adopted a more capability-driven procurement process and developed a revised approach to requirements setting than had been previously used. The new requirements process involved all stakeholders and used the User Requirements Document (URD) and System Requirements Document (SRD).

The URD is equivalent to a SOW and consists of a complete set of individual user requirements for the project. A URD is the means by which the customer is able to develop, communicate and maintain the user's requirement throughout the life of the system. The SRD is equivalent to the project scope statement and is a complete and consistent definition of the entire system to be provided in response to the sponsor's needs in the URD. The SRD also specifies the functionality and performance required. The system of best practice for the development of the SOW indicates the following:

◆ The sponsor or customer takes the lead in the production, refinement and mainte-nance of the URD, drawing on the support of stakeholders as necessary.

◆ The sponsor or customer ensures that verification criteria are identified against each user requirement, and that requirements are prioritized.

◆ The sponsor or customer seeks endorsement of the URD from all the stakeholders, both against their specifically flagged requirements and as a complete integrated document.

◆ Any change of operational need should be reflected in the URD.

Once the policy has been determined as to how the work will be completed, the SOW (URD) can be broken down into more detailed requirements, as defined in the scope statement (SRD), and put out to tender in single or multiple groupings. Each element of the contract will have a separate and discrete contract statement of work to deliver against. The linkage between individual requirements within the URD and the SRD is maintained to show the origin of every demand placed on the system, and how each requirement is met.

For an MOD contract, the SRD defines what the system must do to meet user needs, as stated in the URD. The two documents also provide the basis for advising industry of MOD's requirements for the project. The SRD is also updated to reflect any trade-off decisions and approved system enhancements in response to changes in the URD. The SOW is the key document to which the entire project requirements are traced back, because it states the sponsor's needs.

Example of a statement of work (SOW)

Parties	ABC Ltd, Strand, London WC2 XYZ Ltd, Newersgate Street, London EC2
Project name	Phosphorous
Project dates	1 March 2008 to 31 December 2008
Project locations	London, Frankfurt, New York, Singapore, Shanghai, Santiago
Services and materials	XYZ will design and plan training in strategic sales coverage/account planning and management. XYZ will provide project specialists, working under the ABC project manager. XYZ will supply the following materials: ◆ Psychometric profiling ◆ Senior management interview templates ◆ Video cameras and editing facilities ◆ DVD production, 50 DVDs per location. ABC will provide office facilities, print/photocopying and access to intranet. ABC will provide project support office resources and equipment.

Fee structure	Quarterly in arrears, as per previous contract
Fee	US$440,000 ex. taxes, travel and expenses per quarter
Accommodation	To be booked through ABC intranet site only and approved by project office
Travel	As above
Conditions of payment	Payment dependent upon satisfactory completion of work in each location, to be decided by local management team (and in the event of a legal dispute then by binding arbitration in the London Court of Arbitration)

A case study and an example of the statement of work are given here. In some organizations the statement of work is produced by the key stakeholders in order to outline the business need and product scope. The document may also include information relating to the company's or customer's long-term plans. All of these strands are pulled together for consideration as part of the selection process. Certain experts can also be used to assist in this process. Key stakeholders or users can be involved during the selection process to help assess the series of projects being put forward for consideration. Early involvement and integration of all stakeholders associated with the project should improve the level of communication throughout the organization, as well as producing a more complete and definitive document. If a change to the charter is deemed necessary at a later stage of the project, the whole question of whether to continue with the project must be reviewed.

Develop preliminary project scope statement

Once the project charter has been developed to a level where it could be signed off, the next thing to do is to develop the Project Scope Statement. A couple of observations are needed here to explain how and why to ensure that this is not bureaucracy gone mad. Developing your understanding of scope in partnership with the sponsor and other stakeholders is nothing more than the first step in project planning. Scope is a critically important part of project management, and planning, so it is split out in PMBOK's project integration flowchart as its own step, because it is so important in real life. But if your project is one where scope is well defined in the charter, which could be because the project is small or is of a familiar type, or simply because everyone is clear what it is, then you can ignore this step. It may also help to think of the scope statement, even in its preliminary form, as merely a section of the project plan. It is the first section you should write, because it defines everything else that you will write.

Scope is vital to project management, and 'scope creep' has killed more projects than anything else. Even if you are clear in your mind what the scope of your project is, it needs to be documented so that it can be communicated to others, and ideally key stakeholders, and the project steering committee if there is one, should sign off the scope statement.

Scope means the boundaries of the project, including the methods of acceptance that are to be applied to deliverables. There are three sources of information to use as input to the preliminary scope statement:

◆ The sponsor (the main source of information)
◆ The statement of work (SOW)
◆ The project charter.

PMI says

Scope
'Scope. The sum of products, services and results to be provided as a project.' *PMBOK Guide* (p.375)

Comment: it is often useful in real life to extend the PMBOK definition to include the processes and parts of the organization that will be used to obtain those products, services and results.

The project management team work on the preliminary scope statement to refine and improve it. It is called 'preliminary' because that is the version that gets signed off in the initiating phase of the project, and becomes input to the planning phase. In the planning phase the scope statement is further refined, and becomes part of the plan. Of course, after the project plan is signed off in the planning phase of the project, the scope may still change throughout the project, but changes are then controlled as part of the integrated change control process.

Why spend so much effort on a scope statement? Apart from creating the document called the preliminary scope statement, the main outcome is to ensure that the sponsor and project manager, and other key stakeholders, have the same understanding of the project's scope. It is quite normal in the early stages of a new project for individual understanding of scope to keep changing greatly. If you are the project manager or sponsor or a stakeholder and see the scope changing very fast in the early days of your project, this is normal. What's happening is that your understanding, and that of others, of the scope is developing. The process of producing a preliminary scope statement helps to ensure that the associated dialogue is efficient and structured. Scope definition is critical to the success of the entire project, and it must be established before starting the planning process.

Develop project management plan

No project succeeds without a plan. But remember, the plan is not the project. The plan is there to make the project work. As project manager, use the plan to get the work done; don't drift into acting as if creating and updating the plan is the same thing as doing the project. That attitude will stress you and probably kill the project. But like carbon monoxide poisoning or hypothermia, you won't know that you are suffering from that attitude until it is too late. So, for sponsors among you, watch your project managers and help them steer clear of this risk.

The project management plan consists of all the management plans and performance baselines established by the endorsed project management methodology. Note that the plan should includes baselines, where the type of project warrants it. A baseline is the initial budget or estimate for how long project activities will take and how much resources, including time, people and money, will be required. (See the 'PMI says' box for a fuller definition.) The reason for including a baseline is to ensure that progress against the plan can be measured. In some circumstances, such as projects that are not priorities and are very small, it may not be worth including a baseline, but as a rule, in a project of any size, a baseline should be included, though perhaps not in the initial version of the plan. As changes to the plan are approved, the plan may need to be re-baselined to reflect the changes. As project manager you should ensure that all key stakeholders know what the current baseline is. Avoid the situation, for example, where the project sponsor thinks that the baseline for the project is $1m of spend to go and deliver the summer after next, but the chief executive of the organization thinks that the baseline is half as much and delivery is twice as soon, because the chief executive is working to the old baseline.

The project management plan explains what the project is, why it is worth doing,

PMI says

Baseline
'Baseline. The approved time-phased plan (for a project, a work breakdown structure component, a work schedule, or a schedule activity), plus or minus approved project scope, cost, schedule and technical changes. Generally refers to the current baseline but may refer to the original or some other baseline. Usually used with a modifier (e.g. cost baseline, schedule baseline, performance measurement baseline, technical baseline). ...' *PMBOK Guide* (p.352)

and how it will work. The *how* part is the most important part of the plan, and is about how the project will be executed, monitored, controlled and closed. The project management plan includes outputs produced during the planning process of the project; that is, when you come to write the project management plan, you are not starting from scratch; there should be a number of documents you have already produced by that stage in the project lifecycle that form sections of the plan, for example the scope statement. These may need to be revised and updated in the light of new information which you have learnt since their last versions. Project management is an iterative process, or, more bluntly, it can be a constant struggle to keep on top of changes and keep the plan and reality close enough together so that you and the project team can do your job with the least possible stress.

The plan has two different purposes. It helps you and the project management team control and manage the project, that is, it is a control and management tool. It is also a communications tool, a means to communicate to key stakeholders what is expected of them in order for the project to be a success, and what they should and should not expect of you and the project.

What should the plan look like? What should be in it? This depends on the type of project. The fundamental principle to apply is to make the project management plan reflect the size, complexity, scope and risk associated with the project. A plan to sell mobile phones through athletic shops will focus on consumer behaviour, marketing and the risks of unsold goods and changing fashions. It will have quite a different structure from a plan to build, say, a new nuclear warhead, which will focus on risks of a different kind. Your organization may have templates for project plans of different kinds, and your organization may also mandate that certain sections must be included in project plans. For very small projects, the project charter with an added timeline or Gantt chart may be sufficient for a plan. What matters in a plan is that it will work, that the document that is the plan will enable you and the project team to deliver the project and to communicate the plan to stakeholders in a way that is acceptable to them. It is a mistake to take a template for one kind of project and apply it unthinkingly to projects of another kind. A Google search on the Internet should find a number of good templates for your kind of project. (Examples of project plans can also be downloaded from www.aldpartners.com.)

Key Idea

A Gantt chart is not by itself a project plan

Some people think that a Gantt chart is a project plan. Having a clear aim and clear scope and understanding the risks are at least as important as the Gantt chart. And in order to produce a reliable Gantt chart you need first to have a good work breakdown structure (WBS). A Gantt chart can be a useful part of a project plan, but it is not the most important part.

One reason why so many novice project managers confuse a Gantt chart with a project plan is that Microsoft Project and other software tools are very good at producing Gantt charts. Such tools have a role to play in project management, but before you start using them ensure that you understand how and when to use them.

The project management plan could include, among other sections, separate sections for the following:

- Project organization.
- Scope statement.
- Work breakdown structure.
- Product breakdown structure.
- Baseline documents for cost, schedule, and process improvement.
- Timeline – in Gantt or PERT or other format.
- Quality management plan.
- Human resources plan.
- Communications plan.
- Risk management plan.
- Procurement plan.

Much effort is needed to integrate all these parts into the overall project management plan, and effort is expensive and takes up time. Project integration management is about avoiding unnecessary work by making sure you do only the things that are necessary at the right time. The unnecessary expansion of the project management plan complicates your job as project manager. Work out what sections need to be in the project plan, and make sure that you have them in the plan, but only them. What sections should be in the project management plan depend on the requirements of the particular project, the personal preferences of the sponsor and possibly other stakeholders, and the conventions and mandatory requirements of the organization in which you are managing the project.

The project management plan tells you and others how the project will be done, or, to use language currently popular which means exactly the same thing, how execution will happen. The plan describes what the project is and what principles it will follow. Much of this is unexciting, similar in a way to which side of the road shall we drive on, in that it may not matter which particular principles or approach is followed (e.g. whether project meetings should be on a Monday or on a Friday, or whether to use one software tool or another), but what does matter is that everyone in the project is driving on the same side of the road, so to speak. Much of the value of the project plan comes from setting out this kind of unexciting, but critical, detail. The plan also shows how the project will manage scope, time and cost. The direction given by the project management plan is to specify not only what must occur, but also how it is to be measured, controlled and completed.

It is not necessary to plan the latter parts of the project in as much detail as the early parts. Planning can, and perhaps should be, a rolling process. It often makes sense to plan in detail for the next phase of the project, and leave the plan for the subsequent phases as a sketch or as no more than high-level plans. The advantage of this is that it avoids wasted effort of replanning later phases as new information becomes available and changes affect what is required.

Once the plan is finalized, or nearly finalized, it is common to hold a project kick-off meeting with key stakeholders and the project team, to mark the start of the project and to go through the plan. This meeting is useful from an integration point of view because it is a means to communicate and coordinate matters concerning the project. Such meetings deserve careful planning, and the project manager and sponsor should together decide what they want out of the meeting. Possible aims include verifying risk management plans, building synergies with other projects, or selling the approach or parts of it to individual stakeholders who appear not yet to be fully bought in.

▶ Project planning methodology

A project management methodology is defined as a series of project management process groups and their related processes. The control functions used are also part of the methodology which is then combined to form an overarching approach to the project. The methodology followed by a company could apply a formal set of established project management standards, or it may decide to tailor the processes in a more informal way to suit the project needs. A formal or informal technique can be used, as long as it assists the project management team to develop an effective charter and project management plan. The methodology used is therefore a key input as to how many of the processes will be conducted. The selection of methodology will first be reflected in the project charter.

Key Idea

Project planing methodology

A project planning methodology is a tried and tested standard way of creating a project plan. What matters is that it enables you to produce a practical, reliable plan in an efficient way. Most large organizations have their own methodologies which they have tailored to their needs. The two most successful generic methodologies are the PMI PMBOK and, especially for UK civil service work, PRINCE2.

The three most important things in project planning are to:

◆ keep the project's aim and business needs in mind,
◆ think of scope and scope trade-offs, and
◆ start the planning with a work breakdown structure (WBS).

Chapter 5 says more about scope and WBS.

The biggest mistake in project planning is to start with a Gantt chart. Gantt charts are excellent tools, but can be very dangerous if they are used without first doing a WBS.

▶ Benefits of planning

The benefits of planning should be obvious, but in the real-life pressure when stakeholders may pressure you to cut back on planning time and instead 'get on with real work' you may find it useful to remind yourself, or them, that planning is real work. Here are some benefits of planning:

◆ The process of creating a plan forces people to think about what is involved in the project and their interdependencies. Interdependencies can sink a project if not spotted at the planning stage.
◆ It allows scheduling of usage of scarce resources, both within a project and across the firm.
◆ If there is a plan against which progress can be tracked, then divergence can be spotted and action taken before the situation becomes critical.
◆ A properly thought-through plan is one of the few defences against requests for unreasonable deadlines.
◆ Breaking down a project into separate tasks, each with identifiable outputs and deadlines, allows the project manager to delegate effectively. A well-structured plan makes it easy to give SMART objectives when delegating, and hence also improves the chances that team members will produce the desired output in good time.

- Clearly defined individual tasks are easier for people to focus on than a whole project in which they play only a small part. So structuring a project correctly gives team members satisfying short- and medium-term goals.
- A plan is a communication tool. Customers, suppliers, team members, sponsors and stakeholders can get a common understanding of when outputs will be available and why certain deadlines have to be met.
- Without a plan, things will be forgotten, started late, or assigned to several people to do.

▶ How to plan

How to plan varies much from organization to organization. Increasingly the project planning process is becoming standardized and controlled, and runs on software packages and intranet sites. However, some of the main ideas used are:

- Activity definition.
- Work breakdown structure (WBS).
- Product breakdown structure.
- Gantt or project timeline charts.

It is worth understanding how these things relate. None of the others make any sense unless you have first defined activities. Likewise, for Gantt (timeline) charts or PERT (network) charts to make sense and not to be sources of major risk, it is necessary first to have a work breakdown. Gantt charts, also known as timelines, show elapsed time most readily, and PERT (network) charts show dependencies. You can manage projects without understanding how these things relate to each other and why, but you will have a much easier time and a greater chance of success if you ensure that you understand this and work accordingly in planning your project.

Figure 4.2 shows a very simple Gantt chart for a small project, while Figure 4.4 later in this chapter on page 116 shows a Gantt chart for a much larger project. Figure 4.2 shows how lines can be added to a Gantt chart to show dependencies,

Fig. 4.2 A Gantt chart showing dependency relationship

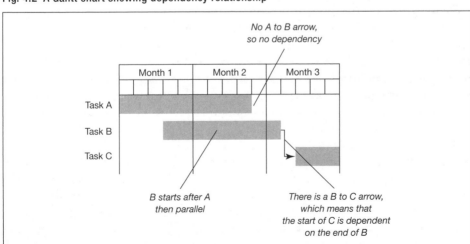

but if your aim is to show timescales, then you may wish to minimize clutter by not adding them. A major problem with most graphical representations of projects is the clutter in them.

▶ Activity definition

An activity is a 'component of work performed during the course of a project' (PMI *PMBOK Guide* (p.350)). An output is the result of an activity or task. It is vital to distinguish between the activity and its output, but it is easy to get confused because activities are often named after the outputs they are intended to produce. Shelling peas is an activity: the bowl of shelled peas is the output. The distinction is important because the arrival of the outputs is the signal that the activity has finished and subsequent activities can begin, subject to the outputs meeting quality standards (that is, being fit for purpose). If the outputs exist and are complete then it is easy for the project manager to know the state of progress on an activity (it is finished). But if the outputs do not yet exist then the project manager must assess how much work remains to be done on the activity, and there is usually much more uncertainty in such progress estimates.

A key concept in project planning is activity duration, which is the time required to complete the activity. Durations can be fixed or variable. A fixed-duration activity takes a fixed length of time from start to end, no matter how much effort is allocated. For example, lead times on specialist equipment might be six weeks, and it will remain six weeks whether we allocate one person, 100 people or nobody at all to wait for it to arrive. Variable-duration activities can usually be shortened by allocating more people to do the work. An example of a variable-duration activity is painting a wall: theoretically, we can halve the time required by doubling the number of painters. Now consider digging a hole. We might be able to also halve the time to dig the hole by putting more people in the task, but if the hole is narrow and deep, there may be room for only one person in the hole.

This simple arithmetic for variable-duration activities is appealing, but it is unwise to try to apply it simplistically to most real projects. Imagine that you had been asked to manage a project to cook dinner. Some activities are fixed duration (cooking times in the oven), but some tasks are variable duration. How much shorter would the dinner project be if you were allocated a team of 10,000 people to help you? Of course, it would take many times longer than if you had a team of three, because you would have to spend so long breaking down the work so that everyone got to do something, allocating tasks, coordinating and supervising. This is why project managers know that trying to speed up a late project simply by adding people will slow it down further. Adding resources can sometimes help, but it must be done intelligently.

People assigned to work on a single activity together must talk with each other and coordinate their work. With only two people on the activity this is a relatively small overhead, but as the number of people rises, everyone must spend more and more time just negotiating with their activity colleagues, and soon very little activity-related work is being done. It is this need for coordination and communication that means every person added to an activity adds slightly less than one person's worth of effort, and also degrades the effort available from those already assigned.

This is one reason why it is so important for the project manager to plan projects so that self-contained activities can be allocated to individuals in such a way that everyone knows the exact scope of their own work, there is a minimum number of multi-person activities, and communication overhead is kept to a minimum.

Project planners use some words in specific ways. The word effort usually means the number of hours or days of work involved in a task or project. It is often measured in man-days. Effort and duration are related but must not be confused. An activity could involve four hours of effort but have a duration of a week if the work is spread across several days or it is a fixed-duration activity. Ten days of effort could be finished after only three or four days of elapsed time if three people share the work – though, for the reasons outlined above, they might put in 11 or 12 days of effort, which consists of 10 days of work and two days of coordination time.

Another favourite word of project planners is resource. Resources are the people, infrastructure and equipment that are made available to the project by the firm. Resources are anything that could be used elsewhere in the firm and that should be booked to make sure that the project can use them when needed. This definition includes things like meeting rooms or project rooms, but by far the most important resources on any project are people. All projects rely critically on their people resources, and it is important to book people for the project in good time, whereas it is often safe to leave planning for things like meeting room access until the last minute. For this reason, many project managers who talk about resources mean people.

During planning, the planner estimates task duration and effort using skill and experience. However, once work is executed, the duration and effort actually required may be different from what was in the plan. Hence we distinguish between planned and actual effort and duration.

▶ Work breakdown structure (WBS)

A work breakdown structure is the easiest place to start with project planning. Creating a WBS will also help you to define the activities – defining activities and creating a WBS are often best done in parallel. A WBS is no more than an enhanced list of all the activities of the project. The enhancements explain how the project is broken down into tasks, groups of associated tasks and sub-projects, and they also give some information about effort or duration.

You may find it convenient and useful to represent the levels of the project breakdown graphically as well as by using the levels of indentation on the work breakdown structure list. This can be done easily by drawing the project structure as a hierarchy of tasks and sub-tasks, as shown in Figure 4.3a. Activities which together constitute a logical sub-project or phase are listed together in the work breakdown structure, under the appropriate sub-project title.

Each activity at each level can always be broken down further, so that it becomes itself a title for a group of constituent tasks. The overall breakdown of the project into phases is given by the first level of titles, and under each phase title, the major blocks of work are listed, each with its constituent tasks. This process of breaking down tasks into ever-finer levels of sub-tasks can continue indefinitely, and it is sometimes helpful to explore what goes on inside activities in this way in order to make sure that we really understand how much work is involved. However, it is also

Fig. 4.3a Example work breakdown structure (WBS) for 'House Build' project

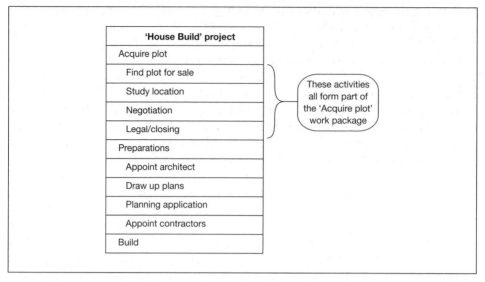

easy to get carried away with this process and end up with a structure with dozens of levels, the lowest of which describe tasks equivalent to 'stand up' and 'open door', as illustrated in Figure 4.3b.

Fig. 4.3b Example of excessive detail in a WBS

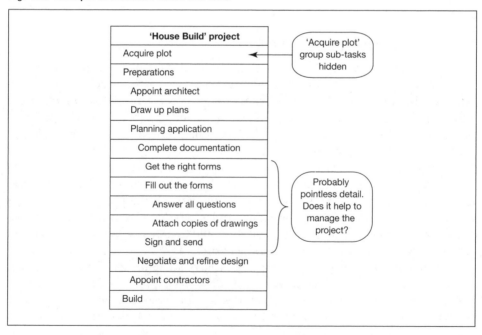

It is extremely unlikely that there will be any value in taking the analysis to this level (the exception may be in generating formal work instructions for standardized factory-like processes, but these do not really fall within the scope of an overall project plan). The task breakdown should be taken to the level where individual tasks for individual people (or for a group that works together) can be identified, with a clear explanation of all the necessary inputs and outputs. In practice, even very large and complex projects do not usually need more than about six levels, and most projects can be satisfactorily represented on three or four.

Fig. 4.3c Example of completed WBS, showing effort and duration in days (d) or weeks (w)

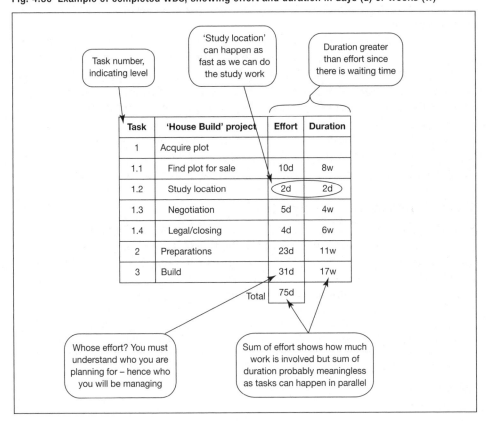

Once the list has been created, we can estimate the time required to do each task and write it next to that task (see Figure 4.3c). The times used should be the effort required for each task so that the total effort required for the project and each sub-project can be calculated simply by adding the column total. It is also useful to record task durations, especially since these will be needed when turning the work breakdown structure into a Gantt (timeline) chart. Durations should be in a separate column from effort to avoid confusing the two. Durations can be entered directly if they are fixed durations, or they can be calculated from the relationship between the effort required and the allocated resources.

It is conventional to give each task in a work breakdown structure a number or other identifying code so that it can be identified in summaries.

Most project planning software packages can produce work breakdown structures, group tasks together into high-level blocks, and let the user enter effort, duration and resourcing information. Task identifier numbers are usually added automatically.

A work breakdown structure is a convenient way to record and group the blocks of work that will make up the project, but it does not contain information about dependencies between tasks, or task sequencing. There is no way to record the fact that task X cannot start until task Y (which is part of an entirely different sub-project) has finished. It tells us how much total effort will be involved, but it does not tell us how long the project will take since it does not tell us which tasks must follow from each other.

Once we have identified the tasks and how long each will take, it is a relatively simple step to add some information about the sequence in which tasks must happen, so that we can get some insight into how long the project is likely to take. For each task, identify the other tasks that provide its inputs and which therefore must be completed before this task can begin. For example, we cannot usually test a solution until it is built, we cannot build it until it is designed, and we cannot design it until the user requirements are known. In project planning language, testing depends on build, which depends on design, and so on. This chain of dependent tasks gives us the first indication of how long the project will take.

▶ Product breakdown structure (PBS)

Sometimes it is useful to do a product breakdown structure (PBS) of the project's product, either to understand the product better or as a way of getting at the work breakdown and tasks necessary. The concept is the same as for the WBS, but the product rather than the work is decomposed.

Table 4.2 gives a product breakdown structure for a sailing boat.

Table 4.2 Example product breakdown structure for a sailing boat

Sailing boat (product)

Superstructure
  Mast and boom
  Rigging
  Sails
  Safety gear on deck
Hull
  Deck
  Cabin/cockpit
  Steering system
  Buoyancy and bilge
Keel

▶ PERT charts

PERT charts, also known as network diagrams or dependency diagrams, are covered in more detail in Chapter 6, Project Time Management.

▶ Gantt charts (also known as timelines)

A Gantt[5] chart starts with the list of project activities in the same format as the work breakdown structure. In line with each named activity we draw a box on a timeline to show when the activity is planned to start and finish. Project planning software packages will do this automatically from the information entered into the work breakdown structure. If you don't have a software package specially for project planning, then a spreadsheet such as Microsoft Excel will do a perfectly reasonable job – as Figure 4.4 shows. Your Gantt chart should show tasks in the right sequence, which you can get from your WBS. Dependencies between tasks can be shown on a Gantt chart with an arrow that links the end of the first task to the beginning of the next, as Figure 4.2 on page 109 showed. Chapter 6, Project time management, says more about dependencies and representing and planning with them.

▶ Project initiation

As the words imply, 'project initiation' simply means starting a project. The reasons for having some methodology around starting a project are as follows:

- ◆ To start a project as efficiently as possible, without reinventing the wheel each time
- ◆ To apply lessons from the wider history of project management to minimize risk
- ◆ To start the project with its end in mind, so that the project (especially the project manager and sponsor) know where it is going.

As a sponsor or project manager, ensure that you know who the project initiator is. The project initiator is the individual or group of people in your organization who has authority to authorize a new project. If you have been in your organization a long time or know it very well, then you will know who the initiator is, but if not, then ensuring that you are clear about who it is may save you much time and effort and avoid you expending effort and building the wrong relationships for getting your project signed off.

PMI says

Initiating processes

'Initiating Processes (Process Group). Those processes performed to authorize and define the scope of a new phase or project or that can result in the continuation of halted project work. A large number of initiating processes are typically done outside the project's scope of control by the organization, programme, or portfolio of processes and those processes provide input to the project's initiating processes group.' *PMBOK Guide* (p.362)

Fig. 4.4 Project Grapple Gantt chart

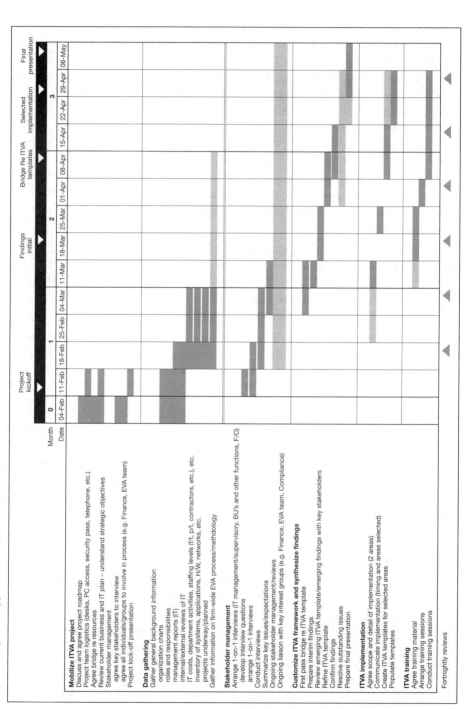

▶ Factors affecting the means of project initiation

How the project should be initiated depends on a number of factors besides lessons from the history of project management and general best practice. There are factors that will vary from project to project. These include the following:

- Whether the project meets a business[6] (or other) need of the organization, or whether it is a risky and speculative project.
- Whether there is only one possible approach to the project or whether there are many possible approaches from which one approach will have to be selected.
- The level of risk in the project.
- The size of the project.
- Whether the project team knows the organization and has experience of the kind of work to be undertaken by the project.

Figure 4.5 shows the effects of the initiating processes.

▶ Understand, document and communicate planning assumptions

Assumption and limiting factors, such as time, cost or resource, must be recorded so that the project manager can manage changes in them. Write them down! A simple way to do this is in a spreadsheet or word processor document: have a simple list of what the assumption is, the date, and for each assumption the main consequences if the assumption is wrong.

Do not think that you will remember changes in key assumptions. And even if you do, no one else will, if their interests and status are threatened by the fact that there has been a change. Write down the assumptions, and show the sponsor. In a large project or a bureaucratic organization, get the assumptions signed off. In the early stages of a project, that is in the initiation stage, it is not uncommon for assumptions about cost and scope factors to change significantly as a better understanding of them evolves. This is normal, but by writing down the assumptions, even if there is consensus that they are merely 'strawman' and are almost certainly wrong, you will protect yourself from being blamed for senior management not realizing that what started as £20,000 for a database is not £2,000,000. More positively than protecting yourself, sufficient a reason though it is, you will be helping key people to develop their understanding of the issues in the project, and quite possibly some key strategic issues facing the organization.

By documenting assumptions and factors early on, the nature of the project can be understood better by all involved. For example, if a project assumes that there will be six experienced middle managers available to join it next June, and before then a 10% headcount reduction is announced, there may no longer be the middle managers available next June, for example, which could have cost, time, risk and quality ramifications, and the time to manage those is as early as possible, not next June. But, to continue the example, if the availability of a few middle managers has not been documented as an assumption, then in the excitement of the headcount reduction its ramifications may get forgotten.

Fig. 4.5 Project initiation, before and after

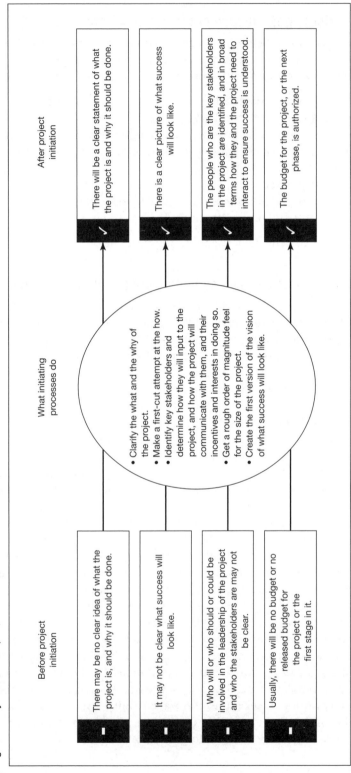

> **Key Idea**

Insurance policy: document all assumptions

For the project manager personally, for their mental health and career, documenting all major assumptions, especially during the planning and initiation phase of a project, is like an insurance policy. It insures you, as project manager, against being a scapegoat when something changes in the world that affects the project. You can turn round and say 'Yes, X has changed, everyone knew that we planned and ran this project on the basis that X would not change, and that there would be major problems if it did'. Ideally this can be followed by 'You decided not to apply resources to planning or creating a contingency reserve for the event that X would change'. Being able to do this has saved many a project manager's career, and bonus.

Direct and manage project execution

This is the 'doing' part of project management. Managing and executing project work should be done so as to meet the project's requirements and objectives, as specified in the scope statement and project plan. Like any management task, the challenge is first of all to execute effectively, that is to reach the objectives, and subject to effectiveness, to execute efficiently, that is at lowest cost and risk. The project manager is the linchpin of project execution. As such, they are involved with the organization and integration of all aspects of the project, from resolving minor issues to ensuring that the path is clear of major obstacles that could halt the progress of the project, and to do this the project manager must work closely with the sponsor.

The project team's efforts must always be focused on the project's aims and deliverables. The project manager must ensure that this focus is maintained, and to do so must check regularly on progress against baseline plans, and manage variation beyond tolerance limits. (See the subsection on 'Corrective and preventive actions' later in this chapter.) Even if the project is managed and directed well, preventive and corrective actions are normal, especially from running the quality process.

Work needs to be controlled, especially so that people do not start work too early. If work is started too early then there is a risk that it will have to be reworked, and sometimes people will want to do work that they find easy or interesting instead of other work that the project needs them to do first. A work authorization system manages this problem. It is used to instruct and direct team members or contractors to start work on a specific work package at a prescribed time. The allocation of when and by whom a work package is started is important to the effective management and control of the project's activities. For larger projects a more rigid system would be in place, purely because of the extra number of moving parts to integrate. The work authorization system is usually an established company process, therefore it is not specifically generated for an individual project.

It cannot be emphasized too much that in managing project execution the project manager must keep in close touch with the project sponsor and communicate with them constantly. It is the sponsor who has the power to protect the project from changes and loss of resources. Keeping in touch means ensuring that the other person understands what you mean.

▶ Requested changes

Requested changes are inputs to the integrated change control process in a project. This may sound obvious, though experience shows it is valuable to remember two points about this. A requested change is just that, a request. It does not mean that the change will be made, or is likely to be made. As project manager you may need to start managing expectation around this as soon as a request for a change to the project is made. Does the person making the request understand that your project does not and cannot automatically accept changes, but that there is a process? This is not bureaucracy, it is good management. (The process can be made bureaucratic, but that is a different matter.) Secondly, these requests go into a system; they are not dealt with on a case-by-case basis. Change requests are normal, and on all but the smallest and simplest projects there will be many of them. It is simply too inefficient not to have a systematic process to deal with them.

A requested change, or, in another style of the English language, a request for a change, should include the following information, and if it does not then your job as project manager is to find out this information:

- Who wants the change?
- Why is the change necessary, or desirable?
- What are the consequences if the change is not made?
- What is the timescale around this change?
- What are the ramifications to the project and to stakeholders if this change is made, and what if it is not made?

During the life of the project, the sponsor or a stakeholder may identify the need to expand or reduce the scope required of the project. The proposed alteration to the project could also impact on the cost or schedule of the project. The set of criteria used to assess the success or failure is contained in the project scope statement, so if a requirement is to be amended in any form, a formal change request must be submitted for consideration. The requested change can be initiated from inside or outside the project, but in either case the Change Control System should be followed for this process. The team will implement only the approved changes, but once again the need to integrate the change is key to the success of the project.

▶ Deliverables

As we know, a project is a temporary endeavour which creates a unique product or service. The deliverables are therefore a set of products or services distinct from what is produced by the normal or everyday activities of the organization. The project management shows what the deliverables are, when they are due, how they will be made, why they are needed and who is responsible for which parts of them. It should also show the processes to be used to review and check the correctness or quality of the product or service. A deliverable can also be used to define a set of customer or sponsor requirements which must be met before approval or acceptance is granted for the project. Once all the planned deliverables have been delivered and accepted by the customer, then the project is deemed successful and project closure procedures can start. If the customer unreasonably refuses to accept deliverables, and the project has documentation to evidence that this is unreasonable, for instance because the deliverables have been produced to agreed requirements, on time and on budget, then the project is still in a very strong position.

PMI says

Deliverable

'Deliverable (Output/Input). Any unique and verifiable product, result, or capability to perform a service that must be produced to complete a process, phase or project. Often used more narrowly in reference to an external deliverable, which is a deliverable that is subject to approval by the sponsor or customer....' *PMBOK Guide* (p.358)

Note that the difference between a deliverable and a work product is that a deliverable can be, but is not necessarily, a kind of work product. A product, in the *PMBOK Guide* definition, is 'an artefact that is produced, is quantifiable, and can be either an end item in itself or a component item ...'. The key difference here is that a product is quantifiable, but a deliverable need only be verifiable. So an increase in sales can be a project's deliverable, because it is a verifiable result of the project, but is not a product. On the other hand, an increase in sales by 10% can be a product. Is this distinction useful? It can be, in some cases. Unless your organization already has particular meanings for these terms, we recommend using the term 'deliverable' as the primary general term for things intended to be created by the project.

▶ Other project integration management tools and techniques

In this chapter so far we have explained what project integration management is and its broad principles. The rest of this chapter gives a summary description of the processes, tools and techniques, inputs and outputs, and other concepts within project management integration. Let us pause just here to clarify these terms, starting with the PMBOK definitions – see the box – and adding to them a few comments.

PMI says

Processes, activities, tools and techniques, inputs and outputs
'Process. A set of interrelated actions and activities performed to achieve a specified set of products, results or services.'

'Activity. A component of work performed during the course of a project.'

'Tool. Something tangible, such as a template or software program, used in performing an activity to produce a product or result.'

'Technique. A defined systematic procedure employed by a [person] to perform an activity to produce a product or result or deliver a service, and that may employ one or more tools.'

'Input. Any item, whether internal or external to the project, that is required by a process before that process proceeds. May be an output from a predecessor process.'

'Output. A product, result, or service generated by a process. May be an input to a successor process.'

All from *PMBOK Guide* (p.350ff.)

The PMBOK definitions given here are as useful as any others. They help us to get clear in our minds what we should be doing at any given time in project management, in the following ways:

◆ Processes answer the question 'What should I be doing now, as a project manager?'
◆ Tools and techniques answer the question 'How should I be doing it?' – the difference between the two terms being that tools are things in the world, such as checklists, software and written procedures, whereas techniques are habits of mind, or in a sense 'mental tools'. The key ideas box gives an example that may help you to remember the difference between tools and techniques.
◆ Outputs answer the question 'Why are we doing it?' in the sense that if the output is not directly or indirectly supporting the aim of the project, then it is not the right output.
◆ Similarly, inputs have value only to the extent that they are necessary for outputs.
◆ And activities answer the question 'Which bit of the project plan should the team be doing now?'

Being clear about such distinctions helps one to avoid the greatest personal risk in project management, which is to drown in the terminology and procedures instead of focusing on what matters. We need to know most of the concepts and terminology, but we need to ensure that we use as little of them as possible at any one time, just the right concepts for the immediate needs of our project. This is especially the case in project management integration, where we need to make everything in the project fit together, but efficiently. In this book we use the term 'concept' to include processes, tools and techniques, inputs and outputs, and also other concepts within project management.

Key Ideas

Tools versus techniques: what's the difference?

Tools are things that exist in the physical world, although tools need not always be physical things. Techniques are in the mind or the body of a person and are also known as the skills of the person (although a technique is a kind of skill that can be learnt by a number of people, rather than being unique to one person).

Consider the great golfer Tiger Woods as an example. His golf clubs are his tools. How he swings them is his technique. Other people can have the same tools, the same golf clubs as Tiger, but that is not sufficient to make them play as well as he. Tiger has mastered the technique of golf to a very high and rare degree, but despite that, without the tools of golf clubs, his technique alone won't move the ball very far, that is, his technique without the right tools won't achieve the objective.

As a project manager, it may be useful to consider whether at a certain point in your project it is investing in tools or techniques, or a mix of both, that will most help your project. Do your golfers have any clubs at all? If they have some clubs, is it going to be better clubs or improvements in technique that raise their game most, within the timescales that matter to the project? There will be different answers to these questions in different cases. Project management training courses, teambuilding, and one-on-one coaching is a way to improve technique; mandating new conceptual tools (or methodologies) and procuring new software tools are ways to improve the tools available.

The rest of this chapter describes the key concepts in project integration management, but only as far as is necessary for project integration management; they are not complete descriptions of each tool. Complete descriptions are given elsewhere in the book. You as project manager should decide whether or not each concept is useful for the project you are running.

You will not need all the tools for any given project. The concepts are:

◆ Processes
  - Develop preliminary project scope statement
  - Direct and manage project execution
  - Monitor and control project work
  - Integrated change control
  - Contract closure
  - Close project

- ◆ Tools
  - – Project management information system
  - – Configuration management
  - – Change control systems (part of configuration management)
  - – Configuration management system
- ◆ Technique
  - – Earned value technique
- ◆ Inputs and outputs
  - – Requested changes
  - – Project management plan
  - – Deliverable
  - – Lessons learnt
- ◆ Other concepts
  - – Project selection methods
  - – Project planning methodology
  - – Statement of work
  - – Drum resources
  - – Hammock tasks
  - – Corrective and preventive actions
  - – Change control board
  - – Administrative closure

Figure 4.6 gives a graphical representation of this list, showing when during the project lifecycle each concept is typically used, or whether it is a hammock task. (Hammock tasks are described below in more detail; they are tasks that run throughout the whole project lifecycle. We are not using this term in quite the same way that the PMBOK uses it, but rather in accordance with the way in which most project managers who use the term use it.)

▶ Project management information system

The Project Management Information System (PMIS) is a system for managing the information needed to run the project. Note the word system – this does not necessarily mean an IT system. Some of the best systems from the project manager's day-to-day point of view are paper based: one can walk around carrying a small notebook or ring binder with key project management documents and checklists; despite the marketing claims of their manufacturers, it is not possible to be as fast and efficient walking around with PDAs or mobile telephones. Note especially that Microsoft Project is not a PMIS. It is a software tool for producing Gantt charts.

The purpose of the PMIS is to assist the project team with the execution of the planned activities listed in the project management plan. Until recently it was the case that few automated software tools were well adapted to the practical tasks of project management at the project manager level, and some sort of manual system was often needed to supplement an automated system; where good and complete systems did exist they were expensive. This is changing, in terms of both falling cost and increasing utility of such systems. Use software tools, but use them as tools – do not get dazzled by them as toys.

Fig. 4.6 Project integration management processes, concepts, tools and techniques, outputs and inputs, showing when they are typically used and what kinds of tool they are

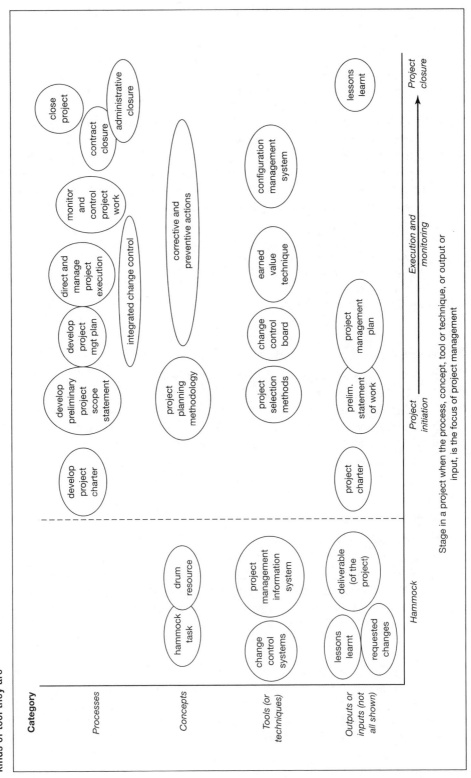

The main requirements of a PMIS are to assist the project manager in the following ways:

◆ To record the aim and scope of the project, so that they stay in scope and can ensure that everyone else in the project does so.
◆ To track changes within the project, so that they control change rather than being at the mercy of uncontrolled change.
◆ To monitor and control the various activities throughout the project from initiation to closure, so that the project gets done.
◆ To summarize project management reports and data (summary reports are also known as a 'management dashboard') so that the project manager can see the big picture and identify trends and events that matter most, and communicate these, with evidence, to the sponsor and other key stakeholders as necessary.

Other functions can include:

◆ Tracking cost, schedule and inventory
◆ Producing management reports
◆ Showing resource levels
◆ Identifying the critical path.

Key Idea

Project management information system (PMIS)
A large amount of information is needed to manage a project efficiently and effectively. The project manager who cannot find their information when they need it won't be efficient and may be ineffective as a result. A PMIS does not necessarily mean an IT system – often having a well-indexed ring binder of key information is more useful than a sophisticated database.

PMI says

Project management information system (PMIS)
'Project Management Information System (PMIS) (Tool). An information system consisting of the tools and techniques used to gather, integrate and disseminate the outputs of project management processes. It is used to support all aspects of the project from initiating through closing, and can include both manual and automated systems.' *PMBOK Guide* (pp.368–9)

One example of a PMIS for smaller projects is Basecamp (www.37signals.com) which is a web-based project and process collaboration system that is inexpensive, effective and easy to use. Basecamp is one of the first of a new generation of tools, and more like it can be expected in the next few years. As ever, a Google search will give a number of others PMIS tools.

▶ Change control systems

However good your plan, it will need to change. You have a choice as project manager: either change controls you, or you control change. The latter is better; the former dooms you. In project management you control change with a change control system. This does not need to be, and should not be, a complex system, but you must have a system. Often a simple spreadsheet will provide most of what you need, with some process around it to use the information in the spreadsheet. An example of the columns in a spreadsheet might be:

◆ Name of change.
◆ Description of change.
◆ Reason change is necessary.
◆ Date raised.
◆ Raised by (name).
◆ Approved or rejected or further information required (pick list).
◆ Date approved.
◆ Approved by (name).
◆ Change actions (i.e. a list of what actions are needed to effect the change).
◆ Owner of change actions.
◆ Next review date or closed date.

If your organization has an IT system for project management then it will include a change control database with fields similar to those above.

The change control system is a component of the configuration management system. Every project must have a plan for how a change would be managed, which is part of the overall project management plan. The change management plan need not be long or complex – two or three lines will do in many cases. For example: 'Once the project charter (and subsequently the plan) is signed off, any changes required to the charter (or plan) will be communicated to the project manager, who will log them in the change control spreadsheet. Every fortnight the sponsor and project manager will review change requests and together with other appropriate people, such as the person making the request, will determine the need for change and evaluate options and make a decision on whether and how to implement changes. Any change requiring or making likely a material increase in the project budget will be presented to the full project steering committee.'

A Change Control Board is a body of people responsible to the organization for evaluating and deciding on change requests. It is usually a sub-group of the project steering committee. Change Control Boards are not necessary in all projects, and typically they will be used only for the larger and more complex projects.

A checklist to ensure that your project has a change control system is:

◆ Do you and the sponsor have a clear idea in your minds of why a change control system is needed?
◆ Do you know how it will work in your project?
◆ Is this documented somewhere?
◆ Is it in the plan?

◆ Has it or will it be communicated to key stakeholders, to manage their expectations of what is and is not likely, or reasonable, in terms of change in the project, from their point of view?

◆ Does your organization have standard forms to be used in change control?

◆ Who is most likely to generate change requests, or to be otherwise involved in the change control system?

PMI says

Change control system

'Change control system (Tool). A collection of formally documented procedures that define how project deliverables and documentation will be controlled, changed, and approved. In most application areas the change control system is a subset of the configuration management system.' *PMBOK Guide* (p.353)

▶ Drum resource

A drum resource is a resource that sets the pace of the rest of the project. The term comes from the analogy of an ancient galley, where the man on the drum set the pace of rowing and thus the speed of the ship by beating the drum[7]. Usually the drum resource is the scarcest resource that is critical to the project. In investment banking this is very often the subject matter expert for risk management: work simply cannot proceed on a project at a rate faster than that allowed by the availability of the risk management experts, who tend always to be in short supply. This means that the most effective way to speed up all projects across the bank is to manage very carefully the availability of the risk managers, the drum resource, to ensure that it is used as efficiently as possible.

▶ Hammock task

There are two different meanings of this term. In this book we follow the more widely used one, which is a task that continues throughout the project, from beginning to end. Time recording, maintaining the issues log and communicating with stakeholders are all examples of hammock tasks. The term comes from the analogy to a hammock slung between two posts, the start post and the finish post[8]. The PMI's PMBOK uses 'hammock activity' in a different way, to mean 'summary activity'. In that sense it is a set of activities reported at summary level, that is, as an aggregate. We do not use the term in that way in this book (and so far as we are aware, knowledge of that use is not something that will make much difference to passing the PMI's exams, for those readers who are interested).

'Hammock task' is a useful term, in the sense of meaning a task that runs throughout the project, because it helps the project manager to be clear in their own minds and to communicate about such tasks. One example of how this helps in real-life project management is that instead of taking up space on a Gantt or PERT chart to show highly important hammock tasks, they can be listed under the heading 'Hammock tasks', thus simplifying the chart and so reducing the risk of confusion, without losing sight of the importance of the hammock tasks.

▶ Integrated change control

No plan survives contact with reality. In real life, you will have to adapt and update your plan to deal with reality. You will have to keep changing your plan right from project initiation though to project completion. If you do not update the plan, then an ever-widening gap between what the plan says and what is actually happening will emerge, and as this gap grows the usefulness of the plan will diminish and the risks in your project, and the risks to your career, will grow. Integrated change control is the process by which you control change in your project. You have a choice: either you control change or it controls you. (We have said this before, but experience from real-life project management shows that it is worth repeating.)

> **PMI says**
>
> **Integrated change control**
> 'Integrated change control (Process). The process of reviewing all change requests, approving changes and controlling changes to deliverables and organizational process assets.' *PMBOK Guide* (p.363)

The sequence of events in a typical change control process is as follows:

- Identify a possible change or establish that a change has already taken place.
- Review the change and understand the reason for and impact of it.
- Approve or reject the change, being sure to involve key stakeholders.
- Modify the plan and baselines accordingly.
- Agree necessary ramifications (e.g. budget increase) with stakeholders.

The integrated change control process can also be used to assess and authorize corrective or preventive actions (see below). Any change needs to be incorporated into the project management plan, and this is a key part of project integration management, because unless this happens coordination and efficiency, which are what integration is about, are lost. The change may also need to be incorporated within the other project documents and plans, such as budgets, risk management plans, work breakdown, communication planning and product specifications. Any stakeholder affected by the change must be not just notified but communicated with sensitively to ensure that all concerned with the project are using the same version of the project management plan. The project must then be managed in accordance with the new project management plan.

▶ Corrective and preventive actions

Corrective and preventive actions help to maintain the project's performance with the specified baselines. Put another way, actual performance may vary from planned performance, and corrective and preventive actions are ways to help the project correct the variance and get back on track. In plain language, a preventive action is something you do to avoid a problem before it happens, and a corrective action is something you do to fix a problem after it has happened.

These ideas are, of course, common sense, like almost everything in project management. The point of making them explicit in project management is to help minimize wasted time by being absolutely clear about things that need to be done and thought about, so that you do not spend time on them when they are not necessary. In any moderately large or complex project, there will be people who for various reasons in effect want to think about preventive actions when what is needed is a corrective one, or to embark on corrective actions before they are necessary. Having a clear categorization of these simple ideas helps integration and saves time.

PMI says

Preventive and corrective actions

'Preventive Action. Documented direction to perform an activity that can reduce the probability of negative consequences associated with project risks.' *PMBOK Guide* (p.356)

'Corrective Action. Documented direction for executing the project work to bring the expected future performance of the project work in line with the project management plan.' *PMBOK Guide* (p.367)

The reporting used in a project should be designed to ensure that the most likely variances are reported and if possible forecast in regular reports. The most basic report (or reports) is the one showing the project's actual spend and actual deliverables produced against the planned spend and planned deliverables, by time.

Any material variance from the planned baseline should be assessed and discussed by relevant stakeholders, including at least the sponsor and project manager. Trivial variances can be ignored. The projects will need corrective or preventive action to address the variance. This action should be agreed through the appropriate mechanism, and that mechanism should be specified in the plan, and then implemented, and the plan and baselines updated. It is important to have a systematic approach to assessing and deciding on preventive and corrective actions, not only because it is simply efficient to do this, but also because if you adopt a different approach each time there is a high risk of unintentionally sending out a negative signal to some stakeholders which will risk turning them against the project. Stakeholders, like all people, prefer consistency in the way in which news that affects their interests is communicated to them.

▶ Project selection methods

It is a fact of management life that there are more things to do than time and resources in which to do them, which is to say that there are more projects to be done than can be done. Therefore every organization has a mechanism for selecting from the large number of potential projects the smaller number to be worked on. This process should be a formal one, because if there is no formal process then the default selection method tends towards chaos, duplication and randomness – in short, a mess. What has this got to do with project integration management?

How projects are selected can affect integration. To take a hypothetical example to illustrate the point, suppose that a $10 million project has been given approval to proceed because firstly, it will deliver a database necessary for compliance with a new regulatory regime, and secondly, it will consolidate three state databases into one regional database. Neither of these benefits will justify the project on its own, but together they justify it. Three-quarters of the way through the project, the new regulatory regime looks as if it will very probably be cancelled before the project delivers, but the sunk costs are such that it is worth proceeding with the project to realize the benefits of the database consolidation. This hypothetical example illustrates two ways in which project selection methods relate to integration.

First, the process of project selection and approval will reveal key interfaces and success criteria for the project, which the project manager needs to track so that the project can change and adapt accordingly. It will reveal these because key stakeholders will be involved or identified in the approval process, and once known their interfaces to the project and their success criteria can easily be determined.

Let's be quite clear: delivering perfectly on the original specifications, even if they don't change, is not necessarily success. Part of the project manager's responsibility, working with the sponsor, is to monitor changes in the external environment that affect the value of the project to the organization, and proactively suggest changes to the project. It will often be that delivering perfectly on the project specifications is in fact success, but it is also common for this not to hold, which is how 'white elephants' arise. This is not a new problem: when armies started using gunpowder, stone castles became obsolete, as they offered no defence against cannon. Before the introduction of gunpowder, to build a castle to plan was to deliver a successful project. The castle was the tangible deliverable, and the business benefit was military defence against the enemy. The moment the enemy started to use cannon, delivering a castle in the old style was a value-destroying activity, even if the castle came in early, below budget and looked wonderful. Castles needed to be fundamentally redesigned to manage the risk of attack by cannon. Fort Brockhurst, Fort Nelson and the other Portsdown forts along the south coast of Britain were initiated by Lord Palmerston in 1859 to address the risk of an invasion, but advances in artillery technology made them obsolete within a few years of completion.

We don't build castles any more, but this kind of mistake is alive and well in project management. Real elephants are an endangered species, white elephants are not. Mankind's ability to produce white elephants is undiminished. You should ensure that your project does not become one.

The three key things from the point of view of project integration management for the project manager to find out from the project selection process are:

◆ Who has an interest in the project?
◆ Why do the project? That is, how is the project expected to add value to the organization?
◆ How will others judge whether the project is a success?

Ideally the project manager will be involved in the project selection process. While organizations should select projects by some objective mechanism that ranks them in order of value of the organization, in real life there may, in some organizations, be some projects that are selected because they are a senior executive's pet project. (This is not necessarily a bad thing: those people may have been promoted or elected in large part because they have been able to see value in projects and other things before there was widespread consensus for them.) In such cases, the integration aspect is the same: the project manager will benefit from understanding that this is the case, and from knowing who are the people close to the senior executive as far as the project is concerned, and why the executive wants the project.

Finally, it is worth making the point that at the very least, as a project manager you should know that your project exists because it has been through some selection process, formal or not. This means that there is a group of people who will be watching your project and have certain expectations of what it will and won't do. Managing those expectations is part of your job. Confound them at your peril.

▶ Earned value technique

A method commonly cited in project management theory as being used to determine the project's performance against the performance baseline from initiation to project closure is called the Earned Value Technique (EVT). Our experience is that it is much less used in real life, but it is useful to know about it even if your organization does not typically use it, for those occasions where someone senior challenges you to justify your project's rate of progress, or to implement a 'more objective' reporting mechanism. It is a useful technique to know about and have in your back pocket, so to speak.

PMI says

Earned value and Earned value technique

'Earned Value (EV). The value of work performed expressed in terms of the approved budget assigned to that work for a schedule activity or work breakdown structure component. ...' *PMBOK Guide* (p.359)

'Earned Value Technique (Technique). A specific technique for measuring the performance of work and used to establish the performance measurement baseline (PMB). Also referred to as the earning rules and crediting method.' *PMBOK Guide* (p.360)

Some project managers use the earned value technique to compare the actual performance of the project against the planned forecast. A reason for using EVT is that it integrates the time, cost and work done. These figures can also be used to reforecast the project's future performance and completion date by applying the project's previous performance. A number of changes or corrective actions are produced after applying this assessment technique, because it is useful to control cost and production activities.

One aspect of control is to establish the cause of any variance shown from the actual versus planned performance figures. EVT uses the baselines stated in the project management plan to determine the level of progress and the variations which may have occurred within the scheduled activities, work packages or control account. Table 4.3 lists the various terms and formulae used within the earned value technique.

Table 4.3 Terms, abbreviations and formulae in the earned value technique

Term	Abbreviation and formula	Definition
Planned value	PV	Estimated value of the work scheduled to be done
Earned value	EV	Estimated value of the work actually completed to date
Actual cost	AC	Actual cost charged for the work completed so far
Cost variance	CV CV = EV – AC	Difference of earned cost minus actual cost. (A positive value means under budget; a negative value means over budget)
Schedule variance	SV SV = EV – PV	Difference of earned schedule minus planned schedule. (A positive value means ahead of schedule; a negative value means behind schedule)
Cost performance index	CPI CPI = EV/AC	A cost efficiency indicator showing the cost value achieved by the project. (A value greater than 1 means that costs are running above budget; below 1, that costs are running below budget)
Schedule performance index	SPI SPI = EV/PV	A schedule completion indicator showing the work completed compared to the planned schedule. (A value greater than 1 means that the project is running ahead of schedule; below 1, that it is running behind schedule)
Budget at completion	BAC	Declared budget for the total project stated at the beginning of the work
Estimate at completion	EAC EAC = BAC/CPI	Total project costs at current forecast
Estimate to complete	ETC ETC = EAC – AC	From current spend, how much extra the cost is forecast to be
Variance at completion	VAC VAC = EAC – BAC	Difference of total project costs minus budgeted costs

Adapted from *PMBOK Guide*, Chapter 7 Project Cost Management, ' p.157ff.

The parameters used may be employed on a period-by-period basis (month-by-month, quarter-by-quarter, etc), or simply on a cumulative basis which runs throughout the project. The selection used depends on the overall timeframe of the project and the assessment criteria applied by the project manager or sponsor.

Let's step back from the detail of these formulae for a moment and ask a few questions. Why do we have these formulae and how should we use them? And what in particular do they mean for project integration management? Simply, these formulae help us to understand, and to communicate to others, where we are in the project. In particular, from the perspective of project integration management, they help us to focus on what is important. For example, imagine a big or complex project where there is too much detail for you to have a reliable intuitive sense of how things are going. You have been asked by the sponsor to help them prepare an *ad hoc* report to the chief executive about your project. You run some numbers, and find that SPI is 1.1, and CPI is 0.9. This tells you that your project is ahead of schedule, but over budget, both by 10 per cent. If that is a problem, then you know that you need to focus your efforts on managing costs rather than, say, speeding up progress. This means you know roughly where to apply your efforts, and how big the problem is. If SPI was 0.5 and CPI was 1.5, you would need to take a different kind of action. In a small project you will probably have a good, reliable intuitive grasp of these things, but even then it may help you to have some hard data to back up your claims. In larger or complex projects, often you need data to understand where you are.

Do you have to use the formulae as presented here? No. These formulae are common sense formulae designed to answer certain key questions, such as 'Are we over or underspent?', 'Are we ahead or behind plan in terms of results produced?' and 'How much of the project have we done so far?'. You can invent your own metrics to answer these and other key questions, and indeed your own organization may already have its own preferred metrics for measuring project progress which are different from the ones measured here. All that matters is that you understand what question you are answering, ensure that the metric does answer it, and finally, apply the metric consistently throughout the project. And from the integration perspective, remember that these metrics are a way to help you focus on just the right things at the right time.

The analysis of variance is not confined to just cost and time. Factors such as project scope, risk and quality can also be assessed for variance from the project's plan. Another area of analysis is to evaluate the trend in performance to determine whether the recent work output is improving or deteriorating with time. The scale of deviation from the planned values is likely to reduce as the project heads towards closure because the team's level of understanding of the project increases, while the risk factor also tends to reduce as the project moves to the final stage of completion.

▶ Configuration management system

The configuration management system is used to track and monitor all the changes within the project management plan. It is used to inform the project team and stakeholders about the current amendment state of each plan and baseline document contained in the project management plan. The benefit of operating such a system is that everyone is aware of the latest version of the schedule and performance baselines.

PMI says

Configuration management system

'Configuration Management System (Tool). A subsystem of the overall project management system. It is a collection of formal documented procedures used to apply technical and administrative direction and surveillance to: identify and document the functional and physical characteristics of a product, result, service or component; control any changes to such characteristics; and support the audit of the products, results, or components to verify conformance to requirements. It includes the documentation, tracking systems, and defined approval levels necessary for authorizing and controlling changes. In most application areas, the configuration management system includes the change control system.' *PMBOK Guide* (p.354)

The configuration management system includes the change control system. The configuration management system also describes the agreed approval levels for the authorization of proposed changes. For example, the project manager may be authorized in it to approve negative variances of up to 5 per cent, the sponsor of up to 15 per cent, with any greater variances to be referred to the Steering Committee. The system also provides an audit trail to check and validate conformance against the requirements. It is not just government bureaucracies in which being able to deliver an audit trail is useful: it is useful in many private sector companies to be able to show that what has been delivered is what people said they wanted, right up to the last minute.

▶ Change Control Board

The project manager is not always the subject matter expert, nor are they in possession of all the facts necessary to make a decision relating to a change request. A Change Control Board (CCB) should be established for a project that is responsible for reviewing all change requests and to decide whether more information is required before the board is able to assess the change. The CCB should consist of the sponsor, stakeholders and the project manager, but expert members could also be included if the change to be reviewed requires someone with a more detailed knowledge of the subject matter. The work of the CCB is therefore to approve or reject changes submitted for consideration, and then to document the recommendations made by the board. Often the CCB is a sub-group of the Project Steering Committee.

PMI says

Change Control Board
'Change Control Board (CCB). A formally constituted group of stakeholders responsible for reviewing, evaluating, approving, delaying or rejecting changes to the project, with all decisions and recommendations being recorded.' *PMBOK Guide* (p.353)

▶ Monitor and control project work

Monitoring and controlling of project work is conducted throughout the project from initiation to closing. This activity is a major control function for the project manager to ensure everything is occurring at the correct time and within cost. Integration of all the process inputs and outputs is key to controlling the project and maintaining the right level of supervision for the project. A larger project will produce a greater number of activities because of its size and complex nature;

therefore an appropriate level of guidance on how to control the planning process should be generated for this purpose. The outcomes from monitoring and controlling the project work are corrective and preventive actions, defect repairs, and recommendations to change the project. All of these changes are considered, assessed and either accepted or rejected for implementation under the banner of integrated change control.

▶ Configuration management

The configuration management system, as a system, is described in a separate section in this chapter. Here we look at the concept of configuration management. The main objective of configuration management is to ensure that the project and any changes to it meet the specified requirements of the project. It is concerned with conformance to requirements, and as such is closely allied to the quality management system. The size and complexity of the project dictates the level of configuration management required. Configuration management is also about confirming the results of the various changes implemented and communicating to all stakeholders regarding the changes approved.

Configuration management = change control
    + identifying and documenting the required characteristics
    or specification of work products
    + auditing conformance to requirements

Key Idea

Change control and configuration management: how they are related?

Change control
+
Understanding the characteristics or
specification of work products
+
Auditing conformance to requirements

=

Configuration management

One of the implications of the difference between configuration management and change control as formulated above is that the people who run the project's change control process do not necessarily need to understand the characteristics of the work products to be produced. This reduces the cost of the change control process, and enables the change control function to be managed as a discrete process.

▶ Lessons learned

Lessons learned are the easiest but the least used way to improve your current project and the projects you and your organization will own in the future. Again, learning lessons from what you have done is common sense. It needs to be part of your project management process because if not, the pressures of day-to-day life make it likely that you will miss out on the easy benefits of learning lessons. Having a formal process also helps ensure that not just you but others learn the lessons. And finally, a lessons learned process in project management is likely to be an essential part of quality management procedures, such as ISO 9000, in your organization.

PMI says

Lessons learned

'Lessons Learned (Output/Input). The learning gained from the process of performing the project. Lessons learned may be identified at any point. Also considered as project records, to be included in the lessons learned knowledge base.' *PMBOK Guide* (p.363)

Lessons learned are collected at all stages of the project, right from the start right up to the finish. Do not put off capturing lessons learned and discussing them until you are 'into the main project', or the chances are you never will. Start the way you mean to go on. This process is vital to continuous improvement of your organization's project management and other processes.

How should you capture lessons learned? If your organization already has a lessons learned process, use that. Have a look on your corporate intranet if you are not already aware of it, failing which, your organization's quality manager should be able to help. If you need to create a lessons learned process from scratch for your projects, be pragmatic and design something that is simple and will work, avoiding over-elaboration. The two main elements are a template for recording the information, and a process to ensure that the information is captured and, most importantly, used to improve your project performance in future.

The template or form to capture lessons learned should include the following information:

◆ Name of the project and date.
◆ Description of the lesson.
◆ Is the lesson something that worked well or badly?
◆ If badly, how could it have been done better? If well, what should be repeated or reused next time? The vital question is what should we do or do differently next time?
◆ Brief rationale for the above, if not obvious.
◆ Some indication of the importance of the lesson, at least whether of high, medium or low value.
◆ To which project management knowledge area is the lesson applicable?
  – In which stage of the project management lifecycle?
  – To which of your organization's processes?
  – To which of your organization's divisions or products?
  – To which of your organization's people?

In designing your process and in your overall approach to lessons learned, consider always human psychology. The aim is to learn from what has happened, both good and bad things, to make the rest of this project and all subsequent projects better, and to make the rest of your career as a project manager, and the careers of everyone else on the project, better than they would be without the lessons learned process. If lessons learned is seen as a threat to people, as a blaming and scapegoating activity, or as pointless bureaucracy, then there is little point in doing it. So you need to manage the way that the process is perceived, and the human element and emotions around it.

The document should outline what worked well, what did not go quite so well and how things could have been done differently. It is useful in larger projects to split lessons learned into categories. Ten possible categories are:

◆ Technical aspects of the project.
◆ How well the project plans and related documents worked.
◆ How useful and timely the project reporting and metrics were.
◆ Causes of variance encountered within the project.
◆ Communication and buy-in issues.
◆ The rationale for and success of particular corrective actions.
◆ Which tools should be used again and which dropped.
◆ Which techniques should be used more.
◆ What project management or other training should be given and to whom.
◆ The performance of the project manager.

Bearing in mind the point above about the human psychology of lessons learned, it may be useful to run the lessons learned process for the last of the above categories in a slightly different way from the others.

▶ Administrative closure

Administrative closure can occur throughout the project, although this would usually take place at set phase breaks within the project. It is typical for small or medium-sized projects to conduct administrative closure at the end of the project, but it must not be concluded until contract closure has finished. In comparison to contract closure, the procedure covered in administrative closure contains only the roles, responsibilities and activities of the project team. The procedure will also establish how the product or service will be transferred to the user. Further elements addressed within administrative closure are how the project will meet the specified requirements, what is necessary to meet acceptance of the deliverables, and finally to confirm the criteria of project completion. The last task is to place all the project plans and information within the company archives for future reference.

▶ Contract closure

Contract closure concentrates on the closure of a contract specifically linked to a project. Contract closure is conducted only at the end of the project, but closure must also be concluded if the contract was stopped or terminated for any reason prior to formal completion. The closure procedure should cover the steps to be followed in order to comply with the terms and conditions laid down in the contract, as well as the criteria listed for contract closure. Contract closure describes the roles, responsibilities and activities of the project team; it also includes stakeholder and customer involvement during the contract closure process. The closure procedure will detail the work associated with the contract, such as ensuring all the payment actions are complete and the cost records are finalized for audit purposes. The final contract performance report should be produced to specify the effectiveness and success of the contract. The procedure could also be used to describe how and when loan equipment is returned to its owner.

Once the project criteria have been met and formal acceptance has been stated, the next stage is to hand over the product or service for which the project was originally authorized. In contract terms, a receipt is required to declare that the project has met the terms and conditions of the contract. The formal basis of a contract means good records must be kept, which includes the contract, list of changes, alterations made to the deliverables and the agreed terms and conditions. All of this documentation is required for normal audit procedures, but it could be important if a dispute arises and legal protection is necessary.

▶ Close project

The closing process is the last of the five process groups, and one element of this is the 'close project' process. The key planning activity conducted under the close project process is to detail how the project will be closed, as well as the procedures required for administrative and contract closure. The two closure procedures will be covered later, but the difference between them is linked to the formality and frequency of the work. Once the technical work is finished, the close project process involves completing all of the activities from the other process groups in order to close formally the project or project phase. Similar close project activities would also be applied if a cancelled project was being wound up, although the requirement to hand over the project, as part of the closing process group, would not be needed.

PMI says

Close project
'Close Project (Process). The process of finalizing all activities across all of the project process groups to close formally the project or phase.' *PMBOK Guide* (p.354)

▶ Summary

Project integration management is the most important of the nine knowledge areas in project management, and is the essence of the discipline. It includes the following activities:

◆ Creating the project charter.
◆ Developing the preliminary scope statement.
◆ Developing the project management plan (i.e. the overall plan).
◆ Directing and managing the execution of the project.
◆ Monitoring and controlling the execution.

◆ Integrated change control.
◆ Closing the project.

The central theme in project integration management is ensuring that everything in the project happens at the right time, that is, coordination, or in other words again, integration. This requires having a plan and baselines, and a system for identifying and approving necessary changes, and making adjustments to the baselines and amendments to the project plans accordingly. Communication is essential to integration, as without the help and support of others nothing will be achieved. Integration is like juggling, and the more complex the project, the more balls there are to keep in the air. If your eye is taken off the ball for any reason, then everything crashes to the floor, including your career. The project manager must retain focus and attention throughout the project to ensure all activities are assessed, evaluated and implemented correctly. The knowledge area of project management integration exists to help you do this.

Further reading

Integration is not a subject that has attracted many writers – yet. It is, however, central to project management and to the highest levels of strategic management. It is a very important subject, and the problems that the US and UK armed forces faced after invading Iraq in the Second Gulf War when civil rule collapsed and the country descended into chaos in places is an example of what can go wrong when integration is not addressed, in that case at the political–strategic level. It is without doubt a difficult subject. Three books and one article that present good practical guidance on how to think for integration, although none of them use that term, are:

◆ Drucker, P. F., 1995. 'The information executives truly need'. *Harvard Business Review* (January–February 1995).
◆ Gause, D.C. and Weinberg, M., 1982. *Are Your Lights On? How to Figure Out What the Problem Really Is ....* New York: Dorset House. This is a classic on identifying and clarifying problems, despite its somewhat folksy style.
◆ Grove, A., 1995. *High Output Management.* New York: Vintage. Chapter 6 is Mr Grove's 12 pages of wisdom on the planning process. The rest of the book is also excellent and much is directly relevant to integration. Andy Grove founded Intel, the silicon chip manufacturer.
◆ Ohmae, K., 1982. *The Mind of the Strategist.* New York: McGraw-Hill. Ohmae's guidelines for thinking through management problems are inherently integrative.

Not all books on project management cover integration, although increasingly they do. Some that are particularly useful are:

◆ Maylor, H., 2002. *Project Management* (3rd edn). Harlow: FT Prentice Hall.
◆ Meredith, J.R. and Mantel, S.J., 2006. *Project Management: A Managerial Approach* (6th edn). New York: John Wiley & Sons.
◆ Young, J., 2002. *Orchestrating Your Project.* Wellington: New Zealand Institute of Management.

Of special interest to IT project management is:

◆ Cadle, J. and Yeates, D., 2004. *Project Management for Information Systems* (4th edn). Harlow: FT Prentice Hall.

Notes

1 PMBOK, 3rd edition, Appendix F.
2 It is not just in the PMI's approach to project management that this splitting out of the charter and the scope statement happens. PRINCE2 and the APM methodology are the same, although the terminology is slightly different, for instance PID in PRINCE2 instead of project charter.
3 Redacted from the definition in the *New Oxford American Dictionary*, 2nd edition, as implemented in Apple Dictionary application, v. 1.0.1. Copyright © 2005 Apple Computer, Inc., USA.
4 Coleridge, Samuel Taylor (1772–1834): *The Rime of the Ancient Mariner*.
5 Why is 'Gantt' not capitalized in full whereas 'PERT' is? Gantt is a proper name, of Mr Henry Gantt, whereas PERT is an acronym, for Project Evaluation and Review Technique. Does it matter? If you write the words as 'Gantt' and 'PERT', you have nothing to lose and you may gain by demonstrating your knowledge of project management. If you do otherwise, you have only downside risk, but it's more important to focus on getting the project done on time and on budget than on this kind of detail.
6 Throughout this book we tend to use the term 'business need', by which we mean a legitimate need of the business, including needs that are primarily regulatory. We also mean by this term the legitimate needs of non-business organizations, such as the charitable, voluntary, government and supra-national sectors – all of which in practice understand this term in their own context.
7 We are grateful to our former colleague Ian Major for relating the origin and meaning of this term.
8 Again, we are grateful to our former colleague Ian Major for relating the origin and meaning of this term.

project scope management

1

2

3

4

5

6

7

8

9

10

11

12

13

▶ Aims of this chapter

This chapter will cover the processes and requirements involved with project scope management to ensure that the work defined by the scope statement, and no extra, is completed and verified to the customer's satisfaction. By the end of this chapter, the reader should:

◆ know what scope management is, and how it relates to project management and the successful delivery of a project;
◆ be able to categorize project activities to confirm that only the designated work is completed, in accordance with the project scope statement;
◆ be able to apply scope definition within project management to ensure scope control, thereby reducing the probability of scope creep within the project;
◆ be able to explain the need for treating project scope management as a distinct knowledge area within project management.

▶ What is project scope management?

Project scope management is the process of determining what work is required to meet the project's objectives, together with the process of controlling the scope of the project. Any planning or work activity not focused towards completing the specified project objective is wasteful and should not be undertaken. Nearly two-thirds of projects are unsuccessful due to difficulties experienced in trying to control the project's deliverables, schedule and budget; therefore the need to manage and control scope is vital to give the project manager a chance of meeting the approved objectives and achieving a successful project.

PMI says

Scope
'Scope. The sum of the products, services, and results to be provided by a project. ...'
PMBOK Guide (p.375)

PMI says

Project scope management
'Project Scope Management includes the processes required to ensure that the project includes all the work required, and only the work required, to complete the project successfully. Project scope management is primarily concerned with defining and controlling what is and is not included in the project. ...' *PMBOK Guide* (p.370)

There are five process groups within project scope management (Table 5.1). These fall in either planning or monitoring and controlling. Scope is a fundamental question in initiating, but there is no process group there because initiation is where the question of scope first arises, and the process group for creating a preliminary scope statement is better classified as integration, rather than managing scope. Once the scope has been defined, albeit roughly and in 'strawman' form, then it can be managed, which is what this chapter is about.

Table 5.1 Five project scope management processes

Initiating	Planning	Executing	Monitoring and controlling	Closing
	1 Scope planning		4 Scope verification	
	2 Scope definition		5 Scope control	
	3 Create WBS			

Process Group

Principles of project scope management

The five project scope management process groups ensure that only the agreed work is done. Doing unnecessary work in the project is sometimes called 'gold plating' and creates waste and unnecessary risk. The project manager's role is therefore to monitor and check that there is no scope creep or gold plating by team members or stakeholders. The priority for the project manager is to complete just the specified work as stated in the project charter and project scope statement. If an additional requirement to the project's scope is considered essential, an authorized and approved change is the only way to get further work added to the project scope statement. Stakeholders may use the 'requested change' route to incorporate an element within the specification that was not included during the initial development of the project scope statement. The project manager must be mindful of any hidden agendas giving rise to the possibility of increasing the project's scope via the back door, so you must consider this when dealing with a request change. If this process is not used, there is no justification to complete the extra work being proposed.

Key idea

Avoid gold plating

Gold plating is an expression that means doing more than the scope requires. Sometimes people think that delivering extra or delivering higher quality than was specified is a good thing. But gold plating creates risk and cost beyond what was agreed and this is waste. Concentrate instead on delivering what was agreed. That is hard enough in real life. If you want to impress by over-delivering, then instead of gold plating deliver either early or under budget.

Scope management is also used to cover the work involved in managing both product and project scope. These two terms are defined as follows:

◆ Product scope is measured against the product requirements, and used to describe the product's features and functions.
◆ Project scope is measured against the project management plan, project scope statement and WBS, and used to specify the work required to deliver a product or service with the stated features and functions.

The point of project scope management is to make sure that only the work required to deliver a successful project is completed, that is processes and knowledge areas, to meet the project's objectives. The individual processes (and the process groups to which they belong) within project scope management are:

◆ Scope planning (Planning).
◆ Scope definition (Planning).
◆ Create WBS (Planning).
◆ Scope verification (Monitoring and Controlling).
◆ Scope control (Monitoring and Controlling).

and Figure 5.1 shows how these fit together.

The initial question to ask is how to go about defining and managing the project's scope, therefore the first task is to conduct scope planning. The work involved in scope planning produces the project scope management plan, which will answer the initial question of how to define and manage scope. The first edition of the scope management plan is not fixed in stone, because the plan can be adjusted and modified to incorporate further issues identified and evaluated later during the planning process group. The next stage in scope management is to expand the detail contained in the preliminary project scope statement in order to generate the agreed project scope statement. Once scope definition has been completed, the project team's main effort is to create a WBS and WBS dictionary from the specified deliverables to break down the work into work packages. A series of inspections and reviews must be undertaken to determine the level of completed work, and then to confirm that the deliverables meet the requirements and objectives stated in the project plans. The final step is to get formal acceptance from the customer for the completed deliverables.

The process in project scope management that covers much of the Monitoring and Controlling process group is scope control. This element of the project management is vital to ensure the specifications listed are met, but not extended. The change control system, as part of scope control, is a documented procedure that defines how the deliverables and documentation are controlled and approved. The trigger for much of the proposed change is caused by the variance of scope performance versus the scope baseline, and the variance data are produced from the project's work performance information. Scope control is therefore used to recommend what corrective and preventive actions are required, and then to update and revise the documents affected by the change.

Fig. 5.1 Project scope management – sequence of processes and activities

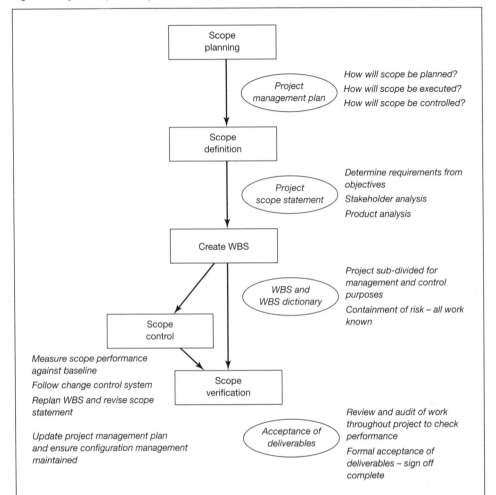

Scope planning

The main aspect to determine during scope planning is how the scope will be specified and verified for the project's objectives. The starting point for this work is the project charter and preliminary project scope statement, which is provided by the project sponsor. Other inputs that would be useful in developing the project scope management plan during scope planning come from the organization's culture and market conditions, the policies and procedures related to the planning process, together with any useful historical information from previous projects. The conclusions of this work should produce a scope management plan that is able to detail how the scope will be planned, managed, verified and controlled for the project.

PMI says

Scope planning
'Scope Planning (Process). The process of creating a project scope management plan.'
PMBOK Guide (p.375)

Factors such as the size and complexity of the project will influence the amount of effort required to complete the scoping process. If an organization is regularly involved with small or similar projects, there may be utility of using a standard template for scope management. Most projects are unique by their nature, although many topics are comparable, so there may be an opportunity to produce a generic template.

▶ Scope definition

As more information is gathered and analyzed from the all the project stakeholders, a better understanding of the project needs is achieved which in turn allows further definition and expansion of the preliminary project scope statement. Once the scope boundaries are set for the deliverables, what is and what is not included within product scope and project scope can be determined. The final output produces the project scope statement, which is a full and detailed document able to describe all the deliverables, the work required to achieve them, the product acceptance criteria and the approval requirements to meet the project objectives. As the words imply, 'scope definition' simply means defining a project. The reasons for having to define the scope of a project are:

◆ to identify the business objectives,
◆ to identify the requirements,
◆ to identify the broad areas of work required.

The work to refine and improve the detail contained in the preliminary scope statement is conducted mainly by the project management team. Their task is to gain the opinions and needs of the stakeholders, and then translate their expectations and objectives into specific deliverables. The discussions and assessments should also be able to determine the priorities assigned to the project's requirements. This knowledge could be extremely useful if decisions must be made regarding issues of trade-off within the 'triple constraint'. Product analysis may also be required to determine what the problems are with an old product, and then to decide on the requirements in order to achieve an improvement. The last stage of the product analysis is to specify the work necessary to achieve the improved requirements for the item. Expert opinion can be included at any stage within the analysis phase to further develop the requirements needed to match the project objectives.

PMI says

Scope definition

'Scope Definition is the process of developing a detailed project scope statement as the basis for future project decisions.' *PMBOK Guide* (p.375)

The project's boundaries, assumptions and constraints are vital factors to be considered during scope definition. The knowledge of what is included within the project work, and what is not, remains key to the project's success. There must be no room to allow personal interpretation, because this could cause a misunderstanding of the work to be completed, or a redefinition of the constraints applied to the project. The initial assumptions and constraints detailed in the project charter are used as the starting point, but further analysis of the project's external or internal restrictions, such as budget profile, resource allocations and schedule impacts due to a plant shutdown, will need to be conducted. This work should also review the accuracy and consistency of the assumptions, as well as expanding the statements included in the project charter. Once again expert advice may be beneficial to determine extra assumptions and constraints that could have been missed by the project team.

The series of analysis activities conducted during scope definition may give rise to a requested change to the project. For example, the extra weight of equipment added to a vehicle that is needed to match the customer requirements may demand an increase in power output of the engine. The proposed response could involve the production of a change request to increase the size, or change the fuel of the power unit. Before any action is taken to amend or change any of the project's plans or documentation, the requested change must be assessed and evaluated by the integrated change control process. If approval is granted to incorporate this change, only then can the scope definition process adjust the requirements specified in the developing project scope statement.

The project scope statement must ensure that all the stakeholders have a common understanding of the project's scope and its objectives. The linkage between individual requirements within the project charter and project scope statement should be maintained to show the justification of every requirement included in the project scope statement, and how each deliverable is to be met. The project charter is the key document which the entire project requirements are traced back to, because it states the sponsor's needs.

Create work breakdown structure

The work breakdown structure (WBS) is a key output from project scope management because it determines what work must be completed to deliver the objectives of the project. Breaking the work down in a systematic way, and using the project team, reduces the chance of missing anything.

The WBS is a hierarchical decomposition of the work to be completed in order to achieve the project's deliverables, although it should not be confused with an organizational breakdown chart. The WBS defines and structures the total scope of the project because it starts from the deliverables as stated for the project. Once the deliverables are listed, the next stage is to decompose the work into smaller sections. Action to break down the work packages further to specific schedule activities can be done, although the number of levels will be determined by the project's size or complexity. The output of this work produces a graphical representation of the work specified in the project scope statement. The WBS is a unique decomposition of the work generated for each project, but a previous WBS could be used as a template for a comparable project because the required deliverables are likely to be similar.

PMI says

Work breakdown structure

'Work Breakdown Structure (WBS) is a deliverable-oriented hierarchical decomposition of the work to be executed by the project team to accomplish the project objectives and create the required deliverables. It organizes and defines the total scope of the project. Each descending level represents an increasingly detailed definition of the project work.' *PMBOK Guide* (p.379)

The reason for breaking down the project to more manageable and defined sections is to enable the project team to estimate the time and costs for each activity or work package. The review and assessment of smaller work packages by project members will provide a better estimate for the overall cost of the project. The same process can be followed to generate the expected time estimates to complete the work; this will also produce a more accurate schedule from which to plan the project. The reasons for creating a WBS for a project are that it:

◆ ensures better control of the work definition,
◆ allows the work to be delegated in coherent packages,
◆ allows the work to be defined at the right level for estimating and control, and
◆ allows the containment of risk.

There are some basic rules to consider when producing a WBS because the resultant diagram achieves a clear indication of the work involved, together with an improved level of buy-in from team members due to their involvement with the work and estimation process. The first rule is to ensure that team members assist the drafting of the WBS in a systematic manner. The next rule to comply with is to make sure that only the work required to meet the project's deliverables is included, and each level should be established before breaking it down further. A key element from this statement indicates that any work not included in the WBS must fall outside the scope of the project. The last rule is to continue breaking down the work until an appropriate level for the project to be managed is reached; the project manager is the only one able to decide this level.

Importance of the WBS

One of the easiest ways to tell the amateur project manager from the professional is the importance they attach to the WBS. An amateur might jump in and start planning using a Gantt chart on one of the popular project management software packages. A professional will do the work breakdown structure first, and maybe also a product breakdown structure.

Much work is needed to produce a complete and thorough WBS, but the benefits of using this approach mean there is less chance of work being missed. The project team will also have a better understanding of the project work, together with the knowledge of where their element fits in to the overall scheme. The wide dissemination of the WBS to all stakeholders will maintain the cooperation and communication link with all those involved, which in turn may help manage the project and expectations. Another vital benefit is the team's buy-in to the document, and the opportunity to ensure everyone remains focused on the outputs of the project.

Once the WBS has been completed, it then becomes a valuable tool for the overall management of the project. The WBS is of particular use when you need to evaluate the impact of a requested change in scope as part of the integrated change control, and also when reassessing the scope of the project due to an approved change. Events can move so quickly when managing a project, so there is a chance that your eye can be taken off the ball. A WBS is therefore a useful reference document to indicate what is and is not included in the project, so control on scope creep is easier to achieve. The layout and structure of the WBS also provides an effective tool to maintain the flow of information to all stakeholders, as well as being used to brief new staff on the status and progress of a project. One element to be finalized by the end of the planning process group is to establish the project's scope baseline, because it will be used to measure the level of success in meeting the project's requirements. The key documents for the scope baseline consist of the project's scope statement, WBS and WBS dictionary.

Scope verification

The process of scope verification is to confirm that the work being completed matches the details stated in the WBS, project scope management plan and project management plan. The inspections used to determine verification of the requirements will usually consist of reviews, audits and user trials.

The final stage of verification involves obtaining formal acceptance of the delivered product or service by the stakeholder, so confirmation is given that the deliverables correspond to the requirements included within the agreed project scope statement and project charter. For example, during a meal in a restaurant your waiter will normally visit your table and confirm that you are enjoying your food.

The reason for this question is to determine whether the food has been prepared and cooked to your satisfaction. If there is no complaint about the meal, the waiter has been able to ensure that payment should be forthcoming because the food has matched the diner's expectations.

If a project has to be terminated early for any reason, the process of scope verification is still required to determine the degree of project success. The verification report should document what was achieved at the point of termination, because this information could establish the start point for possible legal action.

PMI says

Scope verification
'Scope Verification (Process). The process of formalizing acceptance of the completed project deliverables.' *PMBOK Guide* (p.375)

Once the approval of a deliverable is formally declared, documentation should be generated to state acceptance of this fact. (Payment of the restaurant bill is one way to demonstrate customer acceptance.) On occasion, confirmation of acceptance may need to be signed off by both the sponsor and customer before formal compliance is granted. If a deliverable fails its acceptance criteria, a formal document stating non-compliance should be produced instead. The key aspect for any acceptance is to ensure the requirements are met, prior to completing the documentation to state that a deliverable has been achieved. With all the ticks in the right boxes, the project can formally gain sign-off status.

 ## Scope creep

Sooner or later, every project manager develops some finely tuned antennae that are constantly listening for phrases like 'It would be much better if ...'. These phrases have a near-magical power to derail a project, and letting any instance slip through unchallenged can have dire consequences. When people say things like 'It would be much better if ...', they are often about to suggest changing the scope of the project. The suggestion could be to do with timing or, more likely, the performance of the deliverables, but the common theme is that the result will be clearly better and this makes it very easy to agree with the suggestion. It would be foolish not to agree to make things better, wouldn't it?

Key Idea

Scope creep is your constant challenge
If you remember just one thing from this book, it should be that the main risk you face in your project is from scope creep. The sponsor and project manager need to manage scope creep firmly. Scope creep probably wastes more of taxpayers' and shareholders' money than anything else under the sun.

The problem with scope creep is not that any of the suggestions are bad: they are usually entirely reasonable. The problems arise because accepting the suggestion implies changing something about the project objectives, and so the plan and the resources and all the other things that were so carefully matched to the original objectives are suddenly incompatible with the new objectives. Unless it is properly managed, scope creep leads to trouble in one of two ways:

◆ the suggestion is accepted and the project is committed to do things that were not in the plan, usually leading to cost and time overruns, and/or compromised technical quality, or

◆ the suggestion is automatically rejected and the firm loses an opportunity somehow to improve the returns on its investment in the project.

PMI says

Scope creep

'Scope Creep. Adding features and functionality (project scope) without addressing the effects on time, costs and resources, or without customer approval.' *PMBOK Guide* (p.375)

This seems like a no-win situation. The escape route is a scope management process that allows you to keep the project objectives and project plan in line; suggested changes can be accepted but only if the consequences for the plan are also accepted. Before applying the scope management process, it is first necessary to recognize the dangerous suggestions. They can come from all sorts of directions, as the following examples show.

◆ Other staff within the firm might spot parallels between what this project is seeking to achieve and their own needs. A slight modification or enhancement to this project could make it solve a second group's needs in addition to the original user group's, and it might be much more efficient to satisfy this second group in this way than to run an entire project for them alone.

◆ Another common source of problems is the insertion of intermediate target dates or extra intermediate deliverables. These can greatly increase the return on a project investment, but adding a second set of user requirements part-way through often sets the whole project back almost to the beginning, while trying to produce additional mock-ups of the output in time for a public relations event can stop everyone on the team from working on the real outputs.

◆ Project team members are one of the most creative sources of scope creep. People will always try to do their best for the project and for the customer, and it is often hard to get people to understand that delivering output that does no more than meet the requirements is acceptable. Sometimes the behaviour amounts to technical showing off, but it often comes from a sincerely held belief that they know what is best for the end users, despite what was written in the user requirements.

◆ End users can easily introduce scope creep through their feedback on early previews of the project outputs. Non-specialists can have genuine difficulty envisaging a solution before the project starts, and so despite the best efforts of everyone during project definition, users sometimes realize what they themselves want only once a trial version is in their hands. Furthermore, if users get enthusiastic about the project, they can quickly generate a long list of extra things that it should do in order to give them even more benefits. Any and all of these changes to the original project scope may be necessary – but we do need to recognize that scope and effort (and hence cost and timescale) are directly related.

◆ External suppliers can suffer from the same temptations to over-engineer a solution as internal team members. They can also cause problems when they provide cost and time estimates during the definition phase that are based on their own internal capacity at the time the estimates were generated. By the time the project is authorized and the order is placed, the supplier may have other work and so the contract must be given to other suppliers (involving an increase in the supplier management task), or the work taken back in-house (a clear change in the assumptions of work boundaries).

◆ Legal or regulatory change can change the nature of allowable project outcomes overnight. The need to stop and replan and to reconfirm that the new project is still attractive is usually obvious under these circumstances.

One of the most common symptoms of runaway projects is that the requirements stated in the revised project scope statement no longer correspond to the objectives written down in the project charter. So every time that you hear anyone discussing doing things differently from the way you thought they were described in the project charter, alarm bells should sound.

▶ Scope control

The two factors to consider under the scope control process include controlling the impact of scope changes, together with the need to control scope creep. The first stage of evaluation means that a requested change is thoroughly reviewed against the product scope and project scope before passing on to the next process. The justification for a change could be generated from variance identified from the work performance information; the outcome could then determine that a corrective action is required to eliminate the variance. After completing the first evaluation, a requested change or corrective action can only be considered once it has been through the integrated change control process. If the action is successfully approved, the next step is to return to scope control and update the project management plan and components of the scope baseline. If the approved change has an effect on the project's scope, the last stage of the procedure may require you to revise and reissue the project scope statement, WBS and WBS dictionary.

PMI says

Scope control
'Scope Control (Process). The process of controlling changes to the project scope.'
PMBOK Guide (p.375)

Scope management process in action

Technology development projects will usually have a scope management process (often called configuration management) to control the version of the hardware and software that is tested and then distributed to users. It is beyond the scope of this book to try to describe a technology scope management process that would be suitable for use in all circumstances and can supplant those systems already in use. What is described here should be suitable for change control in general projects and should be broadly compatible with most technology change control protocols. The focus of this process is on managing changes to the project as defined in the project scope statement. Such changes might include changes in the following:

◆ Target completion date for the project.
◆ Project costs.
◆ Quantity, quality and performance of the project deliverables, i.e. changes to the user needs.

Changes to project risks are addressed here only insofar as the risk management process may generate risk management actions that require changes in timing, costs or deliverables.

When the project scope statement is authorized, the scope of the project is frozen. Any information which implies that the actual project and that defined in the project scope statement will be materially different should trigger the scope management process. The general process should run as follows:

1 Whenever an action is proposed, consider whether it constitutes a change to the project scope. This is easier to do if you carry a copy of the project charter and scope statement with you wherever you are.
2 Get a written description of the proposed change, with as much clarity as possible. Ideally, the originator should describe the new objectives but you will often find that you will be the one writing down someone else's idea. If this is the case, try to remain neutral and try not to let your views colour what you write. You may find it helpful to list exactly which paragraphs of the project scope statement would need to be altered, and to provide an alternative text. Check this summary with the originator to confirm that it captures their idea, but make clear when doing so that this does not mean that the idea is accepted. Some proposed changes will come from your own analysis of the state of the project and the actions necessary to keep the project in line with the target. Treat these in the same way as other proposed changes.
3 Go back to the project management plan and work out the consequences of accepting or not accepting the change. Focus on timescales, costs, performance of deliverables, and risk. If there are many suggested changes then it will be impractical to repeat this exercise for every one. Under these circumstances, group the suggested changes logically and produce project scenario plans in which one or more of the groups can be actioned independently. It may become clear at this stage that some suggested changes clash with project priorities. For example, they may imply accepting a delay in project completion that is incompatible with

hitting a target launch date that is controlled outside the firm. If this is the case, then such changes should be rejected. A good compromise, if they are otherwise good ideas, is to record them and revisit them once the core project is finished with a view to initiating possible spin-off projects.

4 Discuss the results of the replanning exercise with the originator of the idea and ensure that they understand the consequences of their request. If the originator decides not to pursue the request at this point, then record the decision and move on. If the suggestion would lead to an improvement in the project (lower cost, shorter time, better deliverables, etc.) without any other drawback, then you would expect the requested change to be approved for implementation by the Change Control Board (CCB). The project manager is then required to update and reissue the necessary documents, making sure that everyone involved knows about the change. But usually the suggestion will have a drawback. Discuss this with the project sponsor in the same way as when generating the project charter. If the requested change would mean that the project still makes commercial sense then, depending on procedures in your organization and the authority of the CCB, it may be able to authorize an extension to the work. If a major alteration is required, a revision to the charter may need to be submitted to the programme board for reapproval. The revised project charter should make clear:

  ◆ the new view of likely business benefits, with or without the change.
  ◆ the new view of requirements for resourcing, funding and time, both with and without the change.

5 The programme board will compare the revised charter, and the business payoff implied by the figures with and without the change, with other ways in which the firm can spend its money and resources. If the change is justified then it will be authorized. Sometimes, when the change is a recovery plan that will increase the cost and time of the project beyond that originally planned, the realistic choice for the board is between accepting the change or cancelling the project.

6 If your project gets through this stage and is re-authorized, you can be assured that the firm is committed to the new project, together with the funding and resourcing required.

If a change is accepted, then relaunch the project. Ensure that all team members and all stakeholders know of the new objectives and plan. It would be worth publishing the revised plans so everyone is given the opportunity to see the changes.

▶ Summary

Project scope management is vital to a successful project. Scope creep is the biggest category of threat to projects. You need to manage scope firmly, and this begins with understanding what scope and scope creep are and then planning your scope management. A work breakdown structure (WBS) is an essential tool for this.

You have to manage scope constantly and vigilantly. If you are experiencing a number of scope changes, the ability to identify a common cause and then resolve the problem will prove beneficial in the longer term. It is better to manage scope problems before they happen rather than after the event.

The aim of scope management is to ensure that:

◆ only adequate work is done
◆ unnecessary work is not done
◆ you achieve the project's purpose.

The project manager can manage scope by evaluating requested changes and then making approved changes to the project scope, and making any required adjustments to the performance baselines and project plans. The project manager, perhaps working through the sponsor, has to communicate changes in scope to all stakeholders promptly. The project manager must manage the expectations of the sponsor and stakeholders, because the project's deliverables may have altered or their interests may be affected.

The final part of scope management is scope verification where the project seeks formal acceptance from the customer.

project time management

1

2

3

4

5

6

7

8

9

10

11

12

13

▶ Aims of this chapter

The aim of this chapter is to show you what you need to know to plan and manage your projects to the right timescale to fit the circumstances. It describes the processes of time management in projects, and the related processes from other project management knowledge areas. By the end of this chapter, you should be able to:

◆ list the six processes in project time management, and decide which are relevant to your project;
◆ state the difference between activity definition and activity sequencing and why definition should be done before sequencing;
◆ draw a network diagram;
◆ state two key differences between what is represented on an AOA diagram and on an AON one;
◆ briefly state the principle of rolling wave planning;
◆ estimate resources required for your project;
◆ estimate the duration of your project in two different ways;
◆ develop a schedule for your project;
◆ state what resource levelling does;
◆ control the schedule of your project.

▶ What is time management?

If you lose ten thousand pounds, but some kind soul then gives you another ten thousand pounds, you are no worse off, except for the effect of shock and perhaps the effect of the stiff drink that you had to console yourself before the kind and generous soul appeared. Similarly, if an organization or a project loses twenty computers, and provided the data is backed up, they can be replaced. But time is completely different. If you lose even a minute, you can never get it back again, no matter how much money you spend trying. Time cannot be stored or replaced. As a resource, time is unique in this regard, because all other resources, especially equipment and cash, but also people, can be replaced. This unique feature of time means that the project manager needs to take special care when managing time. The project manager who is poor at managing time will soon put the entire project at risk, by wasting not just their own time but the time of everyone across the project.

▶ Time management in projects

By definition projects are of a transient nature: their lifetime is finite, and their days are numbered. For the project manager this means that the management of time is a crucial skill to master. Even on projects where time to completion is not a hard constraint, poor or non-existent scheduling or time management will affect the remaining project constraints: cost, quality, and customer satisfaction. In short, wasting time not only wastes money, but has the potential to ruin everything, including a project manager's credibility.

Key Idea

Time estimation

'*Time is like a drug: too much of it can kill you*' – Terry Pratchett.

Overestimating the amount of time required on a project can be just as costly as underestimating it.

This chapter covers the project time management process and describes some practical tools and techniques to aid the process. It is important for a project manager to understand timing and scheduling and how to make planning tools work for their project and not the other way round.

The rise of project management as a professional skill has been accompanied by a proliferation of project management software programs. The vast majority of these programs are designed to aid time management; however, as Hobbes said of words, time management software is for the guidance of wise men and the obedience of fools. Software is only an aid to the project manager: the simplest programs can produce highly complex schedules and progress charts, but these are only as good as the plan they are fed into. Experience has shown that projects that proceed with a well-planned, regulated tempo are easier to control than those that move in fits and starts. The underlying reason for this is that real projects do not exist in isolation, but mirror the organizational structure and environment in which they operate. The successful project manager is acutely aware of the drumbeat within his project environment and ensures that he marches in step with it.

Trading time

We have seen that time is unique and that unlike other resources such as money and people, lost time can never be replaced. However, this does not mean that time cannot be traded. By trading time, in the project management context, we mean either giving up time for something else, or giving up something else and getting more time in return. The 'something else' is always definable in terms of scope or cost or risk or quality (The so-called 'triple constraint'). So if you are short of time in your project, you may want to identify options to create more time, and you can start to identify options by considering:

◆ scope – is there a way to reduce the scope of the project so as to create more time?
◆ cost – is there a way to spend more money, that is to increase costs, in a way that creates more time? (That 'buys time'?)
◆ quality – is there a way to reduce the quality of the work to create more time?
◆ risk – what additional risks can be accepted by the project, or what existing risks can be accepted in greater degree, so as to buy time?

The problem can also be the other way around, that is how to trade time by giving up time (that is, taking longer) in order to obtain more of some other resource, such as money or people, or in order to reduce risks or raise quality. An example of trading time in return for money is given in the Channel Tunnel mini-case study.

Case study

Channel Tunnel Rail Link

Though the tunnel that links Britain and France was completed in late 1994, the contract to construct a high-speed link between London and the end of British end of the tunnel at Folkstone was not awarded until February 1996. A consortium called London & Continental Railways Ltd (LCR) was to build a high-speed line from the coast to London and then across London to St Pancras station. The project was to be financed by LCR which would then draw revenues from Eurostar, the train operating company. Construction was expected to start in 1998 and finish in 2003.

At the end of 1997 it became clear that Eurostar's revenues were not going to be sufficient to repay the debts if the project went ahead unchanged, and it was made clear soon afterwards that the government would not make good the £1.2 billion shortfall with a grant. So the money available to do the project had become much less than originally anticipated: cost was out of balance with time and performance.

In June 1998 a solution was agreed that brought cost, time and deliverables back into line. The project was split in two: one part, linking the tunnel with the outskirts of London, would go ahead immediately, and the other part, crossing London, would be delayed. Construction of the first section is on target for completion in 2003, but completion of the entire link is unlikely before late 2006.

The LCR consortium were not the cause of the financing problem, but they had to manage it anyway. At the time they did this it would still have been possible to shut down the project without too much cost, and this was probably their next-best solution after the one that was agreed. The option simply to carry on and hope that it would sort itself out would have cost far more than either of the other options. LCR recognized the severity of the problem and redefined the project so that the new plan met the changed requirements.

▶ Project time management process group

The time management process group is a logical mechanism for taking a project plan and creating a sequence and schedule for producing the project deliverables. The time management process group is required throughout all phases of the project lifecycle. In the initiation phase the schedule is normally derived at a high level. This provides a frame in which the project plan evolves as the project iterates between the planning, execution and monitoring phases, until a detailed schedule for project closure matures.

The time management process group consists of six processes:

1 Activity definition: the deliverables of the project are established at the lowest level and the activities required to achieve them are defined.
2 Activity sequencing: the logical order for the activities to occur is determined and recorded.

3 Activity resource estimating: the resource requirements to fulfil the requirements of the activity sequencing process are estimated.
4 Activity duration estimating: the process by which the durations of the activities are estimated.
5 Schedule development: a frequentative process by which the activity schedule is developed.
6 Schedule control: the process that the project manager employs to keep the project on schedule.

These processes do not have to occur sequentially. It is most effective when all six have been determined at a high level and then refined, until the point when sufficient detail to execute the task is reached. Recognizing when this point is reached is a skill that makes the project manager worth his salt (and from which his salary is derived). In general, the level of detail needed is proportional to its level of risk and uncertainty. For this reason, time management planning should not be carried out in isolation but with the input of the project team who are going to execute the tasks. This ensures that the sequencing and activity duration estimates are as realistic as possible.

Activity definition

Activity definition is the dissection of the work breakdown structure from the project plan into parts whose duration can be meaningfully estimated.

Key Idea

Activity definition
Activity definition is describing the tasks that need to be performed in enough detail to estimate what resources and time will be required to complete them.

The lowest level of the work breakdown structure is known as the work package. Activity definition takes each work package and decomposes it further into schedule activities. These schedule activities are then used to form the foundation of the estimating, scheduling, executing, and monitoring and controlling of the project work. Simply put, activity definition is the breaking down of a project to the level where the duration of individual tasks can be estimated.

Inputs to activity definition

There are six inputs to activity definition:

◆ The project scope statement.
◆ The project management plan.
◆ The work breakdown structure.
◆ The work breakdown structure dictionary.

- ◆ Organizational process assets.
- ◆ Enterprise environmental factors.

The production of the first four inputs to the activity definition process have been described above. These define the project's deliverables and the steps required to achieve them. The project manager's task in activity definition is to divide these steps into a series of activities whose duration can be estimated in a manner that is consistent with the constraints of the organizational process assets and the enterprise environmental factors. Many a large engineering firm's projects have suffered serious schedule delays because project managers did not acknowledge that the organization's procurement system could not produce even simple items without several months' delay. The ability to recognize what is realistically achievable within an organization is crucial to the entire time management process.

▶ Tools and techniques for activity definition

This ability to acknowledge what is and is not possible is often referred to as expert judgement. Expert judgement is one of five tools and techniques used during the activity definition process. The five are:

- ◆ Decomposition.
- ◆ Templates.
- ◆ Rolling wave planning.
- ◆ Expert judgement.
- ◆ Planning components.

Decomposition is a planning technique that breaks the project scope and project deliverables into smaller components, until the project work is defined in sufficient detail to support executing, monitoring and controlling the work. The first experience the project manager has of decomposition is in the creation of the work breakdown structure to create the work packages. In activity definition the work packages are further decomposed to define the final outputs as schedule activities. Note the difference between the schedule activities created by this process and the deliverables from the creation of the work breakdown structure. It is usual for the team members responsible for each work package to undertake its decomposition.

In some cases similar projects may have been undertaken by the organization. In such cases, there may be templates of activity lists available to use on the new project.

Rolling wave planning is a method of planning immediate tasks in sufficient detail to enable work to proceed, while planning later work only to a high level in the first instance and not developing the detail until closer to the time of execution. This is particularly useful when detailed information affecting the later stages of a project becomes known only after earlier work is completed. In the decommissioning of nuclear power stations large savings have been achieved by deferring the planning of demolition work until a full survey of the hazards has been completed. This allows the safety case for demolition to be based on what the actual hazards are, rather than having to assume a more difficult to decommission, worst-case scenario.

Expert judgement comes from an individual or group who have specialist knowledge of the situation in hand. In the case of activity definition, the experts are likely to come from the project team members and other stakeholders who have had experience of this type of project before.

Two planning components are typically used in activity decomposition: control account and the planning package. These components are most successfully employed when there is insufficient decomposition of the project scope to provide a work package within the work breakdown structure. When this occurs the planning component can be used to create a high-level activity schedule for that branch of the work breakdown structure. This is likely to happen when an input to a phase of work is dependent on the unknown outcome of the preceding phases. For example, creating the scaled production process of a new pharmaceutical drug from the lab process can only be commenced once the lab process has been completed. A control account is a management control that integrates scope, budget, actual cost and schedule and compares them to earned value for performance measurement. A planning package is a level below that of the control account.

PMI says

Control account

'A Control Account is a managed control point where scope, budget, actual cost and schedule are integrated and compared to earned value for performance.' *PMBOK Guide* (p.355)

▶ Activity definition outputs

There are four outputs from activity definition. They are:

◆ The activity list.
◆ The activity attributes.
◆ The milestone list.
◆ Requested changes.

The activity list contains all the schedule activities that are planned for the project. At this stage no schedules have been determined and neither have any dependencies. The activities in the list are assigned a unique identifying number, and a description of the scope of work they cover is recorded. This enables the team members to know which activity is being referred to and what exactly is expected to be accomplished during the activity, for example the design specifications for a piece of engineering, or the length of tarmac to be laid in road construction. The activity list is a component of the project management plan and the schedule activities are part of the project schedule.

Activity attributes provide greater information about the activities in the activity list, including activity descriptions, identifiers, predecessor and successor activities, logical relationships, resource requirements, lead times, lag times, constraints and assumptions; in other words, everything there is to know about the activity. These attributes are inputs to the schedule development process.

The third output is the milestone list. This is a list of the schedule milestones throughout the project. There are two types of milestones documented in this list: mandatory, such as being a contractual agreement; and optional, derived from the project requirements or historical information.

Requested changes is the last output from this process. It is likely that during the activity definition process changes to the project plan will be discovered. These changes must be formally documented and requested through the integrated change control process.

▶ Activity sequencing

The activity sequencing process determines and documents the logical relationship of the activities in the activity list. This enables the activities to be ordered coherently and a project schedule built. The main output from activity sequencing is a network diagram; this is used to show clearly the sequence of work and the dependencies between activities and to estimate the duration of the project. A network diagram can also be used for reporting and controlling project progress.

The project manager or a specialized planner can do the sequencing of the project activities. Depending upon the size of the project, this can be done by hand or using specialized project management sequencing software, remembering Hobbes' warning.

Key Idea

Activity definition and activity sequencing
Activity definition describes *what* needs to be done. Activity sequencing describes the *order* to do it in.

▶ Inputs to activity sequencing

There are five inputs to activity sequencing:

- ◆ The project scope statement.
- ◆ The activity list.
- ◆ The activity attributes.
- ◆ The milestone list.
- ◆ Approved change requests.

Except for the project scope statement, these inputs are created in the activity definition process, discussed above.

▶ Tools and techniques

There are five tools and techniques available for activity sequencing:

- The precedence diagramming method.
- The arrow diagramming method.
- Schedule network templates.
- Dependency determination.
- Applying leads and lags.

Precedence diagramming method

The precedence diagramming method creates a network diagram (Figure 6.1) where the schedule activities are represented by nodes, or rectangles, and the relationship between the nodes is represented by arrows. There are four types of dependency and precedence relationships that can be shown using network diagrams. These are:

1 Finish to start – this is where an activity may commence only once the preceding activity has completed.
2 Finish to finish – an activity is able to finish only when the preceding activity has finished.
3 Start to start – the commencement of the successor activity is dependent on the preceding activity also having commenced.
4 Start to finish – this is where the successor activity can be completed only once the preceding activity has commenced.

The most commonly used precedent method is the finish-to-start relationship, while the start-to-finish is rarely used.

Fig. 6.1 Network diagram

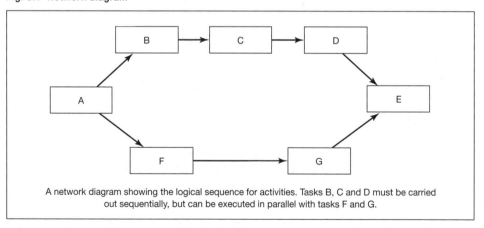

A network diagram showing the logical sequence for activities. Tasks B, C and D must be carried out sequentially, but can be executed in parallel with tasks F and G.

Arrow diagramming method

The arrow diagramming method, sometimes called the activity-on-arrow method, uses arrows to represent the activities and nodes to represent dependencies. This method uses only a finish-to-start method and uses dummies to enable all logical relationships to be clearly represented (see Figure 6.2). A dummy activity is not a real schedule activity and as such has a zero duration value.

Fig. 6.2 Network diagram showing dummy dependency

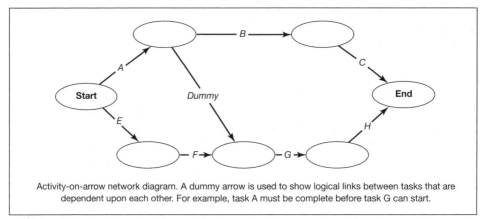

Activity-on-arrow network diagram. A dummy arrow is used to show logical links between tasks that are dependent upon each other. For example, task A must be complete before task G can start.

Schedule network templates

Schedule network templates can be used to accelerate the creation of network diagrams for the project. These can be used for the whole or part of the project and can come from historical data, if similar projects have been performed within the organization before.

Dependency determination

Dependency determination looks at the dependencies to determine the schedule or aspects of the schedule. There are three types of dependencies:

1 Mandatory dependencies often involve a resource limitation and are also known as hard logic.
2 Discretionary dependencies are determined by the project team and are likely to be based on historical information or best practice.
3 External dependencies are those that are external to the project, such as the planning application process in a construction project.

Applying leads and lags

Applying leads and lags is the last tool and technique for activity sequencing. This technique is applied by the project team once the dependencies have been determined. A lead can quicken a successor activity and a lag will delay one.

▶ Activity sequencing outputs

There are four outputs from activity sequencing. The most significant is the project sequence network diagrams. These schematically show the relationship of all the activities required for the completion of the project (e.g. Figures 6.1 and 6.2). The remaining three outputs update the inputs to reflect changes introduced during the activity sequencing process. The complete output list for activity sequencing is:

◆ Sequence network diagrams.
◆ Updates to the activity lists.
◆ Updates to the activity attributes.
◆ Requested changes.

Activity resource estimating

Once the activities required to complete that project have been identified and coordinated into a logical sequence, the next step is to identify the resources required to undertake them. Activity resource estimating is the process by which these resources are identified and quantified. The types of resources will vary from project to project, but may include skilled personnel, money, facilities and equipment. Think about a recent project you have worked on and try to identify the different types of resources used. It is likely that you have identified more than you may have originally thought. Managing and coordinating often competing resources can prove challenging to even the experienced project manager. It is this process, activity resource estimating, that should provide the project manager with the advance knowledge of their requirements before commencing the project. Indeed, activity resourcing can often determine whether a project will proceed. For example, if you are working on a construction project and there is a global shortage of concrete for the next six months, it may be decided to delay the project or cancel the project altogether.

Key Idea

Activity resourcing
The previous processes described *what* and *in which order*. Activity resourcing describes *who* will do the work (people or physical resources).

Inputs

There are six inputs to activity resource estimating:

- Enterprise environmental factors.
- Organizational process assets.
- The activity list.
- The activity attributes.
- Resource availability.
- The programme management plan.

These six inputs can be divided into two groups: the first two tell you what is available to you; and the remaining four are what you need to complete the project. Activity resource estimating is all about matching what you need to what is available.

Resource availability is, simply, information concerning the availability of the resources required for the project. This may include the type of resource, its location and its availability. Your key programmers might be available for the project, but when are they on annual leave? The scope and length of the project will limit the extent to which the information concerning the resources will be valid. Early requirements would be relatively easy to pinpoint in comparison to requirements in two years' time.

▶ Tools and techniques

There are five tools and techniques available to the project manager for activity resource estimating:

- ◆ Expert judgement.
- ◆ Project management software.
- ◆ Alternatives analysis.
- ◆ Published estimating data.
- ◆ Bottom-up estimating.

More than enough ink has been spilled on expert judgement and the limitations of project software, so we will move on to examining the remaining three.

Alternatives analysis

This technique looks at the resource requirements and attempts to determine what alternatives there are to achieve the same result. This could mean choosing between a highly skilled machinist who will do the job in a week but is available for only two weeks a month after the output is required, against a novice but capable machinist, who is available now and will produce the product, but the quality might not be as high as that of the experienced person.

Published estimating data

Project managers can also make use of published estimating data produced by other organizations. These provide regularly updated production rate and unit costs of a wide range of resources, such as trade labour, raw materials, equipment, and so on.

Bottom-up estimating

Bottom-up estimating is a technique that can be used when the activity cannot be fully resourced as is. It involves further decomposition of the schedule activity so that the component tasks can be individually resourced. The use of bottom-up estimating can be seen as an iteration of the activity definition and activity sequencing process groups to achieve the required level of detail. In reality, this iteration will apply to only a few activities and, except in extreme cases, will not require a re-examination of the whole plan.

▶ Outputs

There are five outputs from activity resourcing:

- ◆ Activity resource requirements. This is a documented list of the resource requirements for the successful completion of the project and is the most significant output.
- ◆ Resource breakdown structure. A hierarchical structure of resources by resource category and resource type.
- ◆ Resource calendar. This calendar records resource requirements and availabilities throughout the project, including both workdays and non-workdays.
- ◆ Activity attributes.
- ◆ Requested changes.

PMI says

Resource breakdown structure
'The Resource Breakdown Structure is a hierarchical structure of resources by resource category and resource type.' *PMBOK Guide* (p.372)

Activity duration estimating

The fourth process group in project time management is activity duration estimating. This is the essence of the entire time management process. The preceding processes have defined the what, when and who for each activity: this is the process that determines how long.

Key Idea

Activity duration estimating
The preceding processes have defined the *what, when* and *who* for each activity; this is the process that determines *how long*.

Inputs

There are eight inputs to this process:

- Enterprise environmental factors.
- Organizational process assets.
- Project scope statement.
- Activity lists.
- Activity attributes.
- Activity resource requirements.
- Resource calendar.
- The project management plan.

These inputs have all been described above, as they are used as inputs to the previous process groups. Ideally, the estimating of an activity duration should be carried out by the person doing the work. The role of the project manager is to select the most appropriate estimating tools and techniques and to ensure access to any existing historical or organizational information to assist the estimating process.

Tools and techniques

There are five tools and techniques for the project manager to use when estimating the activity durations:

- Expert judgement.
- Analogous estimating.
- Parametric estimating.

◆ Three-point estimates.
◆ Reserve analysis.

Analogous estimating

Analogous estimating, sometimes called top-down estimating, uses the values of parameters, such as scope, cost, budget and duration from a previous, similar activity as the basis for estimating the same parameter or measure for a future activity. It is frequently used to estimate a parameter when there is a limited amount of detailed information about the project (e.g. estimating in the early phases). Analogous estimating is a form of expert judgement. It is most reliable when the previous activities are similar in fact and not just appearance, and the project team members preparing the estimates have been involved with the previous work.

PMI says

Analogous estimating

'Analogous Estimating is an estimating technique that uses the values of parameters such as scope, cost, budget and duration or measures of scale such as size, weight and complexity from a previous, similar activity as the basis for estimating the same parameter or measure for a future activity.' *PMBOK Guide* (p.351)

Parametric estimating

Parametric estimating allows the project manager to quantify the activity durations by using a simple (often linear) assumption to relate the amount of work to the productivity rate. The productivity rate can be estimated using historical information or expert judgement. Examples of productivity rates include lines of code per hour, metres of tarmac laid per day, bricks laid per hour, or components machined per week. Johnson famously advised Boswell not to turn his land into an orchard on the basis of a parametric estimate: 'we compute in England a park wall at a thousand pounds per mile ... for a hundred pounds you could have forty-four square yards which is very little'.

Three-point estimate

The three-point estimate technique provides an average estimate of the time expected for an activity to be completed. This average is calculated from the most optimistic duration of the activity (O), the most likely (M) and the most pessimistic (P). So, for example, if the optimistic time for a component to be manufactured is 5 days, the pessimistic duration is 12 days and the most likely is 7, the average of these three estimates is 8 days and so 8 days will be used for the duration estimate.

The PERT (Programme Evaluation and Review Technique) estimating technique uses a weighted average to model the duration probability distribution, with M four times more likely to occur than O or P. The PERT distribution is usually normalized by dividing through by 6. For the example given above, the value of the PERT distribution is 7.5 $((5+(4 \times 7)+12)/6)$. The mean of the PERT distribution is M. The variance of the PERT distribution (the expected value of the square of the difference between a given value and the mean) is therefore given by $((P-O)/6)^2$ and the standard deviation of the PERT distribution (the absolute square root of the variance) is $(P-O)/6$. So in the above example, the variance is 49/36 and the standard deviation is 7/6.

Key Idea

The PERT distribution

The PERT distribution is given by $(P + 4M + O)/6$. The variance of the PERT distribution is $((P-O)/6)^2$ and the standard deviation is $(P-O)/6$.

Reserve analysis

The final technique, reserve analysis, examines the risks to the project schedule and builds in buffers or time reserves. Building time reserves into a project should not be confused with padding the project. Padding is a term often used to describe extra slack or waiting time that has been built into a project to cover a lack of realistic knowledge during planning.

PMI says

Reserve analysis
'Reserve Analysis is an analytical technique to determine the essential features and relationships of components in the project management plan to establish a reserve for the schedule duration for a project.' *PMBOK Guide* (p.372)

▶ Outputs

There are two outputs from the activity duration estimating process group:

◆ Activity duration estimates.
◆ Updates to the activity attributes.

▶ Schedule development

Schedule development is the process that enables the project manager to take the time estimates derived in the activity resource and use them to create the project schedule. The project schedule is based on the real calendar; it is in the formation of the schedule where most project plans are confronted by reality. A number of projects have had to be radically revised when it was discovered that the planned delivery date actually falls on 25 December.

▶ Inputs

There are nine inputs to the schedule development process:

- ◆ Organization assets.
- ◆ Project scope statement.
- ◆ Activity list.
- ◆ Activity attributes.
- ◆ Project schedule network diagrams.
- ◆ Activity resource requirements.
- ◆ Resource calendars.
- ◆ Activity duration estimates.
- ◆ The project management plan.

▶ Tools and techniques

There are 10 different tools and techniques for developing the project schedule. Most organizations, and indeed project managers, have a preferred method and the PMI does not profess an opinion upon which is better, or how many of them to use. It is entirely project-dependent. We will discuss each of the methods briefly here, as there are many good books devoted entirely to one or more of these tools and techniques.

Schedule network analysis

The application of this technique results in the production of the project schedule. It comprises a number of different tools and techniques itself, such as the critical path method, schedule compression, resource levelling, critical chain method, what-if analysis, and many more. In fact, this technique encompasses the entire process of generating the schedule. Analysis of the schedule network ensures that points of convergence, divergence, conflicts and other inconsistencies are identified and resolved. It also identifies the late and early starts and finishes for the project activities. For large projects this may be achieved by using a software tool, whereas for small projects, schedule network analysis may be seen as a sanity check.

The critical path method

The critical path method was invented by the DuPont Corporation during the 1950s. A critical path is the sequence of project network elements with the longest overall duration. It is used to determine the shortest time to complete the project. The duration of the critical path determines the duration of the entire project. Delaying an element on the critical path directly influences the planned project completion date. For example, in Figure 6.3, the critical path is 10 days (route A–B–C). The amount of float or waiting time on the project is the time between the tasks not on the critical path finishing and those on the critical path finishing. In Figure 6.3, the float is 1 day. If the duration of task D increases to 8 days then the lower path (route D–E) would become the critical path of 11 days.

Fig. 6.3 Network diagram showing the critical path

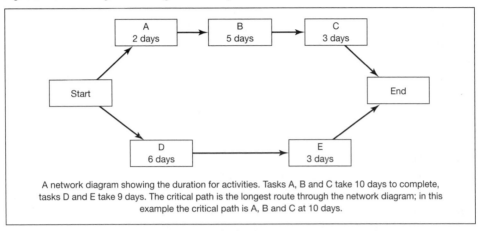

A network diagram showing the duration for activities. Tasks A, B and C take 10 days to complete, tasks D and E take 9 days. The critical path is the longest route through the network diagram; in this example the critical path is A, B and C at 10 days.

PMI says

Critical path method
'The Critical Path Method is a schedule network analysis technique used to determine the amount of scheduling flexibility (or float) on various network paths in the project schedule network, and to determine the minimum total project duration.' *PMBOK Guide* (p.357)

Schedule compression
This is a technique that shortens the time taken to complete the project without reducing scope. Internal and external factors may cause a project manager to undertake this course of action. For example, a product may need to be launched earlier than planned to maintain competitor advantage. There are two techniques that can be used for schedule compression: crashing and fast tracking. Crashing is when cost and schedule are compared to determine how to obtain the greatest amount of compression for the least incremental cost. Crashing may not always produce a viable alternative and can result in increased cost. Fast tracking is a technique where the project manager runs phases of a project concurrently, when originally they would have been run sequentially. It is important to note that there is always a trade-off when changing elements in the project plan between time, scope, cost or quality; fast tracking a plan often increases the amount of risk associated with it.

PMI says

Crashing
'Crashing is a schedule compression technique in which cost and schedule trade-offs are analyzed to determine how to obtain the greatest amount of compression for the least incremental cost.' *PMBOK Guide* (p.357)

What-if scenario planning

When analysing the schedule, it is always useful to ask the question 'what if …?'. If your project is dependent on the delivery of a specific component by a fixed date, you should consider what would happen if it was delayed. What would the impact on the project be if the component was a day late: would this be any different if it was two months late? Working through this analysis is another sanity check on your schedule. It also provides the basis for contingency planning and in some cases may result in scope changes. There are mathematical models, such as Monte Carlo analysis, that can be used for complicated projects.

Resource levelling

Resource levelling is a technique that aligns the schedule to the available resources. For example, your key programme is already committed to a number of projects, so your schedule must be built around them. This may affect the critical path and cost of the project. Another use of resource levelling is to keep spend profiles constant over budgeting periods. This is particularly useful for projects where time is not the greatest constraint. Resource levelling smoothes the peaks and troughs in project resources, making it easier to predict demand over the project life.

Critical chain method

The critical chain method is a schedule network technique that modifies the project schedule to account for limited resources, often by using probabilistic techniques and semi-analytical models to study the network. There are many books and articles that discuss the critical chain method. As a summary, the critical chain method uses network diagrams of the most likely estimate that the tasks will take, determining the critical path. It then builds duration buffers into the critical path at various milestones.

PMI says

Critical chain method
'The Critical Chain Method is a schedule network analysis technique that modifies the project schedule to account for limited resources. The critical chain method mixes deterministic and probabilistic approaches to schedule network analysis.'
PMBOK Guide (p.357)

Project management software

There is a wide variety of project management software available, some for managing a project from start to finish and others to achieve a specific task.

Applying calendars

Project calendars (discussed in integration management) and resource calendars inform the project manager when tasks are to happen and when resources are available. These calendars should be applied to the schedule as it is developed in order to ensure the finalized schedule is feasible.

Adjusting leads and lags

This technique requires the project manager to revisit the leads and lags applied to the schedule and assess whether they are accurate. It is often the case that later on in the planning the project manager will have a better understanding of the time requirements. This will enable them to revise leads and lags set earlier in the planning cycle.

Schedule model

A schedule model is normally a project management software tool used in conjunction with manual methods of project management, to perform schedule network analysis to generate the project schedule.

> **PMI says**
>
> **Schedule model**
> 'A Schedule Model is a model used in conjunction with manual methods of project management software to perform schedule network analysis to generate the project schedule for use in managing the execution of a project.' *PMBOK Guide* (p.374)

▶ Outputs

There are eight outputs from schedule development. The first output is the project schedule. At its bare minimum the project schedule will contain a start and finish date for each schedule activity. It can include target dates and key milestones and can often be presented graphically, using one or more of the following formats: project schedule network diagrams, bar charts (Gantt charts) and milestone charts. The remaining seven outputs are:

- The schedule model data.
- The schedule baseline.
- Resource requirement updates.
- Activity attribute updates.
- Project calendar updates.
- Change requests.
- Updates to the project management plan.

▶ Schedule control

Schedule control is the final process within the time management process group. This process enables the project manager to verify the status of the project, influence proposed changes to the project schedule, identify changes to the schedule, and manage changes to the schedule.

Key Idea

Schedule control
Schedule control is the process by which a project manager works his plan.

▶ Inputs

There are four inputs to this process: the schedule management plan, the schedule baseline, performance reports, and approved change requests.

▶ Tools and techniques

There are six tools and techniques associated with schedule control:

1 Progress reporting. This is the reporting of actual progress against estimated.
2 Schedule change control system. This is a control system that defines the processes and procedures for requesting, accepting or rejecting, and implementing a change to the schedule.
3 Performance measurement. This technique measures actual performance against estimated performance.
4 Project management software.
5 Variance analysis. This measures and analyzes the variance between the estimated and actual schedule.
6 Schedule comparison bar charts. These provide a simple visual tool to enable comparison of schedule activities.

▶ Outputs

There are nine outputs from schedule control:

◆ Schedule model updates.
◆ Schedule baseline updates.
◆ Performance measurements.
◆ Requested changes.
◆ Recommended corrective actions.
◆ Organizational process assets updates.
◆ Activity list updates.
◆ Activity attributes updates.
◆ Updates to the project management plan.

The outputs to schedule control allow time management to be refined, often by iterating once more through the time management process groups.

▶ Meetings and time management

Meetings are important to project managers, both as a proportion of the project manager's total working time, and because of their impact on getting things done in the project. Although the PMBOK's section on time management does not have a heading for meetings, we include meetings in this book's chapter on time management because of their importance to the project manager and we look especially at how to ensure efficient usage of time in meetings.

Meetings as a project management activity are paradoxical in that they are both extremely useful, because they are one of the main ways to get things done through people, and yet they are also a major risk of wasted time. Isn't how to run a meeting or how to participate effectively and time-efficiently in a meeting something that everyone should have learnt early in their career? Ideally so, but in practice many people have not, and so this section of the chapter aims to give some tips for how to manage project meetings effectively, and also how to participate effectively, in order to save time.

▶ Process

The key to a successful meeting is preparation. Quick impromptu discussions require less preparation than formal presentations, but some preparation is always required, if only to think through in your own mind 'What is my aim in this meeting? What do I want?' Indeed the most basic requirements are always to be absolutely clear in your own mind what the issue is, and what you want to achieve by the meeting. What is the one question to which we need an answer? With a good understanding of the issue, it becomes much easier to know what sort of meeting is required. Is it a question that could be answered by one of the project team alone from immediately-available information? If so, go and ask the question at your team-member's desk. Does it involve sharing information between different groups before a group decision can be made? If so, think through who has to be involved and set up a more formal meeting. If you cannot identify the basic issue, then do not take up other people's time to try to find an answer to a problem you cannot pose coherently. Instead, consider holding a different meeting with more limited agenda and attendance, simply to identify what the issue really is. A quick preliminary discussion with one or two other people can bring much clarity to the agenda of a larger meeting without trying to solve the problem identified.

Identifying the core issue should allow you to plan the meeting:

- ◆ Who needs to be present at the meeting?
- ◆ What information do they hold that other people will need?
- ◆ Who needs to be present for reasons of communication or simply to witness that the decision was made rationally?
- ◆ Do we have people with the authority to take the decisions we know will need to be made? (If the right person is simply not available in time, do not just go ahead regardless: try to get the authority-holder to send a named delegate who is given the authority to take the necessary decision in this meeting. Otherwise you may end up having a meeting without any useful outcome).

- What preparation do attendees need to have made, or what information do they need to bring?
- What hardware, facilities, or tests do we need to be able to demonstrate in the meeting, and what does this mean for timing and location?
- When is the earliest possible time for the meeting, given the known availabilities of information and people?
- What preparation do I need to do to make sure that a decision can be taken during the meeting? This may mean, for example, working up a small number of possible actions and their implications, so that the meeting can choose between actions with known consequences. If this thinking is not done before the meeting, then it will be hard to get people to agree that the suggested action is realistic.

Unless the meeting is to be large and highly sensitive, this checklist need not be formal or written down, and it is usually enough just to run through the list mentally. Before any but the smallest meeting, create an agenda. In much the same way as when planning a project, it will be necessary to put people's contributions in some order so that the information is presented coherently. Even if you are only having a 15-minute discussion, it can be helpful to outline a mini-agenda verbally – for example: 'Could each of you explain in no more than two minutes what is happening with this test and what our options are? Once that is clear we will agree which option we will choose.' An agenda keeps the meeting focused on the key issues.

In the meeting:

- Set the scope and objectives. Make clear what is in-scope and what will be left for a different forum.
- Explain the agenda, making clear that everyone will have their say, and that the timing is firm.
- Run the meeting to the agenda.
- Intervene if necessary to keep participants on the topic, to stop disruptive interruptions from parties who have their own agenda, and above all, to keep progress to schedule.

Your colleagues may chat in an unstructured way when you meet socially, but they may need to learn that they will be cut short if they ramble in a meeting.

Do not allow new problems to derail the meeting (unless they clearly change our understanding of the entire project in a way that makes the original purpose of the meeting irrelevant). If new issues emerge, note them and deal with them appropriately; it is likely that most of them would not need a meeting with everyone here, and some would not need a meeting at all. Similarly, do not go beyond the scope of the meeting once you have achieved the objective. As with other critical chain tasks, do not feel obliged to fill the time if you finish early.

If the meeting is just not making progress, you need to make a decision about what to do. Deciding to allow the meeting to overrun is an option but it is not the only option and may not be the best. It may also be possible to reschedule a more focused session now that all the concerns have been aired. Alternatively, you can test the true appetite for a decision by announcing that if no agreement has been reached before the scheduled end time of the meeting, you will close the meeting and make a decision yourself in the best interests of the project. Considerable political sensitivity is required when pursuing some courses of action, since it is often important not only that decisions are made correctly, but also that they are seen to be made correctly. If the project sponsor is in the meeting, you may find it useful to call a short break and discuss the best course of action together.

As the meeting progresses, write down the minutes of the meeting. If it is a larger or longer meeting, appoint a secretary or scribe to do so. The minutes should include:

◆ Date.
◆ List of attendees.
◆ Key decisions or other key information.
◆ Actions allocated to named individuals with agreed timing.

Note that 'Key information' does not mean a transcript of the meeting.

It means information that materially influences the meeting decision. When circulating minutes of the meeting, it is usually much more important that the minutes are promptly and accurately distributed than it is for them to be elaborately formatted. An e-mail or, if it is legible, a photocopied page of a notebook, can contain the same information as a formally typed meeting note.

▶ Summary

The key to time management is for the project manager and each member of the team to remember that whatever they are doing, time is incredibly valuable, and that time is literally money. No one should waste a second.

The best approach to time management is to define what activities need to be done, then work out the sequence in which they should be done, and then what resources are needed to do those activities. This in turn allows the time taken to be estimated, and a schedule put together. Then, when doing the project, control the work so that either it follows the planned schedule, or the schedule is updated.

cost management

1
2
3
4
5
6
7
8
9
10
11
12
13

▶ Aims of this chapter

By the end of this chapter, the reader should be able to:

◆ report the bare minimum cost data about their project without assistance from a cost specialist;
◆ explain the theory of more advanced project cost management, as per PMBOK, to such a degree that the project manager can direct and evaluate the work of a project cost accountant or other cost specialist in a larger project;
◆ present the cost ramifications of any significant scope change or proposed scope change.

▶ Costs matter

Cost management is sometimes seen as a chore in project management rather than a central part of it. While most project managers are required to report actual costs to date against forecast costs, there is much more that can be done in most projects on cost management than that bare minimum. (Costs are not necessarily in monetary terms but can be in terms of days or resources.) On large projects there is usually a project accounting specialist to run the cost management side of the project, but the project manager will still need to understand the principles of project cost management in order to make best use of such a specialist.

There are two different needs for cost management skills in project management. One is the need to set the right budget for the project, that is, to estimate the cost, to understand the risks of inaccuracy in the estimate, and to pick the right level of probable accuracy of the estimates, both for the particular project and for the owning organization. The other need is to manage the project within whatever budget has been set. These are very different needs. You can be an excellent project manager and pursue a great project management career, running the largest projects, without ever acquiring or needing the skills to plan project budgets. And there are people who make a highly successful career out of budgeting for projects without ever getting involved in the project management that follows – corporate and structured finance departments of banks, for example, have many such people. So it is expecting much to cover both subjects in a single chapter. In this chapter we do not attempt to enable you to reach the level of expertise in project budgeting that is required of a bank corporate finance analyst or a professional project budgeteer. The general aim of this chapter is rather to give the practising project manager enough of an introduction to the subject of project cost management so that they know what needs to be done, not so that they can necessarily do it.

▶ Key concepts

There are four key concepts in project cost management. The 'PMI says' box defines these. Note the subtle difference between cost estimating and cost budgeting. Estimating operates at the level of activities, and cost budgeting takes the estimated costs of activities and aggregates them to the project level in the form of a cost baseline.

PMI says

Cost estimating, cost budgeting, baseline, cost control

'Cost Estimating (Process). The process of developing an approximation of the cost of the resources needed to complete project activities.' *PMBOK Guide* (p.356)

'Cost Budgeting (Process). The process of aggregating the estimated costs of individual activities or work packages to establish a cost baseline.' *PMBOK Guide* (p.356)

'Baseline. The approved time phased plan (for a project, a work breakdown structure component, a work package, or a schedule activity), plus or minus approved project scope, cost, schedule, and technical changes. Generally refers to the current baseline, but may refer to the original or some other baseline. Usually used with a modifier (e.g. cost baseline, schedule baseline, performance measurement baseline, technical baseline).' *PMBOK Guide* (p.352)

'Cost Control (Process). The process of influencing the factors that create variances, and controlling changes to the project budget.' *PMBOK Guide* (p.356)

▶ The importance of costs and financial knowledge

Cost always matters. Even on projects where the sponsor and stakeholders say 'Money is no object', which is sometimes true, there will come a time when cost does matter. Costs matter in the private sector because costs come from revenues, and if costs exceed revenues then there is no profit and the enterprise becomes insolvent. In the not-for-profit and government sectors, costs also matter, because although there is no profit, budgets are finite (because resources are finite) and if costs exceed budgets, then insolvency is also the result[1]. It is because costs always matter, in the end, that the skill of financial literacy is so important in management in any organization, commercial or non-profit. The higher in an organization, the more important financial skills become. The reader who is serious about advancing in project management, or in any managerial career, is strongly advised to take a 'Finance for non-financial managers' course if they have not already done so[2].

▶ The bare minimun

The bare minimum that you must be able to report as a project manager is where the project actually is in terms of cost against the planned budget, today. This should be reported accurately in your regular reports to the sponsor, which will normally be weekly or fortnightly. If you are lucky you will have a project support office to work out actuals against planned – as it is called – but even then you must not walk away from responsibility for the accuracy of the report. You must understand it and check that it is right by your own rough calculations.

Table 7.1 is a very simple planned versus actuals report (or variance report). It shows all costs as they are at the date of the report, which is what the words 'to date' mean in the row headings. This contrasts with showing the total planned costs for both phases, that is, planned costs as at the end of each phase. Showing total planned costs would be misleading if shown here in this report instead of planned costs to date, because that would not allow us to calculate variance to date. This distinction is important, often critically important; it is a somewhat like the difference between a runner being five yards behind the leader half-way through a marathon, and being five yards behind the leader as the leader crosses the finish line.

Table 7.1 Example of a project cost report, planned versus actuals
Project PHAEDRUS report, 14 June

	Phase 1: Pilot	Phase 2: Build	Total
Planned cost to date	£20,000	£45,000	£65,000
Actual cost to date	£19,000	£49,000	£68,000
Variance to date	+ £1,000	–£4,000	–£3,000
Notes	Pilot complete, with £1,000 underspent.	Sub-contractor 1 month late. £4,000 additional cost to date for hiring temporary staff because of the sub-contractor delay. A new sub-contractor has started work. The £4,000 may be recoverable from the original sub-contractor, but it may be prudent to budget an additional £8,000.	

Now it is often useful to report the total budget for each phase as well as where the project is currently (or 'to date'). This can be achieved by adding extra rows to Table 7.1, as in Table 7.2.

▶ Scope and cost

Scope is a critical factor in project management. Managing scope creep is one of the project manager's and sponsor's biggest tasks, and a major theme of this book. Stakeholders will always tend to want scope increases or scope changes. This often arises not through deliberate intention, but as a result of improved understanding of the project and its issues, and from people refining or adjusting their expectations. The problem for the project manager is to steer a middle course between on the one hand appearing to say 'no' to every request, and on the other saying 'yes'

Table 7.2 Example of a project cost report, planned versus actuals, with durations and dates
Project PHAEDRUS report, 14 June

	Phase 1: Pilot	Phase 2: Build	Total
Planned duration (weeks elapsed)	8	12	
Planned finish date	10 June	10 August	
Remaining work, planned (weeks)	0	7	
Remaining work, actual (weeks)	0	11	
Planned cost to date	£20,000	£45,000	£65,000
Actual cost to date	£19,000	£49,000	£68,000
Variance to date	+ £1,000	–£4,000	–£3,000
Notes	Pilot complete, with £1,000 underspent.	Sub-contractor 1 month late. £4,000 additional cost to date for hiring temporary staff because of the sub-contractor delay. A new sub-contractor has started work. The £4,000 may be recoverable from the original sub-contractor, but it may be prudent to budget an additional £8,000.	

too readily and then discovering later in the project that there is not enough time or resource to deliver on the additional commitment.

There is only one thing to do in this situation: discuss the requested scope change with the sponsor and project team to determine the likely cost impact, then go back to the person who wants the request and explain the cost ramifications. The type of response is initially 'Let me go away and determine the ramifications of that', after which you discuss with the sponsor and team, so that you can go back and say 'If we made such-and-such a change to the project, the cost ramifications would be $X,000 plus a delay of Y month'. You will of course need to have supporting detail to back up your argument. Although project managers often do not need to know how to estimate costs for an entire project, they should be able to make or supervise others making this kind of revised cost estimate. (The approach outlined in this paragraph is important for both real life and the PMI exams.)

▶ Five rules of thumb for estimating costs

As you progress in your project management career, look for rules of thumb in cost estimation that will help you save time and get a better intuitive feel for costs and cost-related risks in your project. As each industry and organization is different and each has its own characteristics, it is not possible to give a long list of rules of thumb

– what matters and what works in cost estimation in an investment bank will be different from what works in a process industry and from what works in the National Health Service. However, the following five rules of thumb may have some general applicability:

◆ The fully loaded cost of an employee is double their base salary.
◆ All actual IT costs and timescales will tend to be close to double the estimated costs.
◆ Prior probability is the best guide to future probabilities: in other words, the costs, the probabilities of success, and the timescales for the project that you are planning are more likely than not to be the same or close to those in similar previous projects, which means that if you have that historical data, use it in your cost planning rather than accepting any 'but this time it will be different' arguments.
◆ In the absence of any evidence to the contrary, assume that projects have at most a 50% chance of delivering on time and on budget and to user expectations.
◆ Assume 200 to 220 effective working days per year per full-time employee.

▶ A specialist task

When estimating costs the person or team doing the estimating must understand all the details, because one of the most common sources of cost estimation errors is a failure to grasp the details adequately. The WBS dictionary, for example, is something that is omitted in many real-life projects, and yet in real-life cost overruns it is often the case that a cause of the problem is that different members of the project were using key terms to mean different things; it is precisely to avoid that kind of problem that there should be a WBS dictionary. And yet, under real-life time and political pressures, the WBS dictionary is often jettisoned as unnecessary bureaucracy. So, the project manager or whoever is doing cost estimation needs to understand three things: (1) what can be done, in the absence of any constraints on time and resources; (2) what the constraints are in this particular project, especially expectations and political factors; and (3) what the risks of accepting those constraints are in terms of probable sources of error. They must then communicate those risks back to the sponsor and stakeholders, for them to either accept or modify. And of course they would be well advised to document the outcome of such feedback.

Cost estimating is a specialist task, and the reading list at the end of the chapter gives a flavour of what kind and depth of skills are necessary to acquire such specialization.

▶ Cost management process groups

The PMBOK approach to project cost management distinguishes three processes within it. Table 7.3 shows where these fall within the five project management process groups.

Table 7.3 Three project cost management processes

		Process Group		
Initiating	Planning	Executing	Monitoring and controlling	Closing
	1 Cost estimating 2 Cost budgeting		3 Cost control	

In practice, these three processes often run in parallel. For instance, once the project is underway there will be a constant need to re-estimate and re-budget costs as a result of changes and new information which arise during project execution, alongside the cost control process.

Cost estimating

Figure 7.1 shows the inputs, tools and techniques, and outputs for the cost estimating process. Fundamentally, the purpose of the cost management plan is to answer two questions:

◆ How much will the project cost?
◆ How certain is the answer to the question above?

The project manager, the sponsor, the financial control function of the owning organization and the customer will certainly want to know the answers to these questions, and other stakeholders are likely to as well. As a project manager you may have legal liability for ensuring that cost estimates are prepared properly, which means that the workings by which the answers to these two questions were reached should be documented in addition to the answers themselves.

The main point of doing cost estimating is to answer these two questions, which in terms of the outputs listed in Figure 7.1 means the updates to the cost management plan (usually a part of the project plan), and especially the activity cost estimates. We have just explained the need for supporting detail from the legal risk point of view. Another, more positive, reason for keeping supporting detail that underlies the cost estimates is that there may be stakeholders and subject matter experts who can hep to reduce costs or risks by reviewing the details and applying their knowledge and experience to suggest better ways of doing things. Remember that, like so much else in project management, cost estimation is an iterative process and you as project manager are there not to be an expert, but to manage the process. So you should encourage and facilitate a proper debate about cost estimates and risks, in order to improve these iteratively, finding and drawing on the relevant expertise available to the project. And of course you should work closely with the sponsor on this.

Fig. 7.1 The cost estimating process

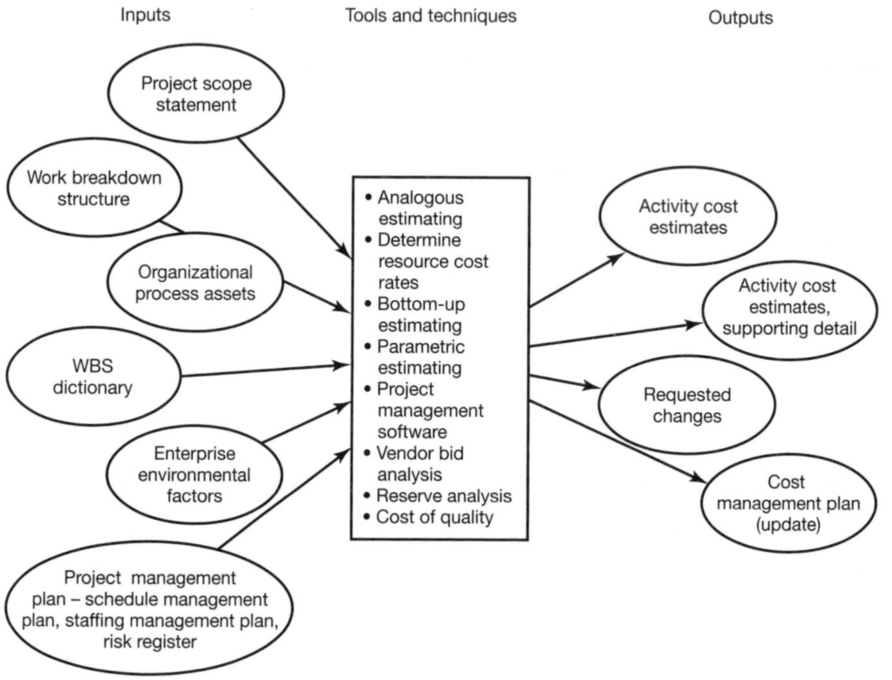

Inputs	Tools and techniques	Outputs

The primary output is the cost management plan and especially the activity cost estimates. These must be supported by the underlying details, and the process of creating the activity cost estimates will lead to updates to the cost management plan and requests for changes. The cost management plan is a part of the overall project management plan.

Adapted from *PMBOK Guide* (p.162)

▶ Accuracy of estimates

The future is inherently unpredictable. In a weather forecast, most people are not interested in knowing how many inches or millimetres of rain will fall tomorrow, they just want to know if it will rain or not. This means they don't need a forecast that is accurate to a sixteenth of an inch of rain, so making a forecast to that accuracy is money wasted. Another problem with weather forecasting is that it suffers the law of diminishing returns, which means that spending more money on trying to improve the accuracy of the forecast produces smaller and smaller gains in accuracy the more extra that is spent. Cost estimating is the same as weather forecasting. Sometimes an accurate cost estimate is not necessary, just something to the nearest order of magnitude. Often at the early stages of planning or initiation all that is required is a rough order of magnitude (ROM) cost estimate, to be refined perhaps as one of the first stages of the project, as the project progresses.

So before you start cost estimating, ensure that you know what accuracy of estimate is required, and check whether the cost is worth it or whether a less accurate estimate might suffice.

▶ Inputs, tools and techniques

The inputs to the cost estimating process listed in Figure 7.1 need no further explanation, as we have explained why the WBS dictionary is an important input, where there is one. Similarly, we have explained the outputs, which together answer the two key questions described above. Let us spend the rest of this section therefore describing the tools and techniques used in cost estimating, as per the list in Figure 7.1 and as that is categorized in Figure 7.2.

Engineering methods

Engineering methods (also known as work-measurement methods) include:

◆ Bottom-up estimating.
◆ Reserve analysis.

Bottom-up estimating is the main technique under this heading; it means building a model or a cost structure from the bottom up.

Reserve analysis means analyzing the project buffer or float, that is the amount of 'just-in-case' reserve that there should be. It can be used for two different purposes in the cost estimation process. First, project cost estimates may include a contingency reserve. Secondly, there are ways to use estimates of reserve to check the overall budget. The critical chain project management methodology places particular emphasis on using and managing a buffer or reserve.

The principal features of engineering methods of cost estimation are as follows:

◆ The method analyzes the costs and times of all the processes, inputs and outputs in the project.
◆ In effect it builds an engineering model of what will be done.
◆ It has the advantage that it is a model of what will be done, and can be developed to a great level of detail.
◆ It has the disadvantage that it is expensive to do, and depending on the project may have a considerable degree of inaccuracy.
◆ Some contracts for projects may specify that this method must be used.
◆ Consulting firms will provide this as a service.

Conference method

The conference method means asking other people what they think. (It is similar to the Delphi technique of information gathering.) Two ways of doing this are:

◆ Analogous estimating.
◆ Vendor bid analysis.

Analogous estimating means finding analogous projects, that is similar ones that have been done before or are at a more advanced stage; in other words, asking what happened last time. The case study gives an example of analogous estimating in use.

Fig. 7.2 The four approaches to cost estimation

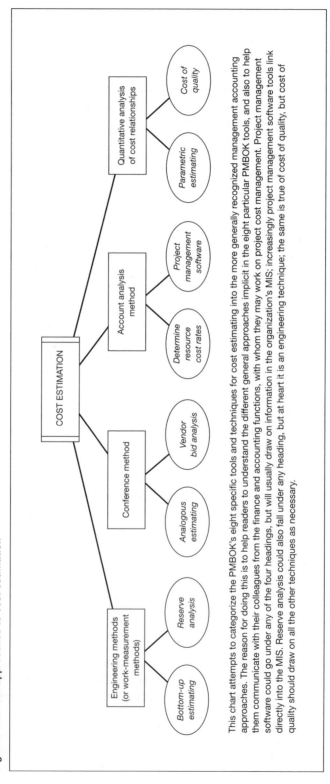

This chart attempts to categorize the PMBOK's eight specific tools and techniques for cost estimating into the more generally recognized management accounting approaches. The reason for doing this is to help readers to understand the different general approaches implicit in the eight particular PMBOK tools, and also to help them communicate with their colleagues from the finance and accounting functions, with whom they may work on project cost management. Project management software could go under any of the four headings, but will usually draw on information in the organization's MIS; increasingly project management software tools link directly into the MIS. Reserve analysis could also fall under any heading, but at heart it is an engineering technique; the same is true of cost of quality, but cost of quality should draw on all the other techniques as necessary.

g

Case study

Analogous cost estimating

Project CHRISTMAS was an internal project with a £1m budget. The project included building a simple Oracle database. Rumours had spread around the organization that the project was lavishly funded. When the project manager for CHRISTMAS went to discuss the likely costs of building a database with the IT department, the head of IT suggested that costs for this database would be in the region of £200,000. The IT department produced much supporting detail, which seemed valid and went into great detail of what was so special about the IT infrastructure in the organization. The project manager went away and made a few telephone calls to friends and colleagues who had built similar, simple Oracle databases – in other words, he did analogous estimating. None of those databases had cost more than £50,000, and the consensus was that £45,000 was a more than adequate budget for the proposed CHRISTMAS database. The project manager went through the supporting detail of the estimate from the IT department, and found several areas where it seemed likely that the project would be paying for things that the IT department would have to do anyway.

The project manager remembered his facilitation skills and intervention training. Although he was certain that the IT guys were trying it on, so to speak, he decided to avoid embarrassing them by making or hinting at any such accusation. Instead, when he met the IT people again for a follow-up on database cost estimates, he suggested several areas either where costs could be cut by using outside contractors, or where costs might be shared with other customers of the IT department, on the basis that they too would benefit. He also politely and non-confrontationally, but definitely, made it clear that he had several estimates for similar work at a quarter of the price, and that that is what he expected. He left the meeting on friendly terms, with IT promising to think about it and get back to him. This they did, the following day, with an estimate of £45,000.

Vendor bid analysis means obtaining one or more bids for the project or parts of it from suppliers and analyzing the cost data contained therein. (Note that to request bids with the sole intention of extracting such data from them, that is, with no real intention of accepting the bid, is to act in bad faith, which is unethical and may create legal and costs risks. Even if these risks do not materialize, when an organization gets a reputation for this kind of behaviour it often finds that good suppliers cease to do business with it.)

The principal features of the conference method of cost estimation are as follows:

◆ The method gets opinions from relevant experts on the likely cost of the project or parts of it, and averages the opinions.
◆ In effect it draws on relevant expertise to make an educated guess as to costs.
◆ Its advantages are high speed and low cost.
◆ Its disadvantages are that it takes little account of new ways of working; it is unsuitable for entirely novel projects; and the audit trail of how the estimate was reached may be insufficiently rigorous for some purposes.

◆ It offers a reasonable approach to cost estimation for many projects, and a good check for all other methods.

Account analysis method
The two particular techniques under this heading are:

◆ Determine resource cost rates.
◆ Project management software.

The principal features of the account analysis method of cost estimation are as follows:

◆ It uses the general ledger and associated MIS to extract data and hypotheses from what the organization has done before to indicate probable costs for the project.
◆ In effect it draws on the organization's relevant historical data as recorded in management accounts.
◆ It has the advantage that it uses historical data from the organization's own actual experience, so the data, where relevant, will be reliable.
◆ Its disadvantages are that it cannot be applied where the data are not relevant, e.g. on a novel project; and that some distortions can arise from cost allocation methodology in the MIS.
◆ It offers a good approach to cost estimation for projects in a programme of similar projects.

Quantitative analysis of cost relationships
The two particular techniques from the PMBOK that fall under this heading are:

◆ Parametric estimating.
◆ Cost of quality.

Cost of quality is in terms of cost estimation a special case of parametric estimating. (The word 'parametric' simply means that parameters or other qualitative factors are used, and in this context it means exactly the same as the term 'quantitative analysis'.)

The principal features of the quantitative analysis of cost relationships method of cost estimation are as follows:

◆ It uses formal methods and historical or other data to estimate costs.
◆ In effect it combines the engineering method with the account analysis method, and possibly the conference method, to create a detailed model of costs.
◆ It has the advantage that is uses the most accurate features of the other three methods.
◆ It has the disadvantage that it incurs the greatest cost, which depending on the novelty of the project may not lead to a better estimate than the other methods.
◆ It offers a good approach to cost estimation for large projects where accuracy in estimation matters, and where there are not strong incentives to distort the estimate.

Cost budgeting

Cost estimating and cost budgeting are both in the planning process group, and they are closely related. Budgeting takes as its key input the cost estimates for activities or work packages that were the outputs of the cost estimation process. The main output is a costed plan. At the beginning of this chapter we noted the difference between cost estimating and cost budgeting: estimating operates at the level of activities, and cost budgeting takes the estimated costs of activities and aggregates them to the project level in the form of a cost baseline. Figure 7.3 shows the inputs, tools and techniques, and outputs for the cost budgeting process; the

Fig. 7.3 The cost budgeting process

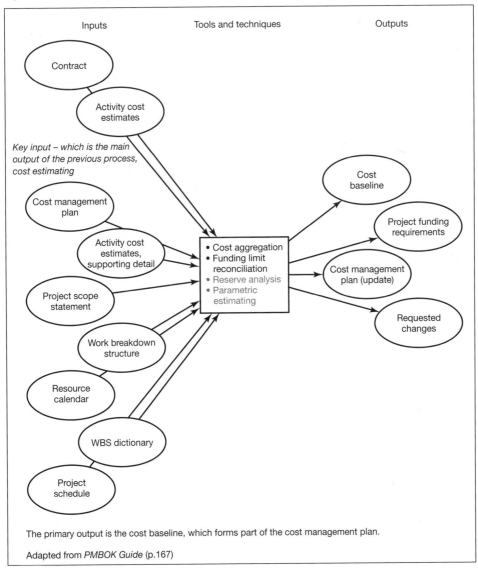

The primary output is the cost baseline, which forms part of the cost management plan.

Adapted from *PMBOK Guide* (p.167)

process is straightforward and needs little detailed explanation, except that it is important to understand the difference between this process, cost budgeting, and the previous one, cost estimating. We say more about this below.

What is the difference between a costed activity and a budget? Take the example of tennis coaching. Coaching one person costs whatever the coach's fee is per hour, but coaching two people might cost the same if the one coach is teaching both people at the same time. And it might be that the coach charges more in summer than at other times. So if your project entails having two people coached in tennis, the cost variables are when they are coached and whether they are coached together. The raw cost data and the cost variables are discovered in cost estimating, and the decision of which cost option to go for and the calculation of the cost ramifications for the project come in the budgeting. Budgeting is also the process in which the project is assigned a cost code and work packages within the project are assigned sub-codes.

For internal projects, the project cost plan must be structured in a way that is consistent with the internal accounting procedures and policies of the performing organization. It helps communications and saves time if externally managed projects also relate easily to the accounting system used by the customer organization. A project manager who is not familiar with the relevant requirements should work through the sponsor to find a contact in the accounting department and get some instruction.

What should the updated cost management plan that is an output of this process look like? Every organization differs, and you should obtain an example of how your organization works. However, it will usually include the following cost information:

- Projected costs at regular periods (typically weekly or monthly) throughout the life of the project, in aggregate and down to the level of cost package.
- Costs for each work package, and costs risks for each package.
- Costs for each resource.
- Mechanisms and criteria for releasing future blocks of conditionally approved project funding.
- Cost warning and indicator limits.
- Budget and accounting codes, authorizations, limits.
- Cost process interfaces between the project and the performing organization.

Cost control

Key Idea

Cost control
The point of cost control is to keep project costs within the agreed budget.

If you have children you may notice that some of them are better at managing their money than others. One child, perhaps, is never short of money and has good financial discipline, whereas no matter how much another works, they are always short. The difference between the two is most probably a matter of cost control. In project management you must ensure that your project has good cost control. Even if it feels as though cost control does not matter, it does, and your career depends on maintaining good cost control in your project.

Project cost control depends on your knowing four things:

◆ Planned costs.
◆ Actual costs.
◆ Causes of variance.
◆ Things you can do to reduce future costs.

There is a surprising number of projects, especially in the public sector, where the project manager does not have a grasp of these things. The questions you need to answer are whether the project is and will be on track in terms of cost, and if not, how big the problem is and what can be done about it.

Fig. 7.4 The cost control process

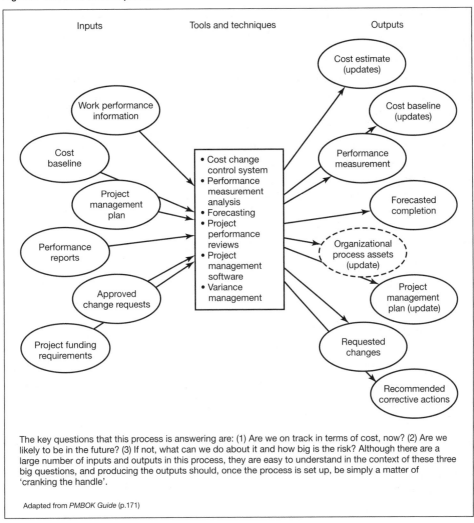

The key questions that this process is answering are: (1) Are we on track in terms of cost, now? (2) Are we likely to be in the future? (3) If not, what can we do about it and how big is the risk? Although there are a large number of inputs and outputs in this process, they are easy to understand in the context of these three big questions, and producing the outputs should, once the process is set up, be simply a matter of 'cranking the handle'.

Adapted from *PMBOK Guide* (p.171)

Figure 7.4 shows the inputs, tools and techniques, and outputs for the project cost control process. Note that project cost control is part of integrated change control. The cost management process is one of the most mechanistic in project management, and the routine part, answering the question 'Are we on track for costs?', should be a reliable but simple and mechanistic process. Your skill and effort should be reserved for identifying cost problems on the horizon of the project, and for identifying options to deal with problems.

The most important thing with cost problems as a project manager is to let the sponsor know as soon as possible. If you hide problems, including cost problems, they don't go away, they get worse.

▶ Summary

Cost management is important in all projects, even if it has been said that 'Cost is no object'. Cost estimating is about estimating the costs of the various activities in the project. Ensure that you know what level of accuracy is required. It is normal in many organizations to start with a rough order of magnitude estimate and then refine down to a more accurate estimate. There are eight different tools or techniques for estimating, the easiest being the conference method, and the most complex parametric estimating. Complex does not necessarily mean better or more accurate, so choose the right technique.

Cost budgeting takes the estimate and works out what it means in terms of a costed and dated plan, so that work packages are costed and cost codes assigned to the project and its elements. It also links the project's accounting into the organization's management accounting system.

Cost estimating and budgeting are part of the planning process group. The third cost management process, cost control, is part of the monitoring and controlling process group, and also part of integrated change control. Cost control is about ensuring that the project's costs stay within the agreed budget for the project.

▶ Further reading

We said at the start of this chapter that the general aim of this chapter was rather to give the practising project manager enough of an introduction to the subject of project cost management so that they know what needs to be done, not so that they can necessarily do it. An indication of the level of knowledge that is necessary for making a career of project financial evaluation and budgeting is given by the standard textbooks for the field, two of which are:

◆ Brealey, R.A. and Myers, S., 1996. *Principles of Corporate Finance*. New York: McGraw-Hill.
◆ Ross, S.A., Westerfield, R.W. and Jaffe, J.F., 1995. *Corporate Finance*. Mason, OH: Thomson/Nelson, Irwin.

The subject of management and cost accounting is an older and larger discipline than project management, and its principles, or comparable general accounting principles, need to be mastered before making any serious attempt on the corporate finance textbooks listed above. Two leading textbooks are:

◆ Hansen, D.R. and Mowen, M.M., 2005. *Management Accounting: The Cornerstone of Business Decisions*. Mason, OH: Thomson/Nelson, South Western College Publishing.
◆ Horngren, C.T., 2005. *Management and Cost Accounting* (3rd edn). Harlow: FT Prentice Hall.

Project managers who come from the IT sector and wish to use project management as a means of escaping from IT might like to consider, after they have qualified in project management, studying for the CIMA management accounting qualification, details of which can be found on the CIMA website at http://www.cimaglobal.com/.

▶ Notes

1 Any reader who doubts that governments, and the UK government in particular, can become insolvent, is referred to the UK War Loan Scandal of the 1930s, when the UK government faced insolvency and avoided it only by wiping out a substantial portion of the savings of the middle classes. Technically, the UK government did not become insolvent, but the consequence for much of the population was arguably even worse than if it had.

2 The author is heartily grateful for this piece of advice, the value of which he can attest, and which he read in the magnificent book by Moran, R.A., 1994, *Never Confuse a Memo with Reality: A Little Book of Business Lessons*. London: HarperCollins.

quality management

1
2
3
4
5
6
7
8
9
10
11
12
13

> ## Aims of this chapter

By the end of this chapter, the reader should be able to:

◆ give the rationale for treating quality management as a distinct subject within general management;
◆ define quality;
◆ list the three processes within project quality management;
◆ explain the value of quality management to the organization that owns the project, beyond the value of producing project deliverables to quality standards;
◆ implement a quality management system in a project;
◆ distinguish between the concepts of quality planning, quality assurance and quality control;
◆ list three indicators of a process or output being out of control;
◆ present the case to a sceptical sponsor for investing in a quality management system in a medium-sized or large project;
◆ understand the personal benefits to the project manager from having some minimum skills in project quality management techniques.

> ## An introduction to the concept of quality

This chapter introduces the idea of quality, which in a sense is an odd idea because it raises the question of whether quality should be a distinct area within project management, rather than quality pervading all areas of it. The chapter begins by answering this question in terms of general management, and then proceeds to set an approach to quality management for projects. Just like the other chapters in this book that cover the knowledge areas in project management or the process groups, this chapter follows the PMBOK approach to project quality management. The PMBOK approach is consistent with the world's main quality management practices, including:

◆ ISO 9000[1] series.
◆ Iskikawa.
◆ Deming.
◆ Juran.
◆ Crosby.
◆ Six Sigma.
◆ Failure Mode and Effect Analysis.
◆ Voice of the Customer.
◆ Cost of Quality (COQ).
◆ Continuous Improvement (CI).
◆ Total Quality Management (TQM)[2].

For a summary of the key features of four of these, see Table 8.1. The PMBOK approach is also consistent with the approaches to quality espoused by:

- Def Stan 05-97[3].
- Review, Learn and Improve (RLI).
- Lean Quality.
- House of quality.
- Quality Value Added (QVA).
- Zero Defects (ZD).
- Baldridge.
- John Boyd/OODA loop.

PMBOK adopts unmodified the ISO definitions for key quality management terms (in recognition of which we use 'ISO says' boxes in this chapter where appropriate, rather than the 'PMI says' boxes). It is not surprising that the list of compatible approaches to quality management is so long, and we have named only a few, because they are all trying to do the same thing. They are worth listing because sometimes as a project manager you may encounter a low-level executive with nominal responsibility for projects or for quality who will try to argue that the approach to quality management that you want to take on your project is incompatible with some mandated standard. One cannot be too sceptical of this type of claim – if you encounter this problem, ask to see the evidence and insist on seeing the details of the argument. The authors' experience of quality management, after a slightly sceptical start, is that there is a great amount in the ISO 9000, PMBOK and other approaches to quality management that can add real value to projects and their project managers, if used intelligently.

Quality is an odd thing to manage. Surely the whole point of management is to do a quality job? As someone once said, if a thing is worth doing, it is worth doing well. And real-life pressures and incentives mean that Oscar Wilde's rejoinder, that if a thing is worth doing then it must also be worth doing badly, is not a factor in management. The question is why have a separate angle on management, including project management, just for quality? Should it not be part of everything we do in management, in business, in government? Let us dispose of a completely uninteresting answer to this question quickly, and then give the real and more substantial answers. The uninteresting answer is that we have a separate field of quality management in project management, or in management generally, because there are standards such as ISO 9000 which we want to comply with. This tick-box answer is not a proper answer to the question.

The question is important because if we are to have quality management as a separate part of project management then there will be a substantial cost, if only in your time as a project manager. That cost must be justified if a project manager is to be asked to spend time on quality management, and the PMBOK and other approaches to project management do ask that. There are two kinds of answer to the question, both of which are different sides of the same coin, so to speak. One answer starts with human nature, the other with the problems of complexity. The reader may be concerned that we have not yet defined what quality is. Let us proceed in answering the question using whatever intuitive notion we have of what quality means, and later we will come to a formal definition.

Table 8.1 Four of the major approaches to quality compared

	Crosby	Deming	Ishikawa	Juran
Definition of quality	Conformance to requirements	Three corners of quality: ◆ the product itself, ◆ the user and how they use the product, ◆ instructions for use	Most economical, most useful and always satisfactory to the customer	Fitness for purpose. Managing for quality requires a trilogy of processes: Quality – ◆ planning ◆ control ◆ improvement
Overall approach	Get it right first time, get the people motivated	Excellence and continual improvement; constancy of purpose; use of statistical analysis	Implement company-wide quality control (CWQC). Talk to the data (use statistical methods)	A project approach: rank the quality problems, and tackle the most significant first, on a project-by-project basis
Approach in detail	The 14 steps: 1 Management commitment 2 Quality improvement team 3 Quality measurement 4 Cost of quality evaluation 5 Quality awareness 6 Corrective action 7 Establish committee for Zero Defects programme 8 Supervisor training 9 Zero defects day 10 Goal setting 11 Error cause removal 12 Recognition 13 Quality councils 14 Do it over again	The 14 points for management: 1 Create constancy of purpose for improvement of products and services 2 Adopt the new philosophy 3 Cease dependence on mass inspection 4 End the practice of awarding business on price tag alone 5 Constantly improve the system of production service 6 Institute modern methods of training on the job 7 Institute modern methods of supervision	The seven tools. 1 Pareto chart: separate out the vital few from the trivial many 2 Cause and effect diagram 3 Stratification 4 Check sheet 5 Histogram (bar chart) 6 Scatter diagram (correlation) 7 Control chart	Two journeys are necessary. Diagnostic journey: 1 Study symptoms 2 Generate theories about causes 3 Do experimental analysis to establish actual cause Remedial journey: 4 Generate possible remedies 5 Select and apply a remedy 6 Consolidate and embed improvements

Table 8.1 Continued

Crosby	Deming	Ishikawa	Juran
Approach in detail *continued*	8 Drive out fear		
	9 Break down barriers between staff areas		
	10 Eliminate numerical goals for the workforce		
	11 Eliminate work standards and numerical quotas		
	12 Remove barriers that hinder the hourly worker		
	13 Institute a vigorous programme of education and training		
	14 Structure top management to push constantly the previous 13 points		

This table summarizes the principal features of four of the main approaches to quality other than ISO 9000. ISO 9000 draws on all of these approaches. The PMBOK seems to draw heavily on Ishikawa's seven tools (and candidates for the PMI exam are recommended to be familiar with all seven and their use in project quality management). Deming's 14 points for management seem a little dated now, but are surprisingly absent from many manufacturing companies in the West to this day. Note the tension in the approaches above between statistical techniques, which imply a need for detailed measurement, and the opposite, to take a qualitative and holistic approach.

Most people, especially in business, are perfectionists. They naturally want to do a high quality job, other things being equal. It is difficult to maintain one's motivation, sense of purpose and pride in one's work if one deliberately tries to do a bad job. There are, however, a number of reasons why even the most able and energetic person may produce a high quality piece of work. And think – who decides what quality is? In project management, as in all business, it is the customer, the organization or person or team for whom the project is being done, not the team or person doing the work, who decides what is to count as a good job, that is, what counts as quality. Some of the reasons why good people working hard to the best of their ability may not produce quality work are as follows:

◆ The customer's requirements were not understood.
◆ The customer's requirements were understood but were not possible to achieve.
◆ The customer's requirements changed.
◆ All other requirements were met but at much greater cost than was necessary (i.e. the implicit cost requirement was not met).
◆ The people doing the work lacked the techniques, experience or skills to do the work well.
◆ The work was done in a way that did not last (i.e. the implicit requirement for persistence was not met).
◆ The final result met quality expectations, but the way it was done upset or disappointed people.
◆ Everything worked out with respect to quality, but the people doing the project were physically or mentally injured in the process.

All of these possible causes of quality failures are consistent with people trying to do a good job, and the last one, perhaps in extreme cases killing oneself through the sheer effort to do a good job, arises precisely from trying too hard to do a good job. Is that a quality failure? Yes, the quality of life of the project team is ruined, and as we shall see the scope of quality management includes more than just the quality of the final deliverable.

Having started from a consideration of human nature, we can see from some of the bullet points above how the problem of complexity also affects quality. When a project is complex, for example it has many stakeholders and a deliverable with many features, it may not be clear what constitutes quality. An excessive focus on satisfying one dimension of quality, say ease of use, may compromise another aspect, say flexibility of use. Quality management is a tool which helps to manage this trade-off.

We finish this introduction by considering why quality should be treated as a separate angle on management, including project management. Let us answer this from the point of view of management generally, as the answer translates readily into project management terms. Management (and project management too) is a unified whole. Financial management is part of management, as is managing people and legal and regulatory management, in the following way. A manager cannot make decisions of strategic importance, or decisions about the general direction and management of an organization, exclusively on the basis of financial factors, while ignoring human factors and legal or regulatory issues. All the different aspects of management need to be considered, certainly at senior management levels and usually at middle management levels, and also in project management. By dividing up the large and difficult subject of management into distinct subject areas – people, finance, leadership, legal and regulatory, marketing and sales, and so on – we are able to make a better job of it. Quality is simply one of the areas within management.

Having set the scene for quality and introduced the notion, let us move to a formal definition of quality within the specific context of project management.

▶ Quality management – an overview of the knowledge area

In project management, the purpose of quality management is simply to ensure that the project meets the needs for which it was created. This is a real problem. Most projects do not meet the aims for which they were created.

There are three processes within the project quality management knowledge area: Quality planning, Perform quality assurance, and Perform quality control. As we expect, these fit into the five process groups in a common sense, even logical, way, starting with planning (Table 8.2). Quality control does not start in initiation because that is too soon; one needs to know what the project is about and have some idea, albeit at a high level, before any value can be added by thinking about quality, so project planning is the right stage in which to start thinking about quality, and one starts by planning for quality. This chapter devotes most space to quality planning, because experience shows that if you get this right, then quality assurance and control are relatively straightforward.

Table 8.2 Three project quality management processes

| | | Process Group | | |
Initiating	Planning	Executing	Monitoring and controlling	Closing
	1 Quality planning	2 Perform quality assurance	3 Perform quality control	

The first part of planning for quality, which is described in more detail below, is to decide what quality means for this particular project and its deliverables, and what the relevant quality criteria are. Once the quality plan is done, which forms part of the overall project plan, there is nothing further to do until the execution stage of the project; and just as with project management as a whole, there is both a doing or execution part and, simultaneously, a monitoring and control part. That is to say, measuring or monitoring how well the project conforms to the planned quality standards is a distinct task from acting on the results of those measurements, just as measuring flour on a weighing scale is a different activity from mixing it with eggs and milk to form a pancake. Shortly we will look at each of the three processes within the project quality management knowledge area in more detail, but first let us define quality.

▶ Quality and quality management defined

It is vital to be crystal clear about what quality means in project management. It is very useful to know the generally accepted meanings of quality management, quality objectives, and quality management system. A slightly easier-to-remember definition of quality than the ISO/PMBOK one is 'conformity to requirements', which is a perfectly good definition for use in real-life project management[4].

ISO says

Quality
'Quality: the degree to which a set of inherent characteristics fulfils requirements.'
ISO 9000 (and also PMBOK)

Note that, on either definition, it is a mistake both to exceed quality as well as to fall short of it. If you deliver a Rolls-Royce car when the customer wanted a Ford, then either you or the customer is paying too much. And it could be that the Rolls-Royce is too heavy a car for the weak bridge that the customer has to drive over on their way home. This analogy illustrates a key point in real-life project management: if you deliver excess quality, then someone, either the project or the customer, is paying for it. This is not to deny that exceeding the required quality usually leads to much less pain for the project manager than falling short does, and when planning your margin of safety always aim high rather than low in terms of quality. But the point is that you should aim to meet or slightly exceed quality targets in your deliverables and processes, and you ought not to aim to exceed them by a great extent, or you will be wasting resources. As well as quality being too high or too low, it is possible to have excess variation in quality. This need not mean a deliverable swinging between too high and too low a standard of quality; it can be a problem where quality is within what is acceptable, but in a different way each time, confounding customer expectations. People, especially customers, tend to like consistency much more than constant surprise when it comes to management.

ISO says

Other key quality management terms defined
'Quality management system: management system to direct and control an organization with regard to quality.' ISO 9000

'Quality planning: part of quality management focused on setting quality objectives and specifying necessary operational processes and related resources to fulfil the quality objectives.' ISO 9000

'Quality objectives: something sought, or aimed for, related to quality.' ISO 9000

'Quality assurance: part of quality management focused on providing confidence that quality requirements will be fulfilled.' ISO 9000

'Requirement: need or expectation that is stated, generally implied, or obligatory.' ISO 9000

'Quality control: part of quality management focused on fulfilling quality requirements.' ISO 9000

Quality planning

We plan in quality management for the same reason that we plan in any other activity, in order to have a sensible, efficient and structured approach to a task. The chief purpose of quality planning is to produce a quality plan, that is, a description of how the project is going to achieve its quality requirement, and also what those requirements are. Like the overall project plan, of which the quality plan is a part, the quality plan serves two purposes: as a plan, and also as a communication tool, especially to engage key stakeholders in the quality management process.

Key Idea

Quality plan
'The quality plan is a vehicle for mitigating risk ....' UK MOD Def Stan 05-97

A quality plan need not be long or complicated or expensive to produce. For small or simple projects, a single paragraph may suffice. Consider the quality plan shown here, used by a London-based company that ran a project to set up a new division to offer training courses to the public. It shows that a quality plan can be short and simple and straightforward. It also shows why it is useful to have a quality plan written down – there can then be no doubt in the minds of those involved what is expected in terms of quality, and everyone is clear what the quality objective is: 60% or more 'Yes' votes. Of course in more complex projects, the quality plan will need to be more substantial.

Example of a quality plan

The quality objective of the new training division is to provide training in XXXX to a level of quality such that delegates and their managers feel that the training was well worth the fee and they will recommend colleagues and friends to attend our courses. We will measure customer satisfaction by using anonymous feedback forms, to be distributed at the end of every course, and the key question will be 'Would you recommend a colleague or friend to attend this course, given its cost? – Yes / Maybe / No'. A 60% 'Yes' recommendation after the second pilot course will constitute success for this project. Before giving the first pilot course to the public, our instructors will all:

1   undergo a one-day course in adult instructional techniques,

2   see themselves on video delivering the course in a dress rehearsal,

3 have been approved as competent to deliver the course by the project director,

and the project director shall satisfy themselves that the dress rehearsals meet a sufficient qualitative standard for proceeding to running public courses.

Let us walk though the steps in the quality planning process, as depicted in Figure 8.1.

Fig. 8.1 The quality planning process

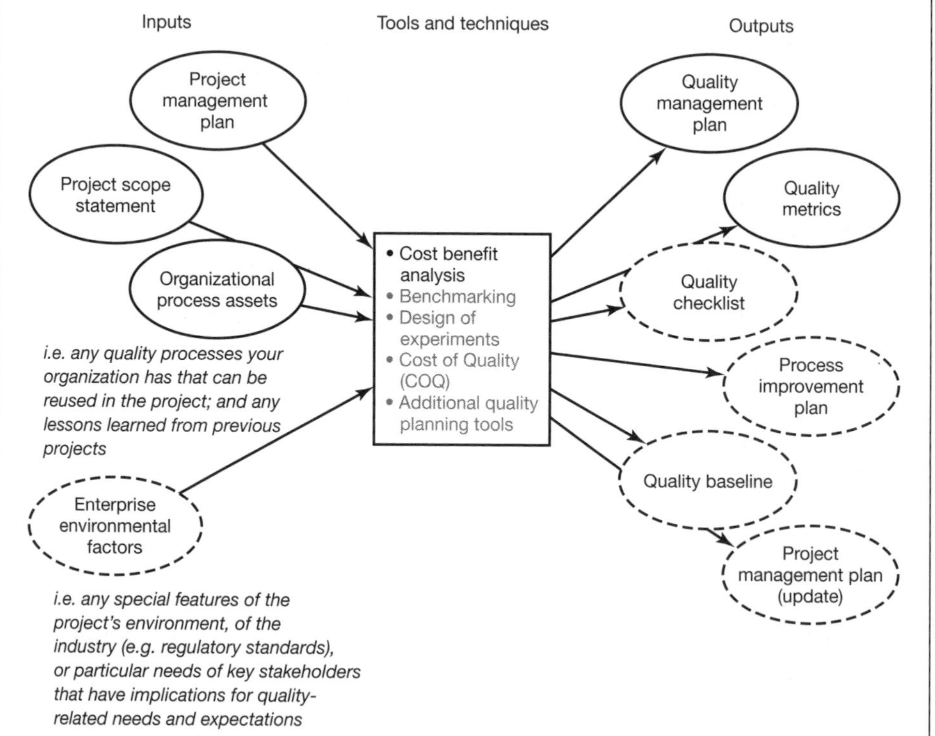

The most important and most commonly used inputs and outputs are in solid ovals, others are in broken-lined ovals. Similarly, the tools and techniques that are most essential are printed in black, the others in grey. Many industries and companies have their own quality planning techniques, and these are recognized under 'Additional quality planning tools. Although that i s in grey, where your organization or industry has such tools and techniques, use them. In the inputs, it is obvious what the project management plan and the scope statement are. The PMBOK terms 'Enterprise environmental factors' and 'Organizational process assets' may be a little cumbersome and obscure, but the notes attached to each of those, above, explain what they are, and they are both useful categories of inputs to the quality planning process. Although the diagram above shows 'Enterprise environmental factors' in a broken-lined oval, implying that generally it is not the most important input to quality planning, an exception of course is in any regulated activity or safety-critical project, where the relevant regulations or legal requirements affecting quality must be used as inputs; in many cases the raw regulations and laws will have been incorporated into in-house procedural manuals, and so should be available as 'Organizational process assets'. The quality management plan is the most important output. It can be sufficient for the update to the project management plan to insert the quality management plan into the relevant place in the project management plan. A quality checklist is very useful, where appropriate, but derives from the quality management plan or the principles in it.

Adapted from *PMBOK Guide* (p.184)

▶ Inputs to the quality planning process

Begin your quality planning by getting together the inputs. The quality plan will be part of the project plan, and quality management is an integral part of project management, so the project plan is an input: do not plan quality in isolation from the rest of the project plan. The scope statement is a vital input to quality planning, because if something is out of scope then you do not need to plan or manage its quality. For example, if the scope of a project to build a database is to build a proof of concept database which will not be used for operational purposes, then there may be a whole raft of quality requirements, for instance to do with longevity, maintainability and data security, which can be ignored. Continuing the example, there are many people in organizations whose job it is to enforce various IT standards on databases, and the quality plan coupled with the scope statement can be an effective way to communicate to them, in a professional and positive way, that in this project those standards and procedures can be ignored. Equally, when something is in scope, the consequential requirements for quality need to be understood and input to the quality planning process. So the scope statement is a key input to the quality planning process.

Figure 8.1 lists two other inputs to the quality planning process: enterprise environmental factors and organizational process assets. Organizational process assets are simply assets your organization has that may be useful as inputs to the quality planning process, such as the following:

- The organization's quality manual, quality plan, quality processes.
- Lessons learned from previous projects or other activities relevant to your project.
- In-house quality experts.
- In-house expertise related to key areas of your project.
- In-house manuals and procedures, including those specifying how your organization is to comply with regulatory and legal requirements.
- Databases and library documents containing standards, policies and procedures.

This input, organizational process assets, illustrates a general point, not just for quality planning but for project management too: do not make a long, expensive and bureaucratic affair out of it. Indeed, if you have to choose, choose too little rather than too much. Judgement and a sense of urgency and efficiency are indispensable; an unthinking rules-based approach is at most one step short of disaster. What does this mean? In respect of finding organizational process assets for use as inputs into quality planning, it means have a quick look around your organization for things that might be useful, and glance quickly through what you find to get a sense of whether it is likely to be useful to your particular project. The loss-making companies and failing government departments of the Western world are full of failed grey men – and they usually are men – who given half a chance will waste weeks and months on pointless documentation and regurgitation of irrelevant details and unnecessary process models. Don't get involved in them, and don't let them clog up your project. Have a quick look in the obvious places for input, do a quick assessment, and bend and adapt it to the needs of your project. Of course you should keep your sponsor informed of what you are doing, and enlist their help in deciding where to look for organizational process assets.

The final input is enterprise environmental factors. This cumbersome term means things like:

◆ Standards that you have to meet because they are mandated by a regulator, a law or an industry body.
◆ Other standard operating procedures and guidance specific to the application area of the project.
◆ Norms and generally expected standards in your organization, or of key stakeholders, which while not directly relevant to your project may create expectations or opportunities to shine for your project.

▶ Tools and techniques used in the quality planning process

Once you have gathered together your inputs you are ready to create your quality plan. The main tool is common sense, otherwise known as cost benefit analysis. There is no point doing quality management if the cost of doing it, in bureaucracy or whatever, exceeds the benefits. To take an example not from project management, if a fire breaks out, trapping you in your office, you want to use the fire extinguisher if there is one and try to escape immediately rather than hanging around conducting risk assessments and working out quality plans, because there is no benefit to doing them; the only possible benefit in that situation is to get you out of danger. That argument can be described as a cost benefit argument. A constant danger in real life where quality management is involved is that the costs of doing quality outweigh the benefits. It need not be so. It is your job as project manager to ensure that if there is a quality management aspect to your project it creates greater benefit than cost.

Do not be put off by the term 'cost benefit analysis'. It does not need special financial skill or complicated spreadsheets, or any spreadsheet at all. It can simply be a matter of writing out a few rows, one for each benefit of using quality management in your project, and describing in words the costs and benefits of so doing. Table 8.3 is an example, from a hypothetical project to build a database for managing legacy documents needed to investigate insurance claims.

Table 8.3 shows the cost benefit argument set out in a qualitative, but objective and verifiable way. Like any plan, the quality plan must have clear objectives, and these are called quality objectives. This is simply saying that you should be clear about what it is you are trying to achieve in quality. Table 8.3 is an example of how not all quality objectives are directly related to the customer. One of the quality objectives concerns the comfort and health and safety of the employees who will use the database. This may have an indirect effect on the end customer, but the primary effect is on the employees, to ensure that they have a comfortable and safe experience when inputting data into the database. This is a valid quality objective. Once you have a qualitative cost benefit case, such as the example in Table 8.3, you can extend it if necessary, and perhaps add more quantification.

Table 8.3 Example of cost benefit analysis in quality planning

Possible quality objective	Cost	Benefit	Comment
1 Contents of database should have same explicit and implicit structure and conventions as our other key corporate databases.	If we use our own staff: overtime costs, one day of training each, but some delay to project because of their limited availability. If we use temporary staff: contractor costs, two weeks of training plus background checks for each – a higher cost option.	1 Confidence that the data are structured and represented in a way that our organization and customers understand. 2 Reduced risk management and insurance costs.	Cost estimates derive from August pilot. Deciding factor is whether we can afford delay in project – right now stakeholders are saying we can.
2 Follow ISO 17799 for IT security.	Minimal. We work that way anyway. The only costs will be some extra documentation and auditing.	We have to do this to meet the requirements of our joint-venture partners, who are paying for the database.	Not a material cost.
3 Provide two large screens instead of a single standard-sized screen for each database user, to increase ease and comfort of use.	Initial, rough cost estimate is £15,000.	1 Improved ease of use: the August pilot showed very strong operator preference for two large screens. 2 Reduced risk of health and safety compensation costs arising from operators using small screens.	Less than 5% variance in cost, probable that benefits from faster working will more than recover this cost. Health and safety litigation risk is small, but last year we lost a similar case at a cost of over £1m. Probably worth going for double screens.

Key Idea

Quality objectives

Quality objectives should be written down. They need not be long, in fact, the shorter and simpler the better. They should be clear and SMART, that is:

S pecific,

M easurable,

A cheivable,

R ealistic – and with

T imings.

The other tools and techniques shown in Figure 8.1 for use in quality planning are essentially special kinds of cost benefit analysis, except that benchmarking can also help to generate options for quality objectives. Benchmarking means looking at what others are doing in the same or similar areas and how well they are doing it, so that you can try to match it. The underlying logic is that if someone else can do it, then you can too, potentially. Benchmarking applies to quality planning in two ways: you can find out what quality objectives others are working to, and you can find out what standards they are meeting or trying to meet for certain objectives. Remember that benchmarking can be both external, that is, against organizations other than your own, and internal, that is, against other parts of your own organization than the project you are managing.

Cost of quality is a refinement of the general cost benefit analysis. Suppose we are running a war and we are using jet aircraft to fight the war. The jet engines break because of quality problems, causing our aircraft to crash. We can (a) do nothing, and keep buying new jets and training new pilots, (b) redesign the jet engines so that they break less often, (c) increase our engineering and maintenance capability, so that we service the jet engines more often, (d) buy a whole set of new jet engines from Clockland, a neutral country with a great engineering tradition. Each of these options has different costs, which need to be judged against the cost of existing quality, that is the cost of keeping on buying new jets and training new pilots. This thinking may lead to generating another option – let us call it (a.i) – which is to buy better ejector seats and parachutes – perhaps we can live with the quality of the jet engines if we can stem the loss of pilots. Just as there is a cost structure in products and services and organizations, so there is a cost structure in quality, and one of the main benefits of the 'cost of quality' approach is that it helps us to understand the cost structure of quality. This enables us to generate options for planning quality.

There are many other techniques and tools that can be used in planning quality, such as design of experiments, linear programming, and brainstorming. Do not be constrained in what tools and techniques you use, be pragmatic: if you have a useful tool or technique, use it. Usually there will not be time to learn a new tool for your project. Use what you already know how to use, or, even better, delegate the task to experts on quality in your organization if they are available. Quality planning is no different from planning as practised in general management; it is merely planning techniques applied to the specific field of quality management. You are likely to find that the tools that are most effective for you are the ones you are already experienced in.

When planning quality, use objective, factual data as inputs to the planning process.

▶ Quality planning outputs

The main output of quality planning is the quality plan. This is not separate from the project plan, but is a section of it. Project planning is an iterative process, so you will start the quality planning process with a version of the project plan that has no section on quality management, and end up with an updated project plan that includes a section on quality. This section is the quality plan; they are not two different things.

Quality plans vary in size according to the size and type of project. A small simple project may have no quality plan or a plan of a few lines. Large complex projects in safety-critical environments may need large and complex quality plans. Even the shortest quality plan should include the following:

- Quality objectives for the project.
- A list of quality standards, tools or techniques to be used.
- A statement of how quality will be measured and what metrics will be used.

If the quality plan is anything more than the smallest kind, it should also include:

- Names of independent reviewers who will be reviewing quality.
- The approach that the project will take to quality assurance.
- The approach that the project will take to quality control.

In large or complex projects there can be great benefits to having peer or external reviews. Even if such reviews are intended to do no more than provide a fresh pair of eyes to look over certain aspects of what the project has done, this can be very valuable. Such reviews fall naturally under the heading of quality management. In some industries and companies external reviews are mandatory. Where there are to be such reviews, the quality plan should describe:

- How the external or peer review will work.
- The objectives of having a peer or external review.
- Its scope.
- Who will be doing the review.
- At what stage in the project it will be carried out.

Having set quality objectives, the project will need to measure performance against the objectives. If it can't be measured it won't be managed, as the saying has it. The quality plan should specify the metric to be used to measure quality. In the context of quality management a metric is a system of measurement. (Note that it is not the measurement itself.) An example of a metric is given by the following instructions:

At the end of the training course for inducting new staff onto the project, the instructor shall hand out the standard end-of-course questionnaire, read the class

the rubric printed on the top of the questionnaire, emphasizing the anonymous
natures of the questionnaire and feedback process, and ask the class to complete
the questionnaire and leave it in the sealed box before leaving the room.
The results will be collated and analyzed by the quality management
department and fed back to the instructors.

This example leaves much of the detail of the metrics implicit in terms such as 'standard … questionnaire', but for this organization it states what the metric is and how it will be deployed on the project. Another example is as follows:

After the final build, the database will be tested by BreakIT Corporation, Inc., the
independent software testing organization, who will perform stress and volume
testing on a Monte Carlo basis to determine the number of users at which perfor-
mance starts to degrade, and the quantitative profile of degradation, especially the
rate of increase in response time delays of entering new data and screen refreshes
with respect to the increase in number of users of (a) the main user screen at levels
of 50, 75 and 100 users, and (b) the data entry screen in the range from 20 to 60
users in five user increments. BreakIT will also record any other test results
that in their expert judgement are likely to be significant, and will produce
a written report of their test findings.

Quality metrics are an essential part of the quality plan. Other possible outputs of the planning process are checklists, a process improvement plan, and a quality baseline. Checklists are a simple but effective tool for improving quality, and are worth using wherever appropriate. Short, simple checklists are best. Where the project plan includes a section for the process improvement plan, updates to it should be an output from quality planning, but in practice this applies only to large and complex projects. The quality baseline is simply the baseline for quality, which is vital because otherwise the metrics will not have any practical meaning. Baselines can be very simple, for example: 'Baseline for SQEP project team members: In April 2006 at the start of the project two of 18 members of the project team had the skills and experience that will be necessary by the December 06 primary test target date.' Or, as an engineering example: 'Mean time between failures for the Mk.IX jet engine systems at the start of the project is 92 days; pilot death/downgrade rates from mid-air Mk.IX failure is 51%.' Both of these examples are baselines that enable improvement, or worsening, of quality to be measured.

▶ The difference between quality assurance and quality control

These are closely related but different. Assurance is primarily about the means by which the project expects to reach its quality requirements, and also about inspiring confidence in key stakeholders that they too can expect the project to do so. Control, on the other hand, is primarily about measuring and testing that those requirements are actually being reached, and interpreting such test and measurement results where quality is not as intended in order to determine the causes and thereby help to identify what can be done to fix quality. IBM describes the difference in the following way:

'Quality assurance focuses on process control and defect prevention activities. Quality control focuses on defect detection and correction activities'[5].

▶ Quality assurance

ISO says

Quality assurance

'Quality assurance: part of quality management focused on providing confidence that quality requirements will be fulfilled.' ISO 9000

PMI says

Quality assurance

'Quality Assurance (QA) is the application of planned, systematic quality activities to ensure that the project will employ all processes needed to meet requirements.' *PMBOK Guide* (p.187)

There are two distinct aspects to quality assurance. One is making sure that quality objectives are met; the other is about giving stakeholders confidence that they will be met. It is possible, but a bad idea, to fail to meet the quality objectives while inspiring confidence that they will be met – that would be nothing more than an old-fashioned confidence trick. Enron[6] became infamous for its skill in this mistaken use of quality assurance. A more honest kind of problem is where the project is meeting quality standards but key stakeholders do not recognize that to be the case. In such a situation, raising quality is not the answer, but communicating the quality that has already been achieved is. So key questions in quality assurance are:

◆ Are we meeting our quality objectives?
◆ And how do we know, and how confident are we in our answer to the previous question?
◆ Who needs to know that we are meeting them?
◆ Are they confident that we are meeting them or can meet them?
◆ If not, what do we need to do?

The 'How do we know?' and 'Are they confident?' questions, above, can be answered in terms of what processes are in place. This is the PMBOK approach, but not every organization or industry is suited to process-heavy thinking, and there are other ways to answer these questions than in terms of processes. For example, simple measurements and long-run histories of actual results may suffice.

▶ The quality assurance process

Figure 8.2 shows the quality assurance process and lists its inputs, tools and techniques, and outputs. Remember that there are two different but related aims in quality assurance: making sure that quality objectives are met, and giving stakeholders confidence that they will be met. The most important outputs of the

Fig. 8.2 The quality assurance process

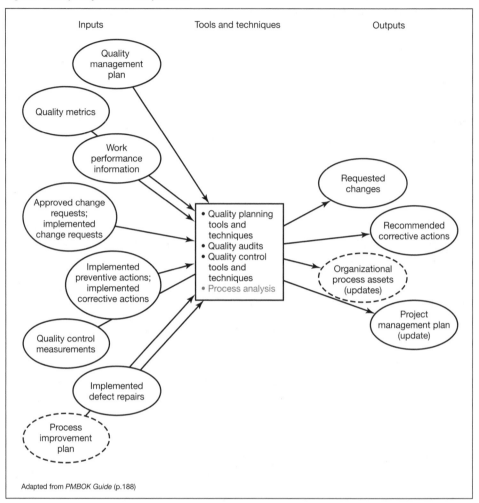

Adapted from *PMBOK Guide* (p.188)

quality assurance process from the point of view of making sure that quality objectives are met are the requested changes and the recommended corrective actions, as these are things that will improve quality. The project plan should also be updated as necessary as a result of the quality assurance process. These outputs can also serve the second aim of quality assurance, giving stakeholders confidence that quality objectives are being or will be met, but sometimes it is quickest and most effective simply to write a report entitled 'QA Report' or similar as an output aimed at this second end. An example of such a report is shown here.

Quality Assurance Report

Prepared for:	M. Ballon
By:	Local Moth Exterminator Co. SA
Date:	10 August 2007

Project Dark Shot

On 5 August 2007 the quality measures being collected by project Dark Shot for tolerance of sprocket manufacturing showed a negative variance against plan by 10% over the proportion of defects allowable in sprocket manufacture. The purpose of this report is to describe what has been discovered to date of the probable causes of this variance and to describe the corrective action planned to remedy the variance in Project Dark Shot.

The project's latest analysis of the defects shows the probable cause of variance as errors in communicating the acceptable tolerances to the Cato Manufacturing Company of Shanghai, subcontractors to the project. Specifically, the acceptable tolerance was specified in centimetres, but had been understood by Cato as a measurement in inches.

Two corrective actions have been initiated. First, the project has met the managers at Cato responsible for the supply of sprockets to the project and confirmed verbally and in writing that all project dimensions are in metric measurements, specifically centimetres unless otherwise specified. Secondly, the project and Cato are reviewing all measurements in the specifications to ensure that the right units of measure are in operation. This will be complete by the middle of next week, and the text of the subcontract will be changed to clarify that the unit of measure is a material item from then onwards. Costs of this variance are minimal so far, and Cato has agreed to bear them.

Local Moth Exterminator Co. SA
Paris

The quality audit is the main tool or technique in quality assurance, besides the quality planning ones, which will have been identified and put in place previously, in quality planning. The idea of an audit is simple, and it can be done very simply, but in real life the word 'audit' can have very negative connotations, and in some organizations the only way to get an audit of any kind – quality or other – done is to use some other word and pretend that it has nothing to do with auditing. The 'ISO says' box gives formal definitions to quality auditing and associated terms; do not worry too much about the qualifier 'independent' in the definition of 'quality audit'. There are degrees of independence from the project, the aim is not to achieve some mythical status of the remotest possible independence in your quality audit, but to achieve whatever degree of independence from you and the rest of the project team is enough to provide either useful information to you as the project manager and to the sponsor, to enable you to manage quality well, or, on the other hand, to be credible to stakeholders as being an objective view of things. Which of these should be the primary consideration will depend on which of the two related but different aims of quality assurance is more important at the time.

Either way, the audit needs audit criteria, and these should normally be the quality objectives, which you will have recorded in the plan. Remember, as we said in the section above on planning, you will probably not have to do or worry about most of this yourself as project manager: in most organizations of any size there will be a quality management staff who either can advise the project on quality management matters, or may even be able to take on responsibility for quality management. If so, the task of running quality audits is exactly the kind of thing in which they can be most valuable to the project.

ISO says

Quality audit and related terms
'Quality audit: systematic, independent and documented process for obtaining audit evidence and evaluating it objectively to determine the extent to which the audit criteria are fulfilled.' ISO 9000

'Audit evidence: statement of facts or other information which are relevant to audit criteria and verifiable.' ISO 9000

'Audit criteria: set of policies, procedures, or requirements used as reference.' ISO 9000

The most important output from the quality assurance process from the project's point of view is a request to change something, because that is how quality problems, indeed all problems, get fixed in a controlled way. Note that the output is a change request, not an actual change, because it should go into the change control process for the project rather than being implemented immediately. Is this bureaucratic? No, it should not be. To implement the change directly and bypass the project's change control process would be to create uncontrolled change, which means increasing risks. The project plan may also need to be updated to reflect the change recommended by the quality assurance process, and this is another output. Although it may not be important from the short-term view of the project, the organization in which the project sits is likely to value the lessons inherent in the recommended changes, which is another output.

▶ Quality control

As is the case for quality assurance, the requirements for quality control will be set out in the project quality plan. Quality control boils down to two questions:

◆ Is the project meeting quality requirements?
◆ If not, what should be done to fix it?

ISO says

Quality control
'Quality control: part of quality management focused on fulfilling quality requirements.' ISO 9000

PMI says

Perform quality control
'Perform Quality Control (QC) involves monitoring specific project results to determine whether they comply with the relevant quality standards and identifying ways to eliminate the cause of unsatisfactory results.' *PMBOK Guide* (p.366)

Fig. 8.3 The quality control process

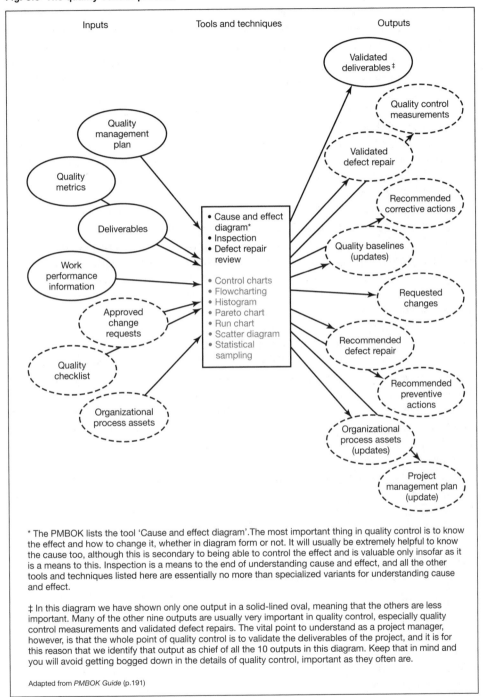

Inputs — Tools and techniques — Outputs

* The PMBOK lists the tool 'Cause and effect diagram'.The most important thing in quality control is to know the effect and how to change it, whether in diagram form or not. It will usually be extremely helpful to know the cause too, although this is secondary to being able to control the effect and is valuable only insofar as it is a means to this. Inspection is a means to the end of understanding cause and effect, and all the other tools and techniques listed here are essentially no more than specialized variants for understanding cause and effect.

‡ In this diagram we have shown only one output in a solid-lined oval, meaning that the others are less important. Many of the other nine outputs are usually very important in quality control, especially quality control measurements and validated defect repairs. The vital point to understand as a project manager, however, is that the whole point of quality control is to validate the deliverables of the project, and it is for this reason that we identify that output as chief of all the 10 outputs in this diagram. Keep that in mind and you will avoid getting bogged down in the details of quality control, important as they often are.

Adapted from *PMBOK Guide* (p.191)

Figure 8.3 shows the inputs, tools and techniques, and outputs for the quality control process. The quality plan and the quality metrics specified in it are of course key inputs to quality control: we have to know what we are to measure and how that fits in to what we want to achieve in quality. The quality checklists and our old friend 'organizational process assets' may also be inputs. If the project has reached that stage yet, then deliverables of course are key inputs, and in any case, information about how the project work is being performed will be an input. Approved change requests need to be inputs to ensure that the quality control process is operating on the project's performance as it actually is, rather than on an out-of-date picture of things.

As the narrative in Figure 8.3 says, the whole point of quality control is to validate the deliverables. The tools used in quality control all have this as their ultimate aim, which boils down to measuring various attributes of quality, and where these fall short of what is required, to gain an understanding of the cause and effect behind this state of affairs so that the project can correct things and achieve the planned level of quality.

Most of the tools and techniques listed in Figure 8.3 are primarily statistical and implicitly assume that the project is an engineering one where there is a wealth of data waiting to be captured. An ideal scenario for these tools is a project in a widget manufacturing company, with machines spewing out widgets, sprockets and furt-wanglers by the million, each with dimensions that can be measured quantitatively. If this is the case, and it often is in project management, then quality control should use statistical techniques in their fullest form. However, there are many projects where quality is important but is more qualitative. The retail experience felt by customers in new shops or on online websites, the emotional intensity of an advertisement, the similarity of a film sequel to the first film in the series, and the value to new hires of a graduate training programme are examples of other things that projects can be set up to achieve, but which are not, at first glance, as amenable to quantitative analysis as our widget manufacturing plant. However, if you understand the principles behind the statistical tools, you will find that the principles are just as applicable to these softer kinds of projects.

Figure 8.4 explains what a cause and effect diagram is and gives an example. This is a one of the most useful presentational tools in quality control, although of course it is not an analytical tool. An analytical QA tool that is not statistical is the flowchart. Figure 8.5 gives the standard symbology conventions for use in drawing flowcharts and Figure 8.6 illustrates their use with an example.

The analytical tools necessary for quality control are mainly statistical, and require a sound grasp of basic probability and statistics (to A-level in UK terms), including concepts such as the following:

◆ Randomness and random noise.
◆ Sampling and effects of sample size.
◆ Mean and standard deviation.
◆ Sensitivity.
◆ Regression testing.
◆ Measures of correlation.
◆ Dependent and independent variables.
◆ Type I and Type II errors.
◆ Degrees of confidence, confidence intervals and confidence limits.

Fig. 8.4 Cause and effect diagram (also known as a fishbone diagram), with example

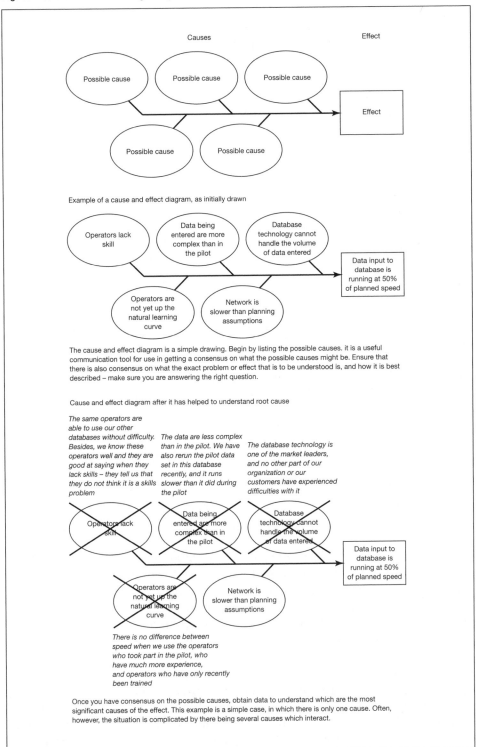

Fig. 8.5 Formal symbology conventions for use in flowcharts

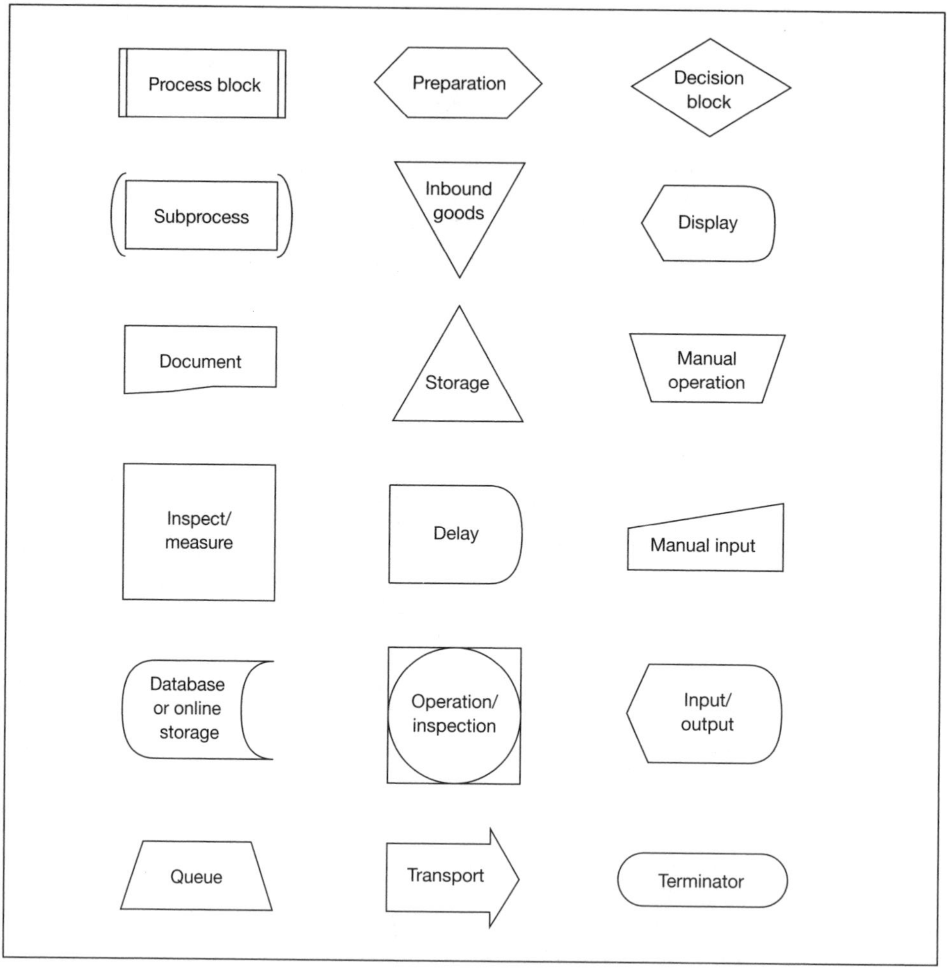

- ◆ Hypothesis testing.
- ◆ T-test.

Textbooks on project management tend to either ignore these statistical techniques entirely, or to give the impression that they are indispensable to project management. There is no shame in being intimidated as a project manager by some of the dry expositions of various statistical techniques on offer within the subject. The purpose of these techniques in quality control on project management is basically to help you understand what level of quality is being attained, and if there is a quality shortfall, to help decide what to do about it. If you are familiar with the necessary statistical theory, great. If not, there is probably not much point trying to pick up bits and pieces of statistical knowledge in a hurry. If you want to learn, an easy way is to confine yourself to what a spreadsheet program such as Microsoft Excel or Lotus 1-2-3 can do, and set yourself a goal of learning one new statistical function every day, or every week. Even more than skill in performing the calculations,

Fig. 8.6 Example of a flowchart, with formal symbols

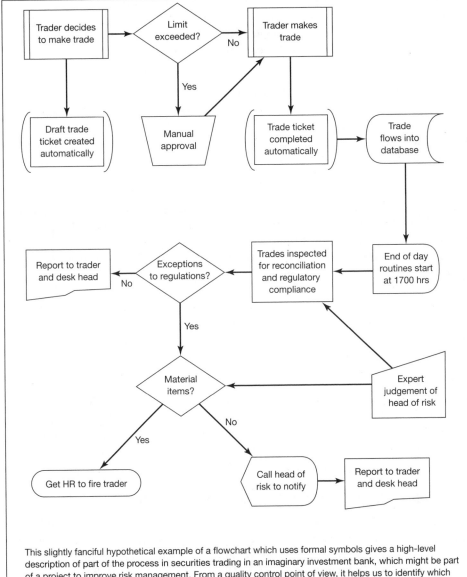

This slightly fanciful hypothetical example of a flowchart which uses formal symbols gives a high-level description of part of the process in securities trading in an imaginary investment bank, which might be part of a project to improve risk management. From a quality control point of view, it helps us to identify which parts of the process are associated with quality problems, or, if that is not yet clear, which parts of the process are and which are not understood, so that we can clarify our understanding where it is not clear, and probably thereby find the problem area. This example also illustrates one of the main drawbacks of flowcharts, which is that they can be messy and unless drawn carefully and using implicit conventions carefully (e.g. how much detail, whether to list all inputs) they may be too vague to help understand the QA problem much.

it is important that you understand the principles behind them, especially what kind of question each technique can answer and its limitations.

This book does not attempt to be a textbook on statistics, but as an example of the kind of thing you need to know in regard to the principles and limitations in statistical techniques, consider the mean and standard deviation. You need to know the following in order to be able to apply this tool to quality control:

◆ The mean is a kind of average, and as such indicates a typical value or set of data.

◆ The standard deviation is a measure of how close any individual datum in the set is to the average.

◆ The standard deviation (represented by the Greek letter σ, 'sigma') is also a measure of how close the set of data, or certain subsets of the data, are to the mean – or to put it another way, how similar or dissimilar the data within the set are to each other.

◆ The mean and standard deviation may not be useful tools unless there is only one characteristic being measured (in technical terms, that the data set is unimodal, not bimodal or multimodal).

◆ The standard deviation is a less and less reliable indicator of how spread out the data are the more unevenly balanced around the mean the set of data is (skewness).

◆ Many risky features of the natural world only follow the normal distribution when it does not really matter, and when it does really matter the normal distribution and standard deviation derived from it are about as useless as an ashtray on a motorbike, only with less resale value on eBay (leptokurtosis).

We will describe one more tool from the PMBOK's list before closing this section on the tools of quality control, and that is control charts. We describe it for two reasons. First, it features prominently in the PMI's exams, but secondly and more interestingly from the point of view of the practising project manager, the ideas behind it, if not the tool itself, are highly valuable in quality control and in general in thinking about project management.

▶ Control charts and the statistical concept of control

The common sense idea of control is all that we need to understand the advanced statistical concepts of control, and it is also, for sound common sense reasons, fundamental to quality control and more generally to quality management in project management. 'Is this project under control?' is the first thing that top management will want to know should a project that one of their subordinates is sponsoring be brought to their attention. There is an obvious difference between a project which is doing badly but which is nonetheless under control, and one which is doing badly and is out of control. Out of control projects often get cancelled, because they need to be to protect the rest of the organization. An out of control project can bring down not just companies, but governments too. Given its significance in plain old common sense thinking, it is not surprising that control has been identified as a vital factor in the health of projects[7].

PMI says

Control

'Control (Technique). Comparing actual performance with planned performance, analyzing variances, assessing trends to effect process improvements, evaluating possible alternatives, and recommending corrective action as needed.' *PMBOK Guide* (p.355)

We may define a project as being in control (Figure 8.7) if all of the following conditions are met:

◆ The sponsor and project manager share the same understanding of what the critical success factors for the project are.
◆ After the initiation phase, there is a project plan, and progress against the plan is being measured regularly, and material variances are both recognized and acted upon to close the gap between the plan and results.
◆ After the initiation phase, there are no changes to the scope of the project that do not go through the integrated change control process.
◆ The sponsor and project manager believe that the project's deliverables are attainable within 10% of planned time and cost – and a reasonable person would agree with them.
◆ There have been no more than two major risks or major unplanned events in the project recently ('major' means 10% of budget or similar, 'recently' means 20% of the total timescale of the project).

The idea of control can be refined in many projects to a point where measurement of some attribute of a deliverable or a process will indicate objectively whether the deliverable or process is in control. In a 10-year project to build a new aircraft, if the actual costs exceed the estimated costs every single month, then we would have little difficulty in saying that costs were out of control, for example. We can extend the idea

Fig. 8.7 Example of a control chart, of a process in control

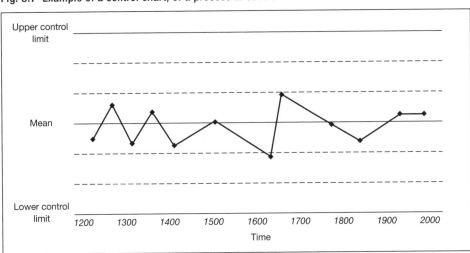

illustrated in that example by using a few elementary statistical tools to build a control chart. Figure 8.8(a) is an example of a control chart 'in control'.

The purpose of a control chart is to give a graphical representation showing whether or not a process or set of deliverables is in control. There are two indicators of being out of control; both are described above. Where do the upper and lower control limits come from? These are defined either arbitrarily, for example a

Fig. 8.8 Control charts: (a) in control; (b) two ways to be out of control

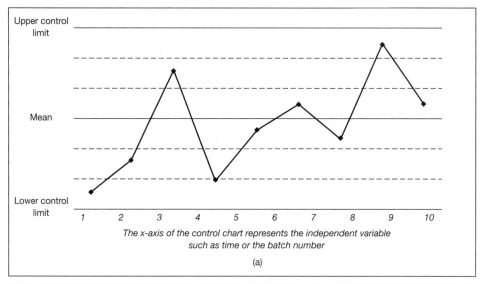

The x-axis of the control chart represents the independent variable such as time or the batch number

(a)

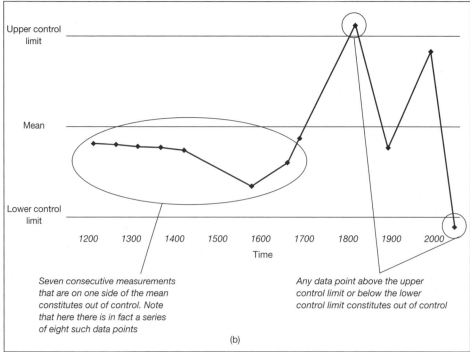

Seven consecutive measurements that are on one side of the mean constitutes out of control. Note that here there is in fact a series of eight such data points

Any data point above the upper control limit or below the lower control limit constitutes out of control

(b)

company may decide that for project costs, a variance of ±10% is acceptable, and anything in excess is out of control, or by some statistical formula, for example by defining anything beyond five sigma or six sigma (five or six times the standard deviation) as being out of control. Note that some other term than 'out of control' may be used, for example 'unacceptable' or 'to be escalated' – but for the purposes of quality control the operative concept is that of control. Why are seven consecutive points on the same side of the mean taken as an indicator of being out of control? Seven points is a convention, but it is based on the idea that we should normally expect measurements to fluctuate around the mean in a random walk, and seven consecutive points on one side suggests that there is a significant non-random factor present. Much of the time it is reasonable to take seven points as an indicator of a control problem (the PMI exams require you to know this). However, there may be cases where this rule of thumb can be changed, for example to consider only a run of data points on one side of the mean, or some number less than seven[8]. Figure 8.8(b) shows two ways to be 'out of control'.

The two main outputs from the quality control process are quality control measurements and, where relevant, validated defect repairs. Updates to the baselines and recommendations for preventive and corrective actions and for changes and defect repairs may also be important outputs, depending on the nature of the project. The full set of possible outputs is given in Figure 8.3.

▶ Summary

Quality is conformance to requirements. The formal ISO and PMBOK definition is 'the degree to which a set of inherent characteristics fulfils requirements'. A project or its deliverables can fail to meet a quality objective in three ways:

- Quality is too low.
- Quality is too high.
- Quality is too variable.

There are three processes within project quality management:

- Quality planning.
- Perform quality assurance.
- Perform quality control.

The purpose of quality management is to add value by explicitly building into your project the idea of quality. This means having a plan for quality and then working to the plan, making adjustments along the way as necessary. In one way, this is no more than common sense, as is the notion of quality; the value of making quality an explicit part of project management is that it can reduce costs and risks and increase value to do so.

Like finance and risk, quality is a sub-discipline of general management with its own distinct tools and techniques. Central to quality management is the quality plan. This should state clearly what the quality objectives for the project are, and how they will be achieved. Key inputs to the plan are the project plan and the scope statement. The quality planning process should consider options for quality objectives, make a selection on the basis of cost benefit tools and techniques, and show how the objectives will be achieved. Being seen to achieve the objectives is as important as achieving them, which is called quality assurance. Quality assurance is about inspiring confidence that quality standards will be met. Quality control, in contrast, is about actually meeting them. Both quality assurance and quality control are essential in quality management, and both depend on having done quality planning.

▶ Further reading

The ISO 9000 and related series, available by electronic download from www.iso.ch, is the definitive reference material for the ISO 9000 quality standard, much of which can be valuable in projects. The elements in the series that are most relevant to project quality management are:

◆ ISO 9000 Quality management systems – Fundamentals and vocabulary
◆ ISO 10005 Quality management systems – Guidelines for quality plans.

The following in the ISO 9000 series may be highly relevant to some projects:

◆ ISO 9001 Quality management systems – Requirements
◆ ISO 9004 Quality management systems – Guidelines for performance improvements.

All ISO standards are published by the International Organization for Standardization in Geneva, Switzerland.

See also the following books:

◆ Coram, R., 2002. *Boyd: The Fighter Pilot who Changed the Art of War*. New York: Little Brown.
◆ Crosby, P. B., 1979. *Quality is Free*. New York: New American Library.
◆ Deming, W. E., 1982. *Out of the Crisis*. New York: Cambridge University Press.
◆ Harry, M. and Schroeder, R., 2000. *Six Sigma*. New York: Random House.
◆ Imai, M., 1986. *Kaizen: The Key to Japan's Competitive Success*. New York: McGraw-Hill.
◆ Ishikawa, K., 1986. *Guide to Quality Control*. Quality Resources.
◆ Juran, J.M., 1992. *Juran on Quality by Design: The New Steps for Planning Quality into Goods and Services* (revised edition). New York: Free Press.

For a quite different view of the Six Sigma movement, see Marsh, Peter, 'When boring beats buccaneering', *Financial Times*, London, 7 June 2006. This is an interview with David Farr, chief executive of Emerson. It can be downloaded from www.ft.com; payment may be necessary.

Notes

1 *International Standard ISO 9000:2000(E)*, 2nd edition, International Organization for Standardization, Geneva, 2000.
2 *PMBOK*, 3rd edition, p. 180.
3 *Defence Standard 05-97*, Issue 2, Ministry of Defence, London, 2002.
4 IBM defines quality this way in some cases: 'Quality can be defined as: conformance to specified requirements, and meeting of customers' expectations.' From IBM Global Services internal paper, 'Quality Plan for Application Domain', Unique ID APP 134, version 3.0, January 2000.
5 IBM Global Services internal paper, 'Quality Plan for Application Domain', Unique ID APP 134, version 3.0, January 2000.
6 Much has been written about the collapse of Enron and its fraudulent officers. One concise article is Jopson, B. 'Accounting for Capitalism after Enron'. *Financial Times*, September 2006. www.ft.com
7 See, for example: *Driving the Successful Delivery of Major Defence Projects: Effective Project Control is a Key Factor in Successful Projects*, The Comptroller and Auditor General, 2005. (Presented to the House of Commons, under Section 9 of the National Audit Act, 1983.)
8 In a random distribution around a mean, there is a 50% chance of any data point being either greater or less than the mean (assuming for convenience that the mean is not itself attainable). The chance of seven data points all lying on the same side of the mean is $(50\%)^6 = 1.5625\%$ (half to the sixth and not the seventh power, because the first of the seven points is a given, i.e. 100% probability; it is the joint probabilities of the next six points all being on the same side that we want).

people management (human resources)

1
2
3
4
5
6
7
8
9
10
11
12
13

▶ Aims of this chapter

People matter. They matter especially in project management, as we shall see. This chapter is about managing the people side of projects, particularly the administration of people – managing people is the central task of management generally, but the administration of people is vital to morale and getting the job done. Administration can be boring at times, but that does not mean it is unimportant. Just try not paying employees and see how long they hang around if you want to test that claim. The aims of this chapter are to:

◆ show why HR management is important in project management;
◆ describe what it is;
◆ enable you to plan and manage the four HR management processes;
◆ identify the key tensions in HR management.

Fig. 9.1 The two great dynamics in project HR management

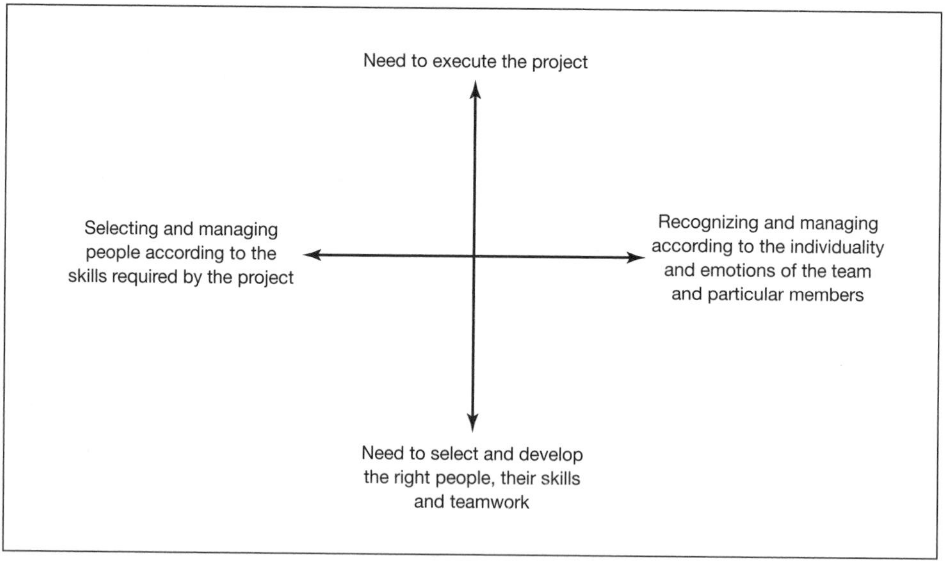

▶ People matter

The diagram in Figure 9.1 shows the two great tensions faced when trying to manage the people side of projects, between getting on with the project and training the project team on the one hand, and on the other between managing people systematically according to objective measures of skills and managing people by playing on emotions and other vital aspects of what makes us human rather than machines. The knowledge area of project HR management contains the tools and techniques needed to manage these tensions efficiently. People do projects, not charts, software, machines or methodologies – and because of this fundamental truth any of the following can transform a perfectly doable project into failure or at best a project over time and budget:

◆ Having the wrong people
◆ Having the right people but not having them working together sufficiently as a team
◆ Having the right people but without having developed their skills adequately.

Project HR management processes

There are four processes in project HR management, which fall into process groups as shown in Table 9.1.

Table 9.1 Four project HR management processes

| | | Process Group | | |
Initiating	Planning	Executing	Monitoring and controlling	Closing
	1 HR planning	2 Acquire project team 3 Develop project team	4 Manage project team	

◆ HR planning is about determining project roles and responsibilities, at the individual level and at the level of how they fit together into a team.
◆ Acquire project team is about getting the right people for the project on board the project.
◆ Develop project team is about taking the individuals acquired by the project in the last process, and improving their individual skills and their ability to work as a team, as appropriate to the project.
◆ Manage project team is about applying the OODA loop (that is, applying a feedback loop – see pages 66–7) to improve individual and team performance in the context of the project and also the organization to which the team members belong.

Key Idea

Managing people
People do projects, and only people. Software, methodologies, and everything else apart from people do not get projects done. People do. So managing people is right at the heart of project management.

▶ HR planning

Human resource planning occurs during the planning phase of the project lifecycle. It is during this process that the project manager identifies the HR requirements for the project. These requirements will include the roles and responsibilities, reporting relationships and a staffing management plan. Figure 9.2 shows the planning process group to have three inputs, three tools and techniques and three outputs. The three inputs to this process group should by now be familiar to you: enterprise environmental factors, organizational process assets, and the project management plan. However, as with all the knowledge areas, different aspects of each input are brought into play for different knowledge areas.

Fig. 9.2 The HR planning process

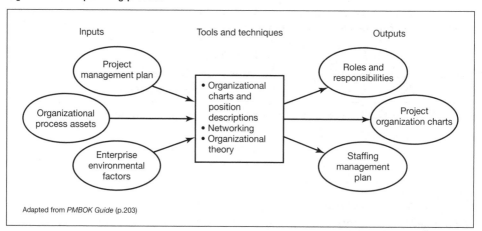

Adapted from *PMBOK Guide* (p.203)

PMI says

Enterprise environmental factors

'Enterprise Environmental Factors. These factors are from any or all of the enterprise involved in the project, and include organizational culture and structure, infrastructure, existing recourses, commercial databases, market conditions and project management software.' *PMBOK Guide* (p.360)

As we have seen before, enterprise environmental factors are any external environment or internal organizational factors that may affect the delivery of the project. In many processes they are 'nice to have' rather than absolutely necessary inputs to the process. However, in the HR processes, and especially in HR planning, it is vital to consider this input, especially legal and regulatory requirements and any that affect morale. The same goes for organizational process assets and HR management processes.

Templates and checklists are particularly useful in HR planning. They can be used to help identify core competency requirements of team members or could show the organizational chart.

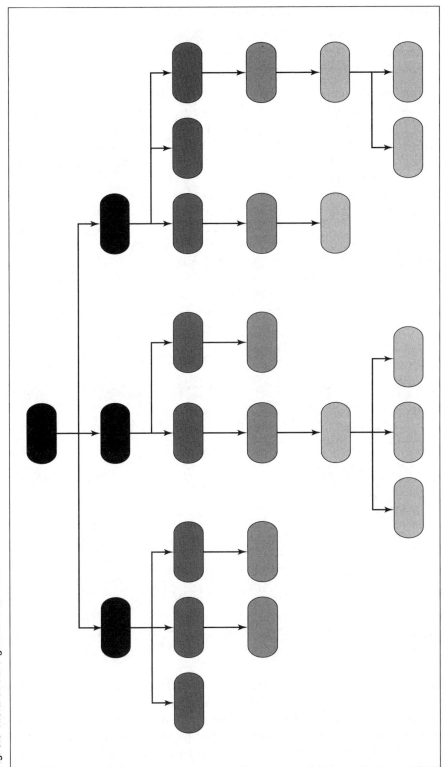

Fig. 9.3 Hierarchical organizational chart

There are three tools and techniques applicable in the HR planning process:

◆ Organizational charts and position descriptions
◆ Networking
◆ Organizational theory.

There are many ways to depict the structure of an organization using organizational charts and position descriptions. There are three main types of organizational charts. Figure 9.3 shows an example of the hierarchical-type charts that are considered to be traditional organizational charts. This has the head of the organization, function, department or group at the top, and their direct reports feeding into them in a top-down diagram.

Figure 9.4 illustrates matrix-based charts, which are best exemplified by the responsibilities matrix. A responsibility matrix lays out the major activities in the project and specifies the responsibilities of each stakeholder involved in a project. It is an important project communication tool because all stakeholders can see clearly who to contact for each activity. Text-oriented formats can be used to provide detailed written descriptions of a team member's roles and responsibilities. Some roles and responsibilities are outlined in other sections of the project management plan. For example, the risk and issue logs will identify the risk and issue owners.

Fig. 9.4 A matrix-based responsibility chart

Activity	Person				
	Abel	Bunty	Casimir	Deepak	Eli
Define requirements	R	A	I	C	I
Design prototype	A	R	I	C	I
Create prototype	I	A	C	R	C
Test prototype	I	R	I	A	C

PMI says

Networking
'Networking. Developing relationships with persons who may be able to assist in the achievement of objectives and responsibilities.' *PMBOK Guide* (p.365)

The second tool or technique is networking. Networking can be done within an organization or external to it, such as at conferences or trade fairs. Networking is generally considered to be an informal affair, and can include lunches, correspondence and conversation. The third and final tool is organizational theory. This is able to provide 'information regarding the ways that people, teams, and organizational units behave. Applying proven principles shortens the amount of time needed to create the human resource planning outputs and improves the likelihood that the planning will be effective' (PMBOK). What does this mean in real life? Very simply, if you are experiencing organizational projects in your team, go and read up on the latest theories: do a Google search of a reputable organizational behaviour site, buy a book on organizational behaviour, or talk to an organizational psychologist. Your aim should not be to become an expert – that is not your job – but to use any existing tools or techniques to solve the problem in your team.

The roles and responsibilities developed during human resource planning should describe the role, the authority level of the person, their responsibilities and the competency required to complete the project activities. The project organizational chart will represent graphically the project team members and their reporting lines. The final output, the staffing management plan, forms part of the project management plan. It is usual for the staffing management plan to include the following:

- ◆ Staff acquisitions processes.
- ◆ Timetables for staffing requirements.
- ◆ Criteria for the release of staff from the project.
- ◆ Staff training needs.
- ◆ Recognition and rewards criteria.
- ◆ Compliances strategies.
- ◆ Health and safety policies and procedures.

Acquire the project team

Figure 9.5 shows the process group for acquiring the project team. The inputs to this process are the organizational process assets, enterprise environmental factors

Fig. 9.5 The acquire project team process

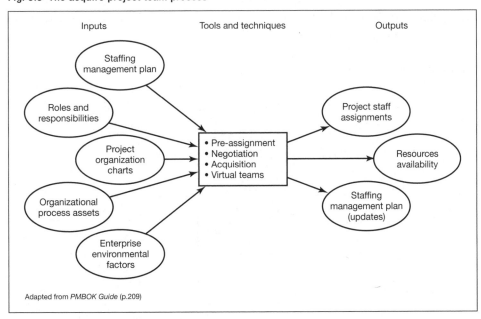

Adapted from *PMBOK Guide* (p.209)

and the three outputs from the human resources planning process: roles and responsibilities, project organization charts, and staffing management plan.

There are four tools and techniques to use during this process. The first technique is pre-assignment. This is where project team members know in advance that they are to work on the project. This often occurs when specific individuals are committed to the project as part of a competitive pitch. The second technique is negotiation. Often the process of acquiring team members requires the project manager to compete for key personnel. Negotiation may occur between competing projects or with functional managers. It is often the project manager's influence within an organization that results in obtaining the required people. The third technique is acquisition. This technique is used when there is no internal resource to fulfil an aspect of the project. The project manager can choose to hire a new employee, engage consultants or sub-contract the work out. The final tool is the use of virtual teams.

PMI says

Virtual teams

'Virtual Teams. Groups of people with a shared goal, who fulfil their roles with little or no time spent meeting face-to-face. The availability of electronic communication, such as e-mail and video conferencing, has made such teams feasible.' *PMBOK Guide* (p.379)

▶ Develop the project team

It is the project manager's responsibility to develop the project team. At the start of a project it is often the case that the team may not have worked together before. The project manager must ensure that the team develops into a group of individuals capable of delivering the project on time, on budget and on scope. The develop project team process is shown in Figure 9.6.

Fig. 9.6 The develop project team process

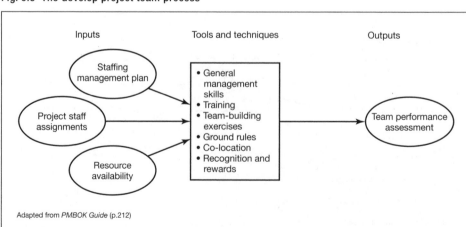

Adapted from *PMBOK Guide* (p.212)

PMI says

Training

'Training. All activities designed to enhance the competencies of the project team members.' *PMBOK Guide* (p.213)

Training can be provided formally, such as obtaining certification, or informally, such as ad-hoc coaching sessions. The third technique is team-building activities. Team-building activities can vary enormously, ranging from a weekly team meeting to a team awayday. Project tasks can also be used for team building, such as the development of the work breakdown structure. The fourth tool is ground rules. It is imperative that the standards for acceptable behaviour are established at the start of the project. In fact the development of the ground rules can be a team-building exercise in the form of a workshop. The project manager must ensure that the team understand not only the rules but also the shared responsibility of enforcing them.

The fifth technique is the co-location of a team. This involves ensuring as many team members as possible are based, ideally, in the same room. If this is not possible, co-location on the same floor or in the same building will often suffice. If it is not possible to have the team in the same building, such as in a multi-country project, other methods must be thought of. One way to achieve this is by the creation of team pages on the organization's intranet. Another is the creation of virtual teams, making the most of novel technology, such as video conferencing and instant messaging.

The sixth and final tool is recognition and rewards. This technique identifies and provides incentives for desirable conduct throughout the project. It is important to reward only good behaviour; for example, working weekends to ensure a software product is ready for the publicized launch date is worth rewarding if the schedule was tight. It is not worth rewarding if the programmer was often absent without notice and was using the weekends to catch up on work. The PMI makes a clear distinction between win–lose and win–win rewards.

PMI says

Win–win versus win–lose

'Win–Lose rewards that only a limited number of project team members can achieve, such as team member of the month, can hurt team cohesiveness. Rewarding Win–Win behaviour that everyone can achieve, such as turning in progress reports on time, tends to increase support among team members.' *PMBOK Guide*

There is only one output from this process – the team performance assessment. As the project team develops, their performance should increase. The performance assessment will evaluate the team's effectiveness by looking at various performance indicators, such as increased productivity, improved competencies, and reduced staff turnover.

▶ Manage the project team

The last process group in this knowledge area is to manage the project team. This process is illustrated by Figure 9.7. This process is concerned with more than just assigning work and telling the team members to go and do it. It involves monitoring the team members' performances, providing feedback, solving problems, managing change, and updating the staffing plan, issue logs, and lessons learned.

Fig. 9.7 The manage project team process

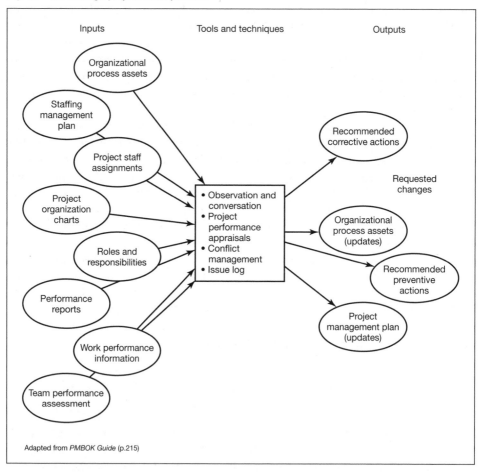

Adapted from *PMBOK Guide* (p.215)

There are eight inputs to this process, all of which have been discussed in either this or previous chapters of the book. They are organizational process assets, project staff assignments, roles and responsibilities, project organization charts, the staffing management plan, team performance assessment, work performance information, and performance reports.

There are four tools and techniques for this process group. Observation and conversation is the first. The project manager uses this technique to understand the mood of the team and to influence them. For example, the project manager may look to see whether a sense of pride arises from meeting a difficult target, or look for interpersonal difficulties between team members. The second tool is project performance appraisals. This is the process by which team members are given feedback on their performance in the project. A popular style of feedback is '360 degree feedback' where an individual is given feedback by a wide range of people, including superiors, peers and direct reports.

The third technique is conflict management. Projects can be particularly stressful environments – doing something new, often to a tight budget and deadline. As such, conflicts are likely to arise. It is up to the project manager to address conflict early. The PMI suggests that the project manager does so in private, using a direct and collaborative approach. Formal conflict resolution procedures should be used only when informal ones fail. However, it is advisable to distribute the formal procedures in outline before the start of the project to enable all team members to have the opportunity to understand them.

The fourth and final tool is the issue log. Issues arise throughout the life of a project and it is extremely advisable to keep a record of them. This enables the issues to be managed in a coordinated way. The information recorded about an issue may include the name of the issue, who it was raised by, the severity of the issue, such as high, medium or low, the issue owner, the status of the issue, and the course of action identified to resolve the issue.

There are five outputs from this process. They are requested changes, recommended corrective actions, recommended preventive actions, updates to the organizational process assets, and updates to the project management plan.

▶ Summary

Projects get done by people, not by tools or techniques or technology. People management, also known as human resources (HR) management, is therefore vital. One of the key differences between professional organizations and small, growth-constrained ones is that the professional organizations select and appoint people according to skills and ability. However, there is a tension between the rationalist approach to HR management, which tries to match the skills and abilities needed to those available in employees, and the emotional side of management. The tools and techniques in project HR management will help you manage this tension.

There are four processes within this knowledge area, starting with planning, in which you plan what people will be needed and how you will develop them as a team and individuals in accordance with the needs of the project and the organization. The other processes are to acquire the project team, develop it and then manage it.

▶ **Further reading**

Bacharach, S.B., 2005. *Get Them on Your Side. Improve Efficiency and Get Things Done.* Avon, MA: Platinum Press.

Blau, P., 1964. *Exchange and Power in Social Life.* New York: John Wiley & Sons.

Buchanan, D. and Huczynski, A., 2003. *Organizational Behaviour: An Introductory Text* (5th edn). New York: Financial Times/Prentice Hall.

Dessler, G., 2004. *Human Resource Management* (10th edn). New York: Financial Times/Prentice Hall.

Fritz, R., 1998. *Corporate Tides: The Inescapable Laws of Organizational Structure.* San Francisco: Berrett-Koehler.

Harrison, M.I., 1994. *Diagnosing Organizations: Methods, Models and Processes (Applied Social Research Methods).* Newbury Park, CA: Sage Publications.

Senge, P.M., 1993. *The Fifth Discipline: Art and Practice of the Learning Organization.* London: Century Business.

Woods, C., 2003. *Everything You Need to Know at Work: A Complete Manual of Workplace Skills.* Harlow: Prentice Hall.

project communications
management

Why communication is important in projects

Some problems of project communication

Ten principles of project communication

A systematic approach to communications mangement

> Communication is the real work of leadership. Nitin Nohria

> The more elaborate our means of communication, the less we communicate. Joseph Priestley

▶ Aims of this chapter

It can be that half or even more of your time as project manager needs to be spent on communication.

This chapter is about how to communicate for your project. That means communicating both within the project team, and also to others outside the project team. There is a view that communication is a less important skill than planning and doing project management. This is not so. If you communicate badly, your project will fail. This is because you will not have discovered all stakeholders, analyzed their needs, and got them on your side. Your project won't have traction with them.

Communication skills can be used immorally as in political spin, but that is not what this chapter is about. Communication is a vital skill, and your stakeholders and your project team deserve decent communication.

By the end of this chapter, you should be able to:

◆ explain why communication is important in project management;
◆ state the tensions that exist in communication;
◆ state the principles of good project communication;
◆ plan communication for your project;
◆ create a stakeholder management plan;
◆ distribute the right information about your project to the right people at the right time.

▶ Why communication is important in projects

> No decision is difficult to make if you will get all of the facts. General Patton

Communication is important in project management because it is fundamental to leadership and management in general, not just in projects. Management's only output is decisions. Decisions can be made well only if they are based on facts, including facts about the opinions of others. Hence communication is fundamental to management, and hence Patton's quote, above. There are special problems arising from the nature of projects in how to communicate, but the reason why communication is important is not specific to projects. However, in terms of your project, communication management is vital for the following reasons:

- Often the demand for reports about the project is large and eats up much of the project manager's time, so anything that can be done to manage this demand helps the project manager.
- People will not understand the project and support it if they do not know about the project, what it is, and what's in it for them.
- As project manager your credibility and power depend upon others understanding that you are competent, for which they need some basis.
- Good communication helps build the project team and its morale, and thus helps to get things done.
- Assumptions in the project plan will change with time, and keeping abreast of changes and adapting the plan and managing the project to cope with changes depends on receiving those changes.
- Your project competes for time and attention with other projects and claims on people's time and attention, so communication keeps your project in people's minds.
- How something is communicated ('bedside manner') is as important as what is communicated – get the 'how' wrong and good news about your project can have the same effect as bad, or, conversely, get the 'how' right and the effects of bad news can be minimized.
- Communication is time consuming and expensive, so make sure the costs are directed as efficiently as possible.

Key Idea

Communication
The ability to communicate effectively is at least as important as technical skill. Communication involves both transmitting a clear message, and listening effectively.

Some problems of project communication

Communication is important but often difficult, again not just in projects but generally. The difficulties arise mainly from six tensions, shown in Table 10.1.

We are not going to give you a recipe for managing these tensions. Sometimes they cannot be managed, and what is required of the project manager is a firm decision on which way to go on one of these tensions. Working through these kinds of tensions is what management is about, and the key thing is to recognize such tensions.

These tensions are more acute in project management than in other work for three reasons, first because of the time pressure in projects; secondly because of the temporary nature of the organization, which means that those communicating have less opportunity to get to know each other; and thirdly, often the stakeholders change or change in importance as the project progresses, which means that communication strategies and plans may in turn need revising.

Table 10.1 Six sources of tension in communication

The need to communicate the complete story or situation	*versus*	The need to be brief
The need to tailor the message to the audience, and to simplify	*versus*	The duty to be open and honest
The need to treat all stakeholders fairly	*versus*	Competing needs and expectations among stakeholders and the need to release some information over time
The need to listen	*versus*	Time constraints and the need to correct at times
Demand for information now, and for a great deal of it	*versus*	The need to release some information over time, and time taken to understand, verify and digest information
The value of showing certainty and clarity in communication	*versus*	The value of a thorough understanding of the subject of communication, which means tolerating ambiguity and shades of grey

▶ Ten principles of project communication

Experience shows that there are 10 principles of communication that a project manager should follow. They are no more than common sense, and most project managers and most managers generally know that these are good communication principles. Following them in the heat of the moment and under time pressure in projects is another thing. The 10 principles are:

1 Know your audience.
2 Know what you are talking about.
3 Pick the right medium for the audience.
4 Recognize tensions in the needs to communicate.
5 Work with the sponsor.
6 Test and adjust.
7 If your message can be misunderstood, it will be.
8 Plan and rehearse.
9 Let people know what is going on, especially your sponsor.
10 Listen and ask questions – understand that communication is two-way.

▶ Know your audience

You would not run a workshop for a board of directors in the same way that you would for entry-level staff in a call centre or for new recruits for the checkout tills at a supermarket. Different audiences have different needs. Who are you communicating to? What is their average age, level of experience in their industry, and knowledge of your project? What do they expect and how do they prefer communication? How educated are they? These are the kinds of questions you must have a feel for.

In the public service senior managers like every communication to be formally documented so that there is an audit trail, because their environment and legal responsibility give them an incentive to want that. The electorate wants it too when there is a mistake or simply an Act of God without a mistake. Investment bank directors, on the other hand, tend to prefer communication that is fast, dense in content and informal – they are free of public accountability and the shareholders to whom they are accountable work through a management chain that relies on judgement.

A key part of knowing your audience is to know their emotions. We are all emotional, every single one of us. Understand the emotions of the people you are dealing with and learn to work with them, not against them. Patton had this to say about emotions in communication:

> It is an unfortunate fact that few commanders, and no politicians, realize the individuality of units and the necessity of playing on human emotion. Speaking of this reminds me that [General Willard S.] Paul once told me, with perfect sincerity, that the greatest moment of his life had been at the Battle of the Bulge when I put my arm around him and said 'How is my little fighting son of a bitch today?' He said that this remark inspired not only him, but every man in the division, and it is highly probable that it did. General Patton

▶ Know what you are talking about

As a project manager you will not be an expert on the subject matter covered in all areas of your project. You lead a team. Often the team members will know more than you on a subject. Where you must be the most knowledgeable is in what is happening in your project, what the plan is, whether there are any gaps between the two and if so how they arose and how they can be addressed. Make sure you know that and can communicate about it, to anyone who asks. So rehearse in your mind, on the way to work every day, what words you will use if you meet the chief executive in the lift and they say 'So – how is the project?'.

What should you say in such circumstances? An answer along the lines of 'Oh, it's OK' gets *nul points*, as they say in the Eurovision Song Contest. If the project is OK, you need to be able to say 'The project is largely on plan. There are some minor slippages but they are not material. We made the pilot test milestone last Friday, 120 users for two hours, with results 7% above planned. The next milestone is in 5 weeks time, in the week before the holiday, and we are on track for that. Are there any particular details you would like to know about?'. Or, if the project is not OK, you need to be able to say something along the lines of 'The project went from green to amber last Friday when we failed to make the test milestone, because only 70 of the 120 planned test users took part in the pilot, which meant the results are unreliable. We are planning a rerun this Friday, subject to final confirmation from Procurement. If we miss that, the project will be downgraded from amber to red. A note to all staff from you would really help us get the extra bodies we need – may I draft a suitable paragraph and send it to you for your consideration?'.

If you don't know what you are talking about, you will not be credible. You must know the things you are expected to know as project manager. For everything else, if you don't know, say so, and make sure you know who it is in your team who does know. If you are asked something that is out of scope, rather than waste time, find a polite way of telling them that it is out of scope.

▶ Pick the right medium for the audience

Different people understand things in different ways. It's no use talking about the vastness of the ocean to someone who has lived all their life in a desert if you want to convey a sense of space – talk about the vastness of the sky or the desert instead. And although a vegetarian chef might understand you if you describe how to roast duck, you are likely to get more of their attention focused on what you are saying if you stick to something vegetarian. Pick the right medium for the audience.

The CEO, for example, is always short of time and is likely to be very quick on the uptake. A brief to them can use a wide variety of language for maximum impact in a short time. Technical specialists may be just as intelligent as the CEO, but can be much more concerned with detail, and uncomfortable going too quickly. You may need to prepare a more detailed presentation for them (not prepare more quickly, which is something else). And finally, consider an audience that swears often. The use of coarse language is often said to be a sign of a poor vocabulary. However, there is little point using your master's level vocabulary if your audience's normal conversational style is to have an expletive for every third word. Know your audience and adapt your style for them. This does not mean swearing every third word if they do, but it does mean simplifying your language and using examples to illustrate your message that will be familiar to them.

▶ Recognize tensions in the needs to communicate

What if your audience contains both the CEO and the rest of the organization, technical specialists and those that use an expletive for every third word? You can't split them up and give three different presentations, nor should you. This is an example of tension in the need to communicate. There are no rules other than know your audience and use your common sense to make a reasonable compromise in your communication piece. Other common sources of tension are between:

◆ short-term versus longer-term needs.
◆ different stakeholders' needs.
◆ different sponsors.
◆ suppliers versus customers.
◆ client-facing versus back-office staff.
◆ sales versus marketing.
◆ compliance staff versus those regulated.

Often these tensions are not fully soluble, but you must at the very least recognize them. The two biggest tensions are the first two in our list. An example of long term versus short term is that some information needs to be kept secret in the short term, and you must be trustworthy and discreet enough to be able to manage such information. As Rudyard Kipling said, 'Most of the Arts admit the truth that it is not expedient to tell everyone everything …'.

Work with the sponsor

All communication from the project is a potential risk to the sponsor. Ensure that all communication from the project is acceptable to the sponsor. This does not mean wasting their time by asking the sponsor to check every e-mail. It does mean the following, however:

- Knowing what the sponsor does and does not want to see in communication, both explicit messages and implicit ones
- Asking the sponsor if in doubt
- Letting the sponsor know your general intentions for communication and the communication plan
- Checking major communications pieces with the sponsor
- Getting the sponsor to send out key messages in their own name.

Test and adjust

For major communications, such as announcing the start of a project, a milestone, or a change in plan, check that what you intend to use to communicate the message actually has the intended effect. Test the message on a few people before sending it out to everyone. Adjust your plans according to the results of the test.

If your message can be misunderstood, it will be

Think how your message could be misunderstood. Look for vague words, unfortunate associations, hidden meanings. Use the test described above to check especially for misunderstanding.

An example of how not to do it was the name used by the USA for military operations in response to the attacks on the World Trade Center on Tuesday, 11 September 2001. The operations were launched under the name 'Infinite Justice'. However, to many Muslims this name is offensive because in their faith Allah is the only one capable of infinite justice. The name was hastily changed to 'Enduring Freedom'. The US had intended to communicate that the military operations were about obtaining justice; the message was understood by some as blasphemy.

Plan and rehearse

This too is an extension of test and adjust. Plan your communication. Rehearse delivering it. This does not need to be complex or expensive or time consuming. In the back of a cab or on the underground or train into work, think through what you want to convey, the words you will use, and some of the likely questions. Mental rehearsal is often the most important thing.

Let people know what is going on, especially your sponsor

'Nobody told me.' 'Nobody asked.' It is up to you as project manager to take the initiative in communication, and most of all you must ensure that your sponsor knows what you are up to. Stealth is good for bats and bombers and assassins, but not for project managers. Do not get a reputation for being a steal manager – no one can see you and you don't appear on the corporate radar. Tell your sponsor what you are doing. This is not achieved though the kind of drive-by messages that timid people use to try to avoid the effort of communicating difficult messages but keep the right to say 'told you so' afterwards. On the contrary, make sure you have the sponsor's attention and that they understand what you mean. That may not be easy but it is your job, what you are paid to do. (Even if you are not paid, perhaps in the voluntary sector, it is still your job as project manager.)

▶ Listen and ask questions – understand that communication is two-way

Communication is not transmission only. It is also receiving and *listening*. Practise listening just as you practise speaking and presenting. Listen with your whole body – eyes, ears, body stance. Ask questions, not to show off but to clarify what is not clear and to show that you are listening. Practise asking questions and get feedback on your style. Table 10.2 lists some common barriers to listening. Find a friend to tell you which of these you may need to work on.

Table 10.2 Barriers to listening

Dreaming: Half-listening until some private association is triggered, then .... (This is particularly common when anxious or bored.)

Derailing: Changing the subject before they have finished.

Mind reading: Second-guessing what they really mean rather than what they are in fact saying.

Placating: Agreeing with everything – but only because you are not really involved.

Filtering: Listening for something specific but ignoring everything else.

Being right: Refusing to listen to suggestions, criticism and comments; not accepting that someone might have proved you wrong.

Judging: You already know that this person isn't worth listening to.

Sparring: So quick to argue or raise counterpoint that they never feel heard. Avoid by replaying what you've just heard.

When trying to get a fix on task status, it is easy to make the mistake of asking 'How far through are you?' After all, that is the information you want. But the person answering knows how long they spent on the task so far and their original time estimate for the task, so the easiest way for them to give you an answer is just to divide effort so far by their original estimate to get a value for progress. If they have worked six days on a task that was estimated at 10 days, they will then answer '60% done' or some equivalent. But in fact there is not enough information to answer the question, because we do not know how much work is left to do as the original estimate might have been wrong or they may have been working ineffi-ciently, albeit unwittingly. So instead of asking how far through the work they are, always ask 'How much more work is there still to do?' If we are six days in and there are still six days of work to do, then the task is only 50% done, not 60%. Framing the question this way also helps them to think about what they are doing from a different perspective – the project's perspective. In communications generally, asking the right question is a powerful skill and one that is well worth developing.

Table 10.3 brings together a few words of wisdom that have been written about communication.

Table 10.3 What others have said about communication

1 Know your audience.	Think like a wise man but communicate in the language of the people.	William Butler Yeats
2 Know what you are talking about.	First learn the meaning of what you say, and then speak.	Epictetus
3 Pick the right medium for the audience.	Words are a wonderful form of communication, but they will never replace kisses and punches.	Ashleigh Brilliant
4 Recognize tensions in the needs to communicate.	Effective communication is 20% what you know and 80% how you feel about what you know.	Jim Rohn
5 Work with the sponsor.	The key to any good relationship, on-screen and off, is communication, respect, and I guess you have to like the way the other person smells – and he smelled real nice.	Sandra Bullock
6 Test and adjust.	Communication works for those who work at it.	John Powell
7 If your message can be misunderstood, it will be.	There is always someone who knows better than you what you meant with your message.	Osmo A. Wiio
8 Plan and rehearse.	To fail to prepare is to prepare to fail.	Anon.
9 Let people know what is going on.	Communication leads to community, that is, to understanding, intimacy and mutual valuing.	Rollo May
10 Listen – understand that communication is two-way.	To listen well is as powerful a means of communication and influence as to talk well.	John Marshall
	What is the shortest word in the English language that contains the letters: abcdef? Answer: feedback. Don't forget that feedback is one of the essential elements of good communication.	Anon.

▶ E-mail alone is not communication

E-mail is great, but e-mail alone is not communication. It can be one of the problems of communication. It is tempting when time is short to eliminate meetings and rely instead on general-circulation e-mails. Both meetings and e-mails have a role but they are not interchangeable. One is an opportunity for two-way communication, and the other is deliberately one-way only. Meetings allow rich person-to-person exchange of information, much of which can be of the non-verbal kind that carries significant meaning. An exchange of e-mails may have some of the characteristics of a conversation, but it loses much of the richness of a real conversation (could you pick up the cues from an e-mail which would allow you to ask '... OK, but isn't there something else you want to talk to me about?'), and because people delay answering e-mails until they are ready it is sometimes slower. (And instant messaging is not the fix to the problem in communications of e-mail.)

IT staff are particularly prone to avoiding human contact and relying on e-mail instead. If you work in IT, take a good look at yourself and ask whether you use e-mail when you could use the phone or walk across the office.

▶ Information gathering

We can all agree with statements like 'The project manager must monitor project progress and take action to ensure that the project stays on track'. But after a few days or weeks of doing the project management job, it is not so easy to agree. Quite quickly, project managers are driven to ask in return, 'Yes, but how? There is just too much happening. I can't monitor everything, and even on those tasks I do monitor I can't tell whether action is really required'. What is needed is a summary of the project status, highlighting tasks that need attention.

Key Idea

Develop gut feel as a communication aid
Learn to develop your gut feel for how things are going, and use it to help know where to focus your communication effort.

For example, a sudden reluctance on the part of a team member to provide a regular progress update is itself a warning sign. It might be simple forgetfulness, but it might mean that the person is worried about the real status of their corner of the project. You need to find out not only the time information, but whether there are any emerging problems.

The sponsor and the programme board face the same problem, but they have even less time to devote to each project. The sponsor cannot and should not get involved in every detail of the project, and yet the sponsor is responsible for safeguarding the organization's investment in the project and guaranteeing the business benefits. How can this be done without checking what is happening several times a day? Both the sponsor and the programme board rely on summary information generated by each project that they supervise. With the right metrics, one can tell a lot about the state of a project or an individual task without having to know the technical detail. The project-level summary information for the sponsor and the programme board is an aggregation of the task-level summary information used by the project manager. Standardization, summarization and systematization are the ways to make the task manageable.

A systematic approach to communications management

So far this chapter has shown why communications is important in project management and the problems faced in trying to communicate in projects. Now let's look at the answer, a systematic approach to project communications management. This section follows the PMBOK approach to project communications management, which is robust and effective. Communication is a broad and deep subject, and entire industries and entire lives are devoted to nothing but communication. A project manager can always learn more about communication, which is a fascinating, practical and valuable subject, but the purpose of a project manager is to manage a project. Communication skills are a means to that end, not an end in themselves. We have had to limit what could be said in this chapter. We have chosen a limit such that you will have a good toolset and pointers for further research into this subject. Table 10.4 shows the four processes in project communication management and how they are categorized within the process groups.

Table 10.4 Four project communication management processes

		Process Group		
Initiating	**Planning**	**Executing**	**Monitoring and controlling**	**Closing**
	1 Communications planning	2 Information distribution	3 Performance reporting	
			4 Manage stakeholders	

Communications planning

The aim of communications planning is to ensure that you communicate the right information to the right people at the right time. Without a plan your chances of doing this are slim. Planning includes finding out the following:

◆ Who wants communication about your project?
◆ Who needs it?
◆ In what format?
◆ What communication channels are available?
◆ What reports should you submit and when?
◆ Who is going to do the work of producing the reports and other communication material?
◆ What are the major communication risks and opportunities?

As well as the formal upwards-reporting channels you should use informal channels to keep people elsewhere in the company informed about progress – particularly if it is good. When the time comes to roll out your hard work across the firm, you will be grateful for the extra supporters.

PMI says

Communications planning

'Communications Planning (Process). The process of determining the information and communications needs of the project stakeholders: who they are, what is their level of interest and influence in the project, who needs what information, when they will need it, and how it will be given to them.' *PMBOK Guide*

Fig. 10.1 The communication planning process

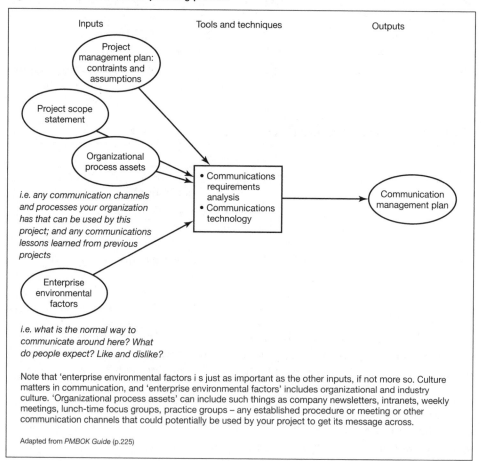

Figure 10.1 shows the inputs, tools and techniques and outputs in project management communications planning. The inputs are self-explanatory and need not be explained further, but one of the tools, communications requirements analysis, merits some discussion, and Table 10.5 is an example of it. See also Figure 10.2 later in this chapter, which lists the processes for information distribution. In planning communications you should understand the information distribution processes available to your project and plan accordingly.

Table 10.5 Example of chart resulting from a communication requirements analysis

Communication needs	Stuart, sponsor	Project team	Steering Committee	Fatima, Financial Controller	Pandora, Procurement	All employees	Frequency	Owner
	◆ Major risks ◆ Milestones ◆ High-level progress ◆ Links to Project OTHER	◆ Tasks for next 1 to 2 weeks ◆ How project is perceived by sponsor	◆ Major risks ◆ Milestones ◆ High-level progress	◆ Financial risks ◆ Actual v. budget variance	◆ Suppliers' performance ◆ Milestones ◆ High-level progress	◆ What's in it for them ◆ High-level progress		
Communication methods								
1. Fortnightly meeting with sponsor	XXX						Bi-weekly	Project manager
2. Fortnightly one-page report (as per company standard)	XXX	X	XXX				Bi-weekly	Project Office
3. Financial annex to (2) above	X	X	X	XXX			Bi-weekly	Project manager
4. Articles in the Company newsletter		X	X			X	Quarterly	Project Office
5. Updates to the project's page on intranet		X	X			X	Weekly	Project Office
6. Monday morning team meetings		XXX					Weekly	Project manager
7. Ad-hoc e-mails as events require					XXX	XXX	Ad hoc	Project manager

Table 10.5 is in three parts. The upper part, 'Communication needs' and 'Stakeholders', lists all the communication needs of each stakeholder in the project, as bullet points under the name or position of each stakeholder. Note that some stakeholders are groups of people rather than individuals. The lower part, 'Communication methods', lists by row each communication method or channel. Each communication channel is rated as meeting each stakeholder's communication needs to a high degree (by a mark 'XXX'), to a low degree ('X'), or not at all (blank). The third part of the chart is the two columns on the right: 'Frequency', which shows how often the communication method is to be sent out; and 'Owner', which lists who is responsible for each communication method.

The point of the chart shown in Table 10.5 is to ensure that the project communicates to everyone it needs to, in the right way, at the right time. The completed spreadsheet, or something like it, should be a section of the communication plan. It may be useful according to the needs of the particular project to use separate spreadsheets for each of the three sections that together make up the example in this table. Note that this table, or tables like it, are used both as tools for planning communication and as part of the output of planning. When using this tool, use it both to show what additional communication methods are needed in order to meet needs, and also to prune methods by identifying any that are redundant if the burden on the project team of reporting is becoming too great. Table 10.6 shows an alternative output.

Table 10.6 Alternative example of chart resulting from a communication requirements analysis			
From	**To**	**Frequency**	**What?**
Project Manager	Sponsor	Weekly	Informal progress note: ◆ Progress and status versus plan ◆ Achievements and problems ◆ Necessary actions
Project Manager	Steering Committee, and Project Support Office	Monthly	Status report: ◆ Progress against plan ◆ Revised cost and time projection
Project Manager	Sponsor	At major milestones or review points	Project review report: ◆ Snapshot of project ◆ Explanation of project decisions ◆ Analysis of other project events and learning ◆ Recommendations

When planning project communications, and also when executing them, all your efforts will be for nothing if you do not plan and act in a credible and trustworthy way. This may require much thought and effort, because of the tension between the need to keep some information confidential and the need to build and maintain trust. But if you understand your obligations and work with your sponsor, there should be no real conflicts here. Trust is very important in communication. The project manager and sponsor, and others involved in project communication, will be able to communicate much better if they are trusted. To be trusted you must seek out information actively, using questions which do not presuppose the answer. When information is made available the project manager must listen, and if it is provided in confidence then either accept it as such or make it clear before it is imparted that you cannot do so. It is easy to agree with all this in principle, but during the hectic lead-up to a project deadline, when communication is most important, it is easy to have a brief conversation without making the effort actually to listen to what is being said and to fail to recognize some of the tensions.

Project managers are the focal point of communications in the project. Good communication leads to efficient working, good morale, and project success. A project whose manager cannot communicate effectively is a high-risk one – which again underlines the need for planning communications. Plan your communications with an eye on maintaining your team's morale.

Good communication involves more than speaking and writing: good management requires receiving information at least as much as transmitting. This too should be a planning factor.

Another factor in planning your communications is the complexity of possible communications channels and communications methods. In a small organization of a few people a purely internal project has simple communications, because everyone can know everything without much cost in time and effort being incurred. But in a large project in a large organization there may be far more possible communications channels and methods than are needed, so there is a choice. In mathematical terms this can be an NP-hard problem – which in plain language means, roughly, don't bother trying to work out with a formula the optimum way to communicate, just use common sense to make a good guess and which channels to use and don't bog yourself down in trying to use too many. Each channel incurs cost to your project in planning and managing. Your sponsor can provide wisdom and guidance.

▶ Information distribution

You've done the planning, now it's time to distribute the information that you want to communicate, and to get feedback. Figure 10.2 shows the inputs, tools and techniques

Fig. 10.2 The information distribution process

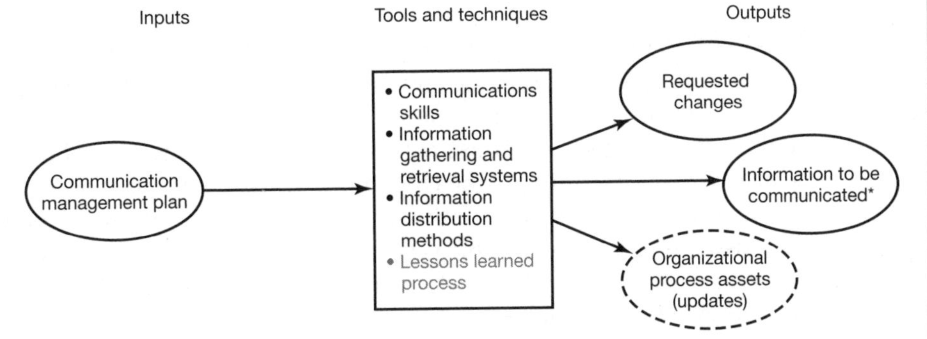

The main effort in the information distribution process is in communication skills. The plan shows what needs to be communicated. The efficiency of this process will depend very much on the information gathering and retrieval systems and the distribution methods, so the project manager should understand what these are – both what is available already and what can be created by the project; effectiveness of communication too will depend to some extent on these, though communication skills can make up deficiencies in effectiveness to a degree not possible in efficiency. The lessons learned process and updates to the organizational process assets should be important, but in real life project management can tend to be treated as secondary in this process under the urgent pressures of the moment.

* *The information to be communicated is not listed in* PMBOK Guide *as an output of this process – but see the section, 'Performance reporting'.*

Adapted from *PMBOK Guide* (p.228)

and outputs of information distribution. Information distribution is the process of executing the communications management plan – as the PMBOK definition here makes clear. Distribution is about executing the communication plan, and there is little to say here that has not been covered above in the section on communication planning, except for two things: first, to emphasize again the importance of how you communicate; and secondly, to say something about requested changes as the output of the information distribution process.

PMI says

Information distribution

'Information Distribution (Process). The process of making needed information available in a timely manner.' *PMBOK Guide* (p.362)

Key Idea

Communications skills

The two vital things in communication are to ensure that the other person:

1 understands what you mean,

2 has a complete understanding (i.e. you have not hidden or evaded something that matters to them).

These things are your responsibility – you must check that both are achieved, and not leave it up to the other person to ask.

▶ How you communicate – further words on communication skills

If you or one of your team who needs to communicate as part of their project duties is weak in communication skills, then consider getting some training: it is a valuable skill and there is much good training available. You might also consider buying a cheap video camera and recording yourself communicating, perhaps not in real meetings but on your own, talking to the camera or with a friend in role-playing. Such an activity would have been prohibitively expensive a few years ago, but costs have fallen and for many people seeing themselves on video is an experience that transforms how they communicate.

▶ Outputs – information

The main output of the information distribution process is of course the information that you are communicating. This should be straightforward, as what should be communicated will have been worked out in the plan, although sometimes you will have to communicate painful news. The techniques and approach to doing that fall under the heading of communication techniques, but the boxed text says more about it.

(Note for those readers preparing for PMI exams: the information being communicated is not listed as an output of the information distribution process in the PMBOK. The omission is perhaps more understandable when one considers the section on performance reporting, which concerns much of the information that is to be distributed.)

Reality, and dealing with it

Failing to deliver their allocated task is *not* the worst crime anyone on your project can commit. The worst crime is having problems and hiding them until it is too late to fix them. Most problems can be solved in a variety of ways, but there are hardly any ways to solve problems instantly; it always takes time. With enough warning most problems can be overcome. But by hiding the problem failure is locked in. By the time the project manager finally discovers what has happened, it is too late for recovery. It is very frustrating to know that a solution would have been possible had the person with the problem spoken up early enough.

The best way to deal with such situations is not to get into them in the first place. A lot of the project manager's monitoring and control tasks centre around avoiding such nasty surprises and maximizing the warning period.

The most basic monitoring and control skills are therefore those of team building and communication. You have got to establish an atmosphere in which people feel that it is safe to report the truth. This will not happen by accident since it runs contrary to many people's instinct. Nobody likes to admit that they have problems and doing so takes courage. Your reaction to the first problem that is presented to you will affect how many others you get to see. If the braver team members get the impression that you are pleased by their openness, then others might be encouraged to involve you in avoiding problems before they get out of control. If the first person to tell you about a potential problem thinks that you think badly of them, you will not get to hear of any more problems. So shouting at people is a good way to have a quiet life for a few weeks. Then all the problems that nobody dared to tell you about will have grown until you cannot fail to notice them even without being told, and you will have a full-scale project crisis.

Your attitude in your day-to-day interactions will govern the quality of the information the team gives you. Go out and look for trouble – but when you find it, manage it like any other task. If you catch things early enough, you will be doing risk management instead of problem management, and the actions can be pre-emptive rather than reactive. In other words, you will be in control rather than just reacting to events. This is a much more comfortable way to run a project.

▶ Outputs – requested changes

When you start executing the communication plan you will discover changes that need to be made to your communications plan, hence requested changes being the main output of the process in Figure 10.2. There will be two reasons to change the communication plan. First, there will be the changes necessary as a result of your plan not working quite as intended, for example the steering committee does not like some particular format. Then there will be changes where the plan was fine but something else changes, such as one of the organization's standard communication templates, or some stakeholder changes their mind about the frequency or format of how they like to receive communication. And of course when things have been running smoothly for a while people tend to want less communication than when surprises and problems have been arising.

▶ Performance reporting

Figure 10.3 shows the inputs, processes and outputs of the performance reporting process – as we have said before, treat the inputs as suggestions and ideas; don't try to find all inputs listed there for every project you run, or you will create a bureaucracy that will kill the project and probably drive you and your team insane. Focus on what matters. Performance is what matters to your stakeholders. You need to consider the following factors in performance reporting:

Fig. 10.3 Performance reporting

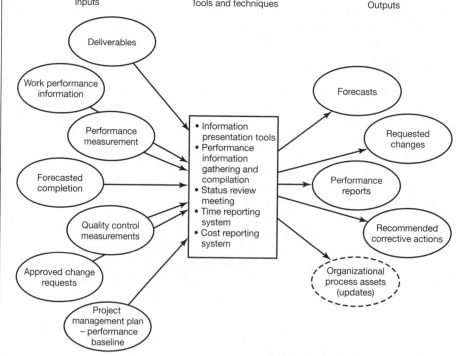

Sponsors and many other stakeholders are always interested in time and cost, so the processes to gather these for your project are important and you should understand how they work and have confidence that they are reporting accurate information. The performance report is the chief output of this process, but the others are all important also. When things go wrong the recommended corrective actions may become the most important output. Revised forecasts too will tend to attract much interest.

Adapted from *PMBOK Guide* (p.231)

- What the stakeholder expects to hear about project progress.
- What the stakeholder wants to hear about it.
- What it is reasonable that they should hear, i.e. actual progress as against the schedule and scope.
- What you want them to understand.
- How to deal with the gaps in the above.

Finding out about and then reconciling all of these is a major task. The tools and techniques of performance reporting are there to make this task easier.

PMI says

Performance reporting

'Performance Reporting (Process). The process of collecting and distributing performance information. This includes status reporting, progress measurement and forecasting.' *PMBOK Guide* (p.366)

Key Idea

Performance reporting

The key idea in performance reporting is to tell each stakeholder how the project is doing in relation to their particular, but valid, interests. 'How it is doing' must include bad news as well as good (see section on outputs – information and the boxed text on reality). 'Valid' means within the scope of the project.

As Figure 10.3 says, time and cost reporting are of particular interest to the sponsor and other stakeholders. The usual way for project managers to track progress is through timesheets or an online equivalent. You should get timesheet information from all of your team at least once a week. However, some time reporting systems only record historical hours spent down to the project level rather than the task level. If necessary, therefore, you may wish to create a project-specific version that allows people to record time on individual tasks and also to give revised estimates of time to task completion, although be sensitive to the costs and possible political ramifications of doing this. On small projects, you can gather this information yourself as part of your regular tours of the project team, without having to use another form, but on large projects some degree of automation will be required.

The sponsor, the steering committee, the managers of other projects that are waiting for your resources, the various stakeholders, and of course the users, are all keen to know how things are going. They aren't likely to be interested in the details that occupy most of your time but they will all want to hear when the project is likely to finish and whether everything is under control. Some of these contacts will need to be informed on an as-needed basis, but as a general rule, reporting should follow standard formats. This saves time in producing them and gets the recipients used to the same format every time, which saves them time and enables them to focus on the actual message rather than the format.

The most significant reporting task for a project manager is the weekly or fort-nightly report to the sponsor. Figure 10.4 gives an example of such a report in one page. The project status report for the Programme Office, where there is one, is almost as important. The project status report is an essential document, but since it contains summary information of what should already have been generated for internal project use, it should be simple to produce. Many sponsors are content to receive a copy of the weekly programme status report without any additional pro-ject progress note. It is good practice to send a weekly note to the sponsor. Sending regular routine notes will make you appear organized, and will mean that, if your project does run into trouble, it will not be the first time that the sponsor has heard about how the project is going. Through being reminded of the project the spon-sor will be better placed to act as project ambassador in interactions with other senior staff. Take the opportunity to raise issues and concerns that do not fit into the project status report format and to ask for support in dealing with any organi-zational, political or resourcing problems that may be emerging.

The design of reports is worth thinking about most carefully. Remember that Gantt charts are good for showing time, PERT charts are good for showing depen-dencies, and milestone charts are often what senior managers want to see. But if someone senior wants to see dependencies by looking at a Gantt chart, it may be

Fig. 10.4 Example of regular project report to project sponsor

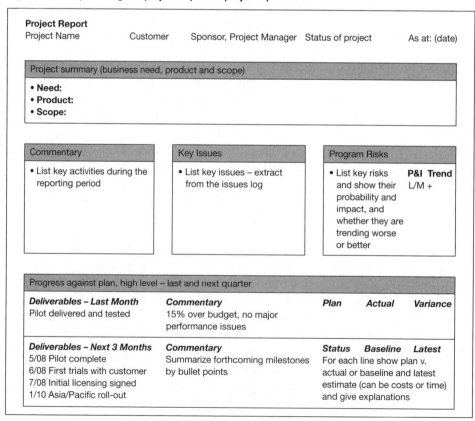

prudent not to argue with them. There are three sources of templates or models: your organization's standard templates, formats or styles preferred by the stakeholder in question, and other templates (such as the ones in this book). Avoid the latter if possible, because it is better to use something that your stakeholder recognizes or something that is a standard in your organization.

▶ Manage stakeholders

Figure 10.5 shows the inputs, tools and techniques and outputs for this process, as per the PMBOK. This diagram is reasonably clear as far as it goes. Another way of looking at the process of managing stakeholders is by keeping stakeholders happy while also keeping the project realistic. There is a tension between these two aims. To keep that tension within manageable bounds, you need to raise issues with stakeholders and either get them to agree a change in scope against their interests, or get the parties to the project (you plus the sponsor plus other affected stakeholders) to agree to extend the scope of the project.

If communication is the most important skill in project management, then stakeholder management is the most important process. Of course you must have a minimum level of competence in actually managing projects, but assuming that, managing stakeholders is the most critical process for success in project management.

There are two parts to getting stakeholder management right. The first is planning, and you will have done this in the communication planning process,

Fig. 10.5 Manage stakeholders

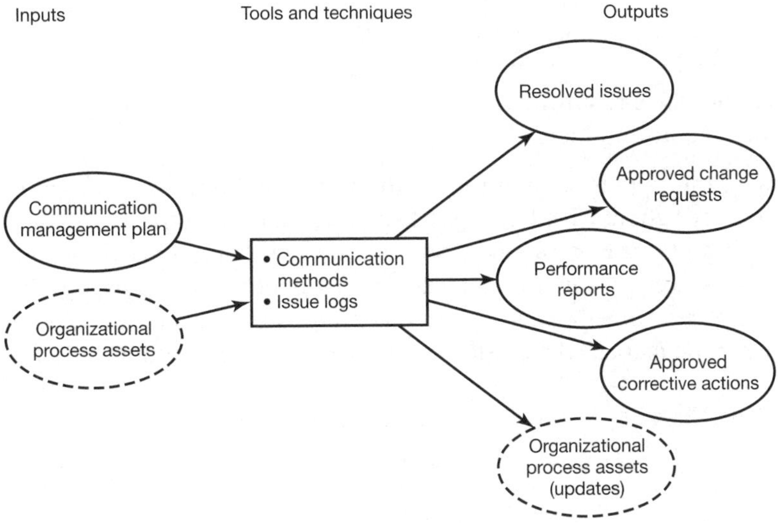

The issue log is vital to everything in this process. It is one of the most important tools in project management. The point of this process is to communicate with stakeholders and keep them and the project happy together. You will need to change their views or how they work at times, and you will need to change your views and how the project works at others.

Adapted from *PMBOK Guide* (p.235)

described above. The next step is how you engage with stakeholders. This comes down to communication skills, also described above, plus how things work in your organization. Your sponsor will probably be an expert at stakeholder management, but if not, or if they are short of time for you, make a special effort to work with the sponsor to get stakeholder management right.

Key Idea

Stakeholder management
The point of stakeholder management is to communicate with stakeholders and keep them and the project both happy. The risk is that you keep stakeholders happy at the cost of expanding scope, or you are too rigid and become seen as unreasonable, thus making them unhappy. So you must strike a balance. To do this you will need sometimes to change the stakeholder's views or how they work, and at other times to change your views and how the project works, and you will also need to cultivate a 'bedside manner'.

▶ Summary

Communication is the most important general management skill. Project communication management is about planning and doing communication to increase the chance of project success and reduce the stress to you and the project team. There are four processes:

◆ Communication planning.
◆ Information distribution.
◆ Performance reporting.
◆ Manage stakeholders.

Most of the work is done in the planning, but you must be prepared to change your plan in the light of what happens when you execute it, in the information distribution and performance reporting processes. The process that can make the biggest difference to your success, assuming competence in the others, is manage stakeholders. Two things to remember especially are to communicate closely with the sponsor, and to look for and manage the tensions that arise in project communications management.

Further reading

Communication is a vast subject and always worth investing in to improve your personal skills or your team's skills.

The book that we recommend most of all, as a must for anyone who makes business presentations, is:

◆ Minto, B., 1995. *The Pyramid Principle: Logic in Writing and Thinking*. Harlow: FT/Prentice Hall.

Some of the many other excellent books for further reading include:

◆ Charvet, S.R., 1997. *Words That Change Minds: Mastering the Language of Influence*. Dubuque, IA: Kendall/Hunt Publishing.
◆ Cohen, A.R. and Bradford, D.L., 2004. *Influence without Authority*. Hoboken, NJ: John Wiley & Sons.
◆ Frank, M.O., 1991. *How to Get Your Point Across in 30 Seconds or Less*. New York: Simon & Schuster.
◆ Harvard Business Essentials Series, 2005. *Power, Influence and Persuasion: Sell Your Ideas and Make Things Happen*. Boston, MA: Harvard Business School Press.
◆ Jolles, R.L., 1993. *How to Run Seminars and Workshops: Presentation Skills for Consultants, Trainers and Teachers*. New York: John Wiley & Sons.
◆ Nutting, J., Cielens, M. and Aquino, M., 1998. *The Business of Communicating*. Maidenhead: McGraw-Hill.
◆ Otazo, K., 2006. *The Truth About Managing Your Career: … and Nothing But the Truth*. Upper Saddle River, NJ: Prentice Hall.

project risk management

1

2

3

4

5

6

7

8

9

10

11

12

13

What is project risk management?

Risk management principles

Risk management planning

Risk identification

Qualitative risk analysis

Quantitative risk analysis

Risk response planning

Risk monitoring and control

▶ Aims of this chapter

This chapter will cover the processes involved with project risk management to ensure that project risks are decreased and opportunities are increased, because every project involves risks. The proper management of risk is acknowledged as a key element to effective project management. The use of risk management should result in the project manager being proactive and in control of the project, rather than the other way round if situations are not planned for. This process will enhance the probability of the project achieving customer satisfaction within the 'triple constraint'. By the end of this chapter, the reader should:

◆ know what risk management is, how it works within project management and its proactive approach on the delivery of a project;
◆ be able to determine the planning and preventive actions required to increase the opportunities and decrease the threats which affect the progress of the project;
◆ be able to apply risk analysis within project management to ensure resources are targeted at the areas identified within the scale of project priority;
◆ be able to explain the need for treating project risk management as a distinct knowledge area within project management.

▶ What is project risk management?

Project risk management cannot eliminate all the risk for a project, but it can ensure the project's exposure to risk operates at an acceptable level. There is always a big storm brewing just over the horizon, but it is the project manager's task to steer round the danger or prepare for it. Some of the risk factors are beyond your control, therefore planning to implement a series of actions should be conducted prior to an unwanted event occurring. Analysis, preparation and planning are therefore key to successful risk management. Many of the major decisions that will have the greatest impact occur during the early stages of the project; however, the information from which to base these decisions is likely to be mostly inaccurate or incomplete. To ensure the best decisions are made for the project, all of the important risks should be identified and assessed as early as possible.

There are also risks which provide the project manager with opportunities, such as the early finish of a module. This prospect could lead to the team starting the next work package sooner, if the resource is planned to be made available.

PMI says

Project risk management

'Project Risk Management includes the processes concerned with conducting risk management planning, identification, analysis, responses, and monitoring and control on a project. The objectives of Project Risk Management are to increase the probability and impact of positive events and decrease the probability and impact of events adverse to project objectives.' *PMBOK Guide* (p.340)

A project risk is generally thought of as a crisis that has not happened yet. Experienced project managers know that risk management is preferable to crisis management – it leads to fewer late nights and ruined weekends. Furthermore, hours spent on risk management are much less stressful than the same time spent on crisis management. The project manager tends to feel in control of risk management activities, but one of the things that makes a crisis uncomfortable is the feeling that the project is out of your control and that you are being driven by events, instead of driving them yourself.

The personal motivation of project managers to avoid stress contributes to sound project management, but project risk management also has more direct and tangible business benefits. Solving problems takes time and money, and if risk management can avoid some of the problems then it is worthwhile. Even problems that cannot be completely avoided can often be mitigated at a lower cost, if some planning is done before they arise. Furthermore, uncontrolled project risks introduce unpredictability into the firm's cash flows that increases the firm's cost of doing business. Hence it makes sense for the firm to provide funds and resources for small additional tasks that may have been identified.

Key Idea

Risk management

Murphy's Law states that 'If anything can go wrong, it will'. Risk management is to prepare and prevent things from going wrong, but if they cannot be avoided there should be a set of actions ready to be implemented which will reduce the impact to the project.

You may hear people argue that 'We cannot predict the future, so we cannot plan for events that may never happen. Anyway we will probably miss the problems that will really cause trouble, so risk management is not worth doing'. But in fact we can often predict much of the future accurately enough and most people have a good instinct for the sort of events that are likely to happen. The fact that we might still be surprised by events is no excuse not to take precautions against those that can be foreseen. If there are a number of uncertainties due to a lack of knowledge, it may be worth conducting an investigation to help identify and determine the potential risks.

Project risk management protects the business by taking a dispassionate view of what might go wrong and what can be done to limit the likelihood and impact of such events. This approach leads to the steps outlined here: the first is to decide how to plan and execute the risk management activities, the next identifies and analyses the sources of risk, and the final step is to develop the required prevention and control measures to be put in place. The overall purpose of project risk management is to increase the probability of meeting the project objectives by the following means:

◆ Creating an awareness of project risks in a timely manner.
◆ Assisting the decision-making process.
◆ Aiding the identification of critical areas of the project.

◆ Determining the level of risk exposure relating to project strategy to better inform the judgement process.
◆ Providing the potential to maximize the opportunities and reduce the threats.
◆ Ensuring the foreseeable risks are proactively managed.
◆ Providing more accurate estimates of project expenditure and timescales.

▶ Risk management principles

The basic principle of risk management is to inform those involved within the project's decision-making process what to look for, what are the key elements to be aware of, who is allocated the specific responsibility for the risk, and what they should do then if action is required. Once the appropriate plans are in place, guidance is provided to assist in the assessment of the issue, together with the appropriate action to take. If an issue can be identified and resolved at a low level, the quicker and easier it can be dealt with, as long as there is a coherent response plan to follow. Escalation of an issue remains vital within this process, because further risk planning or analysis may be needed to reduce or eliminate the potential impact to the project. The risk factors to be assessed and analyzed link the probability that an event will occur to the proposed impact if the event takes place. The individual processes (and the process groups to which they belong) contained within risk management are shown in Table 11.1.

Table 11.1 Six project risk management processes

		Process Group		
Initiating	Planning	Executing	Monitoring and controlling	Closing
	1 Risk management planning		6 Risk monitoring and control	
	2 Risk identification			
	3 Qualitative risk analysis			
	4 Quantitative risk analysis			
	5 Risk response planning			

▶ Risk management planning

Before starting the process of risk identification, the first stage is to establish the strategy for approaching risk management before determining the risk management plan. Risk management planning is required to outline how the risks will be identified, analyzed, monitored, controlled and reviewed. The strategy being applied must be consistent with the priority, size and complexity of the project, as well as the organization's culture and normal working practices. A project would be unlikely to follow a high-risk strategy if the initiating organization usually adopts risk avoidance. The following list of points could be included within the risk management plan to match the strategy:

◆ How the risks will be identified, analyzed and assessed.
◆ How the risks will be defined within the context of their impact and probability.
◆ How risks will be allocated and controlled, decisions taken and actions implemented.
◆ How actions implemented will be monitored and evaluated.
◆ How stakeholders will be involved and informed about the process of risk management.

Key Idea

Risk management planning
Risk management planning should take place as early as is practical because it outlines the processes and their importance for risk identification and analysis.

The formulation of the risk management plan and the definition of the risk process will be headed up by the project manager, but input to the plan should come from the project team, sponsor, stakeholders and experts as appropriate. If the project involves a customer, their thoughts and priorities on the planning process will also affect the project's approach to risk. Much of the planning work should be started as early as possible during the planning phase, because the detail from this process is required to complete the other activities such as identifying, analyzing and planning the risk responses. Without the overarching framework for risk management, the remaining planning work cannot be defined or quantified. Figure 11.1 shows the inputs, tools and techniques and the sole output for the risk planning process.

▶ Risk management plan

The initial starting point for information relating to risk management could be gleaned from historical records, or lessons learned from previous projects. Other useful sources of information are the project charter, letters and papers produced before the approval of the project. The detail contained in these documents provides the background and context for the project, as well as conveying the

Fig. 11.1 The risk management planning process

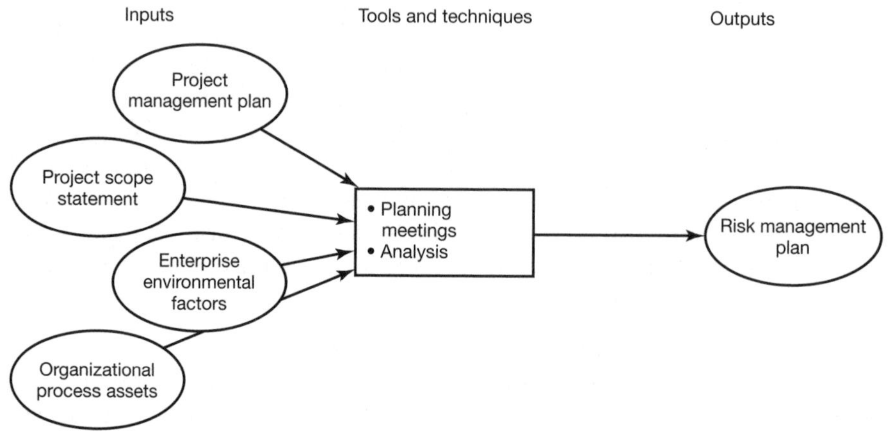

A key discipline in this process is to focus on how to manage risks, not what the risks are, although some experience of relevant risks is necessary to do this, of course. Identifying and managing particular risks comes in subsequent processes.

Adapted from *PMBOK Guide* (p.242)

organization's priorities and tolerance to risk. If the benefits of an early delivery mean that the balance of risk shifts towards 'risk-taking', the risk of fast-tracking the work could be accepted to achieved the required goal. A contingency plan to cater for delays should be prepared to support this more risky approach, but the proposed plan may require the provision of extra funding to provide greater resources to crash the project and maintain the early delivery date. Further project documentation that is key to the production of the risk management plan includes the scope statement and project management plan. Elements contained in the scope statement may mention aspects of the initial risk analysis conducted by the project sponsor.

The various plans included in the project management plan could provide useful inputs to the risk management plan from the WBS, network diagram, communications, staffing and procurement management plans, together with the time and cost estimates versus the project's budget. All of this information can be used to develop the risk management plan, which ultimately becomes part of the project management plan. The risk management plan will therefore define how risk management is to be structured and applied by including the following:

◆ Methodology – how risk management will be performed, taking into account the project's priority, size and complexity.
◆ Roles and responsibilities – people are given specific roles with regard to risk, together with the allocation of certain responsibilities linked to the task.
◆ Budgeting – costs associated with the provision of risk management and contingency planning are included within the cost baseline.
◆ Risk categories – a list of common risk categories used to assist the identification and analysis of risks experienced by the organization, or from other similar projects. The aim is to get a consistent and coherent approach to risk identification.

- Definitions of probability and impact – a declared standard for probability and impact is defined so the level of application is similar for all involved.
- Stakeholder tolerances – from project initiation onwards, the level of risk tolerance must be stated and regularly revised.
- Reporting formats – content and layout of the risk management report are defined, together with its distribution.
- Tracking – how the risk activities are recorded and audited.

▶ Risk categories

Building up a list of the risks on a project is the first hurdle in risk management. It is very hard to manage risks that have not been identified. It can be difficult to get started identifying risks, because the job can seem overwhelming – after all, anything could happen, couldn't it? In fact, risks can be grouped under categories, the significance of which for an individual project is much easier to see. The idea of using a standard list of risk categories is to ensure all the usual areas of risk are covered. Many of the subject headings may not be applicable for your project, but at least each category has been considered. If a project manager failed to follow the company's standard list of risk categories, how embarrassing would it be if a risk from the list appeared on the log without a prescribed response? The benefit of using a standard list in the initial stage of risk identification is to make sure all the common areas, or sources of known risk, are identified and analyzed as appropriate for the project.

PMI says

Risk category
'Risk Category is a group of potential risks. Risk causes may be grouped into categories such as technical, external, organizational, environmental, or project management.'
PMBOK Guide (p.373)

The risk categories can be arranged in a WBS-type framework to form a risk breakdown structure (RBS), with the risk categories replacing the major deliverables of the WBS. The type of risk categories and sub-categories considered to develop a RBS may consist of the following areas.

Technical
These are risks that apply across the project, rather than on specific activities. Examples include:

- Uncertainty about user requirements.
- Technology failure – the possibility that the technology will not work as anticipated.
- Technology advance – a new technical concept may provide benefits to the project.
- Lack of relevant experience that has successfully executed similar projects.
- Degree of innovation required and consequent uncertainty over whether the chosen approach will work.

- ◆ Security and confidentiality.
- ◆ Output quality risk – the possibility that the project output fails to meet expectations. This includes many technical risks, but also risks such as the usage cost of the project output being too high, or the performance being too low, or the quality being too variable.

External

These are external sources that in some way may impact on the project. Some of these are beyond the control of the project manager, but all can be monitored and the project steered round them if they are identified in time. Examples include:

- ◆ User acceptance risk.
- ◆ Failure of a sub-contractor to deliver satisfactorily.
- ◆ Changes in market conditions that may change the commercial attractiveness of the project.
- ◆ Constraints on business activities for legal, regulatory, or environmental reasons
- ◆ Possibility that the market was misjudged – the project might meet all its targets, but customers might not buy.
- ◆ Public opinion of the firm's brand, which may limit or enhance the range of activities that the firm wishes to be seen to undertake.

Organizational

These are threats that could affect the organization as a whole, which in turn could impact on the project. Examples include:

- ◆ Emerging project investment opportunities may reduce the priority allocated to the project.
- ◆ Change in financial status reduces the availability of funding for the project.
- ◆ Competition from other projects competes for limited funding and resources.
- ◆ Mismatch between the skills required and the workers available in the company.

Project management

These are the possible sources of threat or opportunity linked to project management issues that could cause an impact on the project. Examples include:

- ◆ Adjustment to the level of management support and advocacy.
- ◆ Lack of project management knowledge.
- ◆ Change of focus towards project management.
- ◆ Timescale risk – the possibility that the output may appear after the project deadline.
- ◆ Project cost risk – the possibility that the funding required to complete the project exceeds that originally planned.
- ◆ Missing tasks or hidden dependencies in the plan.
- ◆ Resistance to change.
- ◆ Cultural issues.
- ◆ Personality clashes within the team.

The list of risks is there to aid the thinking process, but these should not/ risk areas to consider. There could be risks generated by a new technolo or types of risk not previously experienced by the organization. As a proje.. ager, you must always look beyond the standard list and consider other possible causes of risk that could catch you out.

Risk identification

Once risk planning has been completed, the next stage is to start the process of risk identification. Figure 11.2 shows the inputs, tools and techniques and the sole output for the risk identification process. As in the production of the risk management plan, the task of identifying the project risks is predominately conducted by the project manager, key stakeholders, the sponsor and the project team. Extra assistance can also be gained from subject matter experts, although everyone should be encouraged to identify risks when they are seen. The first iteration of the risk identification process cannot start until the project scope statement and WBS have been created, but a good starting point could be the risks identified within the preliminary project scope statement generated by the sponsor. The whole process does not stop with the production of the initial risk register. Work continues to constantly review and revise the identified risks, because updating the risk register is an iterative process. Always try to involve the project team with the regular risk reviews, because this will encourage a level of ownership and responsibility towards

Fig. 11.2 The risk identification process

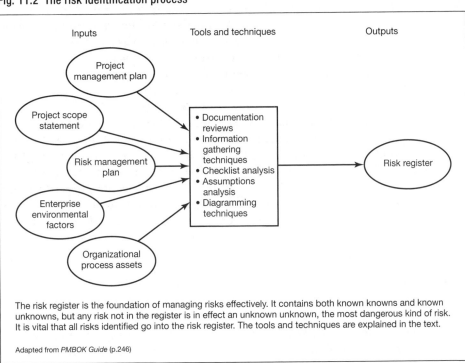

The risk register is the foundation of managing risks effectively. It contains both known knowns and known unknowns, but any risk not in the register is in effect an unknown unknown, the most dangerous kind of risk. It is vital that all risks identified go into the risk register. The tools and techniques are explained in the text.

Adapted from *PMBOK Guide* (p.246)

the risks and their associated responses. As you move through the project's lifecycle, more risks may be identified, while others noted may disappear in time.

▶ Documentation reviews

The first set of tools and techniques used to identify project risk is a full review of the project's plans and documents. This should present the risks covered by the project charter and preliminary project scope statement, together with documents included within the project management plan. The other details to consider, which in some way can be of more importance, are those elements missing from this documentation. All of these documents play their part in the planning and execution of the project, but differences or inconsistencies between the plans and the project requirements could provide signs of risk to the project manager. Risks experienced from other projects could also prove useful as a guide or prompt.

▶ Information gathering techniques

There are a series of basic techniques used to gather information from many sources. The standard approaches used to identify possible risks associated with the project are described in the following paragraphs.

Brainstorming
Brainstorming is a collaborative environment to encourage free association among the project members. Individuals can either call out their ideas spontaneously, or take turns to offer ideas on project risk. The principle of using this technique with stakeholders and team members is to get people to input their ideas on risk, and to feed off points raised by others. A facilitator is best used to control the session, but can also be used to scribe each risk as it is suggested. The initial part of the brainstorming session can be broad, but the risk breakdown structure may be used as a good starting point to target thoughts on specific risk areas. The next stage of brainstorming could involve expanding the identified risks and the definitions linked to them.

Delphi technique
The purpose of the Delphi technique is to obtain information and judgements from experts to come up eventually with an overall consensus. The process does not physically bring the contributors together, but information about risks and their responses is exchanged via mail, fax or e-mail. This technique is designed to take advantage of the experts' creativity, as well as combining the effects of group involvement and interaction. By keeping the group apart during the review process, no one person will have greater influence on the final outcome. If the e-mail system is used to recirculate the anonymous responses on project risk, a consensus can usually be reached within about five days.

Interviewing
The process of interviewing stakeholders and experts to identify project risk remains an important approach. The task of conducting the interview will fall to the project manager, or their team, but time spent gathering risks from subject matter experts and stakeholders could pay dividends in the longer term.

Root cause analysis

Once the task of identifying all possible risks has been completed, analysis of the information may link a single cause to a series of risk outcomes. Further analysis of the identified cause could then uncover more risks to the project. From a proactive approach, if you are able to eliminate the specific cause to some of the risks, effort can then be focused on the remaining project issues.

Strengths, weaknesses, opportunities and threats analysis (SWOT)

The aim of SWOT analysis at this stage should be to isolate the key risks that could have an impact on the success of the project. By identifying the main strengths of the project, this in turn produces specific threats towards its progress. It is also essential to spell out the assumptions made prior to starting the analysis process.

▶ Checklist analysis

The first step for the project manager is to select the required information gathering techniques to identify and specify the risks involved. Once this process has been completed, the checklist can then be considered as a mechanism to double-check your thinking so far. Using the checklist as a final confirmatory test gives the project manager the confidence that all the risk categories have been addressed, although it is impossible to say that every risk has been covered. The checklist can be amended throughout the project's lifecycle, but the final update should occur during project closure to reflect the risks experienced. An improvement to the checklist will prove beneficial for future projects.

▶ Assumptions analysis

A series of assumptions are made at various stages of the project's progress with the information available at the time. Analysis of these assumptions could identify errors or inconsistencies that pose further risk to the project. Assuming good weather conditions in early spring for a building project would certainly increase the level of risk, but also allow justification to challenge the validity of the assumption.

▶ Diagramming techniques

These techniques can be used in the analysis of quality issues when identifying risks. Root cause analysis has already been mentioned for identifying possible causes of risk, but other techniques such as fishbone diagrams, flowcharts and influencing diagrams are useful tools. Looking at the project from a different angle can develop ideas, as well as coming up with other possible risks.

▶ Output of risk identification – risk register

The key output from risk identification, after using some or all of the techniques listed, is contained in the risk register. Once the list of identified risks has been drawn up, a list of potential responses may be produced and fed in to the risk response planning process. New risk categories identified and developed during the risk management process can then be added to the RBS. The risk register is also vital at project closure because the information contained in its pages will be useful to other projects, therefore the need to retain the updated register for the project's historical records must be remembered. The importance of the new categories included in the revised checklist may not help you, but it could assist project managers in the future.

PMI says

Risk register

'The Risk Register details all identified risks, including description, category, cause, probability of occurring, impact on objectives, proposed responses, owners and current status.' *PMBOK Guide* (p.373)

▶ Qualitative risk analysis

As the project manager you cannot deal with all the risks that are identified, or every minute of the day would be spent assessing and planning for risks. The first step is to apply a sift process to label the more important risks to be addressed. This is best achieved by completing some form of subjective analysis for each identified risk. The task therefore involves assessing each risk against an agreed scale of probability and impact, such as low, medium or high. Figure 11.3 shows the inputs, tools and techniques and the sole output (in fact a revision to one of the inputs, the risk register) of the qualitative risk analysis process. Once the qualitative risk analysis has been completed, this information can be used to start the quantitative risk analysis (see below), if this stage of the process is required. The quality of the information being used can distort the results, so the assumptions made do need to be clear, because they can alter the assessment process. Information gained during the interviewing process can be useful in maintaining an unbiased approach to the assessed data. The specification quoted for the level of impact and probability is defined, therefore an increase in its score cannot occur just because the issue is close to the project manager's heart.

This level of analysis is useful because it allows your project to be compared to other projects. The outputs can also lead to your project being selected ahead of others. For an ongoing project, the analysis can be used to give reason for the continued support of the project, or it can justify why the project should be terminated. The information produced at this stage can also be used as an input to the quantitative risk analysis, covered later in this chapter.

▶ Probability/impact matrix

Each risk can be plotted on a risk rating matrix which plots the assessed severity of impact against its probability, so the higher the rating the more important a response is required (Table 11.2). The need to standardize the matrix within an organization is important because the task of risk rating becomes a more repeatable process across all projects. The other benefit of standardization means that people moving between projects will see the same application and layout wherever they are. Standardization is the goal, but there may be a need to adapt the matrix due to

Fig. 11.3 The qualitative risk analysis process

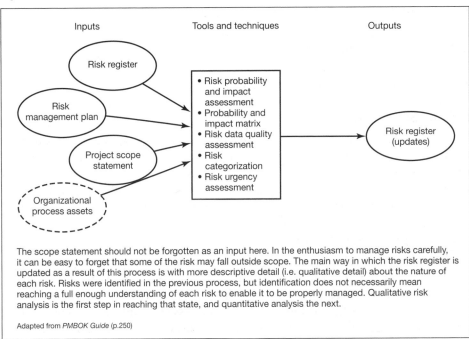

The scope statement should not be forgotten as an input here. In the enthusiasm to manage risks carefully, it can be easy to forget that some of the risk may fall outside scope. The main way in which the risk register is updated as a result of this process is with more descriptive detail (i.e. qualitative detail) about the nature of each risk. Risks were identified in the previous process, but identification does not necessarily mean reaching a full enough understanding of each risk to enable it to be properly managed. Qualitative risk analysis is the first step in reaching that state, and quantitative analysis the next.

Adapted from *PMBOK Guide* (p.250)

the specific nature of the project. If the tolerance threshold is different for elements contained in the 'triple constraint', then a separate risk matrix for scope, cost and time will be needed to cater for their varying level of importance.

Table 11.2 Risk probability/impact matrix

PROBABILITY			
High	Monitor impact	Create a risk management plan	Eliminate risk or mitigate to low impact
Medium	Monitor probability	Create a risk management plan	Eliminate risk or mitigate to low impact
Low	Ignore but log	Monitor probability	Monitor probability
	Low	**Medium**	**High**
		IMPACT	

▶ Risk data quality assessment

To ensure the analysis is correct, the data being used must be as consistent and true as possible. The key question to ask is how confident are you about the accuracy of the data. If you are unsure about the quality of the data, the next action must involve digging below the surface to find out more. Once you are content that you have the right information, you are then able to complete the qualitative assessment. Before starting the assessment process, each risk must be able to provide the answers to the following questions about the data quality:

◆ What level of understanding is there about each risk?
◆ What is the availability of the data for each risk?
◆ What is the quality of the data?
◆ What is the accuracy and consistency of the data?

▶ Risk categorization

Rather than having an overall prospective of the level of risk, you would prefer to know where the majority of the risk is located and what work could be affected. Categorizing the risk means that more definition is provided to aid the project manager in the task. Once it is known where much of the risk resides, risk response planning can use this information to remove a number of risks by eliminating a root cause.

▶ Risk urgency assessment

Certain risks that are identified could pose an immediate threat to your project if early action is not taken to resolve the problem. As an example, if a component requires a long lead time and is needed early in the project, the urgency to start the procurement process to source the item is high. This risk is assessed as urgent, therefore a quick response is necessary to avoid your head being on the block. If an urgent risk is detected during the qualitative risk analysis, the issue should be fast-tracked so the response is quickly planned, developed and implemented to meet the project deadlines.

▶ Outputs of qualitative risk analysis – risk register

The initial risk register produced after completion of risk identification must be updated to include the following outputs from the qualitative risk analysis:

◆ Compare the risk ranking of your project against other projects. The output can be reassessed after completing risk response planning.
◆ Place risks in priority order.
◆ Group risks by categories.
◆ Identify risks shortly requiring additional analysis.
◆ Identify risks to be taken forward for quantitative risk analysis and response planning.
◆ Document non-critical risks within the watchlist and review at regular stages during risk monitoring and control.
◆ Risk trends can be identified if the qualitative risk analysis is redone during the planning process group, or when the project is underway.

▶ Quantitative risk analysis

Once the risks have been prioritized and listed by the qualitative risk analysis process, the next stage can involve analyzing the risks and assigning a numerical rating on the probability and impact of the highest risks. The process is illustrated

Fig. 11.4 The quantitative risk analysis process

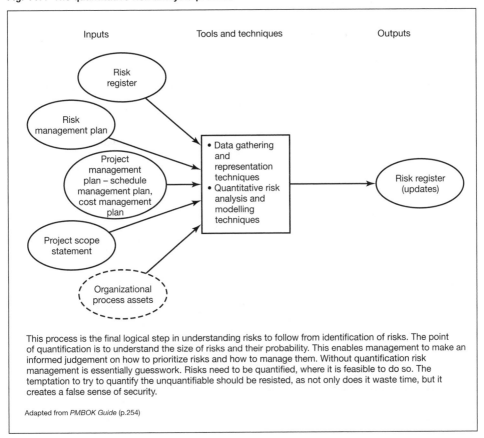

Inputs	Tools and techniques	Outputs

Risk register

Risk management plan

Project management plan – schedule management plan, cost management plan

Project scope statement

Organizational process assets

- Data gathering and representation techniques
- Quantitative risk analysis and modelling techniques

Risk register (updates)

This process is the final logical step in understanding risks to follow from identification of risks. The point of quantification is to understand the size of risks and their probability. This enables management to make an informed judgement on how to prioritize risks and how to manage them. Without quantification risk management is essentially guesswork. Risks need to be quantified, where it is feasible to do so. The temptation to try to quantify the unquantifiable should be resisted, as not only does it waste time, but it creates a false sense of security.

Adapted from *PMBOK Guide* (p.254)

in Figure 11.4. Quantitative risk analysis can also be used to present a quantitative approach when having to make decisions regarding the project, as well as determining which risks warrant a response. It is worth carrying out this process only if the time and cost warrant this level of effort, because there is little point in completing this analysis for a short-term project or risks of a lower priority. For projects where a quantitative approach is essential, there is no need to conduct qualitative risk analysis and the team therefore jumps straight into the quantitative risk analysis. The analysis will generally involve all or some of the following activities:

- Further investigation of the project's highest risks.
- Type of probability distribution to be used.
- Sensitivity analysis to determine the risks likely to have the most impact.
- Determining the level of quantified risk.

Many of the same information gathering techniques, such as interviewing, the Delphi technique and expert judgement used in risk identification, can also be applied for quantitative risk analysis. Other ways to determine the probability and impact of the risks can come from the use of historical records, expected monetary value analysis, Monte Carlo analysis, and cost and time estimating.

▶ Expected monetary value (EMV)

This tool is a statistical concept that calculates the average outcome when the future includes scenarios that may or may not occur. In simple terms it is the percentage probability multiplied by the value of the impact if it did occur. Table 11.3 shows an example.

This type of analysis is commonly used in decision tree analysis (see below). A positive EMV is an opportunity value, but a risk is expressed as a negative EMV.

Table 11.3 Expected monetary value equals cost impact times probability

WBS work package	Probability value	Cost impact	Expected monetary value
X	20%	£10,000	£2,000
Y	50%	£30,000	£15,000
Z	75%	£50,000	£37,500

▶ Monte Carlo analysis

This type of analysis uses the network diagram and estimates to conduct a series of simulations on cost and schedule for the project. It is able to evaluate the overall risk in the project and provides a percentage value that it will be finished by a certain date, or within a specified cost. The simulation can also be used to determine the probability of any activity being on the critical path and to take path convergence into account. The series of complex iterations is normally conducted using a computer-based Monte Carlo program, with the results displayed in a probability distribution form.

▶ Decision tree

Decision trees are used to make decisions about individual risks when there is an element of uncertainty. A decision tree tries to take future events into account when making a decision today. If you are unsure about any decisions, this technique could be used to assist the decision-making process by considering all the implications of each choice. Solving the decision tree provides the EMV for each alternative when all the benefits and subsequent decisions are quantified.

As an example, Company X is considering whether to refurbish an old factory, or to continue running on its existing facility due to the launch of a new product. Figure 11.5 shows the calculated impacts when determining whether the plant works or fails for the production of the new item. It shows that if the refurbishment costs are looked at in isolation, the decision to spend money on the old plant would seem unwise. However, taking just one future event into account, the decision to refurbish the old factory to produce the new item could work out cheaper.

Fig. 11.5 Decision tree for a factory refurbishment

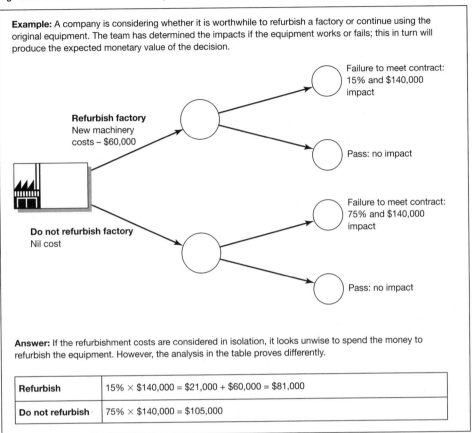

Example: A company is considering whether it is worthwhile to refurbish a factory or continue using the original equipment. The team has determined the impacts if the equipment works or fails; this in turn will produce the expected monetary value of the decision.

Failure to meet contract: 15% and $140,000 impact

Refurbish factory
New machinery
costs – $60,000

Pass: no impact

Failure to meet contract: 75% and $140,000 impact

Do not refurbish factory
Nil cost

Pass: no impact

Answer: If the refurbishment costs are considered in isolation, it looks unwise to spend the money to refurbish the equipment. However, the analysis in the table proves differently.

Refurbish	15% × $140,000 = $21,000 + $60,000 = $81,000
Do not refurbish	75% × $140,000 = $105,000

▶ Output of quantitative risk analysis – risk register updates

During the risk identification process the risk register is raised, but it should be updated in response to both the qualitative and quantitative risk analysis. The updates to the risk register should revise the priority list of quantified risks, together with the amount of contingency and reserves needed to accommodate the risks on the project. Other elements to update may include the realistic and proposed completion dates and project costs versus the time and cost objectives for the project. An update may also alter the quantified probability of meeting the overall project requirements and objectives.

▶ Risk response planning

This process – illustrated in Figure 11.6 – develops the options and actions that could be followed to increase the opportunities and reduce the threats to the project's objectives. It is not viable to eliminate all the risks from the project, nor can you be

Fig. 11.6 The risk response planning process

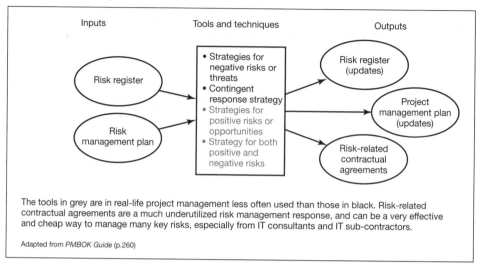

The tools in grey are in real-life project management less often used than those in black. Risk-related contractual agreements are a much underutilized risk management response, and can be a very effective and cheap way to manage many key risks, especially from IT consultants and IT sub-contractors.

Adapted from *PMBOK Guide* (p.260)

expected to plan a response for every risk. The main target is to plan a response for each key risk that has been identified and analyzed as part of the risk management process. Possible responses to the question of what to do for each key risk could be:

◆ Eliminate the known threats before they occur.
◆ Reduce the impact or decrease the probability of a threat occurring.
◆ Increase the impact and probability for an opportunity to occur.
◆ Establish contingency plans for residual risks.
◆ Generate a fallback plan if the contingency plan were to fail.

▶ Risk response strategies

There are certain ways to handle identified risks that involve adjusting the planned approach in order to complete the project. Other strategies used may be reactive, therefore plans are executed if the associated risk occurs. The response strategies for possible threats include:

◆ Avoid – put measures in place to ensure that the risk does not arise, or, if it arises, that there is no impact on the project.
◆ Mitigate – put measures in place to limit either the probability that the risk occurs, or the impact if it does occur, or both.
◆ Transfer – in some instances, it is possible to transfer the impact of a risk to a third party, so that if it does occur, there is no impact on the project. This is commonly done through the commercial terms of sub-contractor contracts which can include penalty clauses to cover the costs of getting the work done elsewhere. Other risk transference tools include insurance contracts.

The response strategies for possible opportunities include:

◆ Exploit – ensure that unplanned opportunities are exploited. If warm weather arrives early and allows building work to start sooner than planned, using staff who are being paid anyway, for example, ensure that the opportunity is exploited and not allowed to go to waste.

◆ Enhance – this is an extension of exploit: rather than merely exploiting the existing opportunity, enhance it. In the example just given, hire extra labour.

◆ Share – if the owning organization is unable to exploit the opportunity itself, perhaps it can partner with another organization that can, and share in the benefits.

The following response strategies can be applied to both threats and opportunities:

◆ Accept – often the consequences of a risk can be accepted. There is no need to avoid all risks, and it is impossible to do so. Some risks should be accepted, and in some cases accepting the risk is the best risk management strategy. For example, the risk that staff may resign: try too hard to keep them and you are likely to end up paying well over market rates for quality and ability.

◆ Contingent response strategy – this means having a response plan to use under certain predefined conditions. There should be a set of indicators and warnings to enable the project team to track those conditions, and if they arise then the contingency plan is automatically implemented. An organization's disaster response plan is an example, though not a project management one, of a contingent response.

Risk monitoring and control

Having identified and understood the risks, the central task of managing them is the monitoring and control process. Many project managers and project team members think that once a risk is in the risk register it is managed. Not so: it is merely identified and partly understood. It then has to be watched, like a sleeping leopard, so that at the first signs of stirring the project can take action to manage the risk. The key thing is to do something, and the right thing. Risk monitoring and control is the process by which you can watch the leopard of risk and act in the right way when it stirs. Figure 11.7 shows the inputs, tools and techniques and outputs of the process.

A surprising number of projects fall foul of risks in the register which are not properly managed. The outputs listed in Figure 11.7 are all aimed at the single end of ensuring that risks in the register do not derail the project. The outputs are reasonably straightforward and self-explanatory. The processes by which they are obtained need more explanation, which is given below.

▶ Risk assessment (also known as risk review)

All projects should have regular risk reviews, to check the current validity and usefulness of the risk register and risk management plan overall. Things change, and no matter how good the initial risk identification and analysis work, new factors or changed circumstances may require them to be updated. This is what the risk assessment does. It can be a standing agenda item in regular project management meetings. It may be useful on some occasions to have a project risk review meeting as a stand-alone event.

Fig. 11.7 The risk monitoring and control process

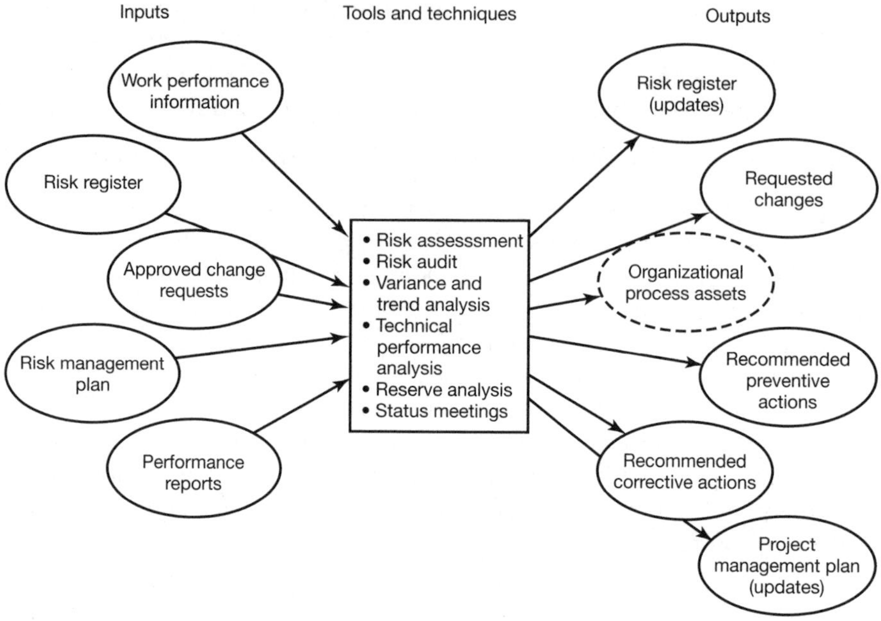

The point of this process is to ensure that the risks in the risk register do not derail the project. (This process is not concerned with risks not in the register; that is the province of the risk identification process.) A surprising number of projects fall foul of risks in the register that are not properly managed.

Adapted from *PMBOK Guide* (p.265)

▶ Risk audit

There are two uses of a risk audit. One is to audit the risk, to have a third party or a friendly outsider come and review the risks and especially the responses and management plans for them, and give an opinion. In a large project or one with major health, safety or financial risks, a risk audit may be a regulatory or contractual requirement. The other use of a risk audit is as a wake-up call to shake people in the project out of their comfortable habits by frightening them. This can be a reasonable control function of the risk audit.

▶ Variance and trend analysis

What was planned progress? What are the actuals? And what is the trend? Is it getting worse or better? Often a graph to show trends is a powerful tool for seeing and understanding what is going on in the project, and also for communicating it to others. Earned value is one metric which can be used for variance and trend analysis; others are schedule performance index and cost performance index. These are described in the boxed text.

Some measures of progress and variance: EV, SPI, CPI

Earned value

Each task in the project should add value in some way. Earned value analysis assumes that the value created is in proportion to the planned effort, and so small tasks add proportionally less value than large ones. It is easy to think of examples where this is clearly not the case, but any other method would be fraught with difficulties over assessing the relative value-add of different sorts of task. At any one time through the life of the project the notional value that has been created is proportional to the percentage of the project that is complete:

$$Earned\ value = budget \times \%\ complete$$

The original project budget is used in order to obtain a value in dollars, pounds or euros. If the project is complete then 100% of the budget value has been created, whereas if the project is less than 100% complete a proportionally smaller fraction of the budget can be claimed.

Project budgets are usually made up of a number of external purchases plus a charge for the time that internal staff are expected to spend on the project. If there are no large external purchases then the budget is dominated by the cost of staff time, so the assumption implicit in the earned value approach that value creation is proportional to effort will hold true. But if the project budget contains large items of capital expenditure then costs are not proportional to effort. Earned value can still be used under these circumstances, but the schedule and cost performance indices will need to be interpreted with care. Some organizations therefore prefer to exclude external purchases when calculating earned value.

Schedule performance index

A key question for a project is where it stands relative to the schedule. This question could be rephrased as 'How much of the progress we should have made to date have we actually made?'. The schedule performance index is defined as

$$Schedule\ performance\ index\ (SPI) = \frac{earned\ value}{planned\ spend\ to\ date}$$

Strictly, this calculation gives the answer to the question 'How much of the value that we should have created to date have we actually created?' but the earlier assumption that progress, value and spending are proportional makes these questions equivalent.

Note that schedule performance is measured in proportion to spending, but planned progress is related to planned spending provided that the project is charged for the time people spend working on it. A schedule performance index below 1 indicates that the project has made less progress than planned. An SPI figure above 1 means that the project has made more progress than planned.

Cost performance index

Project managers and sponsors are also usually interested in project costs. With good recording of the cost of staff time and committed spending, it should be possible to get a good picture of actual costs at any time through the life of the project. But this shows only what has been spent, whereas what people usually want to know is whether spending is higher or lower than what had been planned. Rather than relate actual cost to that planned to date, the cost performance index relates actual cost to earned value. This means that the index is not skewed if a project runs late but still spends what was originally planned. The CPI is the answer to the question 'How much of our spending to date is justified by our progress?'. It is defined as

$$Cost\ performance\ index\ (CPI) = \frac{earned\ value}{actual\ cost\ to\ date}$$

Just as with SPI, figures below 1 are bad, and those above 1 are good. A CPI of less than 1 means that the project has so far cost more than can be justified by progress, and vice versa.

▶ Technical performance analysis

This means analyzing how the technical performance of the project to date compares to the plan. For example, perhaps a project to upgrade an engine planned to enable it to run at a higher temperature than before, say 800°C, so has this been reached or is performance peaking at only 720°C?

▶ Reserve analysis

If you have a ten-week project with a contingency, or buffer, of $10,000, then there is a great difference between the situation in which you have spent $9,000 of the buffer by the end of the second week and a situation in which you have spent $9,000 of the buffer by the ninth week. The first situation suggests that the project is in trouble, the latter that there are no real problems. This example shows how buffer monitoring can be used to monitor risks.

▶ Status meetings

To ensure you get maximum value from risk monitoring and control meetings, participate in them in two ways. Make sure that the meetings are properly administered, so that there is an agenda, you have an aim, and so on. That should be normal. Secondly, listen to your emotions and feel the emotions of others. Does it feel like there are problems? Follow up your gut feelings by looking for evidence, but of course be sensitive to how you do this.

▶ Summary

Project risk management aims to increase the probability and impact of positive events and decrease the probability and impact of events adverse to project objectives. Or, more concisely, it aims to avoid unpleasant surprises or at least to ensure they don't derail the project.

The steps in project risk management, in the proper sequence, are as follows:

1 Plan how to manage risks.
2 Identify the risks.
3 Understand them thoroughly (through first qualitative and then quantitative analysis).
4 Plan responses to those risks that warrant response planning in advance.

So far these are all planning processes. The 'doing' part of risk management is monitoring and controlling, and all planning is wasted without some 'doing'. Don't be one of those people who timidly deludes themselves and everyone else that once a risk is safely documented in the risk register it is managed. The risk register is a vital tool for risk management, but that's only the beginning. The main part of the work is to do something, which happens in the monitoring and controlling part of risk management. Keep the identification and analysis work up to date with regular risk reviews.

project procurement management

1
2
3
4
5
6
7
8
9
10
11
12
13

▶ Aims of this chapter

This chapter explains project procurement management, that is, how to purchase or otherwise acquire a product or service from outside the project and the project team. By the end of this chapter, you should:

- know what procurement management is and how it relates to project management as a whole;
- know when and why procurement management is valuable in project management;
- be able to categorize project procurement activities according to each stage project or process management group;
- be able to apply the standards and procedures associated with procurement management, thereby improving the effectiveness of your project management;
- be able to explain the benefit of treating project procurement management as a distinct knowledge area within project management.

▶ What is project procurement management?

Project procurement management describes the processes required to procure product or services for a project from outside the project. Procure means no more than obtain, just to be clear on terminology. Procurement can entail either entering into a formal contract, such as for purchasing (buying), leasing or hiring, or entering into a non-contractual arrangement, such as an internal requisition or indent procedure, or some other means by which organizations allocate resources internally. Although procuring from outside the organization will normally entail a formal contract, note that procuring from within the same organization as the project may also, at least nominally[1], involve a formal contract, and, less frequently, procuring externally may be on a non-contractual basis.

A key output from the procurement process is often a legally binding contract. Except for the simplest ones, contracts need to be managed and controlled, and often need change control. Examples of common activities performed as part of contract management are passing information to the supplier (for example, to let them know that the project is ready to receive a supply) and checking that payment should be made and initiating payment. The most important control activity is usually to ensure that payment is not made until the project is satisfied that the relevant part of the contract has been met.

Where there is a legal contract, the project needs to operate according to the terms and conditions thereby imposed, or, if these are unacceptable, the project needs to change them. Changing a contract can be difficult and expensive, and may be impossible, so close attention to detail must be applied during the planning and drafting of the contract; once the contract is in place, the focus of the project's effort switches to controlling, managing and administering the procurement processes. We can see from this that there is a natural lifecycle to project procurement management.

In a large or complex project several contracts or other procurement agreements may be running at the same time, and there may be interplays between them. Managing procurement for a large or complex project can thus be a major task in terms of effort, cost and risk.

> **PMI says**
>
> **Project procurement management**
> 'Project Procurement Management includes the processes to purchase or acquire the products, services, or results needed from outside the project team to perform the work.' *PMBOK Guide* (p.341)

▶ Why bother with procurement management?

If you are a project manager who has not yet experienced procurement management, you need to be aware that as your career develops there may come a day when your project includes a significant procurement management element. The tools and techniques in this chapter will make your life easier when that day comes. If you are an experienced project manager and have several projects under your belt that include significant procurement elements, then this chapter can help you benchmark your approach, your personal tools and techniques.

If there is a significant procurement element in your project, then it is very risky to invent a procurement approach on the hoof. In most organizations that should never be necessary as there will usually be a procurement department to assist you, but how much do they know about project management and your project? The project procurement methodology described in this chapter will help ensure a smooth interface with the procurement department where there is one, and will help ensure that there are no gaps between the way they do procurement and the needs of your project in respect of procurement.

▶ How does procurement management fit in the process groups?

The six procurement processes are common sense ones, and boil down to deciding what you need to procure, and then managing the procurement. They all fit into the process groups in a common sense way too (Table 12.1). Note that the table shows the normal model as given in the PMBOK, but you should vary it when necessary. It is the normal model in that, normally, you will not want to or be able to start procurement during project initiation. That is too soon, because you won't know enough about what needs to be procured, and even if you do, at that stage of the project there are many other higher priorities. The right place to start procurement is therefore in the planning process group, because procurement needs to be planned. As we say, there will be exceptions. If procurement is a major part of the project, or there is a particularly long lead time, and time is already tight, then you may want to vary the model above and start working on procurement as part of

Table 12.1 Six project procurement management processes

		Process Group		
Initiating	Planning	Executing	Monitoring and controlling	Closing
	1 Plan and purchase acquisitions	3 Request seller* responses	5 Contract administration	6 Contract closure
	2 Plan contracting	4 Select sellers		

* The *PMBOK Guide* uses the term 'seller'. In this book we use the terms 'seller' and 'supplier' interchangeably, and we prefer 'supplier' because not all parties who supply the procurement needs of a project are sellers: apart from the pedantic (in this context) possibility of hiring rather than buying, in large corporations or government departments there will be intra-organizational suppliers who are not sellers in the conventional sense. If you are taking the PMI's professional exams, think in terms of 'sellers' only. In the real world you will find many organizations use 'supplier' where PMI uses 'seller'.

project initiation. If procurement is a small and very simple part of your project, then perhaps there is effectively no planning to be done. And there are many projects where there is no procurement at all.

Critical factors in procurement

There are three critical factors to consider in project procurement. Ensure that you appreciate them fully in their impact on your project. They are:

◆ Time.
◆ Personal relationships with your own procurement people.
◆ Details of the specifications in the procurement agreement.

Time

Time is a critical factor in most projects. Determining what needs to be procured, specifying it in a way suitable for a contract, and drafting the contract are lengthy processes. Tendering can also be a long process. Sarbannes–Oxley procedures and government contracting rules can further lengthen drafting and tendering. This means that procurement can be a major constraint on the rate of progress in the overall project, and if so will need substantial project management attention. If your project involves procurement make sure that you know the following:

◆ Your organization's processes and typical timescales for procurement.
◆ Sarbannes–Oxley, government or other regulatory impositions on procurement and the likely time consequences.
◆ Who in your department needs to be involved in procurement.

▶ Personal relationships with your own procurement people

If there are documents that need to be prepared for procurement, for example to enable prospective suppliers to prepare their bid submissions, ensure your plan allows enough time. Avoid telling your contract manager 'I need a contract in place tomorrow' – as Toby Young might say, that is how to lose friends and alienate people.

If your organization has a contracts or purchasing department, build relationships in it with the people you will be working with for project procurement. Knowing them and knowing what experience they have helps to avoid delay to projects. These relationships are also important to ensure the details included in the contract are correct and can be verified as required by the project.

▶ Details of the specifications in the procurement agreement

Ensure that the procurement agreement works, which means to say, ensure that it contains the right specifications. It may sound obvious, but check that the product or service specifications, together with any special project management requirements, are actually in the contract or other procurement agreement. Ensure that all the issues are understood by both sides: do this by talking to the supplier before the contract is signed, or getting someone from your project team to talk to them. After talking to them, make a short note of key points from the conversation and e-mail it to the supplier, asking them to verify your understanding. If this sounds like common sense, it is, and it is a reminder that failing to do these simple things is all too often regretted big-time subsequently. Remember that once a contract is made, anything omitted can only be inserted if it is agreed by both parties. So get all your changes in before the contract is signed.

▶ Steps in project procurement management

Figure 12.1 shows the full sequence of processes and activities in project procurement management.

▶ First steps: planning

The very first step, before even starting the process of purchasing a product or service, is to ensure that as project manager you know the organization's procurement and approval process. If you don't know these, then at best you will duplicate work unnecessarily, you will most probably do a worse job of procurement than the established organization would, and at worst you may create legal liability and risk for you personally. If time permits you should ensure that you have a rough understanding of the terms and conditions included in your organization's standard procurement contract. If you don't already know these things, then finding them out is also a way to start developing a working relationship with key people in your organization's procurement department. If you know these things but don't have those relationships, asking again is one way to start to develop them.

Fig. 12.1 Project procurement management – sequence of processes and activities

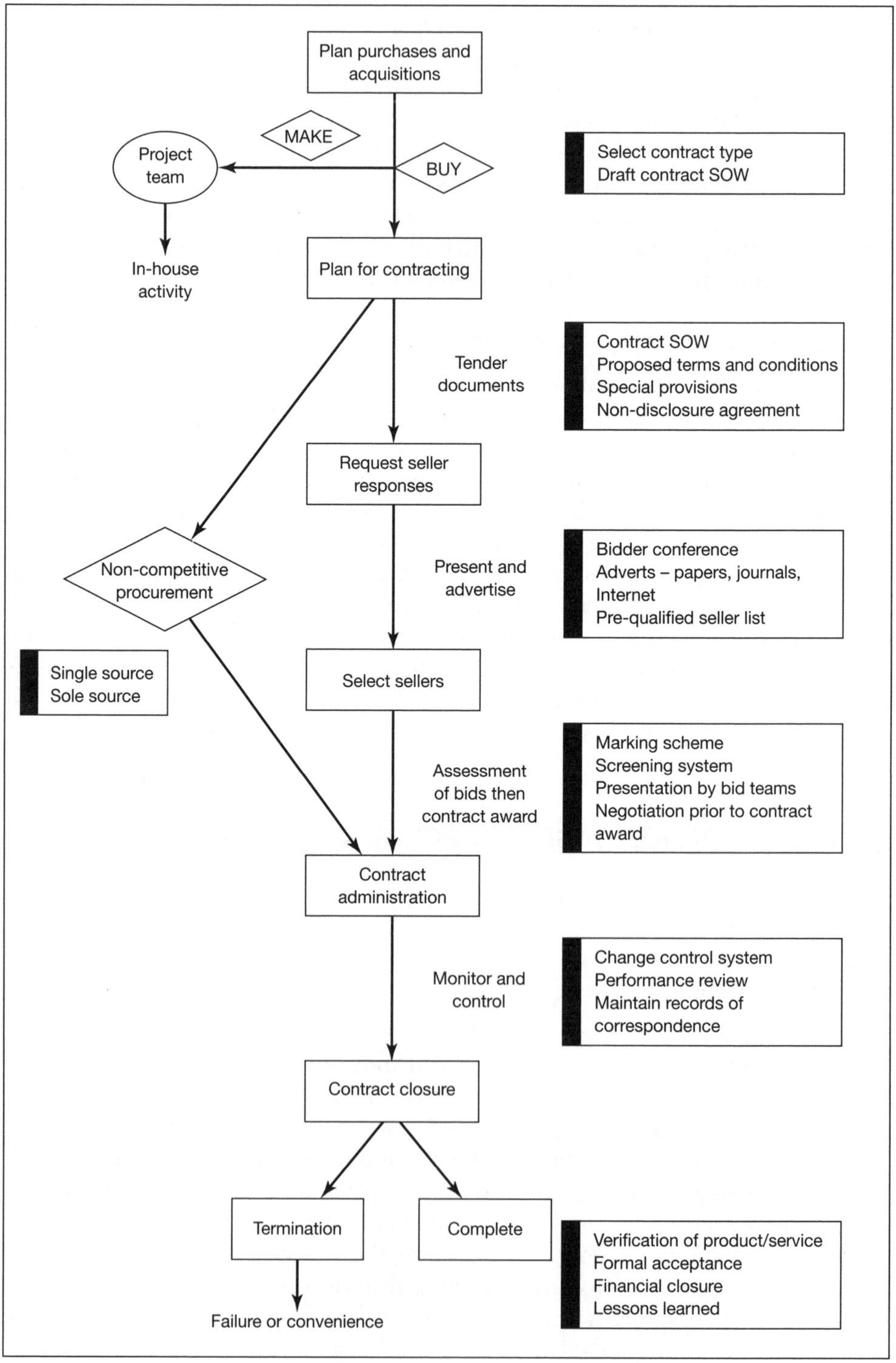

The first two steps in project procurement management (after ensuring that you know your own procurement organization) are:

1 Plan purchases and acquisitions
2 Plan for contracting.

PMI says

Plan purchases and acquisitions

'Plan Purchases and Acquisitions is the process of determining what to purchase or acquire, and determining when and how to do so.' *PMBOK Guide* (p.366)

The objective of procurement management is to procure a product or service necessary to the project. This begins with the first of the six procurement management processes, 'plan purchases and acquisitions'. In this process you decide what goods or services to procure for the project, and how to procure them. It will help to understand why each good or service needs to be procured, that is, how each relates to the final deliverable and business purpose of the project. You should already understand this as project manager, but if you delegate the procurement process, which you might on a large or complex project, you should ensure that the person or team to whom you delegate also has the appropriate understanding. Planning may need to include generating options for procurement and selecting between them, and identifying potential suppliers.

Another decision which may need to be answered in the procurement planning process is the make-or-buy decision. This is a classic general management decision, and it arises in project management too. Table 12.2 gives an example of the make-or-buy decision, highlighting the very common and potentially career-fatal risks in it for project managers, and showing how to manage them down to safe levels.

Planning needs information as an input. Key documents for use as input into the project procurement management processes are:

◆ Project scope statement.
◆ Risk register.
◆ Schedule.
◆ Costs.
◆ WBS.
◆ WBS dictionary.

Once the plan purchases and acquisitions process is completed, or underway, the next process in project procurement management is 'plan for contracting'. The purpose of this process is to produce:

◆ Procurement documents (for prospective suppliers).
◆ Evaluation criteria by which suppliers will be selected.
◆ Updated statements of work.

Prospective suppliers, whether sole suppliers or in a competitive bid, need information about the project's requirements of them, and eventually will need

---

Table 12.2 The make-or-buy decision on procuring a database: an example of how to protect yourself as project manager in make-or-buy decisions

---

An example of a make-or-buy decision, and the personal risks you may face as a project manager involved in it, is when a project needs a database, and the project can:

◆ EITHER buy an off-the-shelf database that meets the requirements almost but not completely,

◆ OR can hire a team of computer database programmers to create exactly what the project wants.

Cost is one factor in such decisions, but risk is more usually a bigger factor. In the database example, the risk in buying something commercially available is that although we think it is a close enough but not exact match for what the project needs, it may turn out to have critical limitations, and on the other hand, the risk in hiring a team of programmers is that they do not deliver what is needed, or deliver late or over budget. As a project manager you are likely to find that you come under pressure to go with the least cost option, and then are personally blamed when the risks associated with that option crystallize. People who were quite happy to back the low cost decision, and even insisted on it, suddenly start to say that all along they knew it was the wrong thing to do, and blame you for not listening. What can you do? The solution to this very common problem is actually quite simple. First, be clear in your own mind that in project management generally, not just project procurement management, your job is not to make such decisions but rather, secondly, to present such decisions to the right people, the right stakeholders, and to provide them with the relevant available information and factors so that they can make a decision. In the case of decisions that no one wants to make, it is your job, working with the sponsor, to ensure that either such decisions are made, or, if they are critical to the project, to consider halting the project until they do, although that is *in extremis*. Thirdly – and this is your personal insurance policy and the bullet proof jacket for your bonus – it is your job to document how such decisions were reached, mainly so that if someone involved in the decision is possibly likely to blame you if things go wrong, you have the documentation to show that you did not take the decision, they did. Ninety nine times out of a hundred, if you run this process and document it, no one will try to blame you anyway.

---

a statement of work and terms and conditions. This information is contained in the procurement documents, which terms may include, for example, requests for information (RFIs), requests for quotations (RFQs), and invitations to tender (ITTs). The details of how to attract and evaluate bidders are the heart of the procurement or purchasing management profession, and fall outside the scope of this book. The various ways to identify potential suppliers include advertising, bidders' conferences, and qualified seller or preferred suppliers lists. That kind of detail should be left to your organization's contracts or procurement department. What you need to ensure from a project management point of view in the plan for contracting step is that you (or the project) have identified and then communicated clearly what needs to be procured, in sufficient detail such that the people doing procurement for you understand it and can use their professional judgement well. Ideally the project will have professional procurement support for the process to plan purchases and acquisitions, who will handle the detail, but the project must be engaged in the process.

Next steps: executing

The next two steps in project procurement management are:

3 Request seller responses.
4 Select sellers.

The project, through the procurement staff where they exist, requests potential suppliers to respond to invitations to tenders or other procurement documentation. Once the deadline for responses arrives (or if no deadline, once enough responses have been received), the process is to assess the proposal for supplying the project and select one or more suppliers. Negotiations may follow, to resolve ambiguities or agree changes to the terms and conditions. When both parties approve the contract, representatives of the project's and the supplier's organizations sign the contract or other supply document.

It is worth knowing that in most advanced economies, including the UK and USA, irrespective of what in-house lawyers and procurement professionals may say, it is now the case that for most kinds of procurement transaction electronic signatures are at least as good and reliable as ink-on-paper signatures (real-estate transactions are the main exception). How prudent or useful it is to argue this point in your project is something you must judge for yourself, but using electronic signatures can save weeks or months on procurement – it is the magnitude of this benefit that justifies mentioning this point of detail here.

Contracts

The point of selecting a seller is to contract with them. Project managers should understand the key features of the main types of contract. The three main types of contracts used are:

- ◆ Fixed price (FP).
- ◆ Cost reimbursable (CR).
- ◆ Time and materials (T&M).

Fixed price (FP) contracts

A fixed price contract involves agreeing a fixed total price for a specifically defined product or service to complete the described work. It is the most commonly used type of contract. The basic form of a fixed price contract is a purchase order that details the goods, what the price is and when it will be delivered. As the buyer, this form of contract has the lowest risk of increasing cost as long as the work has a fully defined scope to deliver against. If the seller signs a fixed price contract, the detail contained in the contract statement of work should be detailed and unambiguous to ensure higher costs are not borne by the seller. The advantage of using this type of contract is the reduced level of work required by the buyer to manage the contract. The buyer will know the price being charged and the incentive lies with the seller to control costs. Most companies have a lot of experience dealing with this type of contract, but extra work is required to produce the contract statement of work. A point to be monitored throughout the contract involves making sure the seller is completing all the work included within the contract statement of work. Another matter to review on a regular basis is the number of changes being incorporated in the contract, the effect of which could be the seller clawing back profit which may have been negotiated away in order to secure the contract.

▶ Cost reimbursable (CR) contracts

For a cost reimbursable contract, the cost risk shifts to the buyer because the total costs are unknown. The seller will bill for the actual costs incurred, plus an agreed fee or percentage of the total sum charged. This type of contract could be selected if the buyer is unable to define fully the scope of work, or the requirements are unknown. IT projects or R&D work can typically fall in this category of contract because their scope is not fully determined. A benefit for the buyer to select a CR contract is that less effort is involved in producing the contract statement of work because it is a simpler document. As stated earlier, the cost risk factor is lower for the seller, so the contract price can be lower compared to a FP contract for a similar package of work. The disadvantage associated with a CR contract is the greater level of management involvement required by the buyer, because extra auditing is required to ensure that invoices match the work and time expended. The other factor to be considered is the lack of incentive to control costs for the seller.

▶ Time and materials (T&M) contracts

The T&M type of contract can be considered an amalgamation of FP and CR. As an example, the rates quoted within the contract for material priced per metre are fixed for the duration of the contract, although the contract's total costs will rise if the

Fig. 12.2 Level of risk experienced by buyer and seller for different contract types

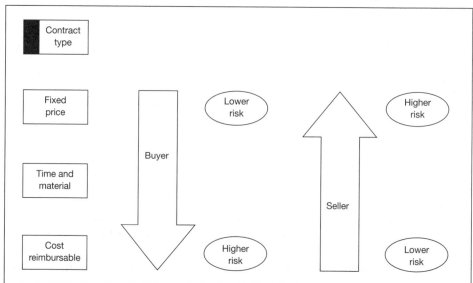

amount of ordered material increases. This type of contract tends to be used for smaller contract amounts and spans a shorter time period. In comparison with the other two contract types, this approach has a medium risk to cost that sits between FP and CR. This type of contract is best considered for smaller projects. It is a good option when wishing to hire staff quickly to expand your team. The drawback of using a T&M contract is the requirement to provide the closest level of supervision.

Figure 12.2 compares the risks to buyer and seller for the three types of contract.

Contract statement of work

The contract statement of work (SOW) is based on specific elements listed in the project scope statement and becomes part of the contract once signed. Until the contract is signed, the contract statement of work remains a live document and can be revised during the procurement process. Each contract statement of work describes an item or service being purchased by the buyer, and is based on information extracted from the project scope. The document must be complete and clearly defined, but the level of detail should reflect the requirements of the work involved. It needs to provide enough detail to enable prospective sellers to decide whether they are capable of delivering the item or service. Building an extension to a school will require a lot of information detailing which building regulations to comply with, together with the specifications of materials to be used. A much less detailed document would be required if you wished to purchase some expertise for the project. The contract statement of work should also include requirements about attendance at meetings, reports to be presented and the distribution of letters and e-mails. If these points are missed, or are not covered in the correct level of detail, trying to get them added to the contract at a later stage will result in extra costs.

PMI says

Contract statement of work
'Contract Statement of Work is a narrative description of products, services, or results to be supplied under contract.' *PMBOK Guide* (p.355)

There are three main types of contract statements of work, but selection will be dependent on the nature of the work involved:

◆ Performance – expresses what the product is required to achieve, rather than detailing how the work is to be done or what its design should be.
◆ Functional – expresses the end purpose or result of the work. It is used in the performance of the work, or it could include the minimum essential characteristics of the product.
◆ Design – expresses exactly what work is to be undertaken, such as build to this drawing.

Contract administration

Contract administration ensures that the supplier conducts the work or service stated in the contract, while the buyer conforms to their requirements included in the contract. If there is more than one contract involved with the project then a key integration task is to manage the various interfaces within the project.

The activities undertaken as part of contract administration can involve the following (see also Figure 12.3):

- Managing the project invoices.
- Completing the change control system.
- Authorizing the seller's work and payments.
- Interpreting the contract and determining what falls inside and outside its scope.
- Verifying that the scope is being achieved.
- Maintaining quality control.
- Updating the risks to the project.
- Identifying and evaluating new risks as they arise.
- Keeping records and correspondence throughout the life of the contract to track changes and to record the reasons behind them.

PMI says

Contract administration

'Contract Administration is the process of managing the contract and the relationship between the buyer and seller, reviewing and documenting how a seller is performing or has performed to establish required corrective actions and provide a basis for future relationships with the seller, managing contract related changes and, when appropriate, managing the contractual relationship with the outside buyer of the project.' *PMBOK Guide* (p.355)

If the work performance information identifies that the seller is failing to meet their contractual requirements, and corrective actions are not able to resolve the issue, the termination clause within the contract could be invoked. For a less severe matter, the contract could be amended by joint consent, although this must occur before contract closure. The change control process would need to be followed for an amendment to the contract, but the instigation of this process could add cost to buyer or seller, depending on the contractual terms and conditions. If either party disagrees with the requested change, there may be the need to resort to the claims administration procedure, as stated in the contract. If the differences cannot be resolved within the terms of the contract, the dispute resolution procedure is the only course open for arbitration or litigation, and the only winners in this case are the solicitors.

Fig. 12.3 Contract administration – activities involved to meet contractual requirements

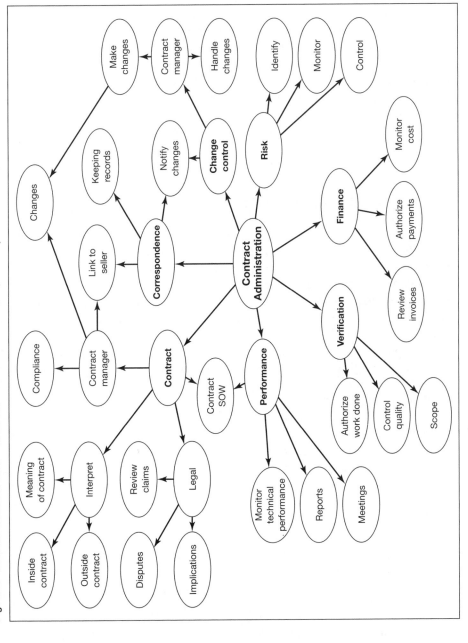

▶ Contract change control system

A contract manager is nominated for each seller and buyer to act as its representative. This person or department is therefore the only individual or group authorized to change or amend the contract. The project team or stakeholders can raise a request for change, but the change control system would be used to review and evaluate the proposal. If the change is approved for implementation, the change request would then need to be formally passed to the seller for consideration. If the impact on scope, cost and time is acceptable to both buyer and seller, the change is then managed as part of the integrated change control process. If too many changes are being proposed to the work package under contract, it may be appropriate to terminate the contract under mutual arrangements and start afresh with a new contract or seller.

▶ The project manager's role

Ideally the project manager will be appointed before any procurement is agreed. One of the aims of the procurement process is to establish the best and most appropriate contract for the product or service. The project manager therefore has a role here, which can include analyzing the concomitant risks to the project before committing to a seller. The output from such risk analysis could involve adding extra work or conditions to the draft contract before it is formally agreed. The project manager should not be working alone on this; if the organization has a procurement or contracts staff, or a legal or general counsel's department, he should be working hand-in-glove with the right person from that department. Ideally, for any but the smallest procurement needs, a contracts manager will be appointed to act on behalf of the project.

Once the procurement processes are underway, the activities and interactions required for the contract can generate their own momentum. The whole contractual procedure could take over and sideline the project manager, therefore a constant flow of communication between the contract manager and project manager should maintain the balance between the project requirements and the demands of procurement.

Key Idea

Working together
The project manager should work closely with the organization's procurement staff, and a procurement contracts manager should be appointed as the specialist to handle contracting and other procurement issues for the project. The project manager should hand over all detail in procurement to them, but should maintain a close working relationship and retain overall decision making on behalf of the project.

Consider whether it will be useful to state in the procurement contract how the project management requirements are to be met by including the frequency and attendance at meetings between the project team and the supplier. Stating in the procurement contract that the supplier will meet the project manager or their designate once a week on Mondays at 0900 from the start of the contract until final acceptance is an effective way to deal with the risk that the supplier may either try not to attend meetings regularly, or try to charge extra for attendance. That kind of detail is the sort of thing that your organization's procurement staff should be experienced in, and if so, use their expertise. Their expertise is also useful in determining what is an appropriate amount of time within the project schedule to allow for conducting procurement contract planning, selection, negotiation and administration. If short-cuts are taken with this process, the ramifications experienced later in the project could be far greater.

We have been saying, above, that as project manager you should delegate the details and day-to-day management of procurement to the appropriate staff in your organization, assuming that there are such people. They are usually very willing, and most belong to one of the professional bodies in that discipline, such as the Institute of Purchasing Managers. However, you must understand what their experience and competence is in broad terms. For example, if your project is procuring an IT database but your procurement department has no IT procurement expertise, and in fact has only ever dealt with suppliers of concrete aggregate and industrial adhesives, you will need to understand and manage the risks that arise from the gap in skills and experience. A less extreme example is if your procurement department has experience of procuring complete IT solutions but your project requires a team of programmers to be hired, then there is probably a skills and experience gap in your procurement department that may be just as critical as in the first example, but it is perhaps harder for you to spot. A checklist of questions to ask of your procurement specialists is:

- What similar procurements have they personally managed before?
- What is different about this procurement?
- What do they think the risks are?
- Where do they think they might misunderstand the risks?
- How well do they know the supplier in question?
- What lessons learnt or industry guidelines exist for this type of procurement?
- What are the common problems in this type of procurement?
- What are the standard moves for managing risks in this type of procurement?
- If the contract manager has no direct relevant experience, can they find and talk to someone who has, to help answer these questions?

The contract manager and not the project manager is responsible for contract negotiations at the day-to-day level. Whether the project manager should foster relationships with the provider depends on how important the provider is to the project and the time available. The project manager should also work with the contract manager to manage any changes to the contract, although it is usually only the contract manager who has the authority to incorporate changes within a contract, because usually they are responsible to the organization, and not the project manager, for procurement.

▶ The special problems of IT procurement

Is IT being procured? IT procurement is usually difficult and stressful, and charac-terized by some degree of failure. If you have experience otherwise, you are very lucky. Most IT procurement ends up costing more than planned at best, being late as a matter of routine, failing to deliver some important aspect of what was speci-fied also as a matter of routine, and not infrequently not working at all. It is not the job of this book to speculate on why this is so, or what the IT industry may do about it[2]. It is the job of this book to ensure that we all understand that IT procurement is so highly risky that it needs special handling and very careful attention in any project. It is conventional to involve IT specialists in the procurement of IT, although whether this reduces the risk at all is debatable, but you will probably be unwise to try to buck this fashion.

If your project involves procuring IT, ensure that your procurement team or con-tracts manager has extensive experience of this, and take special care to ensure that you protect your own position and the project's by documenting everything.

The following principles will be useful in IT procurement:

◆ Insist on seeing a demonstration of all key equipment, programs, interfaces, etc. Do not accept 'canned' or pre-prepared demonstrations; insist on live demon-strations with data from your project.
◆ Do not believe any time schedules for delivering things which do not exist right now or cannot be demonstrated right now. Double them for your planning pur-poses. If they slide, double them again.
◆ Treat cost estimates from suppliers as for time estimates.
◆ When any supplier makes an estimate, get them to put it in writing, and if they don't, you should send them an e-mail documenting what you think they said.
◆ Even if an aspect of a requirement is obvious, such as that a database should have a search function or that a text editor should be able to edit text, make sure this is documented.
◆ Use a set of rules of thumb to help you and the procurement team judge the fair-ness and reasonableness of cost and time estimates from IT suppliers.

An example of a rule of thumb, above, is that a small to medium-sized database should:

◆ if performed in a small company environment, take one man-month to produce at a cost of about £15,000;
◆ if performed for a medium-sized or large company, take one month to produce in pilot form, and should cost no more than £50,000 (the extra cost being the extra bureaucracy involved in communicating with the larger company);
◆ and either way, about half of IT suppliers will try to charge £100,000 for such work.

A good IT procurement manager will have a number of rules of thumb such as these, and will also have a clear enough idea of what 'medium-sized database' and other such terms mean to make the rules of thumb useful.

Case study

Example of the special problems of IT procurement

One of many examples of problems in IT procurement was of a large paint manufacturing plant trying to procure and install an IT system with bespoke software. The levels of data entry, reliability of the hardware and computer interface, together with the number of interactions involved from manufacture to despatch, resulted in the recording system failing to provide both the accuracy and consistency required for quantifying the resources used and the production of management reports detailing volume output and efficiency.

Centralized/decentralized contracting

The two general strategies used to organize a contracting department are either to centralize the expertise into one department, or to decentralize the contract staff by distributing the experts to assigned projects. In a centralized system the contract manager would report to their functional manager and they would expect to work on a series of projects. A decentralized structure has the contract manager reporting direct to the project manager and being responsible for just one project. Each approach has its own merits, but the organization's senior management will decide whether to follow a policy of centralization or decentralization for their contracting staff. The decision is unlikely to be made by the project manager unless there is a compelling argument to change the structure of the contracting department. The main advantage of having a centralized contracting organization is the ability to standardize the company's procedures and processes across the entire department. The main advantage of operating a decentralized contracting department is the allocation of a contract manager to a designated project. The main disadvantage of applying a decentralized system is the difficulty of maintaining expertise and standardization across the organization, because each contract manager is operating in isolation. This approach could also prove to be a less efficient use of contracting resource due to duplication of effort. From a human perspective there is no home department for the contract manager to return to once the project is complete, nor is there a clear career path for the individual to follow. To make a decentralized structure work well, good communication, regular meetings and central training sessions should be set up for all contracting staff within the organization.

Summary

The project manager should be involved in the procurement management process as early as possible, but should delegate day-to-day procurement to professional procurement staff, where they are available. This should result in a contracts manager being appointed from those staff to the project. Procurement is risky and the basis for managing all the risks is to understand and state in the procurement documentation, such as contracts with suppliers, exactly what it is that the project needs. This requires research and analysis. IT procurement is especially risky.

The first step for the project manager is to know the people, experience and capabilities of the procurement people in their organization, and to understand the existing procurement processes and standards and the legal terms and conditions normally used. A key decision is sometimes the make-or-buy decision, and this is usually a matter of which risks are preferable. The project manager's job is to get the decision made by the relevant stakeholders, not to make it themselves. Any time required for procurement management processes must be included within the project's schedule. The work involved to generate the procurement documentation, consider prospective bidders, wait for the sellers' responses, select a seller and then negotiate a contract may often require a significant amount of time to complete.

Work for the project manager continues after the contract has been signed, because there is the need to monitor and control the contract. Administrative activities required to be undertaken involve verifying the scope is being met, checking invoices and paying bills, together with the need to confirm that the seller is complying with the terms and conditions of the contract. Once everything is delivered and completed satisfactorily, or a contract is terminated before the work is completed, the last stage is to conduct contract closure to safeguard the legal interests of both buyer and seller.

▶ Notes

1 A legal entity cannot contract with itself. It may be that within one organization there are different legal entities.

2 But if you are interested, see Nokes, S.M., 2000. *Taking Control of IT Costs*. London: Financial Times/Prentice Hall.

professional
responsibility

What is a profession? What is professional responsibility?

The business case for professional responsibility

The PMI and professional responsibility

Codes of ethics

Aims of this chapter

This chapter explains why project managers have professional responsibility, what that is, and in particular what the PMI's requirements for professional responsibility are. The chapter starts with the broad, general principles of professional responsibility and narrows down to the specifics as defined by the PMI. Those specifics may not be of direct interest to you if you are not a member or not intending to become a member of the PMI, but are the kind of specific statement of professional responsibility which any practising project manager should follow, even if not that particular instantiation. By the end of this chapter, the reader should be able to:

◆ state the fundamental principle of a profession;
◆ state three general principles that guide professional conduct;
◆ explain the business case for being a member of a recognized profession and abiding by its code of practice;
◆ know where to find the PMI's code of conduct and who it governs;
◆ state the two categories and the principles under them of the PMI's code of conduct.

What is a profession? What is professional responsibility?

A profession is defined as 'a paid occupation, esp. one that involves prolonged training and a formal qualification ...'[1]. The first professions were those of clerk in holy orders (that is, priest), lawyer, and surgeon or medical doctor, with accountants, engineers, some architects and patent agents as later additions.

The Hippocratic Oath

The opening words of the Hippocratic Oath – the world's first code of professional ethics – are as follows:

'I swear by Apollo the physician, and Aesculapius, and Hygeia, and all the gods and goddesses that according to my ability and judgment I will keep this oath and code of ethics.'   Hippocrates

The fundamental principle of a profession is that the professional, that is the individual who practises the profession, is paid a fee in exchange for putting their own self-interest to one side and acting in the best interest of the client. This is different, so the argument goes, from a manager or employee of an industrial or commercial concern. The manager or employee has to compromise between their own interest of making a profit and the interest of their customer, which compromise is normally settled by the market price mechanism, and results in the commercial organization supplying at a trade-off in terms of price and quality. This is perfectly normal and sensible, it is merely saying that commercial organizations supply goods at less than perfect quality most of the time because the customer does not want and is not prepared to pay for, most of the time, the best possible quality. Easy-Jet and Ryanair provide excellent services and offer good value, but are not trying to emulate the same quality of customer experience as first class in one of the old-fashioned national flag carriers. To take a different example, not everyone wants to pay for a Rolls-Royce car. The idea is that professions are different because instead of supplying goods or trade services, they are providing an individual's skill and judgement, and reducing the quality of that is not an option, nor is it fair and reasonable, in the same way that filling an aircraft with cheaper seats to reduce price is. Note that the professional can still reduce costs to the client, by spending less time on a task, but this is not the same as reducing quality.

Another difference between a profession and other businesses is that because what is being sold is essentially the output of a human mind, it is much harder to check the quality of the output than is the case with a tangible good. This makes it harder for the client to check that charging is fair. 'Am I certain it really took four man-weeks to write that business case? No, I have to trust you.' In contrast, one can compare prices for a flight on different airlines by simply logging onto the web.

The argument is that a professional's fee is set sufficiently high so that they simply have no need to even think about making a trade-off in terms of quality. In return for the privilege of not having to worry about profit as much as non-professional businesses do, the professional is under a special obligation not to take advantage. That is the fundamental principle behind professional ethics and responsibility. Whether or not project management is a profession, and whether (and by how much) professions differ from non-professions, as has been argued above, are all interesting points, but are outside the scope of this book. The argument was explained as a way of setting the context for professional responsibility, and this book assumes that project management is a profession.

So what is professional responsibility and what is meant by a professional code of conduct? A professional code of conduct is generally a list of behaviours and standards that a professional person declares publicly that they will commit to uphold. Indeed, the term 'professional' has its roots in middle English, as the vow made on entering a religious order, and from the Latin *profiteri*, 'to declare publicly'. In the same way that a medical doctor promises to first do no harm, it is the project manager's responsibility to act ethically, with integrity and professionalism throughout the lifetime of the project and beyond. This often means putting the needs of the project and stakeholders before the project manager's own needs. In order to achieve this, the project manager must understand any legal requirements, ethical standards and stakeholder values that affect or are affected by the project. The PMI requires all entrants to the PMP to sign a declaration committing to abide by the PMI's Project Management Code of Professional Conduct. However, regardless of whether or not the project manager has the PMP certification, they are in a position of responsibility and should act accordingly.

The general principles of professional conduct, whatever the profession, that follow from the above are as follows:

- Put the client's interest first, especially if they clash with your own personal interests.
- Understand what the client wants and what their interests are in relation to your work and your profession.

◆ Know your own competence and its limits, and do not take on work beyond your competence, nor claim to have competence that you do not in fact possess.

The business case for professional responsibility

The previous section made the moral case for abiding by a professional code of practice. There is a related commercial reason, or business case, to do so. In terms of legal liability when something goes wrong, there is a great difference between on the one hand having made a reasonable effort to follow recognized practice but failing to achieve the desired results for the client, and on the other hand not having even tried to follow recognized practice and then failing. The first kind of mistake is treated much more leniently in the courts and by the client, which means less cost and shame if things go wrong, and even if things do not go wrong, lower insurance premiums. Companies that provide project management services are charged lower insurance premiums if their employees are members of a recognized professional body than if they are not.

We believe that the main reason to take professional responsibility seriously is the moral one, but the business case is separately a sufficient reason to do so.

Key Idea

Professional responsibility
As a professional you have a special privilege in your relationship with your client, which is that the client cannot check the quality of what you do in the same way as tangible goods can be inspected and measured. In return for this special power that you have in the relationship, you have a special responsibility not to take advantage and to always do your utmost to work in the client's interest. This includes not holding yourself out as having skills and experience that you do not have.

Understand what your client's interests are, know your own abilities and limits, and do your absolute utmost accordingly to serve the client's interest, putting yours to one side in exchange for your fee.

The PMI and professional responsibility

The PMI takes professional responsibility seriously, and indeed it is one of the main aims of the PMI to increase the professionalism of project management. Accordingly, if you sit the PMP or CAPM exam you will be required to know what the PMI expects. If you are taking the exams, you will be tested on your use of judgement, ethics, and responsibility. Specifically the questions will be based on the following areas:

◆ Ensuring integrity of action and communications.
◆ Contributing to the project management knowledge base.

- Applying professional knowledge.
- Balancing stakeholder interests.
- Respecting differences.

Those taking the PMP exam will be required to sign up to the PMI's code of professional conduct. The PMI says:

> By becoming a PMP certificant, you agree to abide by this Code of Conduct. PMI reserves the right to suspend or revoke the credential of any PMP certificant who is determined to have committed a violation of this Code or otherwise failed to adhere to the tenets of this Code.

You will find a full transcript of this code in the PMP handbook, which is available to download from the PMI's website (www.pmi.org).

The PMP code of professional conduct governs two areas of responsibility for the project management professional:

- Responsibilities to the project management profession.
- Responsibilities to customers and the general public.

The full code of conduct can be found in the PMP Certification Handbook which is downloadable from the PMI website. Responsibilities to the profession of project management include:

- Compliance with laws, regulations, and ethical standards governing professional practice in the state/province/country when providing project management services.
- Recognizing and respecting intellectual property developed or owned by others, and being accurate and truthful in all activities related to work and research.
- Adherence to the policies and procedures of the Project Management Institute in any activity associated with PMI's certification programs.

Responsibilities to customers and the public is concerned with the candidate's responsibility to:

- be truthful, accurate, and technically correct in regards to project scope and other requirements;
- maintain and respect the confidentiality of information in the course of professional activities.

In essence, the professional code of conduct is concerned with your acting honestly and ethically and putting the needs of the project above your own. If you can do this, not only will the questions relating to the code of conduct in the exam be simple, but you will become respected as a professional and trustworthy project manager.

▶ Codes of ethics

Codes of ethics and professional standards are not part-time. There is no point in conning oneself by pretending that one will uphold them 90% of the time, and do what you really want the other 10%. There is no point in signing up to a code of ethics if one does not intend to live by it the whole time.

▶ Summary

- Professionals have special needs and abilities to price less competitively than commercial organizations supplying goods, and special responsibilities follow from them not to exploit the client. This is the moral case for professional responsibility.
- There is also a business case, which is that costs and risks are reduced by being professionally responsible.
- The PMI has a professional code of conduct, to which PMPs must sign their agreement.
- The PMI's code is split into responsibilities to the project management profession and responsibilities to customers and the general public.

▶ Note

1 Apple Computer, Inc., 2005. *New Oxford American Dictionary* (2nd edn). Cupertino, CA: Apple Computer.

appendix A: the critical chain method

This appendix describes the critical chain approach to project management. It differs from the approach given in the book thus far in its focus on managing buffer, or reserve. The central idea behind critical chain is that people naturally tend to add too much buffer or contingency reserve when planning and estimating, for good reasons. But the overall effect is that there is too much slack built into projects, unless this human tendency is tightly managed. Critical chain seeks to make a virtue out of this feature of human nature.

Critical chain has been shown to deliver great benefits over conventional project management techniques, but it differs significantly from other project planning and management techniques. It may be a new way of working even for some experienced project managers. For this reason, only the key points of the technique are summarized here.

The critical chain method evolved from work by Eliyahu Goldratt on improving factory efficiency[1]. Goldratt advocated identifying the bottlenecks in production and concentrating all effort on ensuring that these stages in the production process worked at maximum efficiency, thereby maximizing the efficiency of the overall process (this was an application of his theory of constraints). Goldratt applied and extended this work in the domain of project planning and management, and this led to the critical chain method[2].

▶ Understanding activity durations

When a project is planned, most of the activity durations have to be estimated, and the actual durations of those activities may differ from the original estimate (see Figure A.1). Critical chain provides a means not only to retain control in the face of such uncertainty but also to exploit it.

One of the problems with the uncertainty of task durations is that the variability is predominantly positive: tasks often take longer than the estimate, but are very rarely shorter. There are several reasons for this:

- It is well documented that most people do not fully apply themselves to a task until at least half of the allowed time has elapsed (sometimes known as 'student syndrome'). This is entirely normal, and people may subconsciously or consciously allow for this behaviour in their original estimate. But it means that by the time the real work starts, there is often only just enough time left to complete the work package as it was originally understood, and the slightest problem is enough to push the duration beyond the deadline. Hence there is a tendency for tasks to be completed late no matter how much time is allowed.
- When several workstreams merge together into a single dependent activity, that dependent activity cannot start until the last of the merging workstreams has

Fig. A.1 Activity merge bias

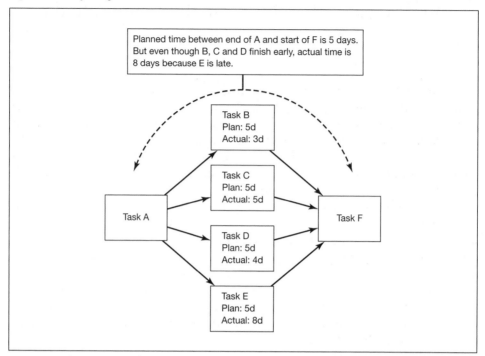

finished. Thus, even if three out of four merging workstreams have finished early, the downstream tasks will start late if the fourth workstream finishes late. All project workstreams must eventually merge together to produce the deliverables, but the fact that only the worst workstream matters means that project duration is again much more likely to be late than early.

- Parkinson's Law[3] states that work expands to fill the time available. On projects, people hardly ever report that a task is completed early, even if their work was of acceptable quality long before the deadline. People may assume that there is some duty to spend the allotted time on the task or they may be tempted to add additional refinements to make the work better, or they may delay delivering the completed work until the deadline because they know that they will be given more work to do if they signal that they are available. Hence project managers rarely get the benefit of tasks being completed early.

▶ Critical chain and activity durations

Critical chain addresses these biases in duration distributions both by addressing the behavioural causes and by turning the variability in task timing to our advantage by exploiting the statistical properties of sequences of uncertain events.

A manager applying the critical chain method will avoid student syndrome and Parkinson's Law by avoiding emphasizing a fixed delivery date when assigning tasks.

Team members are rewarded if they can show that they have delivered as quickly as possible instead of being motivated to deliver on a particular day.

Using classical methods of estimating task durations, the true likely duration of each and every task gets padded with an allowance to prevent embarrassment: unless otherwise directed, most people will give an estimate of the time in which they are almost certain to be able to complete the task, whereas the average time it will take is usually shorter. This protects the estimator because they thereby reduce the chance that they will later be shown to have underestimated. Of course, for the reasons outlined above, the work normally ends up running until the deadline, even though task deadlines include this hidden padding.

▶ Aggregating contingency

The second consequence of task estimates including contingency is that it is an extremely wasteful way to apportion contingency time. The statistics of linked processes are such that it is much better to aggregate the uncertainty into a single pool for the whole project rather than try to protect tasks one by one (see Figure A.2).

Fig. A.2 The cumulative effect of buffers on each task

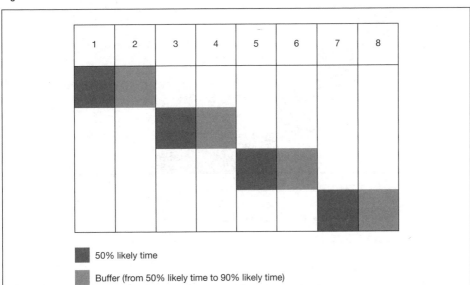

Consider four tasks in series, which have each been estimated to take two weeks to complete. In fact, we know that the two-week estimates are probably the time by which the tasks are 90% likely to complete, and further probing of the estimators reveals that there is a 50% probability that each task can be completed in one week. So the classical estimating method would give a chain of four two-week tasks, for a total of eight weeks.

Using critical chain, we build the plan using the one-week estimates, in the full knowledge that each of these is only 50% likely to be true, to give only four weeks in total. We allow for the uncertainty by adding a 'project buffer' which is shared between all four tasks (see Figure A.3). However, from statistics (see 'Statistics of aggregating tasks' box) we know that the uncertainty of this buffer duration is less than the sum of four individual one-week buffers. We can achieve the same overall level of protection for the project by having a two-week aggregate buffer as we did by having four one-week individual task buffers. So our critical chain plan is only six weeks long overall instead of the eight needed when each task had a buffer, and the two-week saving is due only to taking the buffers away from individual tasks and aggregating them into a single buffer for the project as a whole. Critical chain can shorten a project by over 20% in this way, with commensurate cost savings, without increasing overall risk. This may seem like black magic to project managers trained in other methods, but it is true.

Fig. A.3 The effect of aggregating contingencies is to reduce the total buffer time from four weeks (Fig A.2) to two weeks

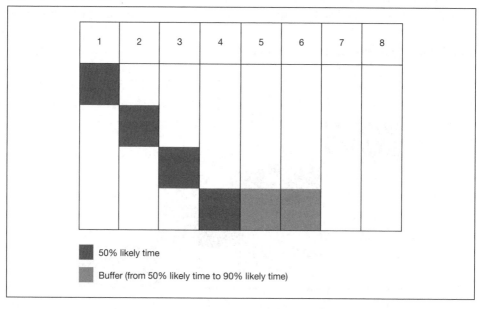

Statistics of aggregating tasks

The amount of uncertainty in a number is expressed mathematically as its standard deviation, SD or σ. It is also common to use variance, SD^2 or σ^2, which is just the square of the standard deviation. If several uncertain processes are aggregated, then the overall variance is the sum of the variances. This is important because if the uncertainty of each number rises linearly, the uncertainty of the aggregate rises much more slowly (with the square root). For example, if four numbers each has a standard deviation of 2, then each has a variance of 2^2, i.e. 4. The sum of the variances is 4×4, i.e. 16, and the standard deviation of the aggregate of the four numbers is $\sqrt{16}$, i.e. 4. Treating each of the numbers separately would face us with a total uncertainty of 4×2, i.e. 8.

The statistics of combining many uncertain events also work to counteract the biases which make individual tasks more often late than early. The Central Limit Theorem shows that, no matter how skewed are the distributions of the durations of individual tasks, the distribution of the aggregated uncertainty will tend towards the symmetrical normal distribution as the number of tasks rises (Figure A.4). In other words, the overall project stands a reasonable chance of coming in early, even if individual tasks have a long tail on the late side (see Figure A.5)!

Fig. A.4 Skewed distribution for a single task

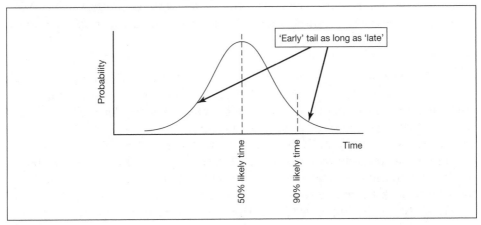

Fig. A.5 The distribution for aggregated tasks tends to the symmetrical 'normal' distribution

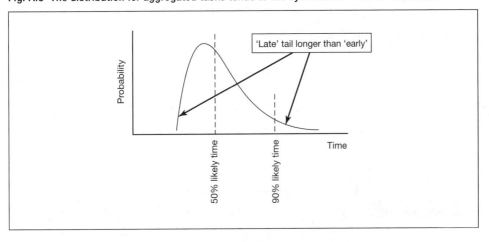

Focus on critical activities

Although critical chain can add much value in planning a project by handling uncertainty more efficiently, it is in helping managers to understand and focus on the critical activities that it has the greatest day-to-day impact during a project.

Because the name 'critical chain' sounds similar to 'critical path', it is tempting to think that they are the same. The critical chain includes all the critical path activities, but whereas the critical path is defined only by task dependencies, the critical chain is defined by both task dependencies and resource dependencies. In other words, it recognizes that the minimum time to complete a project can be driven as much by the limited availability of resources as by task sequencing. Activities not on the critical path can form part of the critical chain if they rely on resources which are in demand elsewhere, and any change in their duration has an impact on the project duration. Much of the thrust of the critical chain method is directed towards protecting the critical chain: anything that affects the critical chain affects the project. The key techniques of critical chain are feed buffers, resource buffers, and eliminating multitasking.

▶ Feed buffers

Non-critical activities must never be allowed to impact on the critical chain. This might happen, for example, when a critical chain activity depends on a non-critical activity that suffers a delay. Critical chain inserts a feed buffer between the non-critical workstream and the critical chain task, so as to insulate the critical chain from the uncertainty in the non-critical workstream timing. This feed buffer is calculated in the same way as for the project buffer, but covers only the tasks on the joining workstream (see Figures A.6 and A.7).

Using feed buffers to protect the critical chain from the non-critical activities frees the project manager from having to use early-start scheduling. (Early-start scheduling means starting all activities as soon as possible, even if they are not crit-

Fig. A.6 Activities merging onto critical chain

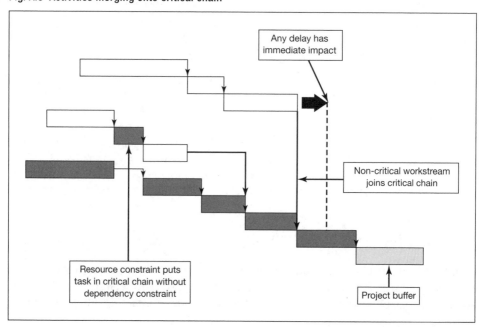

Fig. A.7 Feed buffer

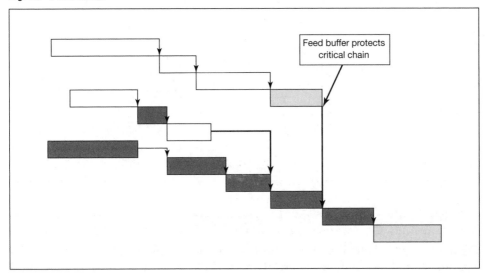

Feed buffer protects critical chain

ical.) During the early days of a project it is often better not to be distracted by having to start many activities at once, and project managers should focus on the critical chain activity that starts the project.

▶ Resource buffers

The critical chain activities must always have all of their resources and inputs available as soon as the preceding task finishes. The simplest form of resource buffer is a reminder flag in the project plan to reconfirm resource availability before the start of each task. When the project depends on another project to release the critical resource on time, it is necessary to include a real buffer period between the tasks on each project. Resource buffers can even take the form of spare or standby staff who are deliberately not assigned to other activities, or, in the case of sub-contract suppliers, cash payments for holding their own staff on instant availability.

▶ Eliminating multitasking

The strict discipline of the focus on the critical chain requires that people should not try to do two tasks at once, especially if one of them is a critical chain activity.

In Figure A.8, all three activities are delivered simultaneously through multitasking, but if resources are allowed to prioritize and do one task at a time, two of the three tasks are delivered early and the third no later than through multitasking.

Fig. A.8 Multitasking

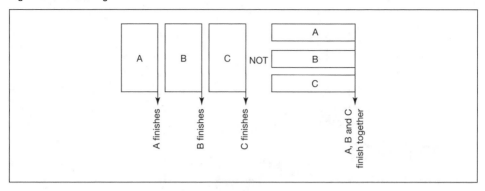

The project buffer as a diagnostic

During the critical chain planning process a project buffer is created at the end of the project and feed buffers are created to separate critical tasks from non-critical ones. During the project the current state of these buffers is an easily understandable shorthand for the status of the project. It is to be expected that projects will often use some of the buffer (after all, the original task duration estimates were only 50% likely times), but managers should take action if it seems likely that all the buffer will be used, since this means that the project will be late overall.

Fig. A.9 Buffer usage and project status

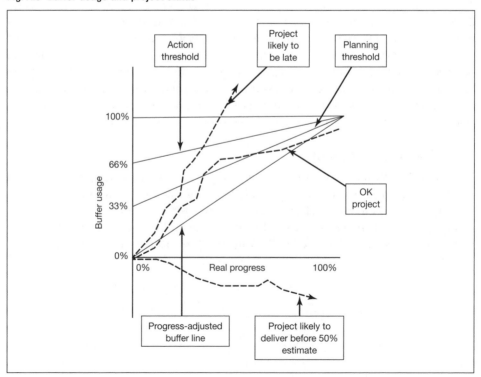

The danger level of buffer usage depends on how much work there is still to be done: 40% buffer usage would be a serious warning sign on a project which is only 15% complete, but is probably not a problem on a project which is 85% complete (see Figure A.9). As a rule of thumb, a project manager should

- plan recovery actions if the buffer usage exceeds one-third of the progress-adjusted buffer (this is the total buffer scaled by the proportion of work remaining to be done); and
- enact the recovery plan if progress-adjusted buffer usage is greater than two-thirds.

Action summary

▶ Planning

1 Create the project structure in the normal way. Pay attention to risks, and take care not to miss out any activities: team members won't have any slack time from task-level contingency time to pick up any extras that are discovered along the way.
2 Gather estimated durations for each task. Start by asking for the time for 90% confidence of success – this is the time most people will give if unprompted. Then ask for the time for which we would be only 50% confident of success (make clear that you fully expect half of these estimates to prove to be low, and you will not regard this as a mistake on the estimator's part).
3 Set the task timing in the baseline plan using the 50% estimates.
4 Allocate resources to tasks and identify the critical chain using both task dependency and resource constraints.
5 Add a project buffer calculated using the aggregated differences between the 50% estimates and the 90% estimates.
6 Add feed buffers to isolate the critical chain from non-critical workstreams. Schedule non-critical workstreams as latest-start rather than earliest-start, so as to make it easier to focus on getting the project up and running at the start.
7 Add resource buffers as required to ensure that critical resources are available when required.

▶ Executing

1 As always: work the plan.
2 Assign tasks to named individuals, but avoid giving exact deadline dates unless absolutely necessary (to meet an externally driven timetable, for example). Instead insist that tasks should be completed as soon as possible.
3 When monitoring progress, expect that 50% of tasks will overrun the 50% likely time, and 50% will finish early. Try not to criticize any team member whose task overruns as long as they started as soon as they had the necessary inputs, they worked 100% on the task (without multitasking), and they passed on their outputs as soon as they were available. Similarly, make clear that you expect tasks that are completed early to be handed over early, so as to get the benefit of positive variation.

4 Use the resource buffers to ensure that critical resources are never idle or unavailable.

5 Monitor usage of the project buffer against actual progress made to determine the true status of the project. Plan for recovery when buffer usage exceeds progress by more than 33%, and enact the recovery plan if buffer usage exceeds progress by more than 66%.

6 Monitor usage of feed buffers to warn of possible impact of non-critical workstreams on the critical chain, and take pre-emptive action before any such event.

Notes

1 Goldratt, E.M., 1992. *The Goal: A Process of Ongoing Improvement* (2nd rev. edn). Great Barrington, MA: North River Press Publishing Corporation.

2 Goldratt, E.M., 1997. *Critical Chain*. Great Barrington, MA: North River Press Publishing Corporation.

3 The law states that 'work expands so as to fill the time available for its completion'. See: Parkinson, C. N., 1958, *Parkinson's Law: The Pursuit of Progress*, London: John Murray; and Parkinson, C. N., 1978. *The Law of Delay: Interviews and Outerviews*, London: Penguin Books.

appendix B: benefits management

The only reason for doing a project is to realize a business benefit. In a sense, therefore, every part of project management is about benefits management, also known as benefits realization. However, it is sometimes useful in the heat of real-life project management to remind ourselves of the benefits realization plan for our project, and some organizations find it useful to treat benefits realization as a distinct part of project management. This appendix sets out the essential of benefits management.

▶ The problem

Projects and programmes are conceived by an organization to achieve something new. Often they fail to deliver the intended benefits. There are many reasons for this: misalignment to corporate strategy; too great an importance placed on deliverables out of context of why they were suggested as deliverables in the first place; an increased focus on meeting deadlines and budgets; or the benefits were simply never identified or planned.

▶ Benefits management

Benefits management is the process by which organizations ensure that they obtain real value rather than merely a set of deliverables from projects. Benefits management is about ensuring that value is defined, identified, agreed upon and realized by the project. It is a very simple idea, and is no more than ensuring that we all remember why we are doing the project. That idea sounds simple when stated like that, but in large, long or complex projects it is easy to lose sight of why we are doing something.

Benefits management comprises five phases:

- ◆ Identification.
- ◆ Analysis.
- ◆ Planning.
- ◆ Realization.
- ◆ Transition.

These phases may be correlated to four of the five phases of the project lifecycle: initiate, plan, monitor and control, and close.

▶ Benefits identification
Benefits identification occurs during the initiating phase of a project. It is an integral part of the project selection process. It is the processes by which the benefits of

a project are identified and qualified against business need. It is not uncommon to compare the benefits of a project against the corporate strategy. If a sponsor is choosing between two competing projects, it will be the one whose benefits are aligned to the strategy that should be picked. In fact if none of the identified benefits of the project can be linked to the corporate strategy, or no benefits can be identified for the project, then the project manager must consider the wisdom in pursuing it at all.

In benefits identification:

♦ State *what* the benefit is, at a high level.
♦ State *why* it is a benefit, also at a high level.

It may also be useful to state the risks, that is, what can happen to invalidate the 'why' above.

▶ Benefits analysis

Benefits analysis is the second phase in benefits management. This phase straddles the initiation and planning phases of the project lifecycle. This phase aims to provide the project manager with a thorough understanding of the benefits to be achieved by the project and metrics with which to monitor and control the realization of the benefits. In benefits analysis you extend the 'what' and 'why' and 'risks' of the identification phase to a finer level of detail, and understand the ramifications and factors that are likely to affect the degree of benefit.

▶ Benefits planning

The third phase in benefits management is benefits planning. This is about the 'how' – how your project will deliver the benefits. The benefits realization plan exceeds the life of the project plan. Where the project plan ends on completion of the final deliverable, the benefits realization plan outlines how the benefits from the project will be transitioned into business-as-usual. As benefits are often realized after the project has finished, so the benefits realization plan must be written to reflect this.

The key thing in benefits planning is to link every deliverable to benefits, and document clearly how the deliverable can create benefits, stating what must be done with the deliverable for that to happen.

▶ Benefits realization

The fourth phase in benefits management is benefits realization and sits within the monitor and control phase in the project management lifecycle. Benefits realization is, at its most basic, the implementation of the benefits realization plan. Realizing the benefits is the *raison d'être* of benefits management. This phase enables the project manager to deliver the benefits in addition to the deliverables.

▶ Benefits transition

The fifth and final phase in benefits management is benefits transition. Benefits transition occurs when the project is completed, but benefits realization is not. Benefits transition is the transition of benefits management from the project into the ongoing operations of the organization. This phase occurs during the closing phase of the project lifecycle. However, due to the ongoing nature of benefits, it is likely to continue to occur after the project is completed. It is for this phase that it is critical that the benefits have been assigned 'owners' beyond the life of the project.

Business benefits

The functions of benefits management are as follows:

◆ To identify and quantify all benefits (and 'dis-benefits') from the project.
◆ To link them to the corporate strategy.
◆ To ensure that all benefits have stakeholder buy-in.
◆ To manage benefit realization proactively.
◆ To monitor and control the planned benefits throughout the project.
◆ To allocate ownership to benefits.
◆ To link planned benefits to project deliverables.
◆ To integrate the benefits into the project plan.
◆ To enable the benefits to move from the project sphere to business-as-usual.

Implementation

Without benefits management an organization will never achieve all the available value from a project. Benefits management permeates every aspect of project management. It is critical at both the initial startup and closedown of a project. The benefits identification process at the beginning of the project enables greater clarity of thought into whether the project is required.

Without considering the benefits that a project would deliver in addition to the deliverables, the organization has no way of knowing whether its resources will be well spent. Likewise, at the end of a project, care must be taken to embed realized benefits and transfer those yet to be realized to the ownership of operations. Too often projects are shut down on delivery of the final deliverables without thought being given to the continued realization of potential or agreed benefits, and it is often the case that the intended benefits are lost.

Summary

◆ Benefits realization is just a small part of benefits management.
◆ Benefits management is a methodology distinct from, but closely linked to, project management.
◆ Only when benefits are managed from conception through to realization can a project claim to have delivered value.

appendix C: PMI exam preparation

Aims of this appendix

This appendix is about preparation for the PMP or CAPM exams. When you have completed it, you should:

- be aware of the two qualifications in project management provided by the PMI, the Project Management Professional (PMP) and the Certified Associate in Project Management (CAPM);
- understand the eligibility requirements for entry to the PMP and CAPM exams;
- know how the exam is structured;
- know what is required to pass the exam and how best to prepare yourself;
- be familiar with the language of the examiners;
- have had experience of practice questions.

What are the credentials offered by the PMI?

The Project Management Institute (PMI) has more than 220,000 members in over 150 countries. It is the world's largest and fastest growing professional body for project management. The PMI has 22,000 members in Europe and 5,000 members in the UK.

The PMI sets standards, conducts research and provides education, certification and professional exchange opportunities designed to strengthen and further establish the profession. The PMI aims to advance the careers of practitioners and enhance the performance of business and other organizations. This it does by running and maintaining two credentials in project management: the Project Management Professional (PMP) and the Certified Associate in Project Management (CAPM). The authors' experience is that both are very valuable.

PMI says

The Project Management Institute
'The Project Management Institute (PMI®) is the world's leading association for the project management profession. It administers a globally recognized, rigorous, educational, and/or professional experience and examination-based professional credentialing program that maintains an ISO 9001 certification in Quality Management Systems.' www.PMI.org

The PMP credential has been specifically designed for experienced project managers. Obtaining this professional qualification shows that the successful candidate not only understands the theory of the PMI PMBOK, but also has had real-life project management experience to the extent that they are able to apply the knowledge appropriately.

The CAPM, by contrast, is an entry-level qualification. No assumption is made as to the actual project management experience the successful candidate has. This qualification is particularly suited to project team members and other stakeholders who would benefit from understanding the language and processes of the PMI PMBOK, but are not yet required to understand its detailed application.

The PMI states that each credential demonstrates that the candidate has:

◆ The appropriate education and/or professional experience.
◆ Passed a rigorous examination.
◆ Agreed to abide by a professional code of conduct.
◆ Committed to maintaining their active credential through meeting continuing certification requirements.

PMP or CAPM?

Determining which credential to apply for is not as straightforward as you may think. It is very tempting to want to jump straight into the PMP. However, there are two hurdles that any budding PMP must jump: actual project management experience and project management education. It may also not be necessary to have the PMP. If you are a project team member or stakeholder, the CAPM may well be sufficient for your needs. Use the flowchart in Figure C.1 to determine the exam for which you are eligible, and see also Table C.1 which lists further details.

Table C.1 PMP or CAPM?

Credential	Educational background	Project management experience	Project management education
PMP	High school diploma or equivalent	7,500 hours in a position of responsibility leading and directing specific tasks and 60 months of project management experience	35 contact hours
PMP	Degree or equivalent	4,500 hours leading and directing specific tasks and 36 months of project management experience	35 contact hours
CAPM	High school diploma or equivalent	1500 hours of work on a project	None
CAPM	High school diploma or equivalent	None	23 contact hours

Adapted from PMI website, www.PMI.org

Fig. C.1 PMP or CAPM decision tree

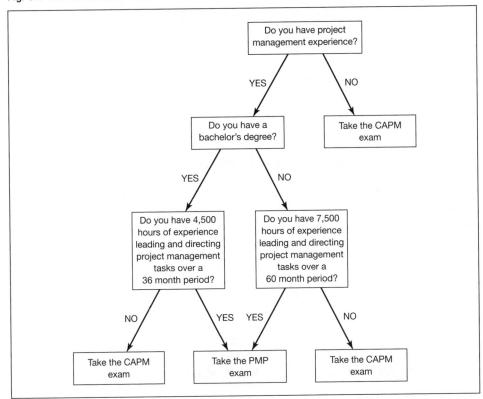

Exam structure

The Project Management Professional (PMP) credential examination measures the application of knowledge, skills, tools and techniques that are used in the practice of project management. The questions are written psychometrically, so there will be some you will be unlikely to answer. 'Psychometric' comes from the Greek *psyche* (mind), *metron* (measure), and means the testing of mental ability such as IQ, as well as interests, attitudes and personality. What this means is that there will be questions that test your ability as a project manager if you are sitting the PMP exam. You will not be able to answer these types of questions unless you have actually 'been there, done that and got the T-shirt'. The questions in the CAPM are more factual, focusing on definition and the processes outlined in the PMI PMBOK.

PMI says

The exam questions
'The PMP and CAPM Examination questions:

- are developed and validated by global work groups of content experts,
- are referenced to current resources from project management textbook sources,

• are monitored through psychometric analysis, and
• satisfy the test specifications of a job analysis.' www.PMI.org

The PMP examination is computer based and has 200 four-option multiple-choice questions to be answered over four hours. The current pass mark is 61%. As this exam tests the project manager's skills, the PMI has broken down the content into the six process groups, shown in Table C.2.

Table C.2 Process groups breakdown in the PMP examination

Project management process	Percent of questions
Initiating	11
Planning	23
Executing	27
Monitoring and controlling	21
Closing	9
Professional and social responsibility	9

Adapted from PMI website, www.PMI.org

Table C.3 PMBOK chapter breakdown in the CAPM examination

Chapter in the PMBOK	Approximate percentage of items on test
1 The project management framework – introduction	4
2 The project management framework – the project lifecycle and organization	4
3 The standard for project management of a project	11
4 Integration management	11
5 Scope management	11
6 Time management	11
7 Cost management	9
8 Quality management	7
9 Human resources management	7
10 Communication management	7
11 Risk management	11
12 Procurement management	7
Total	**100**

Adapted from PMI website, www.PMI.org

Like the PMP, the CAPM examination is also computer based. It is a slightly shorter exam – 150 four-option multiple-choice questions to be answered over three hours – and has a pass mark of 65%. However, in contrast to the PMP exam, where the candidate has to demonstrate their project management skills, the CAPM candidate must show that they have knowledge of the basic terminology, activities, roles and communications. They must also have functional experience in the knowledge areas and be aware of quality management, contract negotiation, the project management processes, methods, policies, rules and external influences. Finally, CAPM candidates must show that they are adaptable, creative and flexible. The exam is broken down by chapter in the PMBOK as opposed to the processes for the PMP exam: see Table C.3.

▶ Preparing for and sitting the exam

REVISE, REVISE, REVISE.

It is that simple. The more you revise, the better you will understand the PMBOK and the more confident you will become. There are many ways of doing this: attending an exam preparation course, learning the PMBOK by rote, using self-study books, etc. The trick to passing the exams is to try to think like the PMI. Download the sample questions on their website to give yourself a feel for the language. There is also a basic knowledge assessment available on the PMI website. This assessment is based on the PMBOK and made up of 100 multiple-choice questions that measure basic but essential project management knowledge. It does not claim to replicate the exam conditions of the PMP or CAPM, and is certainly not as rigorous as the PMP, but it is a good starting point – especially if you have not sat an exam for a while.

On the day itself do not panic. The exams may seem to take a long time, but most people who have sat the PMP have required only between 2.5 and 3 hours in which to complete it. In fact, you will have plenty of time to panic, calm yourself down and then finish the exam should you so wish. Both the CAPM and the PMP exams begin with a 15-minute tutorial on how to use the examination software. This is over and above the three or four hours provided to sit the exam. You will not be able to take anything into the examination room, but will be provided with paper, pencils and sometimes a calculator. Throughout the exam you will be given the choice to mark questions that you may wish to revisit, and you can move backwards and forwards through them. Finally, when you have finished you will be asked several times to confirm that this is the case. Upon the final confirmation the computer will work out your result and inform you immediately whether you have passed or failed, and you will receive a printout of your results. If you have been successful and passed the exam, your certificate will be printed and you will now be certified as a PMP or a CAPM. If you were unsuccessful, the PMI will write to you informing you of the process for resitting the exam.

Examples of questions

There are generally two main types of questions that you will face in the exams: factual questions, such as definitions; and situational questions. It is also important to note that many questions will have superfluous information and others will be on topics you will have never seen before. Try the following 25 questions to get a feel for the language. For exam conditions, give yourself no more than 30 minutes in which to complete the questions.

1 In which project management process group is the project charter created?
   (a) Initiating
   (b) Planning
   (c) Executing
   (d) Closing

2 Which is not an input to the direct and manage project execution process group?
   (a) Project management plan
   (b) Validated defect repair
   (c) Approved change requests
   (d) Resource availability

3 Qualitative risk analysis is ...
   (a) The process of numerically analyzing the effect on overall project objectives of identified risks.
   (b) The process of identifying which quality standards are relevant to the project and determining how to satisfy them.
   (c) The process of prioritizing risks by assessing and combining the probability of their occurrence and impact.
   (d) The degree to which the set of inherent characteristics fulfils requirements.

4 Who has the most power in a matrix organization?
   (a) Project manager
   (b) Sponsor
   (c) Function manager
   (d) Team

5 When should scope verification be done?
   (a) During planning
   (b) Throughout the project
   (c) At the beginning of the project
   (d) At the end of each phase of the project

6 Who bears the risk in a fixed price contract?
   (a) Seller
   (b) Buyer
   (c) Sponsor
   (d) The team

7 Which of the following is not normally part of the contract documents?
  (a) Scope of work
  (b) Proposal
  (c) Negotiation process
  (d) Terms and conditions

8 Who is responsible for quality management throughout the project?
  (a) Team members are responsible for the quality of their work
  (b) Quality manager
  (c) Project sponsor
  (d) Project manager

9 Decomposition of the project deliverables would take place during which of the major project processes?
  (a) Project time management
  (b) Project scope management
  (c) Project risk management
  (d) Project integration management

10 Which of the following defines a project stakeholder?
  (a) Individuals and organizations that are actively involved in the project or whose interests may be affected as a result of project execution or project completion.
  (b) People who used to be part of the project team and still care about the outcome.
  (c) Individuals or organizations that could stop the project if they aren't happy with progress.
  (d) b and c

11 If Earned Value (EV) = £460, Actual Cost (AC) = £380 and Planned Value (PV) = £500, what is the Cost Variance (CV)?
  (a) –£40
  (b) £120
  (c) £80
  (d) –£20

12 A Schedule Performance Index (SPI) of 1.3 means:
  (a) We are over budget
  (b) We are behind schedule
  (c) We are progressing at 130% of the rate originally planned
  (d) We are making £1.30 for every £1 we put into the project

13 As a project manager you are required to have both management and leadership. You need to describe to your sponsor what this means. Which of the following phrases are not correct?
  (a) Leadership is concerned with providing direction, motivation and inspiration to the project team.
  (b) Managing a project is done in order to deliver the results required by stakeholders.

(c) The project manager is the project's leader.

(d) Technical leadership is of primary importance in project management.

14 A company has to make a choice between four projects. Which project is the *best* one to choose?

(a) Project A will take four years to complete and has a NPV of £50,000.

(b) Project B will take seven years to complete and has a NPV of £45,000.

(c) Project C will take six years to complete and has a NPV of £25,000.

(d) Project D will take five years to complete and has a NPV of £32,000.

15 You have been asked to prepare a report on the progress of a new jam pot filling process. You have obtained the last 15 jars from the current production run. Knowing that the control limits for filling the jars are 298.5 cm^3 and 301.5 cm^3, what do the following data tell you?

300.1 cm^3, 299.9 cm^3, 301.4 cm^3, 298.7 cm^3, 299.5 cm^3, 299.9 cm^3, 301.2 cm^3, 299.3 cm^3, 300.2 cm^3, 301.1 cm^3, 300.5 cm^3, 301.5 cm^3, 301.2 cm^3, 300.1 cm^3, 301.1 cm^3

(a) The process is under control. It should not be adjusted.

(b) The process should be adjusted.

(c) The control limits should be adjusted.

(d) The measuring equipment should be recalibrated.

16 As a project manager, you are responsible for encouraging team building. What are the four stages that best describe team development?

(a) Norming, Performing, Forming, Storming

(b) Forming, Storming, Norming, Performing

(c) Performing, Forming, Storming, Norming

(d) Storming, Norming, Performing, Forming

17 Your sponsor has asked for a five-minute briefing on the progress of your project. You have just completed an Earned Value Analysis with the following results: EV: 104600; PV: 124600; AC: 128600. You tell the sponsor that the project is ...

(a) Under budget and under schedule

(b) On time and on budget

(c) Over budget and behind schedule

(d) On time and under budget

18 The main function of a statistical control chart is to help:

(a) Monitor process variation over time

(b) Assess conformance

(c) Set project scope

(d) Identify stakeholder requirements

19 Your sponsor has asked you to review the manufacturing line at Jam PLC. While performing your review you found poor quality control, poorly stocked jam vats and antiquated machinery. How and why would you prepare your results?

(a) Use a Pareto diagram because it will show how many results were generated, by type or category of identified cause.

(b) Use an activity-on-arrow diagram because it shows the dependencies as dummies.

(c) Use a bar chart because the schedule is very important.

(d) Use a fishbone diagram to outline the causes of future problems.

20 You are the project manager on a very complex and lengthy project. Your team is spread across various locations and time zones. A dispute has arisen between two senior members of your team, both subject matter experts in different fields. Senior management have made it clear that your job rides on the successful delivery of this project. Which is the best opening statement you can make when trying to deal with this dispute?

(a) My job depends on this project working, so you are going to get on with it and do as I say.

(b) Let's all take a step back and calm down and focus on the job.

(c) I am far too busy to deal with this now. When I see you both next week I expect you to have resolved your difference.

(d) I am sure that we can come up with a solution that we are all happy with to this problem.

21 The process re-engineering project you undertook at Jam PLC was so successful that production has tripled over the past three months. You have been asked, as an external project management consultant, to project manage the construction of a new distribution centre. You buy in specialist shelf-building expertise on a time and material contract. Halfway through the project you discover that two of your team members assigned to the shelf-building task have charged time without performing any work. Jam PLC is unaware of this. What should you do?

(a) Do nothing, but come up with a backup plan should the customer realize what has happened.

(b) Ask finance why they billed for work not done.

(c) Take the two people off the team immediately and refund the excess charges to the customer.

(d) Try to find another billable task for the two team members and not charge for the work until it equals that already billed for.

22 During your project the scope of product purchased on a cost reimbursable contract has increased. In the contract the supplier's indirect costs are calculated as 35% of the direct costs. What does this mean?

(a) The supplier's indirect costs will increase but the cost of the contract will not.

(b) Neither the indirect costs nor the cost of the contract will increase.

(c) The supplier's indirect costs will not increase but the overall cost of the contract will.

(d) The supplier's indirect costs will increase and the overall cost of the contract will too.

23 As a successful project manager at Jam PLC you have been asked to perform a project management audit throughout the company. Whilst undertaking this

task you find that most of the project plans are neither consistent nor up-to-date. Which of the following statements is true?

(a) Historical information is of no use to the company, as technology and methods change so rapidly.

(b) The project plan is secondary because it is only the results that matter.

(c) The project plan is the result of the initiation phase and once agreed will not change.

(d) Poor planning is one of the major reasons for cost and time overruns.

24 Creating contingency reserves in money and time is an example of …

(a) Risk response planning

(b) Risk identification

(c) Risk management planning

(d) Risk monitoring and control

25 Project costs are under budget when

(a) CPI < 1

(b) CPI > 1

(c) CPI < 0

(d) SPI = 1

▶ Answers

1 a	6 a	11 c	16 b	21 c
2 d	7 c	12 c	17 c	22 c
3 c	8 d	13 d	18 a	23 d
4 a	9 b	14 a	19 a	24 a
5 d	10 a	15 b	20 d	25 b

Key Idea

Revision tips

Set aside dedicated time slots in your diary to revise.

Create a revision timetable.

Start revising with the areas you least understand.

Afterword ten top tips for managing projects

These are our top ten tips for being a successful project manager. They assume you actually have the skills necessary for project management. In other words, these tips are not a substitute for reading and understanding this book and making the effort to apply its lessons in real life. They are tips to help you apply them in real life. We don't claim them to be unique to us or that they would be everyone's choices. They're just things we've picked up, borrowed from others, and sometimes learned the hard way over a combined 50 years of managing projects. If you already do these things, great.

▶ 1 Know your people

Projects are done by teams. Even the simplest of individual projects will require assistance from someone else. The project manager has to lead his team, and to do this well he must know them. Leadership is much more than following the latest fad. You have to know your team and make the effort to continue to do so. How often have we all felt better about ourselves when our boss commented on our non-work activities or asked after our families and actually knew something about them?

Team-building activities are always worthwhile, provided they are well organized. You don't personally have to organize a survival week in the Amazonian jungle. Professionally run centres know how to generate camaraderie in teams and can put together activities appropriate to your team and needs. You can learn a great deal about your team from such events, but just taking your team for a coffee or to the pub can be of enormous benefit, as will actually taking the time to talk to them and remembering some of what they say. If you're managing a project so big that knowing everyone is impractical, ensure they all know you and that your junior managers do know their people.

Tip: Get to know your team. Time and money spent developing your relationship with each of them will pay dividends in the long run.

▶ 2 Cultural and ethical realism

Ethics are a vital part of the project manager's toolset but sometimes ethics assume a nationalistic view of life. What seems ethically correct in a broadly Christian, comfortable, Western society with well-developed welfare systems bears little resemblance to acceptable business practice in other parts of the world. It is arrogant to assume one practice is better than another. Each has developed to reflect local conditions and a view of what is acceptable in the face of wider socio-economic circumstances. The good project manager has to be realistic when it comes to cultural norms. A North American view of 'expediting payments' will not help move along a project in West Africa. Equally, if your culture won't deal with women as equal business partners, don't arrive in New York and expect to carry on in the same way.

This is an area that has the potential to be enormously disruptive. It might be more comfortable to avoid writing or thinking about it, but that would be to duck a critical issue in many projects. Culture and the resulting ethical norms tend to be more deep-seated than even legal or regulatory constraints. Realism in this context is not about asserting your personal view on your whole team or trumpeting every last person's right to freedom and individual consideration. Such approaches are risky and possibly illegal. Cultural realism is about understanding the cultural and ethical realities in which you have to work and steering a path that maintains an acceptable working environment for all stakeholders. You can't please all of the people, all of the time.

Tip: Be realistic with cultural and ethical norms. Don't assume your custom is appropriate in a different culture.

▶ 3 Know the business

The great push in project management is for project managers to be so skilled and professional that they can take on any project and by following the correct techniques and procedures see it through to a successful conclusion. If life were simple and we could trust everyone to do their job and specifications be set correctly and remain unchanged, this would be a possibility. But life just isn't like that. If you're going to get a good grip on a project you have to understand the business. We don't mean understanding the user requirement document; that's relatively easy. We mean understanding the business so you know the overall impact of your project decisions on business activities.

This presents something of a problem. A home-grown expert in the business is unlikely to be an experienced project manager, whilst an expert project manager is unlikely to be experienced in a particular business area. Some large organizations, of course, can afford to develop individuals specifically to fill these roles, but most can't.

There is a pragmatic solution. First, if your company decides you can head up a project despite having had little project management experience, don't feel inadequate because you're new to this role. Work hard on your skills but don't forget the benefits your experience brings to the project. On the other hand, the experienced project manager knows that although he can talk Net Present Value and Critical Path Analysis with the best of them, if he doesn't understand what is important to users he could still preside over a failure even though he might meet his specification. If you know the business you might well run a good project; equally if you've run projects before you might well come to a business and run a good project. If you can do both, though, your chances of succeeding increase enormously.

Tip: If you come to a business to run a project, spend some time learning how it works before you embark on changing anything. It might seem like wasting time but you will reap the benefits later.

▶ 4 Keep everyone happy, or at least content

To be a good leader, for that's what a project manager is, it is not necessary to be popular. It's nice if you are, but it's not necessary. 'Better the devil you know' is an excellent maxim. It is far more important that your team and stakeholders know where you stand on any particular issue, even if they don't like it, than it is for you to sway in your opinions just to be popular.

So, setting aside your own feelings, what about everyone else's? People are all different. Even if you work in an organization with a strong corporate culture, a large industrial company, an investment bank, the army or a major consultancy, for example, you will still find many different types of individual. The trick with running your team is to keep them all happy. It may in fact be an unachievable goal, but you must still strive to accomplish it. Remember, despite what your resource allocation software says, people cannot all be treated the same. Look after the little things. It's amazing how often discontent can spread through a team over the smallest of issues. Fixing a water machine might be a low priority for your building's corporate services department, but if your team all start walking to the next department for a drink you lose their productivity for that time and, more worrying, they begin to form opinions about your view of their worth. We can all remember taking a very serious view of what others considered to be a minor issue. Even if you can't get the water machine fixed, make a public enough fuss so that your team know you care. It's the caring that matters to them more than your failure to achieve the impossible.

Tip: Strive to keep your team content even if you become unpopular in the process.

▶ 5 Communicate in the most appropriate manner

Management by walking around is a good thing, and much human communication is non-verbal. We don't need expensive courses to teach us this, it's a matter of common experience. E-mail may well have been one of the greatest management tools ever invented for virtual teams in diverse locations, but it's also one of the worst for the way in which it interrupts normal human interactions. If, with a little effort, you can communicate face to face, do so. Time spent talking directly to people when things are going well will pay dividends when they are not.

Talking, however, isn't always the best way to get your message across. Newsletters, team notices, minutes of meetings, written briefs and reports all have their place. An experienced project manager has used them all and knows what works best in different situations and, more importantly, what doesn't. Sacking a team member by SMS text message will not build trust between you and the rest of your team. Communication is the project manager's most important skill. The key to good communication is consideration of the needs of the recipient. The CEO is always short of time and is likely to be well educated. A brief to the CEO can use a wide variety of language for maximum impact in a concise manner. Conversely, consider swearing. The use of coarse language is often said to be a sign of a poor vocabulary. However, there is little point using your masters' level vocabulary if your audience's normal conversational style is to have an expletive for every third word. Know your audience and adapt your style for them. This does not mean swearing every third word if they do, but it does mean simplifying your language and using examples to illustrate your message that will be familiar to them.

Tip: Think through how you communicate with every last member of your team and all the stakeholders connected with your project. Be realistic: don't take the easy option. Understand the recipient's ability to receive your message.

▶ 6 Get a grip on the politics early

Internal organizational politics is the bane of a project manager's life. The politics of an organization can prevent a project ever getting going, or worse, can ensure it fails. The last thing you need as a project manager is to discover that your entire project is really just part of an ongoing battle between two business units with hidden agendas.

If you're a project manager within a large organization you should have a reasonable understanding of its politics, but beware a whole new world unfolding before your eyes when you get promoted into the role. And don't say or think 'I don't do politics'; that's about as realistic as saying 'I don't do breathing'. Besides, it's not necessarily a question of whether you do politics, it can be a matter of whether politics is done to you. If you're an employee who sometimes manages projects you should similarly have an understanding of the workings of your company. The worst situation for this is, of course, being a newly employed or contract project manager. Experience helps a great deal, but you still have to gain it. The best advice we ever received on this was to not trust anyone initially and to try to understand the benefits and costs to the decider of each decision taken with regard to your project. This might seem underhand, but if you just sail blindly on and find you are a pawn in someone else's game, your team and your CV won't thank you. Don't appear overtly wary or disbelieving (this will not help you succeed either) but, until you are sure of your ground, don't rush into agreeing or disagreeing with anything without taking time to consider your decision. Sadly, taking too long with your considerations will result in your being labelled indecisive – but then no one said project management was easy.

Tip: Until you understand the politics of an organization for which you are managing a project, don't rush into major decisions based on the advice of individuals or single business units.

▶ 7 Consider the unexpected and allow for it

No one has a crystal ball but we can all think up worst-case scenarios. A good project manager will think these through. You can't ask for a budget to cover all eventualities, but you can have some idea of how you will react if catastrophe strikes. Risk analysis is an excellent tool, but don't just disregard the low-probability risks. How concerned you should be depends, of course, on the criticality of your project. Clearly the development of a pan-European air traffic control system needs a backup plan that facilitates immediate recovery following the complete destruction of its primary site. Similarly, in these days of widespread terrorism, the project manager for a new stock exchange computer system can probably get a budget for several real-time, geographically disparate, reserve locations. Compared to these, a project to develop a new type of toothpaste may appear less critical, but if the future of the company and the livelihoods of its 6,000 employees depend on it, and the development laboratory is flooded, your thoughts on how to keep the project running become critical to a lot of people. And if the world suddenly needs new anti-terrorist toothpaste, it may become very critical indeed. Criticality is a very subjective science when mortgage repayments are concerned.

Tip: Don't worry about low-probability risks but still have a few thoughts on how you will react if they become reality. Unlikely events are only unlikely; they are not impossible.

▶ 8 Don't sugar the pill. Tell it as it is

Making a report of problems poses interesting psychological questions, especially for the person making the report. Most of us are uncomfortable raising an issue as being beyond our abilities or authority to resolve. And unlike good red wine, bad news does not improve with age. It gets worse. If your project begins to experience problems make sure you report the difficulties in an accurate manner. Senior managers and executives do not like surprises.

First, report your problems when they are still just deviations from expected performance, but never just present the problem. Always know why it arose and have solutions even if they are going to be unpalatable. Next, beware cognitive dissonance on the part of your boss. Cognitive dissonance is when the mind cannot accept what the senses are telling it. You might tell him that it's not going to work, but if he believes deeply that it will, he may well just ignore your warnings. Ensure you document your concerns. During the Second World War the infamous British airborne operation at Arnhem went ahead despite information being available to the planners that two SS Panzer divisions were resting in the area. They ignored this because it didn't fit the plans in which they had invested thousands of man-hours – with disastrous results.

Finally, beware your team not telling you what's going on. Ensure you develop a project culture where you don't get surprised either.

Tip: No one likes bad news. When it arrives, as it most certainly will, make sure you and your team deal with it as quickly and pragmatically as possible and document what you do.

9 Consider the practical implications of high-level decisions

How often have you sat there trying to implement a procedure invented by some-one else who clearly had no idea of how you actually worked when they designed it? A key element of project management is meeting the specification as efficiently as possible. As we design increasingly complex systems, however, it is all too easy to generalize about user needs even if only to simplify the specification documen-tation. This is all very well at the high level but doesn't help the poor individual in an unusual but still important situation.

I've just moved into a house with a name and a number. Most companies have software that recognizes one or the other when provided with the postcode, and the postman will deliver with either. Unfortunately, my bank's address software provides the name but their account database expects a number!

Meeting the specification as provided is good project management according to the letter of the law. Raising change proposals that better meet real-world user requirements as your experience on a project grows, however, will mark you out as an individual who adds value. Don't ever find yourself saying 'I don't care whether it works or not – it meets the spec exactly'. You might be right but your future employment prospects will diminish.

Tip: As your knowledge of a project develops, think through what you're doing from an end user's perspective.

10 Be the good guy. Honesty, sincerity and trust

Most people don't like to work with or for someone they consider dishonest or just don't trust. Don't be that person. When you say or do something, be sincere. If you act without sincerity or in a dishonest or untrustworthy manner, you have no right to expect any of your team or your project's stakeholders to act differently. I make no philosophical or ethical point here; it just seems to me that you can't run your project (or indeed your life) if all those with whom you interact feel free to be dis-honest with you because you've set them that example. I can't guarantee that your colleagues and stakeholders will all be honest as a result but at least you'll be head-ing in the right direction.

Tip: Treat others as you'd like to be treated yourself.

Index

Note: figures and tables are indicated by *italic page numbers*; case studies and definition/example/key idea boxes by **emboldened numbers**; and notes by suffix 'n'